The Fall of the Celtic Tiger

The Fall of the Celtic Tiger

Ireland and the Euro Debt Crisis

Donal Donovan and Antoin E. Murphy

OXFORD
UNIVERSITY PRESS

OXFORD
UNIVERSITY PRESS

Great Clarendon Street, Oxford, OX2 6DP,
United Kingdom

Oxford University Press is a department of the University of Oxford.
It furthers the University's objective of excellence in research, scholarship,
and education by publishing worldwide. Oxford is a registered trade mark of
Oxford University Press in the UK and in certain other countries

First Edition published in 2013

Impression: 1

British Library Cataloguing in Publication Data

Data available

ISBN 978-0-19-966395-8

Printed in Great Britain by
Clays Ltd, St Ives plc

It was the best of times, it was the worst of times, it was the age of wisdom, it was the age of foolishness, it was the epoch of belief, it was the epoch of incredulity, it was the season of Light, it was the season of Darkness, it was the spring of hope, it was the winter of despair, we had everything before us, we had nothing before us

... (Charles Dickens, *A Tale of Two Cities*, Chapter 1, 'The Period')

To Elizabeth and Paula

Preface

Although this has been an exciting book to write it has not been an easy task. The Irish financial crisis is now over four years old but its scars are still deeply felt throughout Irish society. Debates about the causes and effects of the events over the last four years along with the responsibility of those involved still continue to dominate the public's attention. New information on many aspects of the crisis and its implications is continuously appearing, a process that doubtless will continue for many years to come. The complexities of the story are still unfolding.

Nevertheless, we felt that it was appropriate to attempt to provide, on the basis of the many different elements that are already known, a broad and systematic treatment of the entire story leading up to and including recourse to the emergency EU/IMF bail out in late 2010. The book seeks to analyse the rise and fall of the Celtic Tiger against the background of some of the vast current and historical literature relating to the evolution of asset market bubbles and the ensuing financial crises and their consequences. Based on a detailed examination of the written record relating to both the international and domestic dimensions of the Irish crisis, it also incorporates the views provided to us by many Irish participants in these events. Hopefully, the overall outcome reflects a balanced and objective assessment.

Although the authors are both professional economists, the book is not targeted at a specialized audience. It is intended to be a readable and accessible work, aimed at the serious, interested reader, both in Ireland and abroad, who is seeking to understand better all of the complex features of Ireland's crisis. Every effort has been made to eschew technical economic or financial terminology—where this may be unavoidable, easily understood explanations in laymen's language are provided. We hope our economist colleagues will excuse any loss in precision or comprehensiveness that this approach might nevertheless entail.

Acknowledgements

The authors are most grateful to the following who gave generously of their time in providing information, advice, and careful review of the content of various chapters: Alan Ahearne, Alan Barrett, Tim Callan, Ronan Coyle, Kevin Denny, Joe Doherty, Paul Gorecki, Jim Higgins, Elish Kelly, Geraldine Kennedy, Anne Nolan, Patrick Honohan, Philip Lane, Seamus McConnell, Brigid McManus, Rafique Mottiar, Carol Newman, Peter Nyberg, Joe O'Connor, John O'Hagan, Roisin O'Sullivan, Shane O'Neill, Conor Rapple, Shane Ross, Frances Ruane, and Diarmaid Smyth.

A special thanks to Richard Curran, Brendan Keenan, George Lee, and Cliff Taylor who kindly agreed to be interviewed on the record for the interviews contained in that part of Chapter 8 dealing with the role of the media.

Many of the above read one or more draft chapters and provided insightful and helpful comments. A particular debt of gratitude is due to Donal Dineen and Paula Donovan, both of whom read the entire manuscript in painstaking detail.

Brian Donovan diligently researched the sections of Chapter 8 dealing with the election campaigns of 2002 and 2007. Eddie Casey, Michael Curran, and Barra Roantree prepared the data and charts used throughout the book with impressive speed and accuracy.

The authors would like to thank the following for granting permission to quote material: The *Irish Times, Irish Independent, Atlantic Magazine, The Economist,* RTE Radio, Penguin Group (USA) for permission to quote from The Road Ahead by Bill Gates, Summersdale Publishers for permission to quote from Keep Calm Sure It'll Be Grand, Warren Buffet for permission to quote from his Chairman's Letter of 2001.

All of the above persons contributed greatly to the final product. Nevertheless, the authors are entirely accountable for any remaining errors of commission or omission. We are of course also wholly responsible for the views and opinions—some of which may prove controversial—expressed throughout.

Contents

Contents

List of Figures

List of Tables

List of Boxes

Acronyms and Abbreviations

AIB	Allied Irish Banks
An Bord Gais	Semi-state gas company
Anglo	Anglo Irish Bank
BoI	Bank of Ireland
CAP	Common Agricultural Policy
CBFSAI	Central Bank and Financial Services Authority of Ireland; often referred to in abbreviated form as the 'Central Bank'
CCTB	Common Consolidated Tax Base
CDS	Credit default swap
CDOs	Collateralized debt obligations
CEBS	Committee of European Bank Supervisors
CFD	Contracts for difference
CSO	Central Statistics Office
Dáil	Lower House of Irish Parliament
DIRT	Deposit Interest Retention Tax
DM	Deutschmark
DSG	Domestic Standing Group
EBS	Educational Building Society
ECB	European Central Bank
ECOFIN	the EU's Economic and Financial Affairs Council:
EDP	Excessive Deficit Procedure
EEC	European Economic Community
EFSF	European Financial Stability Facility
EFSM	European Financial Stability Mechanism
ELA	Exceptional Liquidity Assistance
EMH	Efficient Markets Hypothesis
EMS	European Monetary System
EMU	European Monetary Union
ERM	European Exchange Rate Mechanism
ESB	Electricity Supply Board: large semi-state body engaged in the electricity sector
ESCB	European System of Central Banks, comprising central banks of the entire EU
ESM	European Stability Mechanism
ESRI	Economic and Social Research Institute

EU	European Union
EU/IMF troika	EU/ECB/IMF troika
FDI	Foreign direct investment
Fianna Fáil	until recently, principal Irish political party
Financial Regulator	abbreviated name of **IFSRA**; can also refer to the Chief Executive of the Financial Regulator
Fine Gael	traditionally the main opposition political party in Ireland
FoI	Freedom of Information
FSA: (UK)	Financial Services Authority
FSAP	Financial Sector Assessment Program (of the IMF)
FSR	Financial Stability Report published annually by the CBFSAI
G-20	Group of 20 leading industrial and emerging market countries
G-7	Group of seven leading industrial countries
GDP	Gross domestic product
GNI	Gross national income
GNP	Gross national product
HSE	Health Services Executive
IAVI	Irish Auctioneers and Valuers Institute
IBRC	Irish Bank Resolution Corporation
ICI	Insurance Corporation of Ireland
ICT	Information and communication technology
IDA	Industrial Development Authority
IFAC	Irish Fiscal Advisory Council
IFRS	International Financial Reporting Standards
IFSC	International Financial Services Centre
IFSRA	Irish Financial Services Regulatory Authority (see also Financial Regulator)
IL&P	Irish Life and Permanent Building Society
IMF	International Monetary Fund
INBS	Irish Nationwide Building Society
IPO	Initial public offerings
LTCM	Long-Term Capital Management
LTV	Loan to value
MNCs	Multinational corporations
MOU	Memorandum of Understanding
NAMA	National Asset Management Agency
NCM	New Classical Macroeconomics
NPRF	National Pension Reserve Fund
NTMA	National Treasury Management Agency
OECD	Organisation for Economic Co-operation and Development
Oireachtas	Combined upper and lower houses of the Irish Parliament

Acronyms and Abbreviations

PCAR	Prudential Capital Assessment Requirements
PD	Progressive Democrats
PISA	Programme for International Student Assessment
PSBB	Public Sector Benchmarking Body
PwC	PricewaterhouseCoopers
QEC	Quarterly Economic Commentary published by the ESRI
RHMPS	Review Body on Higher Remuneration in the Public Service
RTE	Radio Telefis Eireann: National radio and television station
S&L	Savings and Loans institutions
SBA	Stand by arrangement
SDR	Special Drawing Rights
Seanad	Upper House (Senate) of Irish Parliament
SGP	Stability and Growth Pact
SLS	Secured Lending Scheme
Taoiseach	Prime Minister
TARP	Troubled Assets Relief Program

Introduction—The Irish Financial Wake

Traditionally the Irish, who can sing the dead to sleep, have been good at organizing wakes. The financial wake of 2008 is another matter. The year 2008 will be known as the year of the great financial crisis, just as 1847 has gone down as 'Black 47', the year when the Great Irish Famine peaked. 'Black 47' involved a massive loss of population and a debilitating legacy of emigration. 'Black 2008', while not as catastrophic in human terms, caused extensive damage to a sizeable part of Ireland's economic fabric and had major repercussions for all parts of Irish society.

The emerging financial crisis crept slowly into the Irish psyche in 2008. At the beginning of that fateful year, notwithstanding some international concern over the developing sub-prime financial crisis in the United States, domestic confidence was still high. In its first assessment, the Central Bank of Ireland forecasted that real gross domestic product (GDP) would rise by about 3 per cent in 2008 and suggested that there would be 'a moderate pick up in growth in 2009 as the restraining impact of the housing sector's adjustment wanes'. The view of the Bank was that Irish economic growth would continue, albeit at a lower rate, and that, despite the incipient downturn in the property sector, there would be a soft landing for the Irish economy. This benign assessment mirrored those made by the International Monetary Fund (IMF), the European Union (EU), and the Organisation for Economic Co-operation and Development (OECD) around the same time.

The year 2007 had been a good one. Economic growth averaged over 5 per cent, unemployment was only 4.5 per cent of the labour force, the budget recorded a surplus and the general government debt to GDP ratio stood at an all-time low of 25 per cent. This was a highly impressive macroeconomic score card. Net emigration, a hardy perennial of the Irish economy and society up to the 1990s, had disappeared and the airports were full of immigrants from Eastern Europe flown in primarily on the hugely successful low-cost Irish airline, Ryanair. But despite the widely acclaimed success, a good part of the underlying economic and financial structure was rotting and would soon begin to fall apart. The 'best of times' would quickly be revealed as the 'worst of times'.

A virus had infected the Irish economy that ended up creating four inter-connected crises: (i) a property market crisis; (ii) a banking crisis; (iii) a fiscal crisis; and (iv) a financial crisis. These interrelated crises would together cause one of the most dramatic and largest reversals in economic fortune ever experienced by an industrial country. Real GDP would fall by 3 per cent in 2008 and by an unprecedented 7 per cent in 2009. Unemployment would triple to almost 14 per cent end-2010 and net emigration—thought to have been banished—would restart on a very sizeable scale. The Irish banking system would undergo a near collapse, necessitating a bailout, first via a comprehensive government guarantee in 2008, and later, by way of massive capital injections to be paid for by tax payers. Recourse would have to be had to large-scale liquidity assistance from the European Central Bank (ECB). As the deterioration accelerated, the budget deficit would jump to an unheard-of 31 per cent of GDP in 2010 and the debt/GDP ratio would quadruple, rising to almost 110 per cent end-2011. Household net worth would plummet.

Notwithstanding emergency efforts to salvage the budget and attempts to assess the true scale of the banking debacle, the underlying erosion of confi-dence in Ireland's ability to handle the damage could not be stemmed. As the second half of 2010 unfolded, the financial markets, the ECB, the EU and the G-7 Finance Ministers—meeting in Seoul, Korea, in Ireland's absence—started to conclude that nothing less than a full-blown financial rescue of Ireland was essential. However, the speed with which the Irish political leadership reacted could not match the rapidly changing financial circumstances.

It was left to the recently appointed Governor of the Central Bank of Ireland, Patrick Honohan, rather than the Taoiseach, Brian Cowen, or the Finance Minister, Brian Lenihan, to announce, in a hastily arranged radio interview from Frankfurt on Thursday, 18 November 2010, the start of the final act of the drama. The Irish government was to enter into discussions later that day to seek a bailout from the troika, comprising the ECB, the European Commission, and the IMF. It was Governor Honohan who ended up informing the Irish people of this unprecedented event that involved the ceding of a major part of financial and economic sovereignty to external institutions. This was a telling testimony as to the extent to which politicians had lost credibility with both the international institutions and the Irish public.

How could an economy with such an impressive macroeconomic record at the start of 2008 be transformed into near receivership by November 2010? This book seeks to provide a comprehensive analysis of the factors that caused the virtual collapse of the so-called Celtic Tiger. It is a complex story, involving many different individuals and institutions, both at home and abroad, and one that understandably has caused huge controversy throughout the length and breadth of Irish society. There is scarcely a household in Ireland that has not been profoundly affected, first by the boom and later, by the need to 'pick up the pieces'. Moreover, the Irish crisis—including the role played by external institutions such as the EU and ECB—has reverberated outside Irish shores and been the subject of considerable commentary and debate. It will be a long time before the dust finally settles on all the issues involved.

0.1 Assigning Responsibility

One objective of this book is to consider two interrelated questions which lie at the heart of the heated debate. First, at whose door can the blame for the debacle be laid? In December 2011, Taoiseach (Prime Minister) Enda Kenny told the Irish people in a televised address that 'you are not responsible for the crisis'.[1] By contrast, Peter Nyberg, in the report of his Commission on the causes of the crisis (Nyberg 2011), concluded that in some sense 'everyone was responsible'. Both statements, along with others dealing with the same theme, provoked strong public reactions at the time, both for and against. The question is of fundamental importance. If the Irish people as a whole was not responsible for the crisis, why should they have to pay for it? Furthermore, if blame should not be laid at Irish doors, it could be inferred that there was nothing fundamentally wrong with Irish economic policy-making that needed to be fixed.

Assigning 'responsibility' is a complex multidimensional issue that calls for a fair and balanced assessment of the roles of the different entities in the economy and society, as well as their mutual interaction. Thus, in considering the process of accountability, there is an important difference between possible criminal wrongdoing and gross errors of judgment. In addition, due weight needs be given to the role of external forces and institutions, in both the boom period and when the crisis began to unfold. At the domestic level, it is useful to keep different concepts of 'blame' in mind. The fact that the citizenry at large may have benefited greatly from the artificial and unsustainable boom, while important, does not necessarily mean that it was, in some sense, directly 'responsible' for it. Apart from the general public, institutions and groups with proven expertise may be specifically charged with certain key roles aimed at safeguarding the public interest. Other, less specialized groups or individuals, such as, for example, politicians or the media, might see their

---

[1] Just a few weeks later, the Taoiseach appeared to reverse course, stating at a symposium in Davos that it was the fact that 'Irish people went mad to borrow . . . which spawned greed . . . and led to the spectacular crash'.

role more passively, as deferring to the assessments of the so-called 'experts'. Distinctions along these lines are difficult but perhaps essential in order to arrive at reasonable and responsible overall judgments.

A second important question needing to be answered is whether, once the potential disaster started to unfold around 2008, there were policy actions or initiatives, other than those actually followed by the Irish authorities, that would have made a difference. How valid, for example, is the often-expressed view that the granting of the guarantee in September 2008, rather than the budgetary excesses between 2002–07, was the main cause of the crisis? Furthermore, even after the guarantee was provided, were there options available during 2009–10 that might have prevented the subsequent bailout by the troika in November 2010? Or was it the case that by 2007, 'the train had in reality already left the station' and that the final outcome was, in some sense, inevitable? This issue requires careful consideration of all the domestic and external forces involved. Indeed, whatever degree of consensus might exist as to the causes of the Irish crash, the discussion as to how it should have been handled continues to be deeply divisive.

0.2 Previous Assessments

Four official reports analysing various aspects of the causes of the Irish banking and financial crisis have been issued, those of Regling and Watson (2010), Honohan (2010), Wright (2011), and Nyberg (2011). These reports, based on inquiries that were not conducted in public, have concentrated on the identification of failures present in specific institutions, namely, the Central Bank, the Financial Regulator, the Department of Finance, and the banks taken as a group. Although comprehensive and detailed, they have certain limitations. First, the analyses by design did not address other key elements such as, for example, the roles played by politicians (both Government and the Opposition), economists, and the media. Second, due to their official nature, the conclusions are perforce presented in somewhat more guarded language than might be the case otherwise.[2] Third, none of the reports deal with events during 2009 and 2010, that is, the critical period prior to the bailout. Conversely, the books published by media commentators on the crisis, such as those of Carswell (2011), Cooper (2011), Murphy and Devlin (2009), O'Toole (2009), and Ross (2009), while also helpful and informative,

---

[2] For example, Governor Patrick Honohan in his report, would doubtless have taken into account (at a minimum subconsciously) that the Report was passing judgments on his immediate predecessor, John Hurley, as well as current Central Bank staff with whom he had begun to work shortly beforehand.

have tended to concentrate more on the personalities perceived to be central to the crisis—developers, bankers, and regulators.[3]

A balanced assessment of the crisis necessitates linking institutions and individuals, including, in many cases, consideration of their possible motivations and incentives, within a more structured framework. This can help identify whether structures facilitated faulty decision making or whether in some instances, individuals may have been in an insufficiently strong position to enforce adherence to institutional rules.

There are also a number of important features underlying the crisis which deserve more emphasis than has been accorded by several of these official reports and books. Firstly, there is a need to pay particular attention to the underlying ideological and institutional forces that fashioned the broader economic and financial environment. These included: the development of ever more sophisticated global financial markets; a huge increase in cross border financial capital flows; changes in mainstream economic thinking that emphasized a 'light regulation' approach and, in the process, minimized the attention paid to issues of financial stability; structural changes in banking that prioritized the sale of loans at the expense of risk management; and, more broadly, financial innovation that created a very large 'shadow' banking system featuring new instruments such as financial derivatives that represented, in Warren Buffett's forceful analogy, 'weapons of mass destruction'. These factors, taken together, help explain why, in many ways, 'Black 2008' was a disaster waiting to happen.

There is an understandable tendency on the part of some—by no means limited to Ireland—to think of the crisis as a somewhat uniquely Irish phenomenon. The scale and extent of Ireland's collapse may well have been unprecedented, at least in recent times. Yet, bubbles and associated financial crises date back to at least as early as the 18th century, when the Mississippi System in France and the South Sea Bubble in Great Britain occurred. In the last two decades of the 20th century, there were 112 financial crises in ninety-three different countries—see Caprio and Klingbiel (1999). Kindleberger and Aliber have noted the accentuation in the number and severity of such crises since the 1960s:

> The inference from the changes in asset prices, the changes in currency values, and the number and severity of banking crises since the mid-1960s is that the lessons of history have been forgotten or slighted. These decades have been the most tumultuous in international monetary history in terms of the number, scope, and severity of financial crises. (Kindleberger and Aliber 2005: 241)

---

[3] Kinsella and Leddin (ed.) (2010) contain several analytical articles dealing with several of the causal elements underlying the crisis.

Unfortunately, the downgrading of economic history and of the history of economic thought in university curricula left little in the form of memory of these events. The dominant economic paradigm that had emerged during the preceding decades, New Classical Economics, proclaimed that people were rational, bubbles were irrational and thus bubbles could not arise. As Reinhart and Rogoff (2009) put it in the title of their book on the history of financial crises, people—in Ireland and elsewhere—came to believe that 'this time is different'.

Secondly, the international dimension that played a major role in the timing of the fall of the Celtic Tiger deserves to be highlighted. 'Black 2008' was not just a domestic Irish financial crisis, it was part of a 'Global Black 2008', involving a near collapse of the US financial system following the bankruptcy of Lehman Brothers that acutely intensified shocks to the global real economy and enormously magnified worldwide financial tremors. Alumina, Bénétrix, Eichengreen, O'Rourke, and Rua in a recent paper describe the shocks to the global economy:

> the decline in manufacturing globally in the twelve months following the global peak in industrial production, which we place in early 2008, was as severe as in the twelve months following the peak in 1929 . . . World trade fell even faster in the first year of this crisis than in 1929–30. (2009: 2)

The financial tremors began with the run on UK Northern Rock and progressed to the major difficulties experienced by the world's biggest bank, the Royal Bank of Scotland, and of Halifax/Bank of Scotland (both very sizeable lenders into the Irish banking system). Europe was witnessing the Icelandic banking catastrophe, the start of other European 'bank rescues', and a slowly developing property and banking crisis in Spain. At the same time, the Greek economy was starting to come apart at the seams.

Thirdly, the official reports—partly due to their terms of reference—have been largely silent on the role of the European authorities (the EU and the ECB) before and during the crisis. There are several dimensions involved: the failure of the EU surveillance process under the Maastricht and Stability Growth Pact to prevent the emergence of large-scale underlying budget deficits such as those of Ireland; the implications for Ireland of the ECB's low interest rate accommodative monetary policy stance; the decision to delegate responsibility for financial regulation to the national level with adverse effects on the ability of the ECB to promote financial stability; the role of the ECB at the time of the controversial guarantee decision of September 2008; and the ECB's position with respect to the treatment of the banking sector debt incurred by the Irish taxpayer as a result of the guarantee.

0.3 A Story of Four Crises

The fall of the Celtic Tiger during 2008–10 is a story of four interrelated crises. It was initiated, first by the collapse of the property market which precipitated a banking crisis and a fiscal crisis, and which then combined to cause the fourth element, the financial crisis (Figure 0.1).

The *property market crisis* resulted from the collapse of a classic asset bubble. The bubble involved massive overvaluations driven by the general view that property represented the fastest and easiest way towards wealth and that, at worst, a 'soft landing' for the market would result. It was financed by over-lending from a banking system that equated profits with the maximization of loan sales, that abandoned portfolio diversification in favour of concentrating on lending to the property and construction sector and that neglected treasury management and the principle of maintaining a reasonable balance between its deposit base and lending. The Irish banks were able to access international wholesale funding in apparently limitless amounts and at very low interest rates. At the same time, they faced little or no effective domestic financial regulation.

The collapse of the property bubble led to the *banking crisis*. The over-reliance on external borrowing exposed the banks to growing liquidity difficulties from mid-2007 onwards which reached a critical point after the collapse of Lehman Brothers in September 2008. This led to a near run on the Irish banks at the end of that month and the granting of the government guarantee in respect of the banking system's liabilities. However, soon thereafter, solvency issues started to emerge and major assistance from the

Figure 0.1 The Fall of the Celtic Tiger: A Story of Four Crises

public purse was required throughout 2009–10 in order to keep the banks afloat.

In parallel, *the fiscal crisis* developed. Government revenue had become hugely over-dependent on taxes related to property transactions—including stamp duty, capital gains tax, VAT, and direct taxes levied on the property sector. Once the property market began to collapse, there was a precipitous fall-off in collections from these sources. At the same time, as economic growth turned sharply negative, rising unemployment imposed further strains on social protection expenditure. Thus even before the fiscal costs associated with the need to recapitalize the banks had been taken into account, the budget moved swiftly from surplus to a massive deficit.

The property, banking, and fiscal crises together led to the *financial crisis* in late 2010, a crisis which involved several elements. First, the banks' increasing inability to access liquidity from the interbank market led to them becoming dependent on funding from the ECB, both directly and indirectly, via the Central Bank of Ireland. By end-October 2010, such ECB/Central Bank lending amounted to €120 billion, equivalent to about three quarters of Irish GDP at the time. Second, from early 2010 onwards, the huge fiscal costs associated with the recapitalization of the banks emerged more clearly. Third, despite various rounds of emergency measures, the underlying budget deficit—abstracting from any banking-related costs—continued to exceed 10 per cent of GDP. All of these elements were reflected in a sharp downgrading of the rating of Irish sovereign debt and the spread on Irish bond yields soared. By early November 2010, all of Ireland's external partners, as well as the G-7, having come to the conclusion that intervention was needed to salvage the situation, insisted that Ireland apply for a bailout from the EU and the IMF. The final act in the drama had come to pass.

0.4 Coping With the Future

The current agreement is set to come to an end and the Irish crisis, as has happened elsewhere, will eventually run its course. But even at this stage it is important to try to look forward. Understandably, much of the current focus has been on the need to adhere to the fiscal and debt targets agreed with the EU/IMF so as to re-establish confidence and restore Ireland's creditworthiness. Yet fulfilling the programme's targets is by no means the whole story. This book does not attempt to deal with the economic and financial developments that have occurred since the November 2010 bailout in any detail. Nevertheless, a number of important issues stand out as one considers the outlook beyond the immediate crisis. For example, what are some of the factors likely to affect Ireland's future growth prospects? Can the euro debt crisis in general—as well as the particular debt burden of Ireland—be tackled successfully? How might Ireland's future relations with Europe evolve in light of current proposals for major architectural reforms of the euro area? And can one discern, even qualitatively, changes in the distribution of income and wealth within Ireland in the wake of the crisis?

Finally, there are the possible lessons to be learned from the current crisis. This is the second time in twenty-five years that Ireland has faced major economic and financial difficulties, (although the 1980s experience did not involve a full blown financial crisis). Can the most recent experience help identify some underlying reasons why economic policy-making has failed so seriously twice in a row? This would seem essential if some other crisis—emanating from whatever unknown source—is to be avoided in the future.

0.5 Structure of the Book

In sum, there is scope for a comprehensive examination of all the interrelated elements underlying the property, banking, fiscal, and financial collapses in Ireland. The analysis should be undertaken at the institutional level and give appropriate prominence to the ideological, historical, and international dimensions. It should address the management of the crisis, including whether there were realistic policy alternatives available that conceivably might have made a difference to the final outcome. It is also important to consider some of the issues and policy challenges that remain, even after the bailout comes to an end. Finally, there is the fundamental question—what lessons can be learned?

This book is organized as follows. The first three chapters provide an historical and ideological background to what ended up happening in Ireland. Chapter 1 discusses the rise of the Celtic Tiger up to 2000, identifying the particular elements that made this period so successful. Chapter 2 provides a broad ideological perspective, by describing the gradual dominance of market-oriented economic philosophies (New Classical Economics and the Efficient Markets Hypothesis), which played a pervasive and influential role in policy thinking in Ireland and elsewhere. Chapter 3 shows how, using as background the approaches of Kindleberger (1978), Kindleberger and Aliber (2005), and Minsky (1978), asset bubbles and associated financial crises such as that of Ireland have been a recurrent feature of many countries and periods throughout history.

The five chapters that follow deal with the specific elements that contributed, in various ways, to the eventual Irish collapse. Chapter 4 describes the evolution of the property bubble supported by increasingly reckless lending by the banks. Chapter 5 considers why financial regulation, at both Irish and European levels, failed to prevent this happening. Chapter 6 and Chapter 7 analyse the roots of the fiscal crisis, at the aggregate level and in terms of specific revenue and expenditure policies, respectively. The roles and influence of three important opinion forming institutions, namely, politicians— more broadly than just the members of the government—the economist community, and the media are assessed in Chapter 8.

The next three chapters are concerned with the unfolding of the crisis itself. Chapter 9 describes the gradually deteriorating economic and financial environment facing Ireland from mid-2007 onwards and the authorities' reactions. Chapter 10 is devoted to a detailed examination of the highly controversial guarantee decision of end-September 2008, including the question of whether feasible and better alternatives were available at the time. Developments, policy actions, and options post the guarantee that preceded up to the granting of the bailout at end-2010 are reviewed and analysed in Chapter 11.

Chapter 12 considers some of the important issues and policy challenges that are likely to be faced in the period ahead. Finally, Chapter 13 attempts to provide some overall conclusions as regards key issues raised in this Introduction.

References

Alumina, Miguel, Agustin Bénétrix, Barry Eichengreen, Kevin O'Rourke, and Gisela Rua (2009) 'From Great Depression to Great Credit Crises: Similarities, Differences and Lessons'. Paper presented to the 50th Economic Policy Meeting, Tilburg. October 23–24.

Carswell, Simon (2011) *Anglo Republic. Inside the Bank that Broke Ireland* (Dublin).

Caprio, Gerard Jr, and Daniela Klingebiel (1999) 'Episodes of Systemic and Borderline Financial Crises', Mimeo. The World Bank. (Washington).

Cooper, Matt (2011) *How Ireland Went Bust* (Dublin).

Honohan, Patrick (2010) *The Irish Banking Crisis: Regulatory and Financial Stability Policy 2003–2008:* A Report to the Minister of Finance by the Governor of the Central Bank (Dublin).

Kindleberger, Charles (1978) *Manias, Panics and Crashes: A History of Financial Crises* (New York).

Kindleberger, Charles and Ron Aliber (revised edn,) (2005) *Manias, Panics and Crashes: A History of Financial Crises* (New York).

Kinsella, Stephen and Anthony Leddin. Editors (2010) *Understanding Ireland's Economic Crisis: Prospects and Recovery* (Berkshire).

Minsky, Hyman (1978) *The Financial Instability Hypothesis: A Restatement*, re-published in *Can 'It' Happen Again: Essays on Instability and Finance* (New York, 1982).

Murphy, David and Martina Devlin (2009) *Banksters: How a Powerful Elite Squandered Ireland's Wealth* (Dublin).

Nyberg, Peter (2011) *Misjudging Risks: Causes of the Systemic Banking Crisis in Ireland*, Report of the Commission of Investigation into the Banking Sector in Ireland, Government Publications (Dublin).

O'Toole, Fintan (2009) *Ship of Fools. How Stupidity and Corruption Sank the Celtic Tiger* (Dublin).

Regling, Klaus and Max Watson (2010) *A Preliminary Report on the Sources of Ireland's Banking Crisis*, Government Publications (Dublin).

Reinhart, Carmen M. and Kenneth S. Rogoff (2009) *This Time Is Different: Eight Centuries of Financial Folly* (Princeton).

Ross, Shane (2009) *The Bankers: How the Banks Brought Ireland to is Knees* (Dublin).

Wright, Rob (2010) *Strengthening the Capacity of the Department of Finance*: Report of the Independent Review Panel, Department of Finance, Government Publications. (Dublin).

Part I
Background

1

The Rise of the Celtic Tiger

Europe's Shining Light

> Headline of *The Economist*, 17 May 1997[*]

One thing is clear. We don't have the option of turning away from the future. No one gets to vote on whether technology is going to change our lives.

> Bill Gates, *The Road Ahead*

In January 1988 *The Economist* published a survey of the Republic of Ireland. The title was 'Poorest of the Rich' and it was accompanied by a photograph of a young girl with her child begging on the street. The opening lines of this survey conveyed a Dickensian bleakness:

> Take a tiny, open ex-peasant economy. Place it next door to a much larger one, from which it broke away with great bitterness barely a lifetime ago. Infuse it with a passionate desire to enjoy the same lifestyle as its former masters, but without the same industrial heritage of natural resources. Inevitable result: extravagance, frustration, debt . . . Ireland is easily the poorest country in rich north-west Europe. Its gross domestic product is a mere 64 per cent of the European Community average. (*The Economist*, 16 January 1988)[**]

Less than ten years later, the tone of *The Economist* had changed. Once again, Ireland was on its front cover but this time with the title 'Europe's shining light'. The lead editorial remarked:

> Just yesterday, it seems, Ireland was one of Europe's poorest countries. Today it is about as prosperous as the European average, and getting richer all the time. (*The Economist*, 17 May 1997)

The transformation of the Irish economy had been extraordinarily impressive. High and sustained economic growth, a very low ratio of debt to GDP (Table 1.1), current account balance of payments surpluses, falling

---

[*] © The Economist Newspaper Limited, London (17 May 1997).
[**] © The Economist Newspaper Limited, London (16 January 1988).

Table 1.1. Ireland: Economic Growth and Indebtedness, 1987–2011

Year	Rate of Change of Real GDP (%)	Public Debt (% of GDP)
1987	3.6	109.2
1988	3.0	107.5
1989	5.6	98.8
1990	7.7	93.5
1991	1.6	94.6
1992	3.6	91.4
1993	2.3	94.2
1994	5.9	88.2
1995	8.9	81.2
1996	7.6	72.7
1997	10.9	63.7
1998	7.8	53.0
1999	9.9	48.0
2000	9.3	37.5
2001	4.8	35.2
2002	5.9	31.9
2003	4.2	30.7
2004	4.5	29.1
2005	5.3	27.1
2006	5.3	24.7
2007	5.2	24.8
2008	–3.0	44.2
2009	–7.0	65.2
2010	–0.4	92.5
2011	0.7	105.0

Source: IMF WEO database

unemployment, net immigration, and a budget surplus are the stuff of macro-economists' dreams. All the key macroeconomic indicators were positive. Ireland, traditionally a laggard behind its nearest neighbour, had achieved a higher per capita GDP than that of the UK.

The metaphor, the Celtic Tiger, first coined by Kevin Gardiner, then working at Morgan Stanley, in August 1994, became the fashionable neologism for the Irish economy. Commentators were fascinated as to how the economy had moved from a 'bleak house' to a 'shining light' phase in such a short time. Many articles were written about the Celtic Tiger as writers hurried to examine the amazing transformation. These were followed by books—Barry (1999), Gray (1997), and Sweeney (1998).

Economic theorists analysed the phenomenon of how Ireland had achieved this new economic growth status. How could a country with a very sluggish performance reach a high growth path so quickly? How could a country with persistently large budget deficits and an extremely high level of state indebtedness—over 100 per cent of GDP—suddenly achieve a budget surplus and a debt ratio of less than 40 per cent by the year 2000? How could a country with chronic mass unemployment and net emigration become one enjoying close to full employment and net immigration? The Irish economy, as it moved towards the millennium, was fascinating, not only because of the extent of the transformation of its growth performance, but also by the rapidity with which this happened.

It would be wrong, as some commentators and politicians have done, to over ascribe to Ireland some unique magical qualities, some 'potion', that caused a low performing economy to become the Celtic Tiger. There were many forces that had been at work to help make Ireland's economy 'catch up' and gradually converge towards the European average. However, while the 'catch up' paradigm explains part of the story, the speed and extent of Ireland's transformation was primarily driven by high-tech multinationals, the vanguard of a major worldwide revolution in information technology. The benefits of this revolution owed much to the phenomenon of globalization and, in particular, to the coming together of two economic tectonic plates, those of the United States and the European Union. This was the spark that set Ireland on the road to rapid prosperity.

Globalization enabled Ireland to take advantage of this revolution and move from the periphery towards the centre of the new global economy. By the end of the 1990s, Ireland had become the second largest exporter of packaged computer software in the world after the United States. Twelve of *Fortune's* top twenty electronic companies and all of its top ten pharmaceutical companies had plants in Ireland. From having virtually no major export manufacturing industries (Guinness, Irish whiskey, and Bailey's Irish Cream constituting exceptions), Ireland had established a sizeable platform for US high-tech companies to compete in the European market.

In this new global economy how meaningful was it to talk of core and periphery, to discuss convergence and catch up? These terms were more appropriate in an industrialized world where transport and communication costs conferred benefits on countries at the core and where investment from core economies could gradually help peripheral countries to converge economically. But in the post-industrial high-tech world, these concepts had started to become anachronistic.

This new economic geography, to use the words of Paul Krugman (1997), turned traditional convergence theory on its head. Ireland had successfully moved from the equivalent of a donkey-and-cart economy to a high-tech economy by leap-frogging over the intermediate hump of industrialization. Indeed, arguably, the absence of a large industrial base actually helped Ireland. This enabled the government to provide significant corporate tax advantages which would have been difficult if a large industrial base paying significant corporate taxes had already existed. Furthermore, the lack of industrialization meant a relative absence of obsolete capital and rigid labour practices.

The Economist's 1988 description of Ireland as a poor struggling economy, though harsh, was realistic. Economic growth had averaged 0.2 per cent over

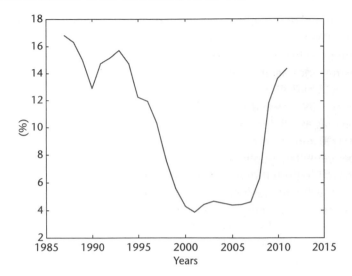

Figure 1.1 Unemployment Rate in Ireland, 1987–2011

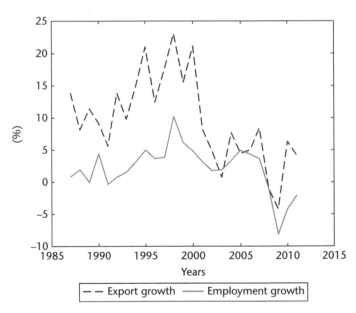

Figure 1.2 Export Growth and Employment Growth in Ireland, 1987–2011

the previous five years, unemployment reached 18 per cent and the national debt had risen to 108 per cent of GDP.

When did all this change? Many identify 1987 as the take-off year for the economy when fiscal retrenchment was introduced to correct for the excesses of the late 1970s and early 1980s (Figures 1.1 and 1.2). Helped by a boom in the world economy, good growth occurred over the following few years. But 1991–1993 produced little by way of a spectacular performance— employment actually fell in 1991—and the familiar pessimistic questions were arising once again. Where was the country heading? Was emigration always inevitable?

Suddenly, 1994 saw a dramatic change. Over the next seven years, real GDP growth averaged 7.8 per cent. During this period, employment grew by more than 500,000 and unemployment plummeted from almost 16 per cent to just over 4 per cent. The public sector deficit moved into substantial surplus and the debt/GDP ratio fell dramatically. An unprecedented boom in consumption and investment was reflected in all forms of expenditure, ranging from new car sales to house purchases.

1.1 The Historical Context

How Ireland's abrupt leap-frogging from a predominantly pre-industrial economy to a post-industrial high-tech economy came about is discussed in more detail below. However, it is helpful first to place these developments in a broader historical perspective.

Three important aspects of Ireland's approaches to economic policy since independence in 1922 deserve to be highlighted:

(i) The fluctuating openness of the economy to trade and capital flows.
(ii) Periodic policy weaknesses.
(iii) The growing Europeanization of the Irish economy.

1.1.1 *The Fluctuating Openness of the Irish Economy*

Ireland is the classic model of a small open economy. The smallness element is self evident as Irish GDP constitutes less than 1 per cent of aggregate European Union GDP. However, Ireland has experienced varying degrees of openness since independence in 1922. In the first ten years of the Irish State, the economy continued its free trading relationship with the UK. Its banking system was also closely linked to that of the UK and, when the Irish Free State pound was established in 1927, it was decided to maintain a one-to-one parity with sterling. Irish labour emigrated without restriction to the UK and capital flowed freely between Ireland and the UK. Agriculture was the main stay of the domestic economy and of exports.

However, when Eamon De Valera assumed the office of Taoiseach (Prime Minister) in 1932, his government's policies sharply reduced the openness of the economy to both trade and capital flows. Restrictions on external trade were intensified during the so-called 'Economic War' with the UK, between 1932–38, when the popular refrain was 'burn everything British except their coal'. Trade was constrained by the establishment of infant industries behind high tariff walls, many of which were maintained even when the Economic War ended in 1938.

The Control of Manufactures Acts of 1932 and 1934—which remained in force until 1957—were a major legacy of that period and sought to copper fasten a protectionist industrial policy. These acts prohibited majority foreign ownership of Irish industry by stipulating that Irish citizens had to control 51 per cent of the voting shares in manufacturing companies. In effect, this prohibited foreign capital from investing significantly in the Irish economy. Although there was no compelling reason for foreign companies to come to Ireland between 1932 and 1957, the restrictions embodied in these Acts implied that that their presence would not be welcomed. As Ó Gráda (1994: 407) noted, 'Fianna Fáil [the governing party] sought to reserve the domestic market for Irish capital'.

Paradoxically, during this period, Irish capital was free to move out of Ireland—at least to the Sterling Area. Capital outflows from Ireland were endemic in the 1940s and 1950s, as the banking sector invested a considerable portion of its deposits in external assets such as British government securities. With foreign capital prevented from investing in the manufacturing sector and the Irish banking system transferring much of its investible resources abroad, it was not surprising to see little Irish economic development during the 1940s and 1950s. Thus, the stagnant economy missed out on the European post-war boom and net annual emigration of over 40,000 occurred throughout the 1950s.

The abolition of the Control of Manufactures Acts in 1957 signalled the beginning of a radical departure in economic policy aimed at welcoming foreign capital to Ireland. In 1958 Dr T. K. Whitaker, the Secretary of the Department of Finance, produced a report entitled *Economic Development*, which was highly critical of the prevailing policy of protecting infant industries and instead proposed the encouragement of foreign capital with tax concessions and other incentives. Moves towards freer trade were initiated through the signing of the Anglo-Irish Free Trade Agreement in 1965 and Ireland's decision to join the European Economic Community (EEC) in 1973.

Membership of the EEC marked the first step in the reduction of Ireland's close economic and financial links with the UK. The process was accelerated by Ireland's decision to join the European Monetary System (EMS) in December 1978, a decision that led to the breaking of the one-to-one parity of the Irish pound with sterling in March 1979. It was given major momentum by the signing of the Maastricht Treaty in 1992. Ireland became one of the eleven founding members of the European Monetary Union (EMU) in January 1999, despite the decision of the UK, its largest trading partner at the time, not to join EMU.

The process of Europeanization, discussed in greater detail below, also had significant implications for policies with respect to international capital movements. From 1979 onwards, the Irish pound, newly linked with the currencies of the Exchange Rate Mechanism (ERM), floated against sterling as the European currencies themselves fluctuated against sterling. In an effort to protect the value of the Irish currency, the Central Bank, in 1979, introduced exchange control regulations limiting capital transactions outside the Sterling Area. However, the growing commitment to European Monetary Union led to the dismantling of these controls in the early 1990s, the last vestiges of which were abolished in 1992. With the introduction of the Single European Market at the end of 1992—Ireland had signed the Single European Act in 1986—the Irish economy *vis-à-vis* Europe had become a fully open economy for commodities, labour, and capital.

There was, however, a significant immediate deflationary impact on the economy in 1992/3. The sterling devaluation of late summer 1992, Ireland's continued trade links with the UK economy and the weakness of the other ERM currencies, led to a period of continued speculative attacks against the Irish pound which had effectively appreciated. The authorities felt obliged to maintain the exchange rate in the narrow ERM bands even after the sterling devaluation. In their attempt to defend the currency, domestic interest rates were raised to very high levels—overnight, money market rates reached as high as 100 per cent—which considerably dampened domestic demand. However, the devaluation of the Irish pound in January 1993 and the move to wider ERM exchange rate bands in August 1993, together with the commitment to EMU, were successful in removing these exchange rate pressures. The more stable exchange rate environment post 1993, together with the growing confidence that interest rates would fall to German levels as European Monetary Union approached, helped boost domestic demand. In parallel, the openness of the economy became more entrenched. Ireland, by the end of the 1990s, had become the second most open economy in the OECD (Organisation for Economic Co-operation and Development), with the sum of exports and imports constituting more than 1.7 times GDP.

1.1.2 Policy Weaknesses

As noted above, the insufficient appreciation by policy makers of the inherent openness of the Irish economy had led to *two* early policy mistakes. The first was the near closure of the economy to trade in the 1930s. This was followed by a second mistake, the continued neglect, until 1957, of the role of international capital in promoting economic growth.

A *third* failure occurred in 1977–81 when the government attempted to stimulate domestic economic growth by Keynesian expansionary fiscal policies without adequate consideration of the consequences for the balance of payments. The government mistakenly believed that fiscal pump priming, by means of tax cuts and increased government expenditure, could push the economy to a high growth path and eventual full employment. This approach did not pay sufficient heed to Keynes's own cautionary views on expansionary policy in an open economy (Keynes 1936). The financing of the high and growing public sector deficits necessitated substantial domestic and foreign borrowing. While faster growth resulted in the short term, much of the budgetary stimulus leaked out of the economy via increased expenditure on imports. Domestic borrowing also exacerbated inflationary pressures. By 1981 the current account deficit of the balance of payments had reached almost 15 per cent of gross national product (GNP) (as against 5 per cent in 1977) and inflation had risen to 20 per cent, far exceeding both UK and average EU inflation of 12 per cent.

The growing macroeconomic crisis was not addressed immediately. Although employing the rhetoric of fiscal retrenchment, domestic politicians were unwilling to take the necessary harsh action. This partly was due to an uneasy coalition mix of the Fine Gael/Labour governments which governed from mid-1981 to early 1987 (except for a short nine-month period of Fianna Fáil rule). The failure to tackle decisively the major macroeconomic imbalances led to stagnant growth between 1982–86 and increasing government indebtedness—over half of which was held externally—which peaked at 109 per cent of GDP in 1987.

The year 1987 was to prove an important turning point from the perspective of the public finances. The new Fianna Fáil government, which had committed itself in the general election of that year to increasing public expenditure, suddenly switched course after being elected and announced a program of major fiscal cutbacks. Despite the electoral support given to Fianna Fáil, most people recognized that retrenchment was unavoidable. Honohan (1999: 85–86) suggested that 'the real fear [on the part of the new government] was of a financial meltdown with foreign and domestic financial market refusal to rollover debt'. The broad public support for fiscal consolidation was epitomized by the commitment of Fine Gael, the main opposition party, led by Alan Dukes, not to precipitate an election provided that the government undertook the required fiscal measures—an approach that became known as the Tallaght strategy.

1.1.3 *The Growing Europeanization of the Irish Economy*

The most important steps taken in Ireland's relations with the European Union and the Eurozone are highlighted in Box 1.1.

Box 1.1 THE GROWING EUROPEANIZATION OF THE IRISH ECONOMY

1973—Ireland joined the European Economic Community (EEC).

1978—Ireland joined the European Monetary System (EMS).

1979—The break in the one-to-one parity with sterling following commitments to the Exchange Rate Mechanism of the EMS.

1986—Ireland signed the Single European Act aimed at establish a full single market by 1992.

1990—Exchange control regulations largely removed.

1992—Ireland signed the Maastricht Treaty and committed to joining the future European Monetary Union. Ireland became part of the Single European Market.

1992/3—The breakdown of the narrow-band ERM of the EMS.

1993—Devaluation of Irish pound.

1997/8—Convergence of Irish interest rates to German interest rates.

1999—European Monetary Union. The irrevocable fixing of exchange rates between the currencies of participating member states. The euro introduced in a non physical form. National currencies of participating countries (the members of the Eurozone) ceased to exist independently.

2002—The new euro notes and coin introduced on January 1.

Europeanization, a key element in the transformation of the economy, was initiated in 1973 when Ireland joined the EEC. The benefits of membership to Ireland's ailing agricultural sector were obvious and the Common Agricultural Policy (CAP) provided farmers with guaranteed prices for many of their products. Ireland also became adept at obtaining and using effectively European structural and cohesion funds which, according to Barry (1999), may have raised Ireland's GNP by 4 per cent. However, there was a reluctance at times to accept the other part of the 'deal' with Europe, namely, adoption of a low inflationary profile and stronger fiscal discipline which Germany had spearheaded. The German Chancellor, Helmut Schmidt, had been instrumental, along with France's president, Valéry Giscard d'Estaing, in launching, in 1978, the EMS, as an intermediate stage towards the target of European Monetary Union.

Paradoxically, as observed earlier, Ireland committed to joining the Exchange Rate Mechanism of the EMS in 1978 at the very time when it had embarked on a policy of fiscal profligacy. The underlying contradiction of committing Ireland to a (relatively) fixed exchange rate regime, the EMS, while simultaneously pursuing excessively expansionary fiscal and monetary expansion, did not seem to concern the political leaders at the time. Instead, the breaking of the one-to-one parity with sterling, in March 1979 was perceived as representing a symbol of success as a nation. Ireland had come of age, many felt, its currency was no longer inextricably linked to sterling and the Irish pound de-coupled from sterling was born. It was also believed that

23

the anchoring of the Irish currency to a Deutschmark (DM) bloc would ensure lower inflation.

The initial anti-inflation assumptions behind the decision to break the link became quickly dated as sterling, due to its enhanced petro-currency status, strengthened and the Deutschmark (DM) weakened. Nevertheless, the 1978 decision represented an important step in the reorientation of Irish economic policy in the direction of an increased commitment to the Continental European countries and reduced dependency on the UK. While this policy did not have an immediate pay-off, it did mean that the later momentum towards European Monetary Union via the Maastricht Treaty represented a seamless move along a spectrum. This evolving commitment to Europeanization contrasted with that of the United Kingdom which continued to maintain an ambivalent attitude towards monetary union negotiations before finally deciding not to participate.

1.2 How Globalization and Europeanization Came Together to Benefit Ireland

While Ireland's economic structure and outlook was undergoing a sharp movement towards Europe, there was an even more significant shift in the US and European Union's economic tectonic plates due to globalization. Silicon Valley in California had become the centre of a virtually unprecedented revolution, driven by new advances in information technology and a host of supporting applications. In the early 1990s, most people did not have portable computers, mobile phones, user-friendly computer programmes, or access to the Internet. The new telecommunications are now part of the everyday working practices of people throughout the entire world and have fundamentally changed traditional concepts of time and distance. Now an entrepreneur based in the Aran Islands on the periphery of Ireland, on the periphery of Europe, may run a business in Prague selling services to New York, Frankfurt, and Tokyo while fishing in Galway Bay. In the world of high-tech, the periphery has lost much of its meaning. In this world, the establishment of a European base from which US multinationals could market their products became a high priority. The search for suitable locations was given special urgency by the creation of the Single European Market and the plan for the move to monetary union via the Maastricht Treaty.

By the late 1980s and early 1990s, Ireland was well positioned to attract a considerable part of US MNCs' (multinational corporations) business. The Industrial Development Authority (IDA) had earlier targeted, in the 1970s and 1980s, emerging MNCs, particularly in sectors such as computers, computer software, telecommunications, pharmaceuticals, and chemicals.

These successful initiatives led to the major expansion of US multinationals into Ireland. By the early 1990s, the high-tech revolution had gathered considerable momentum, with the advent of far more sophisticated and user-friendly computer and telecommunications devices, facilitating a second and more intensive phase of inward capital investment. Also, several large-scale pharmaceutical manufacturing firms began to move their operations to Ireland.

While not the only factor, the new MNCs were attracted to Ireland on account of the continued very favourable corporate tax regime—initially a zero per cent tax rate on the profits of manufactured exports, and, later, a 10 per cent rate, subsequently increased to 12.5 per cent. There were further advantages in the form of capital grants, generous investment depreciation allowances and tax exemptions pertaining to research and development activities.

For US multinationals, Ireland possessed the major linguistic advantage of being English-speaking. However, unlike the other English-speaking member (the UK), Ireland was fully committed to the Europeanization process. The UK's semi-detached approach to Europe came to the fore in 1992 when sterling broke from the ERM and began to float and was later reflected in a refusal to join the EMU. Ireland, with its low corporate tax rates, relatively young English-speaking and computer literate labour force, and fully integrated into Europe through the Single European Market and European Monetary Union, was ideally positioned.

The OECD later noted that 'US investment in Ireland tripled from 1991 to 1993, just at the time of the implementation of the Single European Market programme' (OECD 1999: Note 45). There were 'demonstration effects' in that the favourable experience of the initial group of MNCs encouraged their competitors to follow suit. According to McCarthy (1999), US direct investment in Ireland averaged around 2.75 per cent of GNP between 1994 and 1998. Krugman (1997: 43) calculated that US foreign direct investment (FDI) in Ireland was 50 per cent higher per capita than in the UK and six times as high as in France or Germany. In 1997 Ireland 'ranked fifth in the world as a destination for US direct investment outflows' (OECD 1999:12).

A considerable part of the economic growth witnessed in Ireland in the 1990s thus emanated from growth that was waiting to happen in certain key sectors. Ireland had been able to harness this opportunity successfully. In 1993, the net manufacturing output of high-tech companies in just five sectors (computers, computer software, chemicals, pharmaceuticals, cola concentrates)—companies such as Apple, Boston Scientific, Coca Cola, 3 Com, Dell, Gateway, IBM, Intel, Hewlett Packard, Microsoft, Motorola, Northern Telecom, Pepsi, Pfizer, Schering Plough—amounted to IR£5 billion and constituted 43 per cent of total Irish net manufacturing output (Census of Industrial

Production 1993). By 1996, output of these sectors had reached IR£9.6 billion, equivalent to 53 per cent of total net output. Direct employment in these sectors constituted only some 14 per cent (32,000) of the total labour force engaged in manufacturing activity. However, the indirect employment effect was very considerable as these enterprises utilized a wide range of supporting service industries (see below).

In the introduction to *Understanding Ireland's Economic Growth* (1999), Frank Barry wrote:

> There is widespread agreement by now on the factors that have a role to play in the story . . . Generally included are the long-term consequences of the fiscal stabilisation of the late 1980s, the European Structural Funds, the increased educational attainment of the workforce, continued Irish success in attracting FDI inflows, and the wage moderation and peaceful labour relations that have characterised the last decade. (Barry 1999: 1)

Barry enumerated several reasons that were *necessary* for Ireland's surge in economic growth in the latter part of the 1990s. Honohan and Walsh (2002) have argued that the outstanding performance of the Irish economy in the 1990s was a delayed structural transformation, as the proportion of the population at work outside agriculture and their productivity at last spurted towards levels long achieved by other countries.

It seemed that one could approvingly tick off all the right boxes that provided drivers for the move to a new and sustained economic growth path. The then Taoiseach, Bertie Ahern, ventured his view in 2008 of the magical potion that the Irish had developed:

> Sound, evidence-based policy-making is clearly critical to our economic success, but other factors like workforce adaptability and business innovation have huge roles to play. What we are seeing in this country is that all of the factors which allow us to continue to succeed and to develop are here. So I think the future is bright. (Sweeney 2008: 86)

But as a paradigm of a young, well-educated labour force utilizing European funds along with US capital inflows to produce economic growth in an environment characterized by fiscal and wage moderation, this was incomplete. Such an interpretation places too much emphasis on Ireland's achievements and gives insufficient attention to the major role of developments in the world economy. While the conditions outlined above were surely necessary, the *sufficient* condition, the spark that set off the Celtic Tiger boom, lay in two phenomena, the US revolution in information technology centred in Silicon Valley and the progressive economic and monetary unification across Europe. Ireland started to prosper in the 1990s as illustrated clearly by Figures 1.1 and 1.2, because it was able to adapt to and utilize the enormous forces unleashed by these two developments. Instead of continued isolation at the periphery, as had been the case during the Industrial Revolution and the post-World War II economic boom, Ireland, for once, positioned itself successfully in the centre. Without Ireland intermediating the high-tech revolution between Silicon Valley and Europe, it is quite likely that there would have been no 'Celtic Tiger'.

There were, of course, important specific domestic initiatives that supported these developments. Firstly, successive Irish governments since the 1960s, as a fundamental tenet of economic policy, encouraged foreign direct investment (FDI). Secondly, the IDA successfully identified and targeted emerging high-tech companies across a range of sectors at an early stage, such as computers, computer software, telecommunications, chemicals, and pharmaceuticals. This created important first-mover advantages for Ireland. Thirdly, investment in education produced a solidly educated young labour force. Fourthly, the vitally necessary fiscal retrenchment implemented in 1987 was followed by a sustained period of equilibrium in the public finances. Finally, a 'social partnership' model was introduced that led to wage moderation in return for lowering direct taxation. While this preserved industrial peace and secured important gains in external competitiveness, the approach, as will be seen later, contained major weaknesses that contributed significantly to the eventual fiscal collapse.

Ireland's impressive economic performance during the Celtic Tiger boom, which culminated in growth rates in both real GDP and GNP of 9.3 per cent in 2000, can be illustrated as a series of circles (Figure 1.3). At the core is the circle of the multinationals, the *sine qua non* for growth during this period and which had propelled Irish exports to register record rates of increase—over 21 per cent in real terms in 2000 (Figure 1.2). Radiating out from this circle

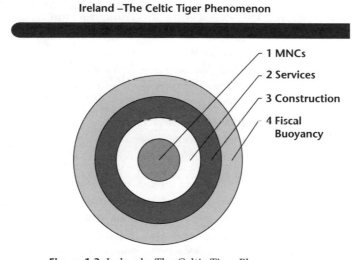

Ireland –The Celtic Tiger Phenomenon

1 MNCs

2 Services

3 Construction

4 Fiscal Buoyancy

Figure 1.3 Ireland—The Celtic Tiger Phenomenon

there was further economic growth from the services sector resulting both from the MNCs themselves and the expanding International Financial Services Centre (IFSC).[1] Both of these required professional services in banking, law and accountancy, hotel and restaurant services, and transport services. The surge in employment by the MNCs, the IFSC and these supporting services sectors fed into a third circle, that of construction. Demand for property in the form of factories, offices, houses and apartments, boomed, stimulated by low interest rates and a wider range of credit facilities available to borrowers.

The fourth growth circle, fiscal revenue, resulted from tax buoyancy and enabled the government to increase expenditure while simultaneously lowering tax rates. By 2000, the top marginal tax rate had been reduced from 65 per cent to 46 per cent, the rate of capital gains tax had been cut back from 60 per cent to 20 per cent, and the capital acquisitions tax rate had fallen from 55 per cent to 40 per cent. The rise in real disposable incomes increased confidence further and the growth of real consumption reached a record high of 10.5 per cent in 2000. By the end of the decade, these mutually reinforcing tendencies had led the Celtic Tiger to what many believed was the start of an eternal golden age.

But matters did not turn out as planned or hoped. As will be seen, the Tiger continued to roar for much of the following decade, but the driving forces were different and the seeds were being sown for an eventual collapse. From 2001 onwards, the MNCs continued to grow but at a much lower pace. In what proved to be a fatal departure from the genuine Celtic Tiger, economic growth started to be largely driven, not by exports—Figure 1.2 illustrates the downturn in the rate of growth of exports from 2001—but by a massive increase in domestic demand. This surge in demand was in turn based on an artificial construction boom and soaring government spending financed on the back of it. The Irish economy moved from high-tech-based growth to a property boom which would cause the previous 'virtuous' construction circle to become a severely distended bubble. The eventual bursting of this bubble towards the end of the decade would puncture fatally all the other circles—apart from the MNC sector—and lead to Ireland's fully fledged financial crisis.

Later chapters deal in detail how, driven by serious failures of policy-making, the collapse occurred. However, as background, it is important to first examine how mainstream macroeconomics had gradually shifted in the direction of emphasizing a highly 'market friendly/deregulation' agenda,

---

[1] The IFSC (International Financial Services Centre) was established in 1987 in the Dublin docklands area with European Union approval. It currently employs over 25,000 people. At the start of 2011 it administered €1.9 trillion in investment funds. It dealt in half of the world's leased aircraft fleet and was the largest provider of cross-border insurance in the European Union.

especially for the financial sector. This aspect, which is the subject of the next chapter, was a pervasive influence on economic policy thinking in very many countries, and plays an important role in understanding the roots of the Irish crisis.

1.3 Conclusions

This chapter has described the rise of the unique phenomenon known as the Celtic Tiger. By the second half of the 1990s, Ireland's rate of economic growth had surged to double digits, a most impressive performance relative to the pedestrian pace of previous decades. The year 2000 witnessed an enviable golden macroeconomic scorecard—continued high growth, low unemployment, a budgetary surplus and a low and falling debt to GDP ratio. The Celtic Tiger had truly arrived. Many reasons have been advanced to explain the growth of the Celtic Tiger. This analysis has focused on how two—sometimes underestimated—factors coalesced in Ireland's favour in the 1990s: first, the emergence of one the most extraordinarily influential events of our times, namely, the high-tech revolution centred in Silicon Valley in California; and second, the growing Europeanization of the Irish economy.

In this unprecedented and exciting environment of high speed technology and communication a new economic geography emerged in which the traditional divisions between economic centres and periphery disappeared. Henceforth a country on the periphery could move, economically speaking, to the centre by attracting high-tech MNC investment. Ireland, a country with no strong industrial tradition, was able to vault from the equivalent of a donkey-and-cart economy to a post-modern high-tech economy without experiencing the intervening phase of industrialization. The IDA enticed newly emerging US companies by offering attractive corporate tax rates alongside the availability of a young, relatively well-educated English-speaking labour force.

Ireland further increased its appeal for MNCs by deepening its links to the emerging European Union. The advent of the Single European Market and the move to monetary union signalled to US MNCs the need to establish European-based centres to produce and market their goods and services. A strong commitment to pro-European policies, in contrast to the semi-detached UK approach to European integration, enhanced Ireland's attractiveness as the only English-speaking member of the European Monetary Union.

Ireland succeeded in capturing a disproportionately large share of US MNC investment, and a number of virtuous interacting circles developed. As exports boomed, employment surged both directly through the MNCs and indirectly through their demand for services such as accountancy, law, hotels and restaurants. The growth in exports and employment boosted tax revenues, enabling the budget to move from deficit to surplus and the national debt to fall sharply. Higher incomes in turn produced further growth in the building and construction sector in response to the accommodation demands of the growing labour force. Alas, as will be seen later, it was in this last property-related circle that the Achilles Heel of the hitherto successful Irish economy would soon start to appear.

References

Barry, Frank (ed.) (1999) *Understanding Ireland's Economic Growth* (London).

Gray, Alan (ed.) (1997) *International Perspectives on the Irish Economy* (Dublin).

Honohan, Patrick and Brendan Walsh (2002) 'Catching Up With The Leaders: The Irish Hare, *Brookings Panel on Economic Activity* (Washington).

Honohan, Patrick (1999) 'Fiscal Adjustment and Disinflation in Ireland: Setting the Macro Basis of Economic Recovery and Expansion' in Frank Barry (ed.). *Understanding Ireland's Economic Growth* (London).

Keynes, John Maynard (1936) *The General Theory of Employment, Interest and Money* (London).

Krugman, Paul (1997) 'Good News from Ireland: A Geographical Perspective' in *International Perspectives of the Irish Economy* (ed.) Alan Gray (Dublin).

McCarthy, John (1999) 'Foreign Direct Investment: An Overview', *Central Bank of Ireland Quarterly Bulletin*, Autumn 2, pp. 55–65.

OECD (1999) *OECD Economic Survey: Ireland 1999* (Paris).

Ó Gráda, Cormac (1994) *Ireland A New Economic History* (Oxford).

Sweeney, Paul (ed.) (2008) *The Celtic Tiger Ireland's Economic Miracle Explained* (Dublin).

2

Ideology and Financial Innovation

> Practical men, who believe themselves to be quite exempt from any intellectual influence, are usually the slave of some defunct economist
>
> John Maynard Keynes[1]

'Black 2008' could be presented in a format writ large as the logical worldwide outcome of a period characterized by excessive innovation and inadequate regulation in global financial markets. The equivalent of a financial nuclear explosion epicentred at the bankruptcy of Lehman Brothers, caused the near implosion of the international financial system and led to what has come to be called the Great Recession. In Ireland's case, the collapse of the Celtic Tiger, although involving important home grown features, was to a considerable extent a reflection of this global approach to economic and financial policy thinking.

To better understand these developments, this chapter traces the intellectual strands underlying the debate on the roles of financial innovation and financial regulation at various times throughout history. There is an inherent tension between these two concepts. The outcome can be instrumental in determining whether economies progress through phases of sustained economic growth or, alternatively, move toward highly unstable environments that can cause asset market bubbles and financial collapses.

The chapter first discusses the emergence of a growing consensus among many prominent economists around the time of the millennium that a new era of economic theorizing and performance had arrived. It then reviews the debate on financial innovation versus financial prudence, in which this emerging belief played an important role. Finally, the chapter considers the broader evolution of a significant part of mainstream economics thinking towards a hybrid conceptual framework combining New Classical Macroeconomics (NCM)

---

[1] Keynes (1936: 383).

and the Efficient Markets Hypothesis (EMH). This approach emphasized the rationality of economic behaviour and the efficiency of financial markets, with the corollary that asset bubbles are unlikely to arise and that financial markets require relatively little regulation.

2.1 The Era of 'The Great Moderation'

In 2003, Nobel laureate Robert Lucas opined, in his presidential address to the American Economics Association, that the 'central problem of depression-prevention has been solved, for all practical purposes'. A year later, Ben Bernanke, then a governor of the US Federal Reserve System (the Fed) and later to become Chairman of the Fed, observed that there had been a significant change in macroeconomic behaviour (Bernanke 2004). He borrowed a term, the 'Great Moderation', first used by Stock and Watson (2003), to describe this apparent new phenomenon. Bernanke presented a variety of possible reasons for the improved performance of the US economy. Perhaps it had been due to structural changes in the form of improvements in technology, economic institutions, or business practices? Or maybe it was due to better macroeconomic policies, particularly monetary policy? Or perhaps it simply resulted from good luck, in that exogenous economic shocks had become smaller and smaller over time? Bernanke favoured the second explanation, arguing that a better understanding and implementation of monetary policy had greatly strengthened the macroeconomic environment. Implicitly, he was paying homage to the then Chairman of the Fed, Alan Greenspan, who had been in office since 1987, for his role in supporting emergence of the 'Great Moderation'. Ironically, Greenspan's approach to monetary policy would later come to be regarded by some commentators as one of the causes of the 2008 financial crisis.

Adding to the general sense of comfort about macroeconomic theory and policy, the chief economist of the International Monetary Fund (IMF), Olivier Blanchard, stated in 2008 that 'the state of macroeconomics is good'. Lucas, Bernanke, and Blanchard, all very distinguished economists, had concluded, that, broadly speaking, depressions were essentially things of the past and that macroeconomics had reached a golden age. Unfortunately, their prognostications turned out to be similar to that of the famous University of Yale economist, Irving Fisher, who forecast some days before the Wall Street Crash of October 1929, that stock prices would rise further, because they were still not reflecting the beneficent effects of Prohibition on American workers' productivity.

Lucas, Blanchard, Bernanke, and many others in the economics profession would have benefitted from reading the earlier words of Hyman Minsky:

Success breeds a disregard of the possibility of failure; the absence of serious financial difficulties over a substantial period leads to the development of a euphoric economy in which increasing short-term financing of long positions becomes a normal way of life.

As a previous financial crisis recedes in time, it is quite natural for central bankers, government officials, bankers, businessmen, and even economists to believe that a new era has arrived. Cassandra-like warnings that nothing basic has changed, that there is a financial breaking point that will lead to a deep depression, are naturally ignored in these circumstances. Since the doubters do not have fashionable printouts to prove the validity of their views, it is quite proper for established authority to ignore arguments drawn from unconventional theory, history and institutional analysis. (Minsky 1986: 213)

2.2 Financial Innovation Versus Financial Prudence

The history of money is personified by the tension between financial innovation and financial prudence. If there is too much prudence and too little innovation, society may be dissuaded from obtaining the finance necessary to support economic activity. On the other hand, too much financial innovation and too little prudence runs the risk of society experiencing the type of cataclysmic shocks that have caused massive economic dislocation and welfare loss since 2008, as well as at many earlier times in history.

Society has greatly benefitted from financial innovation. Goetzmann and Rouwenhorst (2005), contains a fascinating historical analysis, starting with the Babylonian loan tables, of nineteen major financial innovations over the last 4,000 years, while Lerner and Tufano (2011) provide a very comprehensive account of the consequences of such innovation. Without financial innovation, economies would still be using gold and silver coinage, there would be no ATMs, credit cards would be unknown, banks and money/capital markets would not exist, and entrepreneurs would have to rely exclusively on their own retained profits for investment. Financial innovation has undoubtedly led to a vast range of improved practices and technologies for the facilitation of payments and the extension of credit. The challenge, however, centres on how to distinguish good financial innovation from bad.

While *ex post* this may seem easy, *ex ante* it can be a great deal more difficult to determine whether a particular type of financial innovation is appropriate. Furthermore, a given innovation may be effective in solving an immediate problem, but an excess of it over a sustained period may cause serious damage. The concept of credit expansion that transformed the role of banks from just deposit takers to credit creators, was undoubtedly a huge positive financial development for mankind in the 17th and 18th centuries. But history is littered with subsequent cases where credit creation mutated into excessive credit growth that resulted in bank failures and financial crises.

The evolution of sub-prime lending in the US is a good example of the difficulty in distinguishing between good and bad financial innovation. Sub-prime, or non-prime, loans may have been initially a good approach to widen borrowing possibilities to acquire a home for a wide swathe of low income American households. However, Wall Street decided to innovate further by slicing and dicing sub-prime loans before repackaging them in the form of Collateralized Debt Obligations (CDOs). Again, it could be argued—and was at the time—that this was a sound development. Properly managed collaterali-zation enables banks to sell some of their assets in the form of CDOs and to use the funds to extend new loans. When credit conditions are tight, this may be of significant benefit to firms and industries.

However, a significant risk for financial innovation is that it often spawns further innovation when successful. Highly intelligent individuals armed with sophisticated mathematical techniques may decide to add further innovations to those already in existence. Thus, the Wall Street investment banks encour-aged the credit rating agencies—whose rating services were paid for by these same investment banks—to assist in the transformation of risky sub-prime packages from ordinary CDOs into triple AAA ranked instruments. These could then be sold on to a wider range of purchasers. Despite the new pack-aging, this financial transubstantiation did not alter the underlying reality—risky sub-prime loans had just become risky CDOs. When purchasers, many of whom had not bothered to investigate properly what they were buying in the search for quick profits, realized the true nature of CDOs, the bottom fell out of the market. The CDO collapse from 2007 onwards had enormously dam-aging financial consequences worldwide.

A key question, therefore, is, when should the brakes be applied to certain sorts of financial innovation? Andrew Palmer, writing in *The Economist* (25 February 2012), expressed the problem succinctly when he wrote 'Finance lacks an "off button"'. The absence of this 'off' button implies that a delicate balance needs to be achieved between financial innovation and regulation. When asset markets crash, public attention focuses immediately on the 'sins' of the financiers. The righteous, emphasizing the typical costs of the crash—high unemployment, negative economic growth, bankruptcies, and falling living standards—complain that these are the result of imprudent behaviour. This, they argue, calls for more regulation.

While this logic is hard to contest as a general proposition, the difficulty is how far to apply it in practice. Excessive regulation will bring its own costs because it can suppress beneficial financial innovation, including, critics would assert, a blocking of credit expansion. When the financial system experiences funding difficulties, calls for de-regulation, often influenced by powerful lobbyists, are heard. The dilemma is real. An over-cautious regulatory approach can stifle economic growth, while a reasonable degree of innovation applied prudently is necessary to support strong economic growth. The debate on what constitutes the appropriate balance centres to a large extent on alternative behavioural perspectives as to how markets and the people in them work.

2.3 The Evolution of New Classical Macroeconomics and the Efficient Markets Hypothesis

The tension between financial regulation and innovation reflects to a considerable extent differing ideological stances. The espousal of a *laissez-faire* free market approach embraces a concept of an economic universe in which markets generally work, and, moreover, work best when left free and unregulated. From this perspective, regulation tends to be perceived as an unnecessary and damaging form of interference.

The debate on these issues has a long history. The first call for a regime of *laissez-faire* emerged in the late 17th century in France. Louis XIV, concerned about the state of the French economy, assembled a group of merchants and asked them what could be done to re-generate the economy. From the back of this group, a merchant by the name of Legendre cried out *'nous laissez-faire'*— leave us alone. Many in the world of business then and now would identify with this simple request. However, Louis XIV had no intention of heeding this advice since, influenced by the views of his Prime Minister, Jean Baptiste Colbert, he had pursued a strongly interventionist approach to the economy. Even today in France, the term Colbertism equates with interventionism.

However, aside from the business community, other thinkers had started to consider the issue. In the 1690s, a French economic writer, Pierre de Boisguilbert, authored a number of works urging the implementation of a *laissez-faire* approach. By the middle of the 1750s, a group of young administrators, known as the economists—*les économistes*—urged Louis XV, Louis XIV's successor, to pursue a policy of *laissez-faire, laissez passer* (freedom to produce and freedom to trade). Like his predecessor, Louis XV did not accept this advice.

Around this time, the Scottish philosopher, Adam Smith, met with several of these French authors during a trip to France in the 1760s and was profoundly influenced by their thinking. In 1776 Smith's great work, *An Enquiry into the Nature and Causes of the Wealth of Nations,* was published. In his book, Smith argued for minimal interference by the government in the economy. He believed that the market forces of supply and demand acting as a type of invisible hand enabled people to produce a harmonious outcome for society through the pursuit of their own individual self-interest. One of the book's most memorable passages was:

> It is not from the benevolence of the butcher, the brewer, or the baker that we expect our dinner, but from their regard to their own interest. We address ourselves, not to their humanity but to their self-love, and never talk to them of our own necessities but of their advantages. (Smith 1776 [1976]: I, 27)

Smith believed that the pursuit of self-interest could be maximized by limiting the activities of the state to the areas of law and order. Intriguingly, however, Smith recognized the need for a certain amount of regulation in the banking system in order to prevent systemic failures. His views on this issue could have been better heeded by many in the first decade of the 21st century:

> But those exertions of the natural liberty of a few individuals, which might endanger the security of the whole society, are, and ought to be, restrained by the laws of all governments; of the most free, as well as of the most despotical. The obligation of building party walls, in order to prevent the communication of fire, is a violation of natural liberty, exactly of the same kind with the regulations of the banking trade which are here proposed. (Smith 1776 [1976]: I, 324)

The Smithian emphasis on market forces and the self-adjusting role of the price mechanism was further refined by the French economist Léon Walras in the 19th century. Walras presented a highly abstract model (applied to sectors other than banking), showing how the price mechanism could lead to an overall economic equilibrium. However, for the price mechanism to work, at least in theory, a very strong assumption was needed, namely, that there was perfect information about the prices that would clear all markets. This information was provided through an 'auctioneer' who weighed up all the excess demands and excess supplies in markets, raising prices when there was excess demand and pushing them down when there was excess supply. By this process, known as *tâtonnement*, literally a groping towards the equilibrium price, the auctioneer was able to zone in on the prices that would clear all markets.

But if this model works in theory, how far does it work in practice? The differing answers to this question constitute one of the major ideological dividing lines in economics. Economists who believe that markets in reality approximate closely the Walrasian theoretical model, have been classified as neoclassicals and new classicals. Essentially, these economists argue that the price mechanism works effectively and thus urge a policy of minimal governmental intervention in markets.

On the other side of the dividing line, economists, such as Robert Clower (1965) and Axel Leijonhufvud (1968), have argued that the Walrasian approach, while clever and elegant, is nothing more than science fiction.

There exists no magical and mysterious auctioneer who can provide information as to the market clearing prices. Transactors, be they producers or consumers, savers or investors, have to work hard to obtain information on the prices that might clear their own markets. Since the auctioneer is a fiction, this requires labour, time, and money. Transactions in one market may be delayed or cancelled as a result of an inability to find the market clearing price, causing disturbances in other markets, such as those for employment and output. Furthermore, these will have multiplier effects throughout the economy as constraints in one market feed into others. For example, if the market clearing wage cannot be determined in the labour market and the outcome is unemployment, the reduced income of the unemployed decreases expenditure which causes income to decline further and expenditure to follow suit. Thus, the initial unemployment creates further unemployment.

The views of economists who are highly sceptical about the ability of markets to clear continuously have been strongly influenced by the British economist, John Maynard Keynes. Keynes accepted the theoretical possibility that markets could clear but, at best, only with a significant time lag. In perhaps Keynes's best known aphorism, he professed his agnosticism about the speed of market clearing observing that 'in the long run we are all dead'. For Keynes, policy-makers and economists could not tell the public to wait until the price mechanism did its work and we might all no longer be alive. He believed that the Great Depression vindicated the view that, if left to itself, the market could implode, with disastrous consequences for output and employment. Information flows had been massively disrupted during the Great Depression by the 'dark forces of time, ignorance and uncertainty'. Bouts of pessimism reinforcing initial negative sentiments paralysed economic activity. In such an environment, Keynes presented the economic rationale for government intervention in the economy through stimulatory monetary and fiscal policies.

Keynes's book, *The General Theory of Employment, Interest and Money* (1936), provided the macroeconomic policy template for most mainstream policy thinking up to the 1970s. However, doubts then began to arise about the efficacy of his prescriptions because of rising global inflation which was blamed by many on an uncritical acceptance of the Keynesian approach. The intellectual reaction was led by the Chicago-based professor of economics, Milton Friedman, who contended that Keynesian-style monetary and fiscal intervention could be inflationary and have little or no lasting real positive impact. He believed that once the public realized that inflation had been generated, it would seek wage rate increases that would prevent interventionist policies having any effect on employment and output. Friedman, like Keynes, used powerful rhetoric, invoking the words of Abraham Lincoln to show how the public could not be continually fooled by rising prices—'you can fool some of the people all of the time, you can fool all of the people some of the time, but you cannot fool all of the people all of the time' (Friedman 1983).

Friedman, along with another North American economist, Edmund Phelps, also introduced the concept of inflationary expectations explicitly into his analysis. He argued that the possible benefits of macroeconomic intervention existed at best only in the short run and would be quickly outweighed by rising inflation. As a strong opponent of government intervention, he believed that the authorities' role should be limited to keeping inflation in check by controlling the rate of growth of the money supply. He argued that, aside from exceptional shocks—such as the Great Depression, which he blamed on excessively tight monetary policy—economic growth could be achieved by freeing up the supply side of the economy, reducing the size of the public sector, and pursuing de-regulatory policies. Friedman's monetarism, for which he received the Nobel Prize in Economics, shifted policymakers' attention away from unemployment towards inflation. His approach suggested that the market could take care of unemployment, while policymakers could control inflation by introducing a monetary rule linking the rate of growth of the money supply to the growth of nominal income.

Friedman's recommendations were very much in the classical tradition of allowing the market to work. However, his classicism was replaced in the early 1970s by a more extreme form that came to be known as New Classical Macroeconomics (NCM). The inspiration for this approach originated with two of Friedman's former students, Robert Lucas and Thomas Sargent (both subsequent Nobel laureates). Lucas and Sargent contended that economic agents acted rationally when it came to formulating expectations about inflation. In this framework, transactors took into consideration all the information available in the economy to help formulate their inflationary expectations. Lucas and Sargent differed from Friedman by arguing that people would not be fooled even in the short run. In their view, the public analysed government expansionary policy measures and anticipated their consequences. For example, if the government increased the money supply, the rational person would work out that the consequences would be higher inflation. Such an individual would immediately apply for a wage increase to compensate him/her accordingly. Employers facing higher wage demands would have no incentive to increase employment and the desired macroeconomic effects of the expansionary policy would dissipate very quickly. This analysis implied that macroeconomic policy would be ineffective, even in the short run, the so-called macroeconomic policy impotence rule.

A closely related concept, that of credibility, emerged in the economics literature. For macroeconomic policies to be effective, they needed to be believed by the public. If policies were deemed to be credible, they would become self-fulfilling. For example, if policymakers announced a target for inflation, and assuming the public believed in the authorities' willingness and ability to achieve their goal, the target could be achieved painlessly. There could be gain without pain. However, in order to improve credibility, certain major elements of policy making needed to be removed from politicians who could manipulate policies to achieve desired short-run political results.

A further important feature of the more extreme form of NCM was the virtual elimination of money from the analysis. The classical roots of this approach have a long tradition, based on the belief that it is the real economy in the form of the factors of production (land, labour, capital, and enterprise) that is important. Money only acts as a unit of account, useful for establishing a price system, but not much more. Money is seen as a neutral veil, not influencing real activity.

These are strong propositions which become even stronger when money is deemed to be 'super-neutral.' According to this extreme version of NCM, money is completely removed from the stage because it has no economic role. The money supply in the form of currency and bank deposits is seen as responding endogenously to economic needs. Thus, as the real economy requires more money, say, for transactions purposes, the banking system is assumed to automatically provide it.

From the point of view of macroeconomics, the exclusion of money was also associated with the downgrading of finance. If money is unimportant, so also is finance. This created a situation where, in many graduate schools in North America and elsewhere, economics departments worked quite separately from finance departments. Academic economists were largely uninterested in money and finance, while finance departments taught their subject as a way for students to learn to use sophisticated algorithms in order to minimize risk and maximize return. Many of these highly intelligent individuals ended up making a great deal of money working for financial institutions. However, the collapse, in 1998, of Long Term Capital Management (LTCM), a hedge fund involving two of the most distinguished academics in finance, Robert Merton and Myron Scholes, gave an early warning of the limitations of excessive mathematical modelling.

From the 1970s onwards, NCM became the dominant paradigm widely taught in graduate schools in the major North American universities. It had a profound impact on economic policymaking as doctoral graduates found their way into positions of power in government, central banking and international institutions such as the IMF, the World Bank, and the newly established European Central Bank (ECB). NCMs' rejection of stimulatory macroeconomic policies based on the impotence rule implied a strong recommendation that monetary and fiscal policy be removed from the hands of politicians. It was argued that politicians would use macroeconomic policies to seek short-term political gain, without considering the undesirable consequences of their actions.

To restrain these inherent tendencies and provide credibility it was argued that monetary policy should be taken away from governmental departments and put under the control of an independent central bank. It was also argued that fiscal rules should be introduced restricting the size of the budget deficit and public sector debt. An independent central bank would pursue as its overriding objective a low inflation target and would prevent ministers of finance from manipulating interest rates for political purposes. The imposition of budgetary restrictions on deficits and debt, usually expressed as percentages of GDP, would ensure that politicians could not raid the public purse in order to buy votes.

In parallel, the Efficient Markets Hypothesis (EMH) became the ideological soul mate of NCM. Founded by another Chicago University-based economist, Eugene Fama, the essence of EMH is a belief in the efficiency of financial markets. Asset prices are regarded as incorporating all the relevant information that is available so that transactors cannot systematically make excess financial returns from trading. Markets are believed to be self-correcting and adjust for any changes in information. Advocates of EMH conclude that markets are self-regulating and some of its more partisan followers argue that financial regulation is actually redundant. They believe that if the financial market is left to its own devices it will sort out any disturbances. The logical implication of this is the belief that little regulation, or at most 'light touch regulation' is all that is necessary.

NCM, combining with the EMH, led to several major changes in emphasis in macroeconomic policy thinking:

  (i) Less focus on unemployment and growth objectives with greater attention paid to the pursuit of an inflation objective.
 (ii) A shift from demand management policies to supply side policies.
(iii) Enhanced de-regulation of markets so as to free up the supply side of the economy.
(iv) The creation of independent central banks run by technocrats rather than politicians.
 (v) The establishment of fiscal rules involving ceilings on budget deficits and public sector debt.
(vi) An emphasis on light touch financial regulation.

By the new millennium, the influence of the NCM/EMH hybrid was seen in the application of the above elements in many developed economies. The apparent success of macroeconomic and monetary policies based on this broad approach underlay the rather self-congratulatory tone of the assessment of the new economics by Lucas, Bernanke, and Blanchard discussed earlier in this chapter.

The thinking underlying the NCM/EMH hybrid, along with the deeply embedded German aversion to inflation, strongly influenced the basic architecture of the European Monetary Union as embodied in the Treaty of Maastricht of 1992. Consistent with NCM theorizing, the ECB was given the strongest degree of independence of any major central bank. It was also assigned responsibility for pursuing an inflation target. Article 105.1 of the Maastricht Treaty spelt this out:

> The primary objective of the ESCB [the European System of Central Banks] shall be to maintain price stability. Without prejudice to the objective of price stability, the ESCB shall support the general economic policies of the Community as laid down in Article 2.

The primary emphasis on the pursuit of an inflation target and the relegation of all other macroeconomic objectives to, at best, a supportive role, reflects the extent to which NCM allied with the German fear of inflation determined the primary mandate of the new central bank.

As will be discussed in Chapter 5, there was a significant *lacuna* in the Maastricht architecture with respect to financial stability. Under the Treaty, overall financial stability was to be the joint responsibility of the ECB and its constituent national central banks. However, the implementation of financial regulatory policies was left as the preserve of individual countries. This appears to have reflected political resistance to pan-European interference in national prerogatives. Nevertheless, the more subtle influence of 'light touch regulation' ideology was also an important factor. As a result, ensuring financial stability was very much downgraded in policymakers' agendas, which was to have huge repercussions for the global economy, the European economy, and the Irish economy.

2.4 Conclusions

It might be thought that a discussion of the origins and implications of the resurgence of the new liberal market ideology is somewhat superfluous in a book analysing the Irish financial crisis. However, one should recall Keynes's final warning in the closing paragraph of *The General Theory*:

> the ideas of economists and political philosophers, both when they are right and when they are wrong, are more powerful than is commonly understood. Indeed the world is ruled by little else ... Madmen in authority, who hear voices in the air, are distilling their frenzy from some academic scribbler of a few years back. I am

sure that the power of vested interests is vastly exaggerated compared with the gradual encroachment of ideas. (Keynes 1936: 383)

This chapter has explored how 'the gradual encroachment of ideas' provided an underlying economic philosophy that greatly influenced the thinking of policy makers on issues such as the role of monetary policy and financial regulation. At the theoretical level, NCM/EMH thinking rejected the idea that money was important for the real economy. Moreover, assuming a 'great moderation' had been achieved and markets could successfully self-regulate, the approach downplayed the risks to financial stability. The success of macroeconomics was widely, although not universally, heralded.

The architecture underlying the ECB was consistent with the NCM/EMH philosophy. Under the Maastricht Treaty the ECB was charged with pursuit of a single macroeconomic objective, namely, control of inflation, leaving other important goals such as the pursuit of growth and full employment in the hands of politicians and/or to be determined by economic forces. By contrast, financial stability (i.e. ensuring the stability of the banking and financial system) was the collective responsibility of the ECB and the national central banks. However, in practice, national central banks operated in a context where supervisory responsibilities remained vested at the national level. The ECB was not assigned any direct role in promoting or overseeing a pan-European financial regulatory system.

These arrangements might not have mattered greatly if the underlying philosophy that markets could take care of themselves and that light touch regulation would suffice, was valid. The Nyberg Report into the causes of the Irish banking crisis, while not referring to NCM, recognized the dangers emanating from the EMH:

> Financial market and regulatory policies during the Period [covered by the Nyberg Commission's investigation] were influenced by the efficient market hypothesis. This paradigm was widely accepted, particularly in the US and UK, and provided the intellectual underpinning for financial innovation and reduced regulation. One important consequence of the concept was the assumption that self-regulating financial markets tended to remain stable. If the paradigm was accepted without regard to the simplifying assumptions underlying the original theory (a naïve interpretation), quite radical conclusions for policy could be drawn. For instance, strict or intrusive regulation would generally not be needed and could instead, reduce financial innovation and efficiency; a light-touch approach to regulation was the obvious recipe. (Nyberg 2011: 4)

Nyberg equated the EMH with de-regulation and suggested that it was a global approach that influenced a very wide range of individuals and institutions:

The general acceptance of the paradigm of efficient markets also throws light on why most international institutions, foreign analysts, rating agencies, lenders, authorities and commentators were as relaxed about Irish developments as people in Ireland themselves . . . if very large numbers of people also believed in the naïve interpretation of the efficient financial markets paradigm, very few developments in the financial markets would appear unsound or imprudent to them anymore. (Nyberg 2011: 95)

Indeed, Charlie McCreevy, Irish Minister of Finance in the early part of the decade of the 2000s and subsequently EU Commissioner, was a well-known proponent of 'light touch regulation'.

In considering the Irish debacle, some individuals and institutions might claim that 'it was not us that caused the problem, but this complex and esoteric efficient markets philosophy'. Nyberg rejected such a possible defence as 'naïve and opportunistic' and suggested that a good knowledge of history would have prevented people from thinking the way they did:

The Commission accepts that the new, widespread paradigm, as well as the mania in the Irish property market, could create strong pressures for conformity in all the institutions discussed in this Report. However, while this could explain such behaviour, it does not provide an excuse for those who conformed. Only a naïve and opportunistic interpretation of the paradigm, together with a lack of either relevant experience, training or historical knowledge, could possibly have argued for a major dismantling of the traditional prudential safeguards. History is replete with examples of what happens when bankers, authorities and others come to believe that 'this time it is different'. (Nyberg 2011: 98)

The great moderation in the United States was about to turn into the great immoderation. Inadequate financial regulation permitted excessive financial innovation to unleash, in Warren Buffet's phrase 'the financial weapons of mass destruction' that severely damaged Wall Street and produced a global financial tsunami. The NCM/EMH economic ideology provided the basis for what is now widely accepted as an entirely inadequate financial regulatory structure, not only in the US, but also in Europe. Yet history was already replete with examples of how the combination of too much financial innovation, excessive credit expansion and a weak regulatory environment could cause asset market bubbles and financial crises. As George Santayana wrote, 'those who cannot remember the past are condemned to repeat it' (Santayana 1905: vol. 1, 13). The history of financial speculation and asset bubbles discussed in the next chapter provides a further perspective on the events of 'Black 2008'.

References

Bernanke, Ben (2004) 'The Great Moderation'. Paper presented to the Eastern American Association of Economics.

Clower, Robert (1965) 'The Keynesian Counter-Revolution' in Frank Hahn and Frank Brechling (eds) *The Theory of Interest Rates* (London).

Friedman, Milton (1983) *Bright Promises, Dismal Performance: An Economist's Protest* (New York).

Goetzmann, William and Gert Rouwenhorst (eds) (2005) *The Origins of Value: The Financial Innovations that Created Modern Financial Markets* (Oxford).

Keynes, John Maynard (1936) *The General Theory of Employment, Interest and Money* (London).

Leijonhufvud, Axel (1968) *On Keynesian Economics and the Economics of Keynes* (Oxford).

Lerner, Josh and Peter Tufano (2011) *'The Consequences of Financial Innovation: A Counterfactual Research Agenda'*. NBER Working Paper No. 16780.

Minsky, Hyman P. (1986) *Stabilizing an Unstable Economy,* Yale University Press (Yale).

Nyberg, Peter (2011) *Misjudging Risk: Causes of the Systemic Banking Crisis in Ireland*: Report of the Commission of Investigation into the Banking Sector in Ireland, Government Publications (Dublin).

Santayana, George (1905) *Life of Reason: Reason in Common Sense.* Vol. 1 (New York).

Smith, Adam (1776, repr. 1976) *An Inquiry into the Nature and Causes of the Wealth of Nations* (London, Glasgow).

Stock, James and Mark Watson (2003) *'Has the Business Cycle Changed? Evidence and Explanations'* Paper prepared for the Federal Reserve Bank of Kansas City's Symposium 'Monetary Policy and Uncertainty,' Jackson Hole, Wyoming, 28–30 August.

3

Asset Market Bubbles and Financial Crises

> Bankers . . . are merchants of debt who strive to innovate in the assets they
> acquire and the liabilities that they market
>
> Hyman Minsky, 2003

The Irish debate about the banking crisis has at times given the impression
that people believe that it was somehow unique to Ireland, combining a rare
and noxious cocktail involving avaricious bankers albeit assisted by greedy
foreign lenders, over-ambitious developers, and incompetent politicians and
regulators. The Irish case, however, was neither unique nor rare. Kindleberger
(1978, Kindleberger and Aliber 2005) and more recently Reinhart and Rogoff
(2009) have highlighted the regularity and pervasiveness of financial crises
through time and across countries. The behaviour of leading participants in
the Irish catastrophe was by no means atypical of standard asset market
collapses, as the bubble moved from euphoria to distress and to widespread
resentment.

This chapter first considers the theory behind bubble market behaviour and
financial crises in general, followed by a description of several instances of
asset bubbles and collapses. The historical archives are replete with instances
of 'extraordinary popular delusions and the madness of crowds', the title of
Charles Mackay's 19th century potboiler on bubble behaviour from the 17th
to the 19th centuries. History serves as a useful reference point for the later
analysis of the Irish bubble and the subsequent financial collapse.

3.1 The Theory of Asset Bubbles

For some economists, the analysis of asset market bubbles is a subject on
which they choose not to dwell. In the case of followers of New Classical
Macroeconomics (NCM) and the Efficient Markets Hypothesis (EMH)—

discussed in Chapter 2—they are unsettling phenomena. At their peak, bubbles generate asset market prices that are far out of line with fundamental factors and therefore, by definition, unsustainable. People purchasing assets in a bubble are acting contrary to the assumption of rational behaviour under-lying neoclassical economic philosophy. For neoclassical economists, some other explanation of the bubble phenomenon is required, such as that attempted by Peter Garber in his book *Famous First Bubbles* (2000). Garber suggested that there were fundamental factors that could explain the enor-mous price volatility of Dutch tulips in the 17th century and Mississippi and South Sea shares in 1719/20. Once these underlying factors were taken into consideration, price movements no longer exhibited a bubble element.

Not all economists subscribe to the NCM and EMH paradigms. Others find their analytical inspiration in the work of John Maynard Keynes, an econo-mist who certainly did not accept that rationality dominated market behav-iour all of the time. In the famous chapter 12, 'The State of Long Term Expectations', of *The General Theory of Employment Interest and Money* (1936), Keynes showed how markets, concentrating on short-term results and expect-ations rather than the long term, could become extremely volatile. He empha-sized the dark forces of ignorance and uncertainty that could produce waves of pessimism, causing investors and consumers to stall expenditure decisions and set in train reverse feedback mechanisms that could plunge the economy into unemployment and depression. Keynes believed in markets but not in the perfection of markets. For him, there was always the possibility that grit could be thrown into the market mechanism and cause it to malfunction. In such circumstances, he argued for government intervention to prevent initial disequilibria from magnifying into major recessions or depressions.

Keynes was a major source of inspiration for Hyman Minsky (1919–96), a professor of economics at Washington University, St Louis, in the USA. During his life, mainstream economics paid little attention to Minsky's work, regarding him as something of a maverick. This changed abruptly during the recent financial crisis when Minsky came to be viewed as a major interpreter of bubble phenomena. In *The Financial Instability Hypothesis* (2003), building on his earlier work *Stabilizing An Unstable Economy* (1986), Minsky argued that stability is inherently de-stabilizing and that financial systems move from stability to fragility followed by crisis. He contended that the economy can experience stabilizing financial regimes, but that during an associated period of prosperity, the regime may change in a way that generates considerable economic instability. In contrast to monetarists, he emphasized the importance of banking and debt structures:

> the financial instability hypothesis takes banking seriously as a profit-seeking activity. Banks seek profits by financing activity and bankers. Like all entrepreneurs

in a capitalist economy, bankers are aware that innovation assures profits. Thus, bankers (using the term generically for all intermediaries in finance), whether they be brokers or dealers, are merchants of debt who strive to innovate in the assets they acquire and the liabilities that they market (Minsky 2003: 7).

The key insight of Minsky was to link banking, profit making, and innovation in order to demonstrate how increased innovation through monetary creation would produce different debt and repayment structures that could have very significant economic and financial repercussions.

Minsky categorized three types of financing regimes: (i) hedge; (ii) speculative; and (iii) Ponzi. Hedge financing is typically found in a stable economy. Loans are extended by financial institutions when the borrower's cash flow is sufficient to cover interest and capital repayments. The debt that has been issued is stabilizing because the repayment prospects have been accurately assessed and sufficient provisions have been made to ensure that it is repaid.

However, periods of stability may generate further optimism, encouraging borrowers and lenders to become more confident and to move in the direction of speculative financing. Under the speculative regime, borrowers only cover their interest payments and there is a general expectation that asset prices are likely to rise—but not interest rates—so that borrowers will be able to rollover their debt without difficulty.

The apparent increase in prosperity under a speculative lending regime may propel financial institutions towards a third regime, that of Ponzi financing, named after the Italian swindler, Charles Ponzi. This is the riskiest form of lending. Financial institutions lend because asset prices are rising even though the borrowers' cash flow is insufficient to cover either interest or capital repayments. It is assumed that asset prices will keep on rising and that other buyers are prepared to continue to purchase the assets. Transactors, observing the accelerating rate of increase of asset prices, borrow more and the process appears to be self-fulfilling. More formally, Minsky defined Ponzi financing as a 'situation in which cash payments on debt are met by increasing the amount of debt outstanding' (Minsky 1982:67). Loans beget profits, profits improve the equity profile of borrowers who in turn are encouraged to borrow more and the banks to lend more, using as collateral the increased equity value. This process pushes the economy in a highly unstable direction before the arrival of what is now called a Minsky Moment, when the market peaks and then crashes.

The sequential movement from hedge to speculative to Ponzi financing described by Minsky will resonate with many who have lived through the recent Irish experience. As described in Chapter 4, in the first decade of the 21st century, Irish financial institutions began to offer for the first time 100 per cent loan to value mortgages, extended the duration of mortgages to 30 and 35 years, switched from capital and interest repayment mortgages to interest only mortgages, and were willing to provide loans to developers largely collateralized by the apparently never ending rise in the value of their already-acquired property assets. Presciently, Minsky also pointed out that if monetary conditions were tightened, not only the Ponzi financed entities but also those relating to the speculative regime could collapse as net worth would tend to evaporate.

Charles Kindleberger, in his authoritative work *Manias, Panics and Crashes* (1978; Kindleberger and Aliber 2005), built on Minsky's earlier work in a sequential analysis of asset market bubbles:

(1) Some exogenous shock such as a technological development, a war, a natural resources discovery, re-structuring of state debt, or some type of financial innovation, sets in motion a sustained boom in asset prices.

(2) The boom is fed by an expansion of bank credit, increasing the money supply.

(3) As increased demand pushes up the price of goods and assets, new profit opportunities are found and confidence grows. The economy moves into a 'boom or euphoric state'. At this point overtrading is likely to occur.

(4) Overtrading may involve:
   (a) Pure speculation, that is, over-emphasis on the acquisition of assets for capital gain rather than income return.
   (b) Overestimation of prospective returns by companies.
   (c) Excessive gearing (high debt relative to capital or equity), involving the use of low cash requirements for the acquisition of financial assets by means of several variants of margin purchases.

(5) The behavioural element of the bubble changes as neophytes, attracted by the prospect of sizeable capital gains for a small outlay, exhibit 'herd behaviour' and become numerous in the market. At this stage, the process assumes a separate abnormal momentum of its own. Insiders recognize the danger signals and move out of their vastly over-valued assets into money or other more liquid assets.

(6) A financial distress period commences as the neophytes become aware that prices are falling and try to make a rush for the exit. Asset prices fall further.

(7) Revulsion against the depreciating assets develops as financial institutions call in loans and force borrowers to try to sell collateral which depresses asset values even further.

(8) Panic becomes endemic as the market collapses. Calls are made for the government or central bank to intervene as a lender of last resort.

A key element in the anatomy of financial crises is the speed with which markets can change from financial euphoria to distress. One moment optimism dominates, only to be replaced by a dark environment of pessimism and uncertainty. There are triggers in financial market bubbles that can suddenly transform market expectations. But while the pressing of these triggers can affect the timing of the sharp and precipitous falls in asset prices, deeper forces are at work that lead inevitably to the eventual implosion of highly over-valued markets.

It is simplistic to assert that bubbles are caused just by avaricious behaviour, exemplified by neophyte transactors purchasing massively over-valued assets that they know little or nothing about (such as, in the Irish case, foreign holiday apartments bought sight unseen). Certainly, greed plays a part, but it is the manifestation, especially in the later phases, of a process generated by other necessary elements found in many historical experiences. Bubbles inevitably have to be fuelled by excessive credit expansion, usually accompanied by a loosening of prudential regulatory requirements. This includes the increased use of lending instruments with low margin requirements that encourage speculators to leverage the size of their asset-based bets. Not surprisingly, as will be seen, these elements were present in the Irish asset property bubble.

3.2 Bubbles and Financial Crises—An Historical Perspective

The approaches of Minsky/Kindleberger are useful in examining some historical examples of asset market bubbles and associated crises. The first financial crises in Europe started in the early 18th century as debt management exercises[1]. In France a rather extraordinary Scotsman, John Law (1671–1729), despite being a murderer on the run from British justice for killing a man in a duel, became the equivalent of Prime Minister of France for a short period in 1720. His Mississippi System appeared to provide the solution to France's monetary and financial crises. Law introduced paper money into France. He then converted most of the government debt into shares of the Mississippi Company, took over the French colonial trading companies and created a giant conglomerate. The company possessed a very unique asset, namely, the trading rights to French Louisiana, a territory running from the Gulf of Mexico to Canada, bounded by the British to the east in the Carolinas and the Spanish

---

[1] An earlier well-known case of a speculative bubble, the so-called Tulipmania in Holland in the 1630s, is not discussed here as it was limited in its geographic impact and did not entail broader financial repercussions.

to the west by Texas. This vast tract of land constituted half of the area of the US today (excluding Alaska).

In return for transferring their government bonds into shares of the Mississippi Company, shareholders looked forward to income streams from the American territories which were presented as the new Peru, possessing untold mineral and agricultural wealth. The price of Mississippi shares rose from 170 French livres in 1717 to over 10,000 French livres by January 1720. People flocked to Paris to buy and sell a stake. Contemporary prints show them pushing and shoving one another in the narrow winding rue Quincampoix in their haste to transact Mississippi business. As there were few tables or chairs, a hunchback innovatively hired out his hump for signing over the purchase or sale of shares.

Such was the success of Law's Mississippi Company that the British felt bound to follow suit. The South Sea Company was given permission to purchase a substantial amount of the British government debt by issuing shares, the price of which rose from £110 in January 1720 to over £900 in August of that year. Following on the success of the South Sea Company, many fledgling companies issued the equivalent of modern initial public offerings (IPOs) to raise finance for a wide area of activities. These ranged from respectable insurance activities (several of London's great insurance companies date from this period) to more fraudulent activities such as Puckle's machine gun, designed to fire square canon balls, and the ultimate in Ponzi type schemes, 'a company for a project to be announced at a later date'.

The year 1720 saw the peak of stock market euphoria. In January, Law was able to issue options (*primes*) in the Mississippi Company—a 1,000 option giving the purchaser the right to purchase a Mississippi share at 10,000—while London became the centre of new company issues. Financial engineering flourished and Law used the Royal Bank's printing presses to create paper money to drive up the share price. Fortunately, the Bank of England stayed out of the South Sea Bubble, although the Sword Blade Company (which manufactured hollow sword blades) acted as a proxy bank in speeding up the velocity of circulation of money.

Almost inevitably, Law drove his Mississippi System too far and too fast and by May 1720 it had started to collapse. In December of the same year, Law hastily left a bankrupted France, ultimately dying in Venice in 1729. An early victim of financial contagion, between late August and December 1720, the price of South Sea Company shares also plunged and it became impossible to sell the shares of most of the fledgling bubble companies. During this period, an Irish banker and economist, Richard Cantillon, using his own economic insights, made a considerable fortune out of both the Mississippi System and the South Sea Bubble (Murphy 1986) (Box 3.1).

Box 3.1 IRISH ECONOMIST RICHARD CANTILLON: HOW TO USE ECONOMIC THEORY TO PROFIT FROM BUBBLES

In 1729 the Irish-born millionaire, Richard Cantillon, sat down to write a book. Like a latter day Samuel Beckett he was sufficiently linguistically gifted to write drafts in both English and French. The French draft would later be published, in 1755, as the *Essai sur la nature du commerce en général* (*Essay on the Nature of Trade in General*). The *Essai* represented Cantillon's attempt to analyse why Europe had recently witnessed two huge asset bubbles along with their ensuing collapses. These bubbles were those of the Mississippi System in France between 1717–1720 and the South Sea Bubble in Great Britain in 1720. Cantillon had witnessed at close hand both bubbles, enriching himself sufficiently to be classified by the French taxing authorities as a millionaire—the term was coined at the time to describe successful Mississippian millionaires. He had bought shares at low prices and sold them at vastly higher prices, he had shorted currencies and shares and he had taken out put options on English stocks over a frenetic period between 1718–1720. Thus when it came to writing about the financial phenomena of 1720, when both bubbles peaked, Cantillon was not some eighteenth century hack— the 18th century was full of such hacks—chancing his luck with a wide range of opinions on what had happened. Instead he was a professional who had used his economic analysis to identify and exploit weaknesses of the Mississippi System where John Law had attempted simultaneously to expand the money supply, lower the rate of interest, and revalue the exchange rate of the French currency. Cantillon knew that this policy was economically inconsistent and speculated correctly against the French exchange rate. He showed how a dispassionate economic analysis of bubble behaviour could be extremely profitable.

In order to analyse this bubble behaviour, Cantillon, in Cartesian style, started off with a very simple model of the economy supposing that it consisted just of 'one single landed estate'. From this very primitive model of a command, moneyless, and closed economy, he constructed a more sophisticated real sector model incorporating entre-preneur driven market behaviour in a money using open economy. Cantillon juxtaposed the real and the financial economies by grafting different types of financial innovation on to the real economy in order to determine whether such innovation could be successful. He then elaborated how the structure of the real economy could become fundamentally imbalanced by excessive financial innovation. As an example, he presciently showed the potentially catastrophic consequences of sizeable external borrowing.

Cantillon had quickly worked out that financial innovation did not necessarily equate with economic progress. From his perspective, he identified financial innovation as causing shocks involving considerable losses such as the major collapse of the monetary system in France and the near collapse of its counterpart in Great Britain. Cantillon recognized that there was an implicit dilemma between financial prudence and financial innovation. While acknowledging that banks produced benefits to the economy he was not prepared to provide them with an unqualified or over enthusiastic endorsement. Essentially, Cantillon was a metallist, someone who believed in the merits of intrinsically valuable money such as gold and silver. But was metallism the way forward? Ultimately it was discarded as financial innovation produced substitutes in the form of banknotes and bank deposits, financial instruments that played a major role in financing Britain's Industrial Revolution.

The legacy losses of both the Mississippi Company and the South Sea Bubble were considerable. Because of the collapse of Law's paper money system and the shares of the Mississippi Company, a strong aversion developed in France towards financial innovation in the form of banks, credit, paper money, and capital market issues. France returned to a very conservative financial system that relied on gold and silver as the currency, and introduced legislation that made it extremely difficult to tap finance from the capital market.

Great Britain was more fortunate. The South Sea Bubble did not involve a monetary collapse as the Bank of England had stood apart from the activities of the South Sea Company. However, the Bubble Acts of 1720, introduced by a zealous Parliament concerned with the lack of financial regulation, made it almost impossible for new companies to issue shares. As in France, these 'anti-Bubble' Acts would remain in place for over a hundred years, greatly limiting the potential for capital investment. They became a classic example of the damage that could result from excessive financial regulation. However, the serendipitous non-involvement of the Bank of England in the market collapse enabled Great Britain to innovate considerably in money and banking during the 18th century, which in turn ensured continued access to finance for merchants and the British government. Controlled expansion in money and credit helped to sow the financial seeds for the incipient Industrial Revolution, while the financing of government debt enabled Britain to punch above its weight and contributed to the creation of a massive empire. Overall, the prudent innovation introduced into the banking sector provided a structured financial base for Great Britain's successful economic development.

The asset market booms and collapses of the early 18th century were followed in the second half of the 18th century by crises arising from the need to finance two revolutionary wars of independence. In the 1770s, the breakaway colonists financed the US War of Independence by means of a newly issued currency and government bonds. However, over-issuance of the currency led to it becoming worthless, giving rise to the expression 'not worth a continental'. In France, the newly created paper money, the *assignats* (initially collateralized by confiscated church lands and property), financed the first part of the French Revolution between 1789–93 but again, through over-issuance, led to hyperinflation. The message from both experiences was that financial innovation could be used to finance successful political revolutions, but at a clear risk that this might lead over time to substantial inflationary pressures.

The 19th century was characterized by periodic banking collapses in both Great Britain and the United States, as well as asset market bubbles. A notable example involved speculation in railway shares across Europe, following development of the steam engine technology. A large number of new companies were established to finance railway lines that criss-crossed countries and continents, many of which proved to be unviable economically and financially. Their shares now represent worthless memorabilia in the attics of many houses.

World War I left a legacy of Germany's first hyperinflationary experience as the German government used the printing presses of the Reichsbank to finance an expanding budget deficit. The speculative bubble in US shares that burst on Wall Street in October 1929 ushered in a collapse of the US banking system, which in turn generated the Great Depression. The 1929 stock market crash led to a period of great financial uncertainty. Runs on banks developed and the US's fragmented unit banking system was incapable of meeting the panicked demands of depositors seeking to withdraw their funds. Additionally, the US Federal Reserve System, instead of providing liquidity to the market and lowering interest rates, did the opposite, thereby aggravating the crisis. The impact on the real economy was enormous and the unemployment rate reached 25 per cent by the early 1930s.

Ultimately, there appeared to be two major lessons for banking and financial policy arising from the Great Depression. Firstly, a system of deposit insurance was required to help avoid runs on banks. Secondly, the US Central Bank (the Federal Reserve System) needed to act as a lender of last resort to the banking system and pump liquidity into the financial markets at low interest rates so as to maintain or restore confidence.

These solutions, guaranteeing bank deposits and giving the Federal Reserve a more interventionist role, helped protect the US financial system's deposits against banking runs. However, they also raised serious moral hazard issues. Moral hazard happens when individuals are induced to behave in a certain way that is costly to others because of the provision of safety nets intended to protect the common good. Thus, the guaranteeing of deposits—in the public interest—by the US Federal Deposit Insurance Corporation came back to haunt the US taxpayers during the 1980s. Following deregulation under the Garn-St Germain Depository Act (1982), the Savings and Loans institutions (S&Ls) competed for deposits by offering more attractive interest rates and diversifying lending away from home mortgages. Unfortunately, many of them rashly offered excessively high interest rates and invested the proceeds in a property market boom that ultimately collapsed. Easy money could apparently be made by taking over an S&L, borrowing money at high interest rates and investing the proceeds in dubious or fraudulent projects where funds tended to disappear. The American depositor, given the government guarantee on a deposit up to $100,000 at each financial institution, naturally had sought the highest rate of interest for his deposits and had paid little or no attention to the riskiness or financial viability of the institution concerned. The result was an enormous bill of $140 billion for the US taxpayer—see

Akerlof, Romer, Hall, and Mankiw (1993). Thus, deposit insurance can, and in this case did, create significant moral hazard risks.

The second moral hazard issue associated with post-Depression interventionist policies arose from the view that certain financial institutions were of systemic importance to the economy and therefore could not be allowed to fail. In October 1987, the Dow Jones stock market index fell by over 30 per cent over two days, registering its biggest ever daily loss of 22 per cent on so-called 'Black Monday'. Academic opinion is divided as to the causes of the crash. Programme trading, the use of complex buy/sell computer trading order schemes to help limit possible losses, was identified as one of the main explanatory factors. As the market fell, programme trading triggered off further sell orders which in turn produced a downward cascading price effect.

The Federal Reserve, under its newly appointed chairman, Alan Greenspan, showed that it had learnt from the experience of the 1930s and acted swiftly to bail out financial institutions that were facing a potentially serious loss of confidence. By lowering interest rates and aggressively pumping liquidity into the system, the Fed quickly stabilized financial markets. The stock market recovered rapidly and those who purchased shares on 'Black Tuesday' subsequently made considerable gains. In 2001, after the terrorist attacks on the Twin Towers situated in the centre of New York's financial district, the Federal Reserve System once again came to the rescue of Wall Street, providing sizeable liquidity to the highly destabilized market.

Federal Reserve Chairman Greenspan demonstrated both in 1987 and 2001 that the Federal Reserve System was prepared to actively intervene in financial markets as a lender of last resort so that the US financial system would not be allowed to fail. This approach, which came to be known as the Greenspan 'put' option, implied that the US authorities, would always be willing to bail out systemically important banking institutions by providing easy credit facilities at times of financial distress. However, it accentuated the problem of moral hazard. Some institutions, in the absence of an appropriate regulatory framework, could engage in increasingly risky activities in the knowledge that they were too big to fail and that the Fed would always be on hand if difficulties arose. The 'too big to fail' versus moral hazard debate peaked in September 2008 when the Federal Reserve System, in conjunction with the US Treasury, allowed the major US investment bank, Lehman Brothers to file for bankruptcy. As will be seen in Chapter 8, the global fall-out from this highly controversial decision was enormous and, although it did not cause the crisis in the Irish banking system, greatly helped accentuate its timing later that month.

3.3 Conclusions

This chapter has discussed how traditional classical approaches to economic theory have great difficulty in explaining the undeniable existence of bubbles that, by their nature, imply irrational behaviour. However, a Keynesian interpretation of market failures can go a considerable way towards understanding bubble phenomena. The subsequent work of Kindleberger, and especially of Minsky, are instructive in outlining the different stages of an asset bubble. In particular, Minsky's analysis of the way changes in financing from hedge financing to Ponzi financing can lead to a highly destabilized economy is a most useful template for the analysis of many current and recent financial crises.

The brief historical perspective provided here illustrates, contrary to the predictions of NCM and the EMH, how repetitive asset market bubbles and financial crises have been through time and across countries. History shows the extent to which bubbles can develop and, when they burst, cause, in many cases, the collapse of financial systems and massive macroeconomic disorder.

However, the apparent solutions have in turn created their own problems. In some instances, over-restrictive approaches to regulation have stultified the development of money and capital markets. In others, interventions have raised moral hazard issues depending on whether institutions are deemed as 'too big to fail' or 'too big to save'. The policy debate on these issues intensified in the wake of the financial crisis of 2007–2008 and is far from resolved.

In considering a main theme of this book, namely, the attribution of responsibility for the Irish financial crisis, it is important to keep in mind throughout that the crisis was by no means historically unique. Virtually all of the major Western economies have suffered similar experiences at one time or another. Unfortunately, as the title of Reinhart and Rogoff's (2009) book aptly summarizes, throughout history those eagerly participating in bubble behaviour are invariably convinced that 'this time is different'. As will be seen in the chapters that follow, Ireland proved to be no exception.

References

Akerlof, George A., Paul M. Romer, Robert E. Hall, and N. Gregory Mankiw (1993) 'Looting: The Economic Underworld of Bankruptcy for Profit'. Brookings Papers on Economic Activity, vol. 1993, no. 2.

Garber, Peter (2000) *Famous First Bubbles* (Boston).

Keynes, John Maynard (1936) *The General Theory of Employment, Interest and Money* (London).

Kindleberger, Charles (1978) *Manias, Panics and Crashes: A History of Financial Crises* (New York).

Kindleberger, Charles and Ron Aliber (revised edn.) (2005) *Manias, Panics and Crashes: A History of Financial Crises* (New York).

Minsky, Hyman (1982) 'Can it Happen Again', *Essays on Instability and Finance* (New York).

Minsky, Hyman (1986) *Stabilizing an Unstable Economy* (Yale).

Minsky, Hyman (2003) 'The Financial Instability Hypothesis' Working Paper No. 74, published in Philip Arestis and Malcolm Sawyer (eds) *Handbook of Radical Political Economy* (Aldershot).

Murphy, Antoin (1986) *Richard Cantillon, Entrepreneur and Economist* (Oxford).

Reinhart, Carmen and Ken Rogoff (2009) *This Time its Different: Eight Centuries of Financial Folly* (Princeton).

Part II
The Causes of the Crisis

4

The Banks and the Property Market Bubble

Moderation is a fatal thing. Nothing succeeds like excess.

Oscar Wilde

As described in Chapter 1, by the start of the new millennium, the Irish economy appeared to have achieved the status of a high-growth Asiatic economy operating in Europe. While the groundwork for the emergence of this growth phase had been prepared in the 1980s, the rise of the Celtic Tiger began in earnest in 1994 and finished in triumph in 2000, when both GDP and GNP growth averaged 9.3 per cent. Ireland had successfully linked in with the remarkable technological revolution at Silicon Valley and created a European platform for US multinationals to export into Europe. Combined with sound macroeconomic policies, this had created a virtuous cycle: unprecedented rapid economic growth; an increase in population; and a dramatically changed fiscal environment in which tax rates were falling alongside a spectacular reduction in public sector debt ratio—from 109 per cent of GDP at its peak in 1987 to 25 per cent by 2006. The Irish economy had been transformed. Both at home and abroad, confidence was at an all-time high, reflecting the view in some quarters that Ireland had produced a unique macroeconomic mix that could be bottled and sold externally.

Nevertheless, some seven or eight years later, by 2007–08, the dream had been shattered and the Celtic Tiger appeared to be dying a painful death. Ireland's aspirations to be a model of sound economic and financial management for the rest of the world seemed to lie in ruins. Many elements ultimately contributed to the disaster. However, this chapter deals with the original source of the crash, namely, the unchecked emergence of a property bubble financed by the reckless lending of the banks. All of Ireland's subsequent economic and financial woes—the insolvency of the banking system, the unrestrained expansionary fiscal policies, the need for the fateful guarantee in September 2008, and the final recourse to the external bail out in November

2010—had their roots in the extraordinary rise and fall in Ireland's property market.

As the decade of the 2000s began and the success of the Celtic Tiger was at its height, there were a number of unsettling interrelated developments. First, exogenous external forces—especially the collapse of the dot.com bubble in 2000 and the downturn of the US economy in 2001–02—were at work that would slowly but steadily switch the pattern of Irish growth from an export-led boom to one reliant on domestic demand. Instead of maintaining momentum based on competitive exports, people became seduced by the idea of building more and more houses, hotels, apartments, leisure centres, and other amenities for each other. Second, this switch was accentuated by a deliberate policy shift. In late 2001, just as the earlier Irish property market boom during the rise of the Celtic Tiger was starting to peter out, the government, bowing to pressures from builder/developer lobbyists, rashly adopted a wide range of fiscal incentives aimed at countering the decline. These measures encouraged the excesses in the construction sector that were to characterize the years 2002–07. Third, the banks, following Ireland's entry into the euro area, discovered unlimited sources of cheap external wholesale funding. With an appetite for quick profit-making, they started to cast caution to the winds and climbed eagerly aboard the property bandwagon, initially lending 'innovatively' for residential mortgages, but soon extending not just millions but, in some cases, billions, to the riskiest clients, builders/developers.

As the decade progressed, all these negative tendencies—described in greater detail below—became mutually reinforcing and the virtuous cycle at work in the period of the rise of the Celtic Tiger, described earlier, became a vicious one. The original Celtic Tiger had become muted and an artificial boom—one driven by builders, builder developers, and compliant bankers—was in the process of unfolding.

4.1 The Dot.com Bubble Collapse in 2000 and the Slowdown in the US Economy, 2001–02

The growth of Silicon Valley in the 1990s was characterized by vast flows of financial capital as seed capitalists and financial institutions tried to link in with the high-tech growth miracle. The successes of entities such as Apple, Intel, Microsoft, and Oracle, encouraged the search for their successors as the exciting possibilities of networking and brand-building through the internet had become apparent. For a period, it appeared that all a company needed to do was to append a dot.com to its name and then make an initial public offering at some outrageous price. The fact that the company had no earnings and was leaking cash flow at a very fast pace did not deter the market. Many of the shares were massively overvalued and on 10 March 2000, the Nasdaq Composite Index peaked at about 5,000, double its value of the previous year.

The resulting crash of these newly established dot.com companies took a great deal of gloss off the internet boom throughout 2000 and 2001. Combined with the outbreak of war in Iraq, it led to a sharp downturn in the US economy and in world trade. This, in turn, had a significant impact on the performance of Irish exports. At the same time, Ireland's external competitiveness started to show signs of weakening. Reflecting various social partnership and public sector benchmarking agreements (see Chapter 7), unit labour costs began to rise above those of trading partners, a tendency that would become much more pronounced as the decade progressed. Although total exports were still increasing in real terms, the rate of growth declined sharply, from an average of almost 20 per cent during 1998–2000 to 4.5 per cent in 2001–03, and 5.7 per cent between 2004–07. Table 4.1 contrasts the export performance of exports for the three years 1998–2000 with that for the three years 2001–03. The weakening was mainly due to a fall off in the demand for exports from the multinational sector which constitute the vast bulk of total exports. It appeared that the export-led sector was beginning to lose its overriding dominant influence on Irish economic growth.

4.2 The Property Market Downturn of 2001 and the Government's Policy Response

Property prices, linked to the extraordinarily impressive economic growth performance from 1994 onwards, had been rising at a rapid rate up to and including 2000. This price rise suddenly stopped in 2001, although for various reasons this was not captured properly by the official statistics, which showed a continuing increase.[1] The extent of difficulties in the market may be seen by re-reading the property pages of Irish newspapers of the time. For example, at the end of 2001, the *Irish Times* reported that the annual number of residential property auctions in Dublin had dropped by almost 50 per cent, to the lowest level since 1994.

> a total of 815 auctions were held in the greater Dublin area this year [2001], down from 1,547 in 2000, and from a peak of 1,804 in 1998. Of those 815 properties, just over 25 per cent were sold under the hammer with a further 17 per cent sold in post-auction negotiations...House prices across the capital have dropped by

---

[1] According to the official statistics, between 2000 and 2001, new property prices rose from €169,000 to €183,000 and second-hand prices from €206,000 to €228,000 (Budgetary and Economic Statistics, 2011). However, these data contain several weaknesses and have never been considered a reliable guide to the actual prices at which transactions occurred.

Table 4.1. Volume Growth in Irish Exports of Goods and Services

	Volume Growth (%)
1998	23.1
1999	15.6
2000	21.1
2001	8.2
2002	4.8
2003	0.8

Source: Central Statistics Office (CSO), Dublin

between 5 and 20 per cent, according to industry sources. (*Irish Times*, 6 December, 2001)

The estate agent Sherry Fitzgerald, in its annual property review, estimated that prices for new property fell by 4.6 per cent across the country in 2001, with a sharper drop of close to 10 per cent for second-hand houses. As auctions had effectively stalled and many properties could not be sold due to the prevailing pessimism, these figures were most likely underestimating the full extent of the market decline.

There were a number of reasons for the downturn. The first, as noted above, was the puncturing of the US dot.com bubble and the growing realization that Ireland's export-led boom, closely linked to the progress of Silicon Valley, had started to stall. Secondly, Irish agricultural exports had become badly affected by measures introduced to prevent the spread of an outbreak of foot-and-mouth disease in the UK to Irish livestock. This episode added to the growing pessimism about the overall state of the Irish economy.

Cassidy and O'Brien, in an article on 'Export Performance and Competitiveness of the Irish Economy', synopsized these developments:

> The slowdown began with a number of adverse shocks to the Irish and global economies in 2001. These included the foot-and-mouth problem for Irish agriculture, which also had a significant impact on the tourism sector, and the downturn in the global information and communication technology (ICT) sector. (Cassidy and O'Brien 2005)

On 11 July 2001 the *Irish Independent* ran a headline 'Drop in second-hand house prices confirm slowdown' which was followed two days later by another headline 'House prices take first dip in years'. The stories were based on the Irish Permanent/Economic and Social Research Institute (ESRI)'s survey that indicated that house prices had fallen in Dublin for the first time in six years. A week later, the then Taoiseach, Bertie Ahern, during a trip to Brazil announced that the Irish economy was battling against a dangerous slowdown. In early August, Gateway, a major MNC computer company, closed down a plant in Galway with the loss of 1,000 jobs. Writing under the headline 'Economy Stalls with No Signs of Soft Landing', economist Moore McDowell, observed:

> There is an increased degree of unease about the property market, and increased concern over the potential consequences of a property market downturn, even if it is only short-lived. (*Irish Independent*, 1 August, 2001)

Another economist, Fiona Adkins, working for Hibernian Investor Managers, wrote an article headlined 'Why I Believe the Great Housing Boom is Over'. She noted the extent to which the IT setbacks were affecting the property market adversely and wrote that, according to reports, prices at the very top end of the market had fallen by as much as 15–20 per cent. She predicted a major downturn:

> Confidence in ever-rising housing prices has completely cracked and I believe this is the end of the great Irish house price boom. (*Irish Independent*, 17 August 2001)

If this was bad news, there was much more to come. In September the traumatic events of 9/11 caused the Irish property market and confidence in the Irish economy to fall further. The destruction of the Twin Towers at the centre of New York's financial district created a massive loss of confidence both in the United States and internationally which added considerably to global economic pessimism.

Had the Irish property market peaked in 2000? Had it experienced just a housing boom linked to economic fundamentals or had it become a property market bubble? Certainly, there were possible bubble characteristics in the property market at that stage. The average price of a new house had risen by 133 per cent, from €73,000 (all figures are rounded to the nearest 000) in 1994 to €169,000 in 2000. Second-hand house prices had increased even faster, from €70,000 to €191,000, a jump of 173 per cent. In Dublin, the growth in property prices had been even more marked. Between 1993 and 2000, the average price of new houses rose by 170 per cent, from €82,000 to €222,000, and that of second-hand houses by 199 per cent, from €83,000 to €247,000 (Budgetary and Economic Statistics 2011: Table 72). Overall, in the six years between 1994 and 2000, the rate of increase in property prices was far higher than that experienced between 2001–07. Could it then be said that the period 1994–2000 was characterized by even greater bubble behaviour than that of 2002–07? If so, why did this bubble not burst completely in 2001 when property prices started to fall?

There are several factors to consider. Firstly, the increase in house prices that took place between 1994 and 2000 was linked closely to the exceptionally high overall economic growth rates of the Celtic Tiger boom. Real incomes had risen sharply, net immigration was taking place for the first time in Ireland's history, employment and labour force participation had increased, and people felt more secure about acquiring rather than renting property. Secondly, mortgage lending was financed domestically through the deposits of financial institutions and at interest rates that in real terms turned out to be higher than those in subsequent years. Both the availability and cost of funds that could be borrowed to finance a 'speculative bubble' were constrained. Third, the mortgage lending during this period was based for the most part on the traditional model, involving loan to value (LTV) ratios that did not exceed 80 per cent, forcing the borrower to find 20 per cent of the purchase price. Up to this point, the banks' lending had been relatively prudent, based on attracting sufficient domestic deposits and backed by significant collateral (the average LTV ratios were: 67 per cent in 1997, 63 per cent in 1998, and 62 per cent in 1999—see Somers and Corrigan (2000)) in an environment of high and sustained economic growth. In other words, the property market had generated a boom rather than a bubble.

Nevertheless, in 2001 there was the real fear that a significant fall in property prices could be in the offing. At this point, the property slowdown should have been interpreted as a necessary wake-up call to purchasers that prices would not inevitably always move upwards. The decline in prices that had taken place during 2001—highlighted by an inability to sell properties at auction during that year—gave breathing space to dampen down speculative property-related activity and to stabilize the construction sector at a sustainable level.

Unfortunately, however, the 2001 downturn was not seen as a signal to guard against excess. Instead of battening down the hatches, both the government and the financial system did the opposite and provided a range of new measures to reignite the market. The policy response was to introduce a wide range of fiscal incentives that, when linked to the gradual change in the banks' approach to financing, helped develop a bubble that in the process would end up infecting many sectors other than just property.

Traditionally there had always been a very close alliance between Fianna Fáil, the dominant government coalition partner, and builders and developers. As prices weakened in 2001, these builders and developers lobbied government ministers intensively—including no doubt in the iconic Fianna Fáil tent at the Galway summer race festival—to introduce a new package of measures to reflate the property market. Their efforts met with very considerable success. The Budget for 2002, introduced in December 2001, provided an early Christmas present as it contained major concessions in the form of interest relief on borrowings for residential rented properties. Specifically, interest accruing on and from 1 January 2002 on borrowed monies employed in the purchase, improvement, or repair of rented residential properties, was to be allowed as a deduction against *all* rental income in calculating rental income for taxation purposes. Furthermore, this interest relief was to be

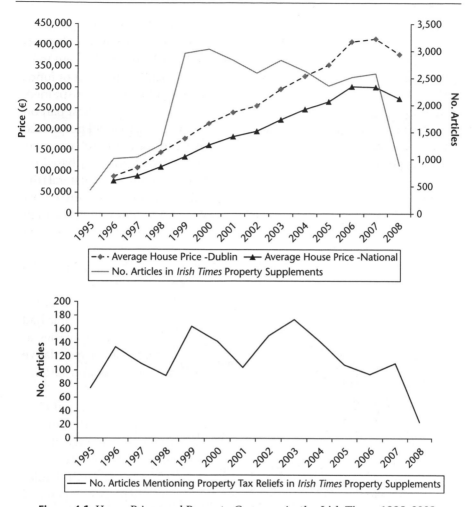

Figure 4.1 House Prices and Property Coverage in the *Irish Times*, 1995–2008

available for money that was borrowed in respect to both Irish and foreign residential properties acquired to rent. The measure, which was counter to the recommendations of the first Bacon report, reversed the restriction that had been introduced by the Finance Act 1998. Together with a reduction in stamp duty that was also announced in the Budget, it provided an enormous encouragement to investors in the residential rented property market. Figure 4.1 summarizes data on the extent to which articles in the *Irish Times* mentioned property or property tax reliefs during 1998–2005. The number of these references peaked in 1998–99, before falling significantly, but then grew rapidly in 2002–03, as readership interest in the topic gained momentum consequent on the changes in tax relief introduced in the 2002 Budget. As purchasers of the buy-to-let properties bid up prices, the prices of private (owner-occupied) properties increased in a similar fashion, due to competition. At the start of 2003, Marian Finnegan, chief economist at estate agents Sherry Fitzgerald, estimated that the market had risen by 20 per cent in 2002. She remarked that:

> The restoration of mortgage interest relief for investors, combined with the reduction in the rate of stamp duty, resulted in an immediate restoration of confidence in the performance of the market and a surge in the demand for property (*Irish Times*, 2 January 2003).

4.3 The Rise of the Builder/Developer

Many commentators have tended to interpret the Irish property market bubble as a homogeneous phenomenon. However, this approach needs to be refined in order to identify accurately the dominant virus that accentuated the crash of the banking system after the bubble burst. From 2002 onwards, property prices started to move upwards again, heralding a second phase of the boom but one that very quickly was transformed into a bubble. The character of this second phase was quite distinct from the first phase prior to 2000. Mortgage loans to finance the residential property market grew again at a fast pace, aided by the new fiscal incentives, low interest rates, and financial innovations in the form of tracker mortgages, 100 per cent—and sometimes higher—LTV mortgages, and extensions of the length of loans to thirty years or longer.

This continuing rise in residential property prices, although very significant, was not the most important spoke on the speculative wheel that caused a true property market bubble in the years from 2002 onwards. The rapidly surging house prices, of course, helped to spur profit-seeking builders and developers. However, if the boom had been solely confined to the residential market, what subsequently happened would, arguably, have been manageable. It was the lending of ever increasingly large sums of money to developers that would contribute greatly to the banks' losses.

Something considerably more sinister than the extension of residential property mortgages on unduly generous terms had started to permeate the market. Massive direct lending, amounting to several multiples of the financing of residential mortgages, had begun to occur. This represented a distinct shift, to use the Minskyian terminology—see Chapter 3—from speculative to Ponzi-scheme financing. Henceforth, the essential criterion to justify continued lending was that of ever appreciating asset prices.

Table 4.2. Mortgage Lending by Irish Banks (billions of euros)

	2003	2008	Growth Rate (%)
AIB	13.2	31.6	139
Bank of Ireland	30.9	60.1	95
Total	44.1	91.7	108

Table 4.3. Property and Construction Lending by Irish Banks (billions of euros)

	2003	2008	Growth Rate (%)
AIB	11.1	47.9	332
Bank of Ireland	6.6	35.6	439
Anglo (Loan development book)	18.4	74.1	303
Total	36.1	157.6	337

Table 4.4. Rates of Growth of Property and Construction Lending by AIB and Bank of Ireland (per cent)[1]

	2004	2005	2006	2007	2008
AIB	32	53	41	32	32.0
Bank of Ireland	63	34	40	46	20.0
Anglo Loan Book	34	41	45	34	9.9

[1] AIB statistics are for December to December; Bank of Ireland statistics are for March to March; and Anglo statistics are for September to September

The relative importance of this type of lending is illustrated by data for the three largest domestic banks, Allied Irish Banks (AIB), Anglo Irish Bank (Anglo), and Bank of Ireland—see Murphy, 2012.[2] The data (see Tables 4.2–4.4) differ significantly from those contained in the Nyberg Report in that they cover all financing provided by these institutions, both domestically and internationally. By contrast, the Nyberg Report's data relate only to domestic lending by the six Irish institutions, that is, they exclude international lending—for example to the UK, European, or US markets—by their subsidiaries. Figures on the lending by foreign-based subsidiaries, which are mainly supervised by the regulatory authorities of the countries where they reside, are not normally published by the Central Bank of Ireland.

[2] The biggest bank in Ireland at the time was actually the German-owned bank, Depfa, which had transferred its head office to the IFSC in 2002. It was taken over by the German commercial property company, Hypo Real Estate, in 2007, a takeover that was to prove extremely costly for the German taxpayers.

However, it is important to include the international lending of the Irish banks in their total lending because of the consequences for overall liquidity and solvency. Charles Goodhart, a former member of the Bank of England's Monetary Policy Committee, astutely encapsulated the issue when noting that 'banks are international in life but national in death'. Bad international loans, even if they were mainly the supervisory responsibility of another jurisdiction, will end up just as prominently on the balance sheets of the banks as bad domestic loans. When the taxpayer was forced to shoulder the burden of the overall insolvency of the Irish banks, the total bill reflected the excesses not only of their domestic, but also of their international, lending.

Data compiled by the National Assets Management Agency (NAMA) on total bank lending (domestic and international) to the property sector comprise two components: (1) residential mortgages; and (2) loans to property and construction, essentially loans to developers. The available data do not permit a two-way breakdown between domestic and international, on the one hand, and residential and property lending, on the other. As Anglo was not involved in residential mortgages, the analysis is confined to AIB and Bank of Ireland.

Total mortgage lending by the two largest Irish banks rose by 108 per cent between 2003 and 2008, from €44.1 billion to €91.7 billion. The figures include the lending activities of the Bank of Ireland's mortgage lending UK subsidiary, Bristol and West. In 2008, 55 per cent of Bank of Ireland's mortgages were in the UK and 45 per cent in Ireland.

However, total lending to the property and construction sector by the three biggest Irish banks rose much more sharply, from €36.1 billion to €157.8 billion in the same period. Table 4.3 shows the extent to which the property boom metamorphosed into a predominantly builder/developer bubble between 2003 and 2008. By 2003, Anglo, which specialized in loans to this sector, had captured a sizeable chunk of the profitable fast growing builder/developer market. The surge in the share price and market valuation of Anglo presented a threat for the more conservative Irish banks, AIB and Bank of Ireland. Rather than assessing carefully the risky nature of Anglo's loans to the property and construction sector, both AIB and Bank of Ireland worked aggressively to emulate Anglo's performance.

The phenomenal rates of growth in the loan book of Anglo (34 per cent (2004), 41 per cent (2005), 45 per cent (2006), 34 per cent (2007), and 10 per cent (2008)-shown in Table 4.4)) should have sent warning signals, not just to the Financial Regulator and the Central Bank, but also to AIB and Bank of Ireland. Instead, both these banks jumped onto the most speculative part of the bandwagon. Thus, while AIB grew its mortgage book by 139 per cent between 2003 and 2008, its property and construction lending expanded by 332 per cent. Bank of Ireland, despite the widely held perception that it was a conservative lender, increased its property and construction lending by 439 per cent, at an even faster pace than AIB, albeit from a lower base, and much more rapidly than the (just under) doubling of its mortgage lending. That said, in AIB's case it appears that the drive for profits led it to lend far greater amounts for land and site developments, lending that subsequently would contribute in a major way to its insolvency. Anglo, boosted by its continuing success, more than tripled its lending during the period.

The data in Tables 4.2–4.4 demonstrate that increases in property and construction lending to developers (domestic and international) played the more dominant role in the expansion of banks' balance sheets. Between 2003 and 2008, total mortgage lending by AIB and Bank of Ireland grew by €48 billion, whereas the total property and construction lending by AIB, Bank of Ireland, and Anglo increased by €122 billion. These figures contrast significantly with those presented in the Nyberg Report which, using domestic lending data only, depicted residential mortgage lending growth of €56 billion (from €35 billion to €91 billion) and commercial and property lending growth of €64 billion (from €12 billion to €76 billion). Considering only the latter data, the conclusion could have been drawn that the property bubble was caused in near equal measure by residential property lending alongside commercial and property lending. While this might be true so far as the bubble within Ireland was concerned, once one considers all of the banks' lending, a different picture emerges. Total lending to the property and construction sector by these three banks dwarfed mortgage lending. That said, the impact of the lending by subsidiaries on the later insolvency of the banks depended on the relative incidence of default on loans in this category.

The data published by the Central Bank during this period did not allow outsider observers to distinguish clearly between the different categories of lending engaged in by banks, including that by their subsidiaries abroad. Aside from the executives and boards of the banks (and, perhaps, the Financial Regulator), the extent to which the type (and as will be seen below, the nature) of lending had changed, was not widely known. For example, Anglo, which would ultimately prove to be 'the baddest of the bad,' gave the impression that its activities were balanced across a range of different sectors of the economy. Nyberg emphasized that this was not in fact the case:

Notwithstanding this description of itself as a broadly based business bank, in reality Anglo actually catered for a relatively limited number of customers, many of them in the property development sector. (Nyberg 2011: 22)

4.4 From Speculative to Ponzi-style Financing

Hyman Minsky's analysis of asset market bubbles, outlined in Chapter 3, cogently illustrates the three stages experienced by the Irish property market: (1) hedge financing; (2) speculative financing; and (3) Ponzi financing. The funding of the first stage of the property market boom between 1994 and 2000 appears to have been largely in the form of hedge financing. Banks prudently vetted borrowers' ability to pay both the interest and capital on their loans and imposed LTV ratios that provided a significant margin in case of default.

However, the financial system then evolved to a more speculative form of financing. External competition played an important role in the process. The growth of the economy encouraged foreign institutions—for example, Bank of Scotland (Ireland)—to enter the Irish financial market and introduce innovations such as 100 per cent mortgages and tracker mortgages that made it considerably easier for property buyers to acquire funding. A follow-the-leader model developed, with the domestic banks attempting to protect and grow their market share by offering similar financial inducements—high LTV mortgages were accompanied by interest only loans and by equity release programmes.[3] Property prices continued to rise, lenders became primarily interested in the borrower's ability to service the interest due, rather than repay principal. This constituted the second phase, namely, speculative financing.

In parallel, the banks encouraged many of their older managers, who were well versed in risk management, to retire, to be replaced by younger staff who were inadequately trained (training programmes had earlier been cut back as a cost-saving exercise) and with no knowledge of the credit cycle. This younger staff was incentivized to grow the banks' loan book by sales-based bonuses. The boards of the banks, encouraged by their shareholders, set objectives often in the range of 20 to 25 per cent growth in gross earnings per share, targets that could be met only by ever-increasing lending. Those working in the banks were encouraged to borrow from their own banks—why give business to other banks—which led to a number of banking executives holding sizeable property and site portfolios. This change in banking culture was evident at the top echelons, with one senior manager at AIB later reporting that at the height of the bubble, there was no specialist in risk management on the board of the bank.

There was a further breakdown in the financial institutions' protective mechanisms. Auditors did not identify the risks inherent in the banks'

---

[3] Under these programmes, borrowers were permitted to utilise the paper gains associated with their previous property acquisitions to pay whatever deposit might be required for their next purchase.

changes in lending practices. Audit staff sent to examine the balance sheets were often young and inexperienced who tended to accept unquestioningly the interpretation of the accounts presented by management. Thus, even though auditors were required to present a 'true and fair' account, the underlying destruction of the banks' balance sheets went essentially unnoticed.

The auditors of the three biggest Irish domestic banks were Ernst and Young (Anglo), KPMG (AIB), and PricewaterhouseCoopers (Bank of Ireland). At the peak of the banks' market capitalizations in 2007 Anglo was worth €13 billion, AIB was valued at over €20 billion, and Bank of Ireland was worth close to €19 billion—a total of €52 billion. Anglo—described in 2010 by the *Banker* as the worst bank in the world—was bankrupted by the financial crisis, AIB became almost fully nationalized, and the Irish state ended up owning 15 per cent of Bank of Ireland whose shares fell from over €18 in 2007 to 10 cents in 2012. Shareholders have witnessed over €45 billion wiped off the market capitalization of the three biggest Irish domestic banks. Additionally, the Irish state has had to re-capitalize these banks to the extent of €64 billion. One would have thought that these enormous losses and taxpayers' injections would have warranted an explanation from the three firms in question—as to how their 'true and fair' accounts of the Irish banks up to 2009 were so out of line with reality. Although the firms may argue that they were constrained by international accounting rules (see Section 5 below) this is not an excuse for not even, as a minimum, drawing specific attention to the clear limitations of their approach.

Interestingly, PricewaterhouseCoopers (PwC), the Bank of Ireland's auditors, was asked by the Regulator (IFSRA) to provide reports on Anglo Irish. These reports on Anglo, dated 27 September 2008, 27 November 2008, and 17 December 2008, are incorporated in PwC's *Project Atlas—Anglo Irish Bank Corporation Extracts* (dated 29 February 2009). Some extracts from these reports are worth presenting. On 27 September 2008 PwC was reporting:

> According to August [2008] management information almost all of the Bank's [Anglo] loan book, equating to c. 99% of total customer loans, is considered by management to be performing. 0.6% of the bank's loan book is classified as impaired but significant security is in place to minimize the Bank's loss given default. 2.6% of the book is classified as 'Watch', i.e., loans are performing but require intensive management to ensure that the bank does not incur any loss.

The extract for 27 November 2008 states that 'Management have asserted that the bank [Anglo] only underwrites loans based on a thorough understanding of the client'. Regarding management, it went on to add:

> We were informed that Anglo's senior management team has significant experience in banking, underwriting, risk and wider financial services. Most of the senior

underwriters have in excess of 15–20 years lending risk experience in the sector and relevant markets and have worked through previous economic cycles.

On the question of interest roll ups, the report observed:

In common with other banks, Anglo provides interest roll up facilities when providing development facilities where supported by expected future cash flows. The extent to which interest rollover is permitted in any given case is determined by policy limits, including the strength of the individual client, other cash flow and security and underlying asset values. Management indicated that interest rollover is continually assessed by relevant lending directors and Group Risk Management and may be extended where deemed appropriate, for example, as underlying asset values increase or to reflect the strength of a borrower or as part of a restructuring. This would be consistent with our sample reviews of the larger loans, particularly longer term Irish development land plays.

The above speaks for itself. The Nyberg Report expressed considerable concern about the inadequacies of the financial institutions' auditors:

The Commission would have expected a bank auditor, exercising necessary professional skepticism to have concerns where there were growing property and funding exposures, combined with material governance failings. This combination of factors should, in the Commission's opinion, have raised questions for the auditor about the sustainability of a bank's business, the extent of concern necessarily involving judgement. (Nyberg 2011:56)

With no meaningful internal or external audit controls and in the absence of any effective action by the Financial Regulator (see Chapter 5) the speculative financing phase quickly transformed itself into Minsky's third phase, Ponzi financing. Financial institutions believed that the most profitable area for lending was in property and construction. Very sizeable loans to this sector involved the payment of up-front fees which translated immediately into the bottom line of increased profits. In addition, interest rollovers—one of the strongest indicators of a Ponzi financing phase—started to become a dominant feature. Finally, under equity release programmes, previous borrowings by developers became the basis for further borrowings. It sufficed for them to demonstrate the apparent rise in the value of their holdings, including sites, acquired earlier.

There was a significant link between the banks' lending and the value the market placed on their share prices. At this stage, the property market bubble had created a secondary bubble in the share price of Anglo. Driven by a sales-based bonus culture, Anglo had built up a base of apparently successful builders and encouraged them to become developers who were prepared to borrow even more, using the equity release arrangements described above. The faster the expansion of its loan book, the greater the apparent surge in the bank's profitability—particularly via fee income—and the higher its market valuation. AIB and Bank of Ireland very quickly adopted the Anglo model.

Such was the success of Anglo at the time that then Senator Shane Ross urged investors at the annual general meeting of the Bank of Ireland in 2005 to make the managing director of Anglo Irish, Sean Fitzpatrick, Governor of the Bank of Ireland. Although Ross's proposal was rejected, his enthusiasm for the Anglo model, along with his continued endorsements of the lending policies instigated by Michael Fingleton, head of the Irish Nationwide Building Society (INBS), was replicated across the boardrooms of the other institutions. Anglo's continuing growth, combined with further penetration of the market by the UK-owned banks, Ulster Bank and Bank of Scotland (Ireland), raised shareholder concerns about the direction and leadership of AIB and Bank of Ireland. There was even a worry that one of the latter could become a target for a takeover by Anglo. In 2003, Michael Buckley, then the CEO of AIB, remarked that Anglo had joined AIB for breakfast but was now eating its lunch. Between 2000 and mid-2007, Anglo had increased its market capitalization by an astonishing amount, from €0.6 billion to €13.3 billion. In 2007, financial consultants Oliver Wyman nominated Anglo as the best bank in the world (Carswell 2011: 97).

In this new banking environment, a culture of loan expansion dominated the agendas of financial institutions' board meetings. Proper risk management had noticeably been removed from the high table where the big property and construction borrowers were constantly feted by the financial institutions. A new group of apparent developer heroes, such as Gerry Barrett, Sean Dunne, Gerry Gannon, Ray Grehan, Paddy Kelly, Bernard McNamara, Sean Mulryan, Michael O'Flynn, Joe O'Reilly, Derek Quinlan, Sean Quinn, and Noel Smyth, emerged as the high priests of the boom. Their initial successes enabled them to leverage their equity gains for ever larger loans which meant bigger fees and profits, increased bonuses, and constantly escalating share prices. A virtuous cycle appeared to have developed, allowing the sector to expand seemingly without limit as successful builders mutated into even more successful builder/developers.

The concentration of lending to a small group exacerbated credit risks. Anglo had a limited circle of very high net worth property developer clients. Nyberg would later report that the 'aggregate exposure to the top 20 customers as at 31 May 2008 equated to circa 50 per cent of the Irish loan book of €41.7 billion' (Nyberg 2011: 32), implying an the average loan to their top twenty property developer clients of over €1 billion. According to a report by accountants PwC, in May 2009, the thirteen biggest borrowers from Anglo owed a total of €13.9 billion (including €2.3 billion lent to Sean Quinn and his family, €1.7 billion owed by Joe O'Reilly and his Castlethorn company, and over €1 billion each provided to developers Gerry Gannon, Sean Mulryan, Bernard

McNamara, and Michael O'Flynn). INBS overtly attempted to model itself very closely on Anglo and grew its commercial property lending from €2 billion in 2000 to €9.8 billion in 2007, mainly in the form of site financing. In September 2008, lending to INBS's top 25 customers represented over 50 per cent of its total lending (Nyberg 2011: 33).

The commercial loans to developers were classic Ponzi-type loans, predicated on the assumption that the property market would continue to grow seemingly for ever. Borrowers were not required to make any principal repayments or even, in the later stages, to pay interest on their loans because of the recourse to interest rollovers. Under the equity release arrangements already described, the paper gains arising from successful projects could support the granting of a further and bigger loan.

The prices of urban and rural sites throughout Ireland began to explode. Hotels were bought near the centre of Dublin at dizzying prices. Jurys Hotel and the adjoining Berkeley Court, in the heartland of Dublin 4, were sold for €379 million in the latter half of 2005, representing an implicit land valuation of €54 million an acre. In March 2007, the Burlington Hotel, also in Dublin 4, was acquired for £288 million. The hotel chain, Jurys Inns, was purchased in June 2007 for €1.2 billion with the aid of a loan of €1 billion from Anglo. These hotels were acquired to be knocked down so as to free up sites for new high rise commercial property ventures. The site of a former glass bottle company at Ringsend, close to Dublin's River Liffey, was purchased for €412 million in 2006. Estate agents CB Richard Ellis estimated that when developed, the site could produce sales and rents of €1.8 billion from over 2,000 apartments and a million square feet of letable commercial spaces. They assumed that two bedroom apartments could be sold at €625,000 each and three bedroom apartments for €850,000 (Carswell 2011: 90). A number of owners of well-known manufacturing or retail establishments decided to branch out into property acquisition, several with disastrous outcomes which in turn affected the financial viability of their original business.

Successes in Ireland led developers to the confident belief, shared by their bankers, that they could replicate the success overseas. Irish banks were willing to finance a spire-like building which, when constructed in Chicago, would become the highest building in North America. Budapest's landmark Gresham Palace hotel was bought and re-built by an Irish developer. Land sites and commercial units were purchased across Europe in the rush to acquire property gold. Irish developers acquired wide swathes of property in London, including the Savoy Hotel, costing £750 million, and the disused Battersea Power station site.

These entrepreneurs formed consortia with members of well-off professional groups—accountants, barristers, dentists, doctors, medical consultants, and solicitors—so that they too could benefit from the boom, while also exploiting tax advantages. Financial presentations—some by a former tax inspector—were given to high-income earning individuals at early morning breakfast meetings in Dublin hotels. Attendees were encouraged to participate in highly leveraged property syndicates that would acquire new development land at home and abroad that could be turned into future shopping malls, industrial units, and hotels and leisure centres.

It was difficult to avoid hearing long discussions about the amazing riches that had been, or shortly would be, acquired by those who had been lucky enough to sample the road to easy prosperity. Taxi drivers, realizing that they were priced out of the Irish property market, sought to acquire, sight unseen, apartments and sites in exotic locations such as Bulgaria, Cape Verde, and Mumbai. When this started to happen, some began to realize, as multimillionaire Joe Kennedy did with his shoeshine boy in Wall Street in 1929, that a Minsky Moment had arrived.[4] By 2006, collective madness had hit the property market and the Irish financial system. The bubble, with the builder/developers leading the charge, had reached its apogee. This had little to do with wealth creation, as largely was the case in the earlier Celtic Tiger period, but reflected Ponzi financing where prosperity apparently could be achieved simply by exchanging one piece of property or land for another.

The bankers and developers were not alone in pursuing property acquisition. A cast of supporting groups ranging from estate agents to the newsprint media helped puff the market to new high levels. Estate agents and valuers linked up with the banks to provide property valuations that supported further equity release programmes. These estate agents and valuers pushed up values relentlessly, conning purchasers into the belief that there had been a complete metamorphosis in the Irish property market that justified the ever increasing prices of property. In some cases, where estate agents questioned this mood of unbridled optimism, warning against excessively high valuations that could place the borrower at risk in the event of a future downturn, banks threatened the agents with the loss of their business. The property supplements in newspapers began to resemble telephone directories and the number of property-related articles soared (Figure 4.1). The *Irish Times* itself plunged massively into the property market at the height of the bubble, paying €50 million to acquire myhome.ie, an internet property company, in mid-2006.[5]

---

[4] Kennedy decided to sell all his shares shortly before the Wall Street Crash of 1929, after his shoe shine boy had begun to offer him tips on how to make money quickly on the stock exchange.

[5] The broader role of the media during this period is examined in Chapter 8.

4.5 Funding the Banks

The discussion thus far has focused on the nature and scale of the risky lending by the Irish banks, that is on the assets side of their balance sheets. But where did the money come from to finance all this frenzied activity? Banks can fund loans by attracting retail deposits, by borrowing in the form of either wholesale deposits or bond issuance, or by changing the growth and composition of their reserves. In the traditional banking model, growth in lending was funded largely by obtaining more retail deposits. However, in Ireland, the increase in retail deposits throughout this period fell far short of the amounts needed to finance the banks' extraordinarily fast pace of lending.

This funding gap was met by large scale recourse to external wholesale borrowing. There was a chicken/egg element to this process. Was it the ready access to cheap international money that led to the increase in the banks' lending? Or was it the increase in the banks' lending that dictated increased recourse to international wholesale borrowing? This issue is of considerable importance because, in the aftermath of the crisis, some commentators viewed foreign banks as having, in their words, 'shovelled' money at Irish financial institutions. Thus, just as the domestic banks engaged in imprudent lending, so also did foreign lenders in providing the funding that made this possible. From this perspective, there was a strong element of co-responsibility on the part of both the Irish banks and foreign banks. This provided the basis of the argument that Irish taxpayers should not end up footing the entire bill for the banking collapse—others should also shoulder some of the burden. This issue, which also involves the role of the European authorities (particularly the European Central Bank), is returned to in later chapters.

It should be borne in mind, however, that, following the inception of the euro and the disappearance of exchange rate risk, all other countries of the Eurozone had similar access to the vast international pool of wholesale liquidity. This did indeed open up hitherto untapped funding sources at low interest rates that were eagerly availed of by the Irish banks. But it is noteworthy that most of the other Eurozone countries, particularly those in northern Europe, did not borrow on the unprecedented scale that Ireland did. Were their central banks and regulatory authorities more aware of the potential dangers involved and did they discourage it? Or was it a case of different cultural approaches?

The acquisition of property was higher on the agenda of the Irish than, for example, that of Germans, who appear more content to rent their homes and apartments. Moreover, unlike in most other countries, as the boom gathered pace, many segments of the Irish population appear to have concluded that the easy path to wealth lay in the acquisition of even more property, whether in the form of holiday homes, buy-to-let properties, or participation in bank-financed consortia that could leverage further acquisitions, in Ireland or elsewhere.

The gap between the banks' lending and their retail deposits rose from €26 billion in 2002 to €129 billion by 2008 and was met by wholesale funding, largely from abroad. The traditional constraint of linking loans to deposits had disappeared. The banks' loan to deposit ratios rose to over 150 per cent in many cases. Irish Life and Permanent's ratio reached an extreme of 275 per cent, implying an almost total dependence on wholesale funding. There appeared to have been no concern amongst the banks that this particular source of borrowing might dry up. As Nyberg observed:

> the banks commonly assumed that access to funding would continue unchecked. The Commission was repeatedly assured that, during the Period, there was little or no concern with banks' deteriorating loan/deposit ratios or the absolute amounts of wholesale funding being accessed as balance sheets expanded and leverage grew. (Nyberg 2011: 40)

However, as will be shown in Chapter 9, difficulties began to emerge from late 2007 onwards as liquidity tightened in international financial markets. Combined with the deteriorating reputation of Irish banks, this forced a shift to short-term wholesale funding which, because of the need for continued roll-overs, caused even greater problems when markets started to dry up completely. Nyberg noted that, in certain cases, the Treasury management arms of the banks accentuated the move to shorter-term financing because of the lower cost. However, such short-term profit maximization considerations were very much at odds with the need for the banks to have a more balanced maturity funding structure.

In addition, the capital component of the liabilities side of the banks' balance sheets evolved in two negative ways. In order to grow the capital base, recourse was made increasingly to subordinated debt, rather than share-holders' equity. According to Nyberg, the capital of the Irish domestic banks increased from €18 billion in 2000 to €47 billion in 2007, mainly due to the use of subordinated debt.[6] While this instrument had the immediate advantage of improving the banks' earnings per share, as with wholesale funding, it had to be re-financed over increasingly shorter maturities, thereby weakening the banks' capital structure and accentuating their vulnerability.

The second distortion was exogenous in character and resulted from changes, starting in 2005, in the International Financial Reporting Standards (IFRS) accounting rules which applied to all European Union companies. The

---

[6] See Chapter 10 for a discussion of the concept of subordinated debt.

modifications, aimed at constraining the banks' ability to artificially reduce their tax liability, stipulated that loss provisions could only be made where there was objective evidence of loan impairment. This effectively meant that banks could not make provisions for possible losses in the absence of evidence showing that these losses were actually occurring. Even as the financial clouds darkened in 2007 and 2008, the banks could claim that, even if they had so desired, they were constrained from making additional provisions in anticipation of a possible financial rainy day. On the other hand, there is no evidence to indicate that the subject was raised by the Financial Regulator, perhaps because it might have given a worrying signal to the markets.

Both the Honohan and Nyberg reports argue that, if it had really been thought to be necessary, despite the IFRS constraints, the banks could have been required by the Financial Regulator to increase their provisioning.[7] This did not happen. Instead, as Nyberg (2011: 43) noted, the Irish banks were able to increase their capital by an additional €3.5 billion as a result of the (at least perceived) constraints arising from IFRS accounting rules. This in turn increased their lending capacity by over €30 billion. These pro-cyclical accounting conventions proved to be highly damaging in the Irish case. Instead of encouraging prudential provisioning against possible losses in the downturn of the cycle, they in effect enabled the banks, to continue to over-expand lending.

Over-reliance on external wholesale borrowing, excessive use of shorter-term subordinated debt, and under-provisioning for possible loan losses left the balance sheets of the banks in a particularly weak position to cope with the nuclear winter that hit international markets in the final months of 2008. They would find themselves in a classic bind. Increasing liquidity problems would direct attention to their growing insolvency. In turn, heightened market concern about the viability of the banks would cause capital flight, further exacerbating the problem that policymakers faced in September 2008.

This is illustrated by movements in the cost of credit default swaps (CDS) for Anglo in September 2008 (Figure 4.2).[8] On 1 September 2008 a CDS for Anglo cost 302 basis points. By 18 September it had risen to 583, and by 29 September to 731 basis points. This was a clear sign of major unease in international money markets about the state of Anglo at the time which culminated in an inability to roll over maturing deposits (see Chapter 9).

---

[7] 'In later stages of the boom, when the relevant property markets had already began to turn down, regulators could have required more provisions to be taken, thereby inducing the banks to consolidate their capital, for example by limiting dividends, or by issuing new capital' (Honohan, 2010: 106).

[8] Credit default swaps are a rough measure of the market's evaluation of the cost of insuring against default by a government or financial or corporate entity. The data need to be interpreted with caution as in some cases, the market for CDS is relatively undeveloped, with only a small volume of trading taking place.

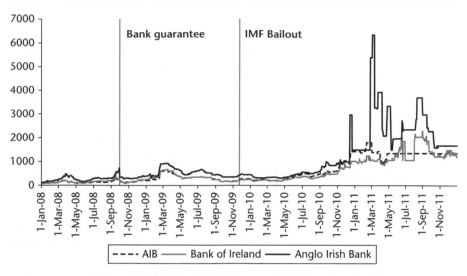

Figure 4.2 Irish Bank CDS: January 2008–January 2012

The old adage, 'as safe as a bank', was to be seriously questioned. The banks' problems were greatly accentuated—or perhaps more accurately accelerated—by the collapse of Lehman Brothers in early September 2008. However, the assertion that this event was largely responsible for the Irish crash was categorically rejected by the Honohan report. In other words, the Irish disaster 'was an accident waiting to happen'.

4.6 Conclusions

This chapter has highlighted how the original Celtic Tiger phenomenon changed utterly from 2002 to 2008. The Tiger that had been driven by multinational investment, peaked in the golden year of 2000. The multinational sector's growth rate stalled in 2001 due to the dot.com collapse, the shock of 9/11, and a growing lack of global confidence. After a temporary fall in 2001, the Irish property market, which should have been left to reach a stable equilibrium on its own, was resuscitated by the political decision to grant significant fiscal concessions in the 2002 Budget. From then on the property market slowly but surely became a bubble that ended up infecting all sectors of the economy.

The ignition of the bubble was given impetus as the Irish banks, following the apparently successful role model of Anglo Irish Bank, massively increased their lending to the property sector by availing of an apparently infinite pool of liquidity from international wholesale markets. Encouraged by the apparent success of Anglo, the other Irish banks joined in lending to developers intent on transforming building sites into a new form of gold. In many cases these soon became Ponzi-type financing schemes.

The excessive concentration of lending to the property sector was matched by short-sighted decisions on the banks' funding side. The traditional reliance on retail deposits was replaced by large scale recourse to short-term wholesale funding and the banks' loan to deposit ratios soared. Vulnerabilities were heightened by greater reliance on short-term subordinated debt to help improve the capital base. The banks apparently saw no reason (nor were they given any by the Regulator) to strengthen their capital by provisioning against possible losses reducing dividends, or raising additional equity.

All these factors combined to create a classic Minsky-type outcome. It took the wave of international financial turbulence, culminating in the collapse of Lehman Brothers in 2008, to pull the trigger. But the seeds of Ireland's property and banking disaster had been sown for some considerable time beforehand. The question was only when, not whether, a 'Minsky moment' would arrive.

References

Budget and Economic Statistics (2011) Department of Finance (Dublin).

Cassidy, Mark and Derry O'Brien (2005) 'Export Performance and Competitiveness of the Irish Economy', *Central Bank of Ireland Quarterly Bulletin*, Number 3 (Dublin).

Carswell, Simon (2011) *Anglo Republic: Inside the Bank that Broke Ireland* (Dublin).

Honohan, Patrick (2010) *The Irish Banking Crisis: Regulatory and Financial Stability, 2003–2008*, A Report to the Minister of Finance by the Governor of the Central Bank (Dublin).

Murphy, Antoin E. (2012) 'Ponzi Financing and the Property Bubble', *Irish Times*, 13 June.

Nyberg, Peter (2011) *Misjudging Risk: Causes of the Systemic Banking Crisis in Ireland*, Report of the Commission of Investigation Into the Banking Sector in Ireland, Government Publications (Dublin).

Somers, Michael, and John Corrigan (2009) 'The Irish Economy'. Paper presented in Paris, June 2000.

5

The Failure of Financial Regulation

> Nobody made a greater mistake than he who did nothing because he could only do a little.
>
> Edmond Burke[1]

The previous chapter described the increasingly reckless lending policies of banks that fuelled Ireland's extraordinary property bubble and ultimately led to their financial downfall. The obvious question then arises. Why did the supervisory institutions that were supposed to oversee and ensure the stability of the Irish financial system not prevent this excessive lending? To answer this question, it is necessary to assess the responsibility of the regulatory authorities at both the domestic and European levels.

Both the Honohan and Nyberg reports dealt extensively with the role of the domestic authorities, that is, the Financial Regulator and the Central Bank. However, they did not address a second key dimension, namely, the role of the European authorities. The debt crisis revealed fundamental flaws in the design and implementation of the architecture of the euro area. As discussed below, any successful currency union needs, as a minimum, three key features: first, a common monetary policy that commands sufficient support among member states; second, a system of financial regulation to ensure effective macro-prudential supervision; and third, a structure to prevent the pursuit of unsustainable fiscal policies by individual members. While, in the case of the euro area, the first element was present, the second turned out to be, in effect, largely absent in many cases, partly due to the devolution of financial supervision to the national level. This chapter deals with these two aspects. The third element, namely, the failure of the Maastricht Treaty and the Stability and Growth Pact to restrain fiscal excesses, is discussed in the next chapter.

---

[1] Summersdale (2012).

5.1 The Role of the Irish Financial Services Regulatory Authority (the Financial Regulator)[2]

In late September 2008, the Financial Regulator reassuringly reported to the Minister of Finance that there was no cause for significant concern regarding the state of the Irish banking system. The banks had met all prudential requirements and, according to the joint financial stability assessments of the Regulator and the Central Bank, were well placed to meet any adverse exogenous developments, including the effects of what was confidently predicted to be a 'soft landing' for the Irish property market. At the time of the fateful guarantee decision on 29 September 2008, the Financial Regulator, Patrick Neary, continued to assert unequivocally the view that the difficulties that the banks were experiencing were only of a liquidity nature and that no issues of possible bank insolvency needed to be considered.

Thus, the Regulator failed to identify the underlying financial vulnerabilities of the Irish banks, let alone take vigorous action to address them. The Honohan and Nyberg reports discussed in some depth the major weaknesses that were largely responsible. These can be grouped under three broad headings: (a) an excessive reliance on procedures, as opposed to substance; (b) a reluctance to take decisive action even when problems were identified; and (c) broader factors that appear to have constrained the ability and willingness of the Regulator (and the Central Bank) to adopt a more aggressive approach.

Before dealing with these elements, it is helpful to outline briefly the history surrounding the creation of the Financial Regulator in May 2003 and its (complex) relationship with the Central Bank. Until then, financial supervision of credit institutions had been undertaken by a dedicated department within the Central Bank of Ireland. Before and during the decade of the 2000s, much debate took place throughout the EU as regards the relative merits of retaining the supervisory function within national central banks, establishing an independent regulatory authority (as in the UK and a number of other EU Member states), or devising some kind of 'hybrid arrangement', such as the Irish structure.[3] The practices followed varied considerably across EU states, partly reflecting historical factors and political traditions.

In the case of Ireland in 1999, in the wake of public disquiet over various financial scandals involving the banks (overcharging borrowers and facilitating

---

[2] The Financial Regulator was originally called the Irish Financial Services Regulatory Authority (IFSRA) before being subsequently renamed. However, throughout this book, the term 'Financial Regulator' is used, regardless of the date. Unless otherwise indicated, the term 'Financial Regulator' (sometimes referred to as the 'Regulator') refers to the institution. Also, for shorthand purposes, in this book, the CBFSAI is often referred to as the Central Bank (or, on occasion, the Bank).

[3] For a thorough review of the theoretical and institutional pros and cons associated with alternative approaches, see ECB (2001).

tax evasion for some customers), the McDowell Report recommended—by majority decision—the creation of a new 'green fields' regulator and the removal of any direct supervisory responsibilities from the Central Bank. This proposal was in line with the changes introduced in the UK that involved the establishment of the Financial Services Authority (FSA) as an entity quite distinct and independent from the Bank of England. The Central Bank of Ireland and the Department of Finance members of the McDowell Committee did not support the Report's proposals and, after a long debate, a compromise was reached. A separate Financial Regulator was set up within an overall new structure of what was to be called the Central Bank and Financial Services Authority of Ireland (CBFSAI). The Regulator was not a division of the CBFSAI and both the CBFSAI and the Regulator were governed by independently appointed Boards. However, a majority of the Board members of the Regulator, including its Chairman and Chief Executive of the Financial Regulator, also sat on the CBFSAI Board which was chaired by the Governor.

The two institutions operated under the same roof and shared overhead resources such as technology, human resources, and premises.[4] From a formal legal perspective, the Regulator was autonomous but not independent of the CBFSAI, as it did not have a distinct legal personality. The two 'wings' of the CBFSAI generally operated fairly separately without apparent major conflicts. However, in one crucial respect, namely the preparation of annual financial stability reports published by the CBFSAI and which therefore involved both the Central Bank and the Regulator, serious weaknesses emerged, as will be seen below. In the event, the onset of the crisis led to a move away from the 'independent regulator' approach, at least in the UK and Ireland where the responsibility for financial regulation is now unambiguously vested in the Central Bank.[5]

5.1.1 *Reliance on Procedures Rather than Substance*

The approach adopted by the Irish Financial Regulator was fully consistent with a broadly prevailing philosophy at the time (including in the UK) of 'principles based regulation'. This stressed the importance of ensuring sound internal governance structures and procedures in each institution, as opposed to delving into the substance of the banks' activities. In line with the Efficient Markets Hypothesis discussed in Chapter 2, it was implicitly assumed that self-regulating financial markets would remain stable and that intrusive regulation of financial institutions was unnecessary and could stifle financial innovation.

---

[4] Various practical aspects of these arrangements are discussed in Honohan (2010: 34–42).
[5] In Ireland's case, the separate Boards of the CBFSAI and the Regulator were abolished under new legislation passed in 2010 and replaced by a single Central Bank Commission.

Although the worldwide financial crisis has cruelly exposed the theoretical and empirical limitations of this approach, its potential defects were not considered sufficiently seriously beforehand by most economists or policymakers.

While the conceptual underpinnings of the 'light financial regulation' philosophy (sometimes referred to as a 'principles' approach) were not explicitly outlined by Irish policymakers, it was *'de facto'* followed.[6] This framework was consistent with the government's broader deregulation agenda, itself inspired by European and much worldwide thinking (see chapter 2). The Regulator's main task was to try to ensure that appropriate internal arrangements were in place within the relevant financial institutions. If this was the case, these entities could then be assumed to act in their own enlightened self-interest and conduct their affairs in a responsible manner.[7] Competition and the discipline of the market could be relied on to avoid errant or reckless financial behaviour. Consistent with this approach, the Honohan report refers to a deferential approach on the part of Regulator staff who most likely were not sufficient either in numbers or technical expertise to challenge the confident assertions of the bankers.[8]

By the time the crisis broke, the Regulator had little substantive information on the extent and nature of the banks' true exposures. To illustrate how this came about, Honohan (2010) documents in detail the approaches adopted in the reports of two important sets of representative bank inspections undertaken by the Regulator. The first set of reports, covering 2005–07, depicted significant deficiencies in the banks' commercial property lending activities. However, rather than assessing their likely adverse impact on the financial health of the banks, the weaknesses were characterized in terms of inadequate structures and procedures. The second in 2007 (referred to as the '5x5 Big Developer Exposures Inspection') dealt with what subsequently turned out to be a crucial aspect of the banking crisis, namely, large-scale commercial

---

[6] Regulator officials would probably object to the term 'light' as it connotes an attitude of indifference. However, regardless of issues of motivation, in practice the approach was the opposite of 'heavy handed', as it did not come to grips with the detailed substance of much of the banks' activities.

[7] The content of a letter (described in Nyberg (2011)) from the Regulator to Irish Nationwide Building Society (INBS) in December 2004 is a good illustration of the approach that tended to be followed. The letter states that while the Regulator had some concerns with respect to the risk profile of INBS' lending portfolio, from its perspective the issue was for INBS to ensure that it had appropriate procedures and structures in place to effectively handle this risk.

[8] It has sometimes been suggested that the problem stemmed from a shortage of staff within the Regulator. While this may have been the case (and the large-scale expansion in the numbers of Regulator staff after the outbreak of the crisis lends this credence), both the Honohan and Nyberg reports note that there is no evidence that the Regulator sought authorization for increases in staffing from the Department of Finance who was responsible for approving its budget. Nor did the Regulator indicate at any stage that this was essential in order to be able to fulfil its mandate effectively. In other words it appears to have been relatively content with the 'light regulation' approach and the resources that it had at its disposal to implement it.

lending by the banks to developer clients. Again, the reports revealed major concerns about inadequate loan appraisal procedures and the lack of reliable assurances relating to personal guarantees. However, the reports did not analyse the macro-prudential implications of these key weaknesses.

In neither of the above examples were the possible implications for the solvency of the banks or the potential risks for overall financial stability brought to the attention of the Boards of the Regulator or the Central Bank. More generally, as Whelan (2009) has stressed, the risks associated with excessive concentration on property-related loans (see Chapter 4) appear to be have been completely underplayed by the Regulator, who drew satisfaction from the fact that the banks met all capital adequacy requirements throughout.[9] It eventually proved necessary for the authorities to request a consultancy report from PricewaterhouseCoopers (PwC) in September 2008 to determine the real situation of the banks. It is very hard to understand why the information in the PwC report had not already been acquired and analysed by the Regulator long beforehand. The decision to call in PwC at that point was a possible indication that the Department of Finance may have begun to lose confidence in the technical expertise and judgement of the Regulator.

5.1.2 A Reluctance to Take Decisive Action

The overall weaknesses of the Regulator's approach were highlighted by two further important issues that the Regulator had identified but only partially followed up. The first, serious concerns regarding governance, surfaced repeatedly with respect to Irish Nationwide Building Society (INBS) and, to a lesser extent, Anglo Irish Bank.[10] However, despite observing these weaknesses, according to Nyberg (2011: 63), the Regulator 'remained hesitant to take effective action even when the engagement with INBS resulted in little material change. And as a result, the very significant risks inherent in INBS's business model...had time to develop essentially undisturbed'. Although the Regulator could and should have attached conditions to the licence of an institution such as INBS, or even withdrawn those licenses altogether, this

---

[9] Whelan (2009) quotes from the Basel II framework document: 'A risk concentration is any single exposure or group of exposures with the potential to produce losses large enough (relative to a bank's capital, total assets, or overall risk level) to threaten a bank's health or ability to maintain its core operations...Risk concentrations are arguably the single most important cause of major problems in banks'.

[10] According to Nyberg (2011: iv), 'Governance at these banks fell short of best practice. While procedures and processes in Anglo existed on paper, in certain cases they were not properly implemented or followed in practice. It appears that, at least in the latter years, only a handful of management were aware of all activities of the bank. At INBS, a number of essential, independent functions either did not effectively exist or were seriously under-resourced'.

avenue was not pursued. One reason appears to have been a general reluctance to take decisive action unless a legally watertight case could be made, presumably for fear of a reputational damage if a legal victory was not assured.[11] In the case of INBS, Honohan (2010: 17) observes that 'while it was understood by all that [the central management figure, Michael Fingleton] was politically well-connected [and that] unconscious factors may have been at work, [Regulator] management and directors agree that there is no evidence of political representations being made on his behalf aimed at influencing regulatory decisions'. It is up to readers to draw whatever conclusions they may wish from this observation.

The second issue arose from the fact that the Regulator was not totally impervious to the possible risks involved in the splurge of property-related lending indulged in by banks. In 2006, after considerable discussion and debate spanning eighteen months or so—which included seeking, as required under the CBFSAI statute, the approval of the Governor of the Central Bank—the Regulator introduced increases in the risk weights to be applied to certain categories of property-related lending.[12] However, this measure is widely acknowledged to have been more of a 'shot across the bows', rather than a serious attempt to curtail lending sharply. It was a case of too little too late—indeed, the increase in risk weights was only fully implemented in mid-2007, after the property boom had peaked and, in effect, 'the horse had already bolted the stable'.

This action was the only across the board initiative taken by the Regulator. Other possibilities, for instance, the application of non-statutory sectoral credit limits or the imposition of ceilings on loan-to-deposit ratios, were not pursued. Such measures, although apparently not considered statutorily enforceable, could have exercised a significant dampening effect, if they had been backed up by strong moral suasion, including public support from the Central Bank. The same could have been true in the case of a public campaign by the Bank to discourage high loan to value (LTV) ratios or a call for extra provisioning against possible future loan losses by the banks. The statistics (highlighted in Chapter 4) on bank lending to the property sector and more specifically to developers, along with the increasing reliance by the banks on foreign borrowing, should have sounded alarm bells. The fact that they did not do so is a serious indictment of both the Central Bank and the Regulator at a crucial time.[13]

---

[11] However, as noted by Nyberg, even if a case had been lost, this would have been useful in clarifying the Financial Regulator's powers or in demonstrating the need for additional legislative powers in order to be able to fulfil its mandate.

[12] See Honohan (2010: Box 7.1) for a full discussion.

[13] Even as regards ensuring good corporate governance (the 'bread and butter' of principles-based regulation), there was significant resistance to putting in place stricter measures as regards

5.1.3 *Other Forces at Work*

If there had been a sufficient will and a greater sense of urgency, much more could have been done by the Regulator and the Central Bank to identify and address many of the fundamental problems as the bubble started to develop. But while the 'principles approach' contained serious inherent weaknesses, there were other forces at play. First, tighter regulatory requirements applied to the six domestic Irish institutions would likely have placed them at some competitive disadvantage—or so they would have claimed—*vis-à-vis* non-Irish institutions eagerly seeking to raise their share of the booming Irish property lending market. It might also have cast some cloud over the 'light regulation' reputation of the International Financial Services Centre which was very strongly supported by the government.

However, such fears should and could have been tempered. As Nyberg (2011) pointed out, there was no evidence that the Regulator ever contemplated approaching the UK FSA or the European Committee of Bank Supervisors to alert others to the risks their own institutions might be incurring in the Irish market. Moreover, while the mandate of the Central Bank/Regulator was to promote the development of the financial services sector in Ireland, the Central Bank Act is quite explicit that this is to be done in such a way as not to affect the Bank's objective of 'contributing to the stability of the financial system'. Finally, if indeed measures to tighten regulation of domestic banks had led to a reduction in their market share, in hindsight the likely outcome would have been that non-Irish banks would have ended up bearing a larger proportion of the costs of the banking disaster, to the ultimate benefit of savings to the Irish taxpayer.[14]

A second aspect was that the Regulator would have required broad support from others, including prior explicit approval of the Central Bank Governor, in respect of any more 'aggressive' regulatory measures under consideration. However, as will be seen below, the Central Bank separately held the view, as expressed in the Financial Stability reports, that there were no major concerns regarding the financial stability of the system. Moreover, the Secretary General of the Department of Finance who, presumably, had no reason to think otherwise, was an *ex officio* member of the CBFSAI Board.

Third, the possibility of a sense of urgency emerging in favour of greater action would have been dealt a blow by the reports of the IMF Financial Sector

---

Directors' Compliance Statements, a Corporate Governance Code, and the application of an Administrative Sanctions Procedure (see Honohan 2010: 48–60).

[14] It is also true that closer cooperation between the Irish authorities and the UK FSA could have led to lower losses being incurred by the Irish subsidiaries of UK entities such as Ulster Bank. However, in the main, supervision of these entities was not the direct responsibility of the Irish Financial Regulator.

Assessment Program (FSAP), especially the report published in August 2006.[15] The methodology used—perhaps inevitable given the small number of IMF staff involved and their short stay in Ireland—was similar to the approach of the Regulator itself and focused more on procedures rather than detailed substance. Although some risks arising from the banks' exposure to the property market and their reliance on wholesale funding were noted, the overall IMF judgement was positive about the apparent financial stability of the Irish banking system:

> ... financial institution profitability and capitalisation are currently very strong, with Irish banking sector profits among the highest in Western Europe. Reflecting their good performance, the major Irish banks receive upper medium to high-grade ratings from the international ratings agencies... [As regards the Financial Regulator itself, it noted] the significant achievements in the prudential framework [and an] organisational structure and a consistent corporate culture that are likely to enhance financial stability (IMF 2006).

It is not surprising that Honohan (2010: 92) remarked: 'In hindsight such an unwarrantedly favourable report by an authoritative international body was clearly unhelpful'.

Finally, given that the boards of the commercial banks have been heavily criticized publicly on account of the banks' activities, it is relevant to question the role of the Boards of the Central Bank and the Regulator. These comprised prominent persons from all strands of Irish society, including finance, business, academia, and the trades unions. It is unlikely that most of these non-executive directors had the professional experience or analytical capability to pass informed judgements on what was happening with the banks and the property market. It is true that specialized expertise in this area was not plentifully available, at least within Ireland. Nevertheless, apart from possible non-Irish appointees, inclusion on the Boards of Irish academics such as Patrick Honohan (with extensive expertise acquired at the World Bank in financial sector matters and later appointed Central Bank Governor), Alan Ahearne (who had been a staff member of the US Federal Reserve and became a member of the Central Bank Commission in 2010), or indeed the economist Morgan Kelly, would have added an important external analytical perspective. In the event, as Nyberg implies, with perhaps one or two exceptions, most Board members were content to go along with the prevailing consensus.

---

[15] See Honohan (2010: 6.29–6.6.36) for more extensive coverage of the report's contents and findings.

5.2 The Central Bank

The Financial Regulator was responsible for micro-prudential matters, namely, the development and implementation of the regulatory framework at the level of individual institutions. The Central Bank was charged with systemic financial stability matters, that is, 'analysis of the micro-prudential where appropriate as well as the macro-prudential health of the financial sector' (Honohan 2010: 38). The main instrument for fulfilling this function—often referred to as macro-prudential supervision—was the Financial Stability Reports (FSRs) published annually between 2004 and 2007, in line with requirements in other euro area states. The FSRs were published by the CBFSAI after discussions between high level staff of the Central Bank and the Regulator and approval by a joint Board meeting of the two institutions. However, in practice, preparation of the FSR was undertaken by a small group of economists working within the Central Bank.

The internal processes, the coverage and analytical content of issues and the key conclusions of the FSRs are discussed extensively in Honohan (2010: Chapter 6). The main elements can be summarized:

(i) The central messages of the annual FSRs, including that of 2007, were unwavering and broadly speaking, sanguine. The reports noted at various stages vulnerabilities of the banking system associated with strong credit growth, high indebtedness levels and the outlook for house prices. Although there were concerns that financial stability risks had on balance increased between 2005 and 2007, the general thinking is best illustrated by the conclusion of the 2007 FSR:

> However, the central expectation, based on an assessment of the risks facing both the household and non-financial corporate sectors, the health of the banking sector and the results of in-house stress testing is that, notwithstanding the international financial market turbulence, the Irish banking system continues to be well placed to withstand adverse economic and sectoral developments in the short to medium term (CBFSAI 2007: 11).

(ii) The FSRs contained considerable discussion of house prices, with the 2007 FSR concluding that 'the central scenario is, therefore, for a soft landing'. The possibility that the price fall that had already taken place was the harbinger of much greater future falls was not entertained. The analytical evidence on the topic relied largely on the proposition that 'fundamental factors', such as economic growth, low levels of Irish home ownership in the past and demographic influences, broadly explained the rise in prices that had occurred. While it was recognized that these fundamental factors might be tapering off, the overall assessment was cast in terms of the 'soft landing' scenario, implying a prospective price decline of only up to 15 per cent or so.

The methodological issues raised by this approach, as well as counter evidence available from other sources at the time, were reviewed in detail by Honohan (2010: 6.12–6.18). The paper by the academic Morgan Kelly (see Chapter 8 for a more extensive discussion), which argued that, based on OECD evidence, house prices could be expected to fall by 50 per cent in real terms, 'rather than acknowledging the red flag raised, elicited what now appears as a somewhat defensive response' (Honohan 2010: 84). Other 'contrarian' evidence, including from academic Alan Ahearne (also see Chapter 8), was not seriously considered. Within the Central Bank itself, there is clear evidence of a desire to engage in 'group think' and to censor or cast aside evidence that could cast doubt on the benign scenario described above. Thus, the 2007 FSR did not contain an update of any of the calculations contained in earlier FSR reports, but instead essentially asserted the validity of the 'soft landing' hypothesis. In particular, important internal Central Bank staff calculations showing estimated house price overvaluations of 35–40 per cent as of various dates in 2007 were ignored.

(iii) Central Bank staff studies in 2006–07 raised concerns regarding the commercial property market, drawing attention to the sharp rise in price/earnings (rent) ratios and the strong (positive) correlation between prices in different segments of the market. These concerns, while noted, were not given major prominence in the main body of the FSRs and were not reflected, at least in any explicit sense, in the overall conclusions that favoured a positive outlook for the banking system. This omission partly reflects the lack of awareness and/or appreciation on the part of the Central Bank/Regulator of the implications of the risky nature of the concentration of bank lending to major developers. Nor did it take full account of the growth in banks' international lending (i.e. lending by their subsidiaries abroad) highlighted in Chapter 4 and which paints a considerably more worrying picture of the totality of risks incurred by the banks.

(iv) The Nyberg report noted the more general 'group think' tendency within the Central Bank which discouraged internal contrarian information or opinions that ran counter to the desire to convey a relatively positive message. Apart from the neglect of important analysis on housing prices noted already, this extended to significant pressures to tone down the drafting of the FSRs. The report describes the 'apparent lack of interest in fostering critical debate within the confidential confines of the Central Bank on stability issues . . . [and] the signs that, reinforced by the relatively hierarchical structure of the [Bank] a climate of self- censorship had become prevalent in CBFSAI policy work' (Nyberg 2011: 68).[16]

(v) The 2004 and 2006 FSRs contained the results of various 'stress tests' applied to the banks. Although in line with international best practice, the shocks employed 'did not capture the scale of what could and did happen' (Honohan 2010: 94). While many generally accepted limitations of stress testing were noted in the main body of the text, the overall conclusions contained an unduly favourable assessment of the capacity of the banking system to survive potential shocks. Quite apart from the published stress tests, it is particularly unfortunate that, even on a strictly confidential basis, no internal work was done by Central Bank staff to analyse the implications of possible worst case scenarios. Such analysis could have deepened the Bank's appreciation of the potential for a major disaster and better prepared it for dealing with the eventual crisis.

Both the Honohan and Nyberg reports convey the impression that apart from analytical weaknesses, there was a desire on the part of the Central Bank (shared by the Regulator) to adopt a cautious approach publicly and to avoid doing anything that could 'rock the boat' or create market turbulence. While this may be seen by some as a legitimate consideration, there is no evidence to indicate that any less sanguine, blunter, assessments were provided privately by the Central Bank to the government.

Why, it may be asked, was the Central Bank so silent on the possibility of an emergence of a serious problem? Most senior Bank officials may genuinely have believed that there was no cause for major worry. But apart from this, for the Central Bank to have expressed greater concern, either publicly or privately, would have involved 'swimming against the tide' of widespread public opinion that the riches associated with the property bubble could continue and that the market would not crash. Given this climate, it is questionable whether, in the absence of overwhelming compelling evidence—by which time, by definition, it would be too late—the Central Bank would have been willing to 'spoil the party' and run the risk of public opprobrium. Both Honohan and Nyberg emphasize that for this to have happened would have required a technically strong and sufficiently independently-minded Bank leadership. This leadership was unfortunately missing, certainly to the extent needed, during this period. The long-standing tradition in Ireland, namely, that the post of Central Bank Governor was filled quasi-automatically by the retiring Secretary of the Department of Finance, who did not necessarily have any experience of banking and finance, must surely have played some role.

---

[16] Another underlying problem appears to have been long-standing tensions between the non-specialist Central Bank staff and management and the economist staff as regards the perceived value added in practical terms, of the latter to the Bank's activities.

5.2.1 *The Relationship Between the Central Bank and the Financial Regulator*

The structure of the CBFSAI (encompassing the Central Bank and the Financial Regulator), it could be argued, did not facilitate the identification and effective management of micro-prudential or macro-prudential stability problems. However, while the structures were cumbersome and led to some practical and administrative complications at times, both Honohan and Nyberg concluded that this aspect, in itself, was not a decisive factor. The somewhat unwieldy framework should not have blurred the key issue of overall responsibility.

In this context, Nyberg (2011: 66) discussed a (somewhat strange) view presented to the Commission, namely, that it was not the primary responsibility of the Central Bank to evaluate problems in domestic financial markets emanating from the behaviour of individual institutions. According to such a view, under the division of labour embodied in legislation, although the Central Bank was charged with overall financial stability matters, the Regulator was responsible for identifying and raising institution-specific problems with potential systemic significance. Since the Regulator, for whatever reason, did not do so in the pre-crisis period, it was suggested that the Bank could not have been expected to detect such problems itself. Moreover, for the Central Bank to be seen as enquiring into the Regulator's activities might have been viewed as an unacceptable intrusion into its autonomous status. Such a perspective implied that the responsibility of the Central Bank for not preventing what happened is lessened considerably.

However, the above reasoning was rejected by the Commission's report which observed that:

> when combined with the 'static' approach of the FR [Financial Regulator] in assessing individual institutions it [such an approach] could—and did—create a situation where financial stability problems could not be addressed or prevented. Financial stability should be the overriding objective and the Central Bank (as well as other responsible authorities) should do whatever is reasonably necessary to maintain it . . . [by] mid- to late-2005, on the basis of available data at a macro level, there were more than ample grounds for the Central Bank to have pursued a closer and more intensive dialogue with the Regulator than actually occurred. The aim would have been to determine, in sufficiently good time, whether the macro warning signals also indicated a pattern of unsound lending behaviour by banks (Nyberg 2011: 66–67).

In this context, the Honohan report, in describing the complex structures involving the Central Bank and the Regulator, also made a number of relevant observations. It noted that, while licensing and prudential legislation were the responsibility of the Regulator, the latter had a duty to act in a manner consistent with the CBFSAI's functions—including the Governor's role in contributing to financial stability—and, if necessary consult and act with the Governor's approval on matters pertaining to financial stability. The relevant legislation also provided that the Governor be empowered to authorize a CBFSAI employee to undertake certain supervisory acts and to issue public guidelines as to the policies and principles required of the Regulator in order to perform CBFSAI functions. These provisions for close involvement of the central banking functions in supervision matters were included at the suggestion of the European Central Bank, which in turn regarded the powers— although they were never used in the period in question—as fundamental and believed that they should be made the most of in practice.

It is not seriously disputed that in the final analysis, the Central Bank was the 'last line of defence' and had a duty to do whatever was required to ensure that the Regulator was discharging its own responsibilities appropriately. The failure of the financial stability process in Ireland was not due to issues 'falling through the cracks' because of complex administrative structures. The chairing by the Governor of the Central Bank of the Board of the CBFSAI, the 'overseeing' institution, with six persons from the Financial Regulator as members of the Board, left little doubt as to where, substantively, ultimate responsibility lay.

5.3 The Role of the European Central Bank

The Irish approach to micro-prudential regulation and macro-financial stability described above needs to be assessed against the background of that adopted by the euro area as a whole. As noted earlier, the three pillars necessary for the successful functioning of the eurozone were: (a) a common monetary policy; (b) measures to ensure effective financial sector regulation and promote macro-prudential stability; and (c) structures and processes to prevent individual members from the pursuit of irresponsible fiscal policies. The first two pillars are, or could have been, the responsibility of either the European Central Bank (ECB) in the case of (a) or the European System of Central Banks (ESCB)[17] in the case of (b).

---

[17] The ECB is the central bank for Europe's single currency, the euro, and the corresponding Eurosystem comprises the ECB and the national central banks (NCBs) of all 17 member states who have adopted the euro. The ESCB comprises the ECB and the NCBs of all 27 EU member states.

5.3.1 *The Common Monetary Policy*

By definition, a common currency area requires that monetary policy be entrusted to one institution, in this case, the ECB, analogous to the conduct of monetary policy by a national central bank issuing an independent currency. The Maastricht Treaty established the ECB's political and operational independence and set as its primary objective, the maintenance of price stability (see Chapter 3).[18] ECB statements issued from time to time specified the inflation objective more precisely, in terms of a specific quantitative target. In recent years, the ECB has aimed at keeping inflation at 'around' 2 per cent per annum. The ECB has a number of instruments at its disposal, principally the maturity and interest rates attached to various lending facilities, to help achieve this goal.

The ECB has by and large succeeded in achieving relative price stability. Since the euro area's inception, consumer prices on average have risen by about 2 per cent per annum. As in any common currency area, ECB monetary policy was inherently a 'one size fits all' concept. The ECB's low interest rate policy was based on average inflation throughout the union which mainly reflected developments in the largest countries, especially Germany. The generally prevailing low interest rates were of significant benefit to German efforts to boost their economy in the wake of reunification in the early nineties.

However, the ECB's common monetary policy framework did not suit Ireland for most of this period. Throughout the 2000s, Irish inflation was higher than the European average and led to a sharp loss in external competitiveness. At the same time, rising property prices caused interest rates on loans to turn sharply negative in real terms. This in turn encouraged more borrowing and lending, fuelling the property bubble further.

If Ireland had not been a member of the euro area, the appropriate response in the case of 'overheating' and the risk of a bubble emerging would have been to tighten monetary policy significantly. Such an option was of course unavailable. However, to 'blame' the ECB's monetary policy for the Irish bubble is to misunderstand entirely the concept of a currency union. Euro area monetary policy can no more be set with Ireland specifically in mind than could US Federal Reserve monetary policy be decided on the basis of a jump in prices in one particular region of the United States. Moreover, there does not

---

[18] From time to time, national politicians (notably in France) have criticized what they view as the ECB's excessively narrow mandate, namely, the focus on inflationary objectives to the neglect of broader considerations involving, for instance, growth or unemployment. The ECB has typically rejected (or ignored) such criticisms by asserting its independence from political influences and pointing to the Treaty's explicit provisions on this issue. Any change in ECB policies would have required unanimous approval by member states which, given general German insistence on a conservative approach to monetary policy, was not likely to have been forthcoming.

appear to be any evidence that Irish political or financial leaders, let alone the general public, at the time complained that ECB interest rates were too low and urged that they be raised.

5.3.2 Financial Supervision

The second 'pillar' of a successful currency union is arrangements to ensure that appropriate prudential supervisory procedures are in place throughout to safeguard macro-financial stability. As the crisis has highlighted, there are two basic reasons why this key element cannot be left only to the national level. First, given the highly integrated nature of financial markets, problems experienced by a domestic financial institution may cause a significant loss of confidence that will quickly spill over to other parts of the union. Second, it could be argued that, provided that the costs of a bailout of a troubled domestic bank are met within the national fiscal limits implied by the Stability and Growth Pact (see Chapter 6), the problem of fiscal 'free riders' would not arise. However, this view was naïve and illustrated the very weak architecture underlying the Maastricht Treaty. The Treaty did not envisage the potentially huge fiscal repercussions of banking failures leading to the assumption of the banks' debt by the sovereign. Ireland is a major example of the practical reality that governments, when confronted by a perceived imperative need to bail out a bank or banking system in difficulties, have little option but to override budgetary deficit limits. Moreover, the higher fiscal deficits may cause damaging spillover effects for others by raising the possibility of a sovereign becoming unable to meet its obligations. It is not surprising that these issues have been brought to the forefront since the outbreak of the crisis and have called into serious question the approach taken by Europe with respect to financial banking supervision since the euro area's inception.

The topic of European-level involvement in financial supervisory matters had been the subject of a long and complex debate. The Delors Report (1989: 22), which laid out the road map for European monetary union, recommended that 'the System would participate in the coordination of banking supervision policies of the supervisory authorities'. However, there was considerable national opposition to any strong role being given to the ECB, or any similar institution, in this area. As a result, the basic tasks which the Maastricht Treaty stipulated to be carried out through the ESCB (in practice this applied only to the euro system) included:

> to define and implement the monetary policy of the euro area to conduct foreign exchange operations ... to hold and manage the official foreign reserves of the Member States; and to promote the smooth operation of the payment systems (Maastricht, Article 105.2).

These tasks do not include any reference to financial supervision. However, Articles 105.5 and (especially) 105.6 of the Maastricht Treaty do provide for the possible involvement of the ECB. Article 105.5 states that the ESCB 'shall contribute to the smooth conduct of policies pursued by the competent authorities relating to the prudential supervision of credit institutions and the stability of the financial system'. But in practice, Article 105.6 states that the Council of Ministers *may* [authors' italics] entrust the ECSB with 'specific tasks concerning policies relating to prudential supervision of credit institutions and other financial institutions with the exception of insurance undertakings'. This provision does not make any distinction between macro- and micro-prudential supervision.[19]

There is no evidence available indicating that the possibility of the application of Article 105.6 was ever pursued vigorously in the decade prior to the crisis. Invocation of the provision would have required the unanimous agreement of all members of the Council of Ministers—over twenty in all, depending on the time period. This was extremely unlikely, given the opposition of several countries. The UK remained strongly against European involvement in the supervision of institutions based in the City of London, even after the crisis broke and the issue became the focus of much attention. Thus, were the ECSB to have sought to exercise a direct role in banking supervision, this would have been essentially 'blocked', given the Treaty provision in question. Neither, for broader reasons, was there a political appetite for modifying the Treaty itself, assuming this had been thought necessary, which did not appear to have been the case.

As a result, in the period leading up to the crisis and for some time after, financial supervision was construed as essentially a national responsibility, a matter for each Member State, including Ireland, to execute.[20] There was no possibility of assigning to the ECB, for example (or another EU body), the power to issue binding rules or decisions on national supervisors. The main pan-European institution established was the Committee of European Banking Supervisors (CEBS), a forum intended, *inter alia*, 'to promote supervisory cooperation, including through the exchange of information'. There is nothing on the record to suggest that this group played any significant role in identifying or addressing prudential problems at the national level.[21]

---

[19] The implications of this provision have been subject to extensive discussion (see, for example, UK House of Lords, EU Committee 2009).

[20] Following the outbreak of the crisis, various reports were commissioned which called for a strengthening of centralized European involvement in supervision. However, most of these recommendations (e.g. those of the Larosiere Report) would involve modification of the Maastricht treaty and/or invocation of Article 105.6.

[21] A search of this Committee's website does not reveal any documentation in the public domain relating to potential regulatory problems in individual countries. As noted above, the Irish Financial Regulator did not raise the issue of potential competition in the property market

The most that could be done by the ECB was to emphasize to national central banks their responsibilities for promoting financial stability and, in that context, to advise the inclusion of provisions in domestic legislation empowering central banks to intervene as needed *vis-à-vis* the domestic regulatory authority. As noted above, an initiative by the ECB took place at the time when legislation was drafted to establish Ireland's CBFSAI in 2002. It is very likely that the financial situation in Ireland was the subject of regular internal discussions within the ECB in the pre-crisis period. However, there is no evidence available, at least publicly, suggesting that the ECB held significantly different views from those contained in the CBFSAI's Financial Stability Reports.

Why did national authorities oppose the granting of greater supervisory responsibility to the ECB or some other pan-European institution, a stance reflected in the weak provisions of the Maastricht Treaty and the continued resistance to application of Article 105.6? Part of the explanation, as was the case for the UK, lay in a principled objection to any encroachment of sovereignty by Brussels and/or Frankfurt, including because this might place their financial systems at a competitive disadvantage. Another part was the view that national regulatory institutions were quite capable of dealing with any issues that might arise without outside surveillance or monitoring. A further aspect may have been an underestimation of the size of cross-border financial flows and the degree to which they might end up contributing to havoc in domestic financial systems.

There was another, perhaps more fundamental, issue of principle which quickly came to the fore as calls for a reform of the European financial regulatory system mounted in the wake of the crisis. It was argued that supervisory powers should not be transferred to a pan-European body so long as responsibility for 'bailing out' any troubled financial institution remained, in the absence of a European-wide fiscal institution, a national prerogative. This view—a reversal of the aphorism 'you make your bed and you lie on it'—found particular resonance, given the explicit 'no bailout' clause in the EC Treaty at the time. However, it subsequently lost much of its force given the abandonment of this 'no bail out clause' and the establishment of European financial rescue mechanisms such as the European Financial Stability Facility and the European Stability Mechanism. But throughout much of the last decade, any talk of jettisoning the no bailout clause and, for example, financing recapitalization of European banks under a common funding arrangement—as currently contemplated—would have been very far from most policymakers' or the public's minds.

from less regulated foreign firms at the CEBS, which could have been a logical forum to discuss such a matter.

As discussed in Chapter 12, it is not surprising that the June 2012 EU leaders' Summit agreement to establish a pan-European regulatory system was accompanied by calls for a parallel pan-European resolution regime for troubled financial institutions. The 2008 global financial crisis has forced the eurozone leaders to face up to the inadequacies of the Maastricht Treaty with respect to financial stability and to re-structure the eurozone's architecture accordingly. At the same time, while it can be argued that the presence of a pan-European surveillance system is a *necessary* condition for promoting financial stability, it may not be sufficient. Many would claim that even if such a structure had been in operation prior to the crisis, there could still have been questions as to whether it would have possessed the necessary expertise or authority to prevent what actually happened.

While the Irish view on these issues over the years is not well documented publicly, it is likely that Ireland did not differ from many other countries in resisting any encroachment on national supervisory responsibilities. A major reason would have been fears that this would interfere with the 'light regulation' approach that encouraged the rapid expansion of Dublin's International Financial Services Centre. This aspect is of some importance in the ongoing debate as to the apportionment of responsibility for the Irish crisis. A number of commentators have rightly criticized the absence of a pan-European approach to supervision as a significant contributing factor. But to go further and invoke this argument in order to 'shift the blame' from Ireland to Europe is valid only to the extent that the Irish authorities strongly advocated such an approach but failed. Consistent with a general bias in favour of minimal interference from Europe, there is no evidence available indicating that this was the case.

5.3.3 *The Absence of Contingency Planning*

The ECB did, nevertheless, undertake its own macro-prudential supervision for the euro area as a whole, drawing on individual national Financial Stability reports such as those prepared by Ireland. However, it failed to identify the problems (Whelan 2009). The overview of the ECB's Financial Stability Review published in June 2007 (just before the cracks appeared in the global financial system) concluded that:

> With the euro area financial system in a generally healthy condition and the economic outlook remaining favourable, the most likely prospect is that financial stability will be maintained in the period ahead (ECB 2007).

The ECB's inability to assess and anticipate possible looming problems thus was no different from that encountered at the national Irish level. Largely due to its benign assessments, the ECB also followed national approaches in failing to develop in advance effective contingency plans for dealing with any major pan-European banking difficulties. As discussed in Chapters 10 and 11, this led to a situation where, once the crisis broke, countries such as Ireland were left to their own devices to deal with the emerging problems as best as they could. Writing two years later, Whelan remarked:

> The crisis has demonstrated that that the European Union's current agreed procedures for dealing with financial crises . . . are completely inadequate. The result has been a sequence of *ad hoc* interventions, the scale and nature of which have varied widely across countries, with governments directing their fiscal support almost completely [to] their own domestic banks (2009: 3).

Ireland ended up as the first country to experience the costs associated with the absence of contingency planning and an effective pan-European crisis resolution mechanism. But it turned out to have been by no means alone. It was only much later, in 2011–12, that the European authorities (including the ECB) began to attempt to develop a more consistent and coordinated approach to handling national banking issues with systemic implications.

It is not known publicly whether the ECB in fact undertook some internal confidential work on contingency planning which might have included a critical assessment of Ireland's situation. The issue is complicated by the ECB's exceptional secretiveness about its activities. For instance, although in earlier years the IMF had followed a similar approach, over the last two decades it has devoted considerable efforts to self-examination and improving transparency and public communications. Not long after the crisis began, the IMF issued a report very critical of the internal weaknesses that led to its failure to foresee the crisis. It is unfortunate that the ECB has not conducted, at any rate publicly, a similar self-assessment. This could provide an informed analytical basis for judging relative European and national responsibilities for the crisis and could identify key lessons to be learned for the future.

5.4 Conclusions

The immediate responsibility for the failure of regulatory oversight to prevent the Irish banking disaster is distributed over a few specific institutions. Those directly charged with national supervision of the domestic banking system, and in promoting financial stability, in essence, the Financial Regulator and the Central Bank, respectively, have to shoulder a large part of the blame. However, major faults in the design and implementation of the architecture of the Eurozone, along with the passive attitude of the European authorities, also contributed to the lax domestic financial regulation that prevailed in many member countries, including Ireland.

The Irish government's decision at the start of the decade to establish a somewhat unwieldy 'hybrid' structure of financial regulation, involving a semi-independent Financial Regulator under the overall umbrella of the CBFSAI, did not help matters. However, this was not the root cause of the problem. It is clear, as the Nyberg report emphasized, that despite some administrative complexities, the final responsibility for ensuring the overall stability of the Irish financial system rested with the leadership of the Central Bank. This was also the unambiguous position of the ECB of which Ireland was a member.

A large part of the problem was the approach to supervision followed by the Financial Regulator. The 'principles approach', which was similar to that adopted in the UK, stemmed from the prevailing ideological conviction, discussed in Chapter 2, that regulators should not seek to delve deeply into the activities pursued by lending institutions. The general view was that the latter could be left largely to their own internal devices, provided that appropriate internal governance structures were in place and they complied with a limited number of financial norms such as capital adequacy requirements.

The Regulator thus focused mainly on process rather than substance and failed to investigate or detect the true nature of the banks' irresponsible practices, in particular, the highly risky concentration of their property lending, especially to developers. When (occasionally) questionable procedures were detected, the likely implications for the overall financial viability of the institutions, or for the financial system as a whole, were not followed up or analysed. Moreover, even in a case such as the INBS, where serious long-standing governance problems were identified, the Regulator showed little appetite to pursue issues aggressively. This appears to have been partly due to an undue aversion to legal risk. In any event, the debacle associated with INBS, in particular, illustrates the intrinsic failure on the part of the Regulator to take the decisive action expected of it.

The Nyberg report rightly highlighted the failure of the Central Bank to work closely with the Regulator and detect and address key underlying problems. Moreover, on the macro-prudential front, the Bank consistently engaged in wishful thinking that all would be well in the end, despite the mounting evidence of a massive and dangerous exposure to property lending financed by large-scale foreign borrowing. Group think was present at the highest levels and contrarian internal voices were given little exposure at key decision-making times, most noticeably, during preparation of the Bank's 2007 Financial Stability Report. The possibility of a looming disaster was not and apparently could not be contemplated and no work was undertaken, even on a confidential basis, to consider the implications of and plan for the contingency that the 'comfortable consensus' might not come about. A reluctance to risk 'rocking the boat' and run against the prevailing tide of political and public opinion surely played a role. Nevertheless, a willingness and ability to use the best available expertise and analytical resources to present serious alternative scenarios (including highly uncomfortable ones) is an essential prerequisite for the leadership of an independent and effective central bank.

Driven by the overriding objective of controlling inflation, the Maastricht architecture overlooked the issue of financial stability, and allowed it to remain in practice the preserve of national authorities. Nor did it take into consideration the possible takeover of banking debt by the sovereign because of banks' systemic importance, together with all the implications that this would entail.

The European institutions, by their passive attitude thus indirectly contributed to allowing fatal weaknesses, such as those that emerged in Ireland, to go unchecked. They at no point appear to have taken a proactive approach in Ireland's case, relying, it seems, on the benign assessments provided by the Irish Central Bank, backed up by the Regulator. Nor does it appear likely that the Irish authorities would have supported any moves to assign a greater role to Europe in financial supervision or to involve, say, the ECB, directly in domestic macro-prudential matters. That does not mean necessarily that greater European involvement would in itself have been a panacea. Indeed, the assessment of the ECB (or some similar body) could possibly have been similar to that of the Irish authorities. This judgement is borne out by the very positive conclusions in the ECB's own euro area financial stability report published in mid-2007. For whatever reasons, the ECB, too, together with the IMF, was assessing developments through rose-coloured spectacles.

References

CBFSAI (2007) *Financial Stability Report.*

Delors, Jacques (1989) *Economic and Monetary Union in the European Community.*

European Central Bank (2001) *The Role of Central Banks in Prudential Supervision.*

European Central Bank (2007) *Financial Stability Review,* June.

Honohan, Patrick (2010) *The Irish Banking Crisis: Regulatory and Financial Stability Policy, 2003–2008,* A Report to the Minister of Finance by the Governor of the Central Bank, Dublin.

House of Lords (2009) *The Future of European Financial Regulation and Supervision,* EU Committee.

International Monetary Fund (IMF) (2006) *Financial Sector Assessment Report,* August.

Nyberg, Peter (2011) *Misjudging Risk: Causes of the Systemic Banking Crisis in Ireland,* Report of Commission of Investigation into the Banking Sector in Ireland, (Dublin).

Summersdale Publishers Ltd (2012) *Keep Calm Sure It'll Be Grand,* (Chichester).

Whelan, Karl (2009) 'The ECB Role in Financial Supervision', UCD Centre for Monetary Research, WP09/15, October.

6

The Makings of a Fiscal Crisis

When I have the money, I spend it . . . when I don't, I don't

Charlie McCreevy, former Minister of Finance, 2002[1]

The state is the great fiction whereby everybody attempts to live at the expense of everybody else

Frederic Bastiat[2]

Chapters 4 and 5 described the creation of the Irish property bubble, fuelled by fiscal incentives and increasingly reckless lending behaviour of the banks, accompanied by what one might best describe as 'benign neglect' on the part of the Central Bank and the Financial Regulator. The collapse of the property market was soon followed by an emerging banking crisis which, in turn, accentuated a third, underlying, fiscal crisis. These different elements culminated in the fourth crisis, the full blown financial crisis, that led to the emergency bailout from the EU/IMF in late 2010.

The roots of the Irish fiscal disaster were initiated by a political decision, implicitly shared by all political parties, that the fruits of the boom should not be confined to those involved directly in property. Policies were adopted by successive governments that involved a significant reduction in non-property-related taxation (essentially direct taxation) and a major sustained surge in government expenditure. They were sustained largely by the property boom itself and continued rapid overall economic growth, a great deal of which came from the construction sector. When, inevitably, the bubble burst, the 'fiscal emperor was left with no clothes'. The dramatic deterioration in Ireland's budgetary position from 2008 onwards was virtually unprecedented in the history of post-war industrial countries. As discussed below, this

---

[1] O'Toole (2009: 22). This remark has been very widely quoted in the domestic and foreign media subsequently. Although it has never been contradicted by McCreevy, the precise venue and date of the statement remains somewhat obscure.

[2] 'L'Etat' in the *Journal des Débats*, 25 September 1848, English translation.

deterioration was quite separate from the additional burden that arose later when the fiscal costs associated with bailing out the banks had to be reckoned with.

6.1 The Causes of the Fiscal Meltdown

The build-up of the fiscal problem prior to 2008 was largely unnoticed at the time by politicians, the public, outside commentators, and international bodies. The collective domestic reaction of politicians and most of the economist community and the media was largely one of indifference—see Chapter 8. At the European level, as discussed below, the Maastricht Treaty and the Stability and Growth Pact, which were intended to rein in potential fiscal excesses, turned out to be seriously defective. A lack of political will to follow through on sanctions for errant fiscal behaviour, the failure to identify the true structural imbalances in public sector finances, and the absence of sufficiently strong preventative mechanisms, were fundamental weaknesses of the eurozone fiscal architecture.[3]

In the case of outside assessments, some modest cautionary notes were sounded by the IMF and the OECD regarding overreliance on the construction sector and declining external competitiveness. However, these had little impact on the general perception that overall fiscal management was excellent. The 2006 OECD report concluded that that 'the fiscal position is healthy' (OECD 2006: 10) and that 'Ireland had continued its exemplary economic performance' (OECD 2006: 1). Its 2008 report (OECD 2008: 8) observed, as the crash was emerging, that 'the economic fundamentals remained strong'. Further praise was lavished by the IMF in 2007 which assessed Ireland's economic performance as 'impressive', even 'remarkable' (IMF 2007: 19). Although the OECD (2006: 10) referred in 2006 to 'large downside risks to fiscal policy', neither organization came remotely close to envisaging the catastrophe waiting in the wings.[4]

Ireland's fiscal balance moved from a surplus of 0.1 per cent of GDP in 2007 to deficits of 7.3 per cent and 14 per cent of GDP in 2008 and 2009, before soaring to an unheard of 31.2 per cent of GDP in 2010 (Table 6.1). Even abstracting from the one time costs of bank recapitalization, the 2010 deficit amounted to almost 11 per cent of GDP. How could a fiscal reversal of this magnitude have come about in such a short time? And why were more

---

[3] The previous chapter discussed the other weaknesses in the euro system's architecture relating to financial regulation and financial stability.

[4] Appendix A contains a detailed review of the assessments and policy advice provided by the IMF and the OECD in the years preceding the crash.

Table 6.1. Ireland—General Government Budgetary Aggregates, 2000–11 (% of GDP)

	Total Revenue	Total Expenditure	Surplus (+)/Deficit (−)	Surplus (+)/Deficit (−) Excl. Banking Assistance Measures	Government Debt
2000	35.9	31.2	4.7	4.7	37.5
2001	34.0	33.0	0.9	0.9	35.2
2002	33.1	33.4	−0.3	−0.3	31.9
2003	33.6	33.1	0.4	0.4	30.7
2004	34.9	33.5	1.4	1.4	29.4
2005	35.4	33.8	1.7	1.7	27.2
2006	37.2	34.3	2.9	2.9	24.7
2007	36.7	36.6	0.1	0.1	24.8
2008	35.5	42.8	−7.3	−7.3	44.2
2009	34.8	48.8	−14.0	−11.8	65.1
2010	35.6	66.8	−31.2	−10.9	92.5
2011	35.7	48.7	−13.1	−9.4	108.2

Source: Department of Finance

warning signals not raised, or to the extent that they were, why did they attract little or no attention?

The root causes of the problem were twofold. First, the government largely abandoned a counter-cyclical fiscal policy throughout most of the first eight years of the decade. In other words, as revenues soared, expenditure was boosted simultaneously. This approach was exemplified best by the famous (or perhaps infamous) quote of then Minister of Finance Charlie McCreevy in 2002, 'when I have the money I spend it . . . when I don't, I don't'. Although there was an initiative by Minister McCreevy to put revenue aside for a 'rainy day' through the creation of the National Pension Reserve Fund (NPRF), financed by an annual budgetary transfer equal to 1 per cent of GNP, this was insufficient to stem a major ramp up of public expenditure. Secondly, because the budget's cash position was in broad equilibrium on average during the period, there appeared to be no cause for major concern. It was implicitly assumed that the property boom would continue largely unabated and that economic growth, while inevitably slowing, would still be maintained at reasonably high levels. By 2007, the ratio of gross debt to GDP was only 25 per cent, which was thought to provide a comfortable cushion in case of any unexpected difficulties.

The process was well summarized in Addison-Smyth and Quinn:

It is evident that tax revenues were on an unsustainable level in recent years due, in large part, to structural imbalances within the economy, mainly associated with the housing market. The excess growth in the latter culminated in large and transitory tax revenue windfalls, which ultimately proved unsustainable . . . This meant that, even abstracting from the economic cycle, the actual General Government Balance in those years was artificially inflated, thus painting a

> misleadingly optimistic picture of the sustainability of Irish public finances. Furthermore, in light of consistently robust increases in government spending in those years and tax cuts, it fostered an overreliance on asset based tax revenues. (2010: 222)

The specific revenue and expenditure policies referred to above and that caused Ireland's fiscal meltdown are described in detail in the next chapter. However, the IMF's 2007 report on Ireland illustrates vividly how the true underlying position of the public finances had become concealed. Although the issue was not discussed in the text, the report contained a table referring to the so-called structural deficit, that is, the 'cyclically adjusted, and including one-off factors' budgetary position (IMF 2007: Table 4). According to the IMF estimates at the time, this measure showed a surplus averaging 1.9 per cent of GDP during 2005–06, while a surplus averaging 0.5 per cent of GDP was projected for 2007–09.

Yet two years later, in a remarkable *volte face* the IMF concluded in its 2009 report that essentially the same indicator, the structural budget balance, had in reality shown a *deficit* averaging 5.6 per cent during 2005–06 (IMF 2009: Table 3). Even more alarmingly, this revision showed that the structural budget deficit reached around 9 per cent of GDP in 2007 and no less than 13 per cent of GDP in 2008, as opposed to the small structural surpluses that the IMF had calculated two years earlier.

How could such a 're-estimation' by the IMF have led to such hugely different interpretations of the same historical budgetary data for the period 2004–06? Most of the answer lies in the fact that, at the time of the first assessment in 2007, the IMF, along with almost all other commentators, did not envisage a property crash that would bring with it the collapse of a significant part of the rest of the economy. If the IMF had done so, the temporary windfall nature of much of the revenue surge would have been revealed, and with it the extremely precarious underlying budgetary situation. By 2009, when the IMF undertook its second assessment, this reality had become starkly evident for all to see.

The conclusions of the IMF in 2007 proved exceptionally misleading but, as with many aspects of the Irish crisis, this only became clear *ex post*. Moreover, in fairness, there was virtually no one—among the Irish economist community or elsewhere—drawing attention to the extent of the vulnerability of the public finances at the time. Nor, as discussed below, did the commitments made by Ireland under the EU Maastricht Treaty and the Stability and Growth Pact which were intended to ensure a prudent fiscal policy, exercise a meaningful restraining impact.

The analysis of the causes of the overall Irish financial crisis needs to keep the key role of the unprecedented budgetary deterioration clearly in focus.

Several commentators have suggested that, without the costs directly attributable to recapitalizing Ireland's broken banks, the state's overall financial situation would have remained manageable and recourse to a bailout would have been avoided. Furthermore, it has been asserted that the bailout of the banks resulted from an enormous 'policy error' of granting the comprehensive bank guarantee in September 2008 (see chapter 10). Thus, according to this view, the guarantee was largely responsible for the financial crisis that propelled Ireland 'into the clutches' of the EU/IMF troika (as the EU/ECB/IMF troika is usually referred to), with the budgetary collapse playing only a relatively minor part.

This line of argument that places the blame for the current major fiscal difficulties experienced by Ireland largely on the banking system's losses is not consistent with a careful examination of the evidence. It also distracts attention from recognizing the extent to which most of the population benefited from the pre-crisis expansionary budgetary policies and underplays the degree to which these policies became, and remain, unsustainable.

Ireland's budget deficit, even when abstracting entirely from the costs of the banking disaster, reached almost 12 per cent of GDP by 2009. A deficit of this magnitude constituted an enormous problem, requiring painful adjustment over many years. In the meantime, public debt has had to rise inexorably due to further unavoidable borrowing in order to maintain the functioning of the government.

The assertion that most of the accumulation of government debt was a result of taking on the banking debt is not supported by the facts. O'Brien (2012) reports on a survey of the Department of Finance, independent academic economists, financial sector economists, and left-leaning economists as to estimates of the share of the debt accounted for by bank-related debt as of end-2011. Their calculations ranged from a low of 21 per cent to 28 per cent[5]. Moreover, these ratios will fall in the future. The amounts considered necessary for the banks have already been fully expended and counted as part of the debt, while the financing of prospective budget deficits will continue to add to indebtedness for some years into the future.

A more comprehensive, forward-looking analysis of this issue is contained in McArdle (2012), who also examined the path for net (as opposed to gross) debt. The net debt position was derived by taking into account the fact that a significant part of the recapitalization of the banks was funded by a drawdown of liquid assets held by the NPRF and the National Treasury Management

[5] The total amount of capital injected by the state as into the banks amounts to €64 billion. Of this, some €31 billion is accounted for by the promissory note issued as payment of capital to Anglo and INBS and is included in the state's gross debt. The remainder, which was paid to AIB, BoI, and IL&P, was financed by a drawdown of liquid assets held by the NPRF and NTMA at the time. This amount is therefore not counted as part of gross debt, but serves to increase net debt since the state's liquid assets have been run down.

Agency (NTMA).[6] The data show that three-quarters of the total projected increase in Ireland's net debt position between 2008 and 2015 is accounted for by the need to finance budget deficits, as opposed to bank recapitalization.[7]

This sharp prospective rise in debt (to over 90 per cent of GDP by end-2010) was bound to cause considerable nervousness on the part of market lenders. Countries facing such unfavourable debt dynamics—extremely large under-lying budget deficits and uncertain growth prospects—run a clear risk of facing difficulties in continued access to market funding. O'Brien (2012) noted that Portugal, with a public debt level close to that of Ireland after excluding banking sector-related debt (which was relatively minor) was forced, six months after Ireland's bailout, to follow the same route.[8] In Ire-land's case, the need for emergency assistance from official lenders at some stage was always a distinct possibility, even if, somewhat implausibly, all of the debt relating to banking losses could have been made to disappear. That said, as will be seen in Chapter 11, the crystallization of the full costs of the banking disaster proved to be a major, if not decisive, element determining when the bailout finally was triggered.

6.2 The European Dimensions and the Failure of Maastricht

From the outset of the euro area project, it was accepted that, for any currency union to operate effectively, individual member states must pursue respon-sible fiscal policies. The reasons for this are worth repeating. As an independ-ent central bank, the European Central Bank (ECB) was entrusted with the maintenance of low inflation and the safeguarding of the common currency. Were members to run large fiscal deficits and/or build up unsustainable debt positions, the ECB's ability to implement a prudent monetary policy as well as the external reputational value of the euro would come under significant pressure. Moreover, although this was formally forbidden, in the event that fiscal mismanagement was to reach the point that a direct 'bailout' to a member state would become necessary, the costs to taxpayers of the donor countries might prove insupportable.

In other words, the costs stemming from irresponsible fiscal and/or debt policies on the part of some euro area members would end up being borne by

---

[6] As O'Brien also notes, the more comprehensive calculations for net debt should also allow for a partially offsetting effect in the form of some of the state's investment in the banks.

[7] Governor of the Central Bank Patrick Honohan stated (Cooper 2011: 63) soon after the bailout that bank debt represented only 6 per cent of the total debt increase foreseen under the agreement. While details were not provided, it appears likely that he was referring to gross debt only and his estimate is therefore less than the McArdle figure of around 25 per cent.

[8] However, it could be argued that Portugal's productivity levels are lower than Ireland's, while its capacity to attract foreign direct investment is more limited.

those who had been more restrained. This creates a classic 'free rider' issue, namely, the ability of someone to transfer a good part of the consequences of his/her foolish actions to others. Failure to prevent profligate fiscal behaviour on the part of some will also inevitably undermine the political support essential for the survival of the currency union. Indeed, this is precisely what started to happen once the euro area fiscal and debt crisis began to unfold.[9,10]

Mindful of this key aspect, the Maastricht Treaty, which applied to all EU members and established the so-called Maastricht criteria—also known as the convergence criteria—was signed on 7 February 1992. Subsequently, the Stability and Growth Pact adopted in 1997, specified that countries participating in the European Monetary Union—that is those opting to eventually join the euro area—must meet the Maastricht criteria and also established procedures and sanctions in the event that these were not fulfilled.

The two criteria relevant for fiscal policy were:[11]

- An annual budget deficit (covering general government, i.e. including local authorities) no higher than 3 per cent of GDP.
- A national debt to GDP ratio lower than 60 per cent (or approaching that value).

The Maastricht criteria, at the time of their introduction, were subject to some criticism that they did not take account of temporary factors and should have been applicable over an economic cycle rather than in any given year. While in principle valid, the force of this objection was subsequently weakened significantly by the fact that most of the many countries not meeting the criteria, did so for periods well beyond the economic cycle.[12]

The story was indeed dismal (Table 6.2). As of end-2010, all but six of twenty-seven EU countries (four of seventeen eurozone members) were in

---

[9] The calls from some quarters (including from several EU political leaders) for the ECB to act as a lender of last resort to sovereign euro members in debt difficulties and for the issuance of eurobonds illustrate the kind of political tensions that can arise. Other countries, notably Germany, have strongly resisted these proposals, arguing that they would involve transferring the costs of irresponsible policies to other governments and/or the ECB which would in turn risk inflationary pressures. It could also represent a clear contravention of the Treaty establishing the ECB which rules out direct lending by the ECB to governments. Architectural issues relating to the eurozone are dealt with further in Chapter 12.

[10] As discussed in Chapter 5, an additional missing element was ensuring that effective regulatory arrangements were in place so that national domestic banking sectors remained sound. Otherwise, a troubled banking system could cause almost irresistible pressures for intervention, thereby adding to fiscal difficulties facing the government and/or further compromising a national central bank as well as the ECB.

[11] The criteria also covered national inflation rates and long term interest rates, as well as specific procedures relating to the period prior to joining the euro area. However, none of these elements turned out to be particularly contentious.

[12] Nevertheless, setting fiscal deficit criteria to take account of cyclical factors has been a key element of both the updated 'Six Pack' agreement of November 2011 and the subsequent Fiscal Compact Treaty (see Chapter 12).

Table 6.2. Compliance with Maastricht Fiscal Criteria, 1998–2010[1]

Country	Budget deficit as a per cent of GDP (2010)	Past Periods for Breach of 3% Deficit Limit	Debt as a % of GDP (2010)	Past Periods for Breach of 60 % debt limit (and not decreasing)
Austria	−4.5	2004; 2009–10	71.9	1998–99; 2008–10
Belgium	−3.8	2009–10	96.0	2008–10
Bulgaria	−3.1	2009–10	16.3	
Cyprus	−5.3	2004; 2009–10	61.5	2004; 2010
Czech Republic	−4.8	2005; 2009–10	38.1	
Denmark	−2.5		42.9	
Estonia	0.2		6.7	
Finland	−2.5		48.4	
France	−7.1	2002–2004; 2008–10	82.3	2003–05; 2007–10
Germany	−2.5	2001–05; 2009–10	83.0	1998–99; 2002–05; 2008–10
Greece	−10.3	1998–2010	145.0	1999–2001; 2004–10
Hungary	−4.2	2004–2010	81.4	2005–10
Ireland	−31.2	2008–10	92.5	2009–10
Italy	−4.6	2001–06; 2009–10	118.6	2005–06; 2008–10
Latvia	−8.2	2008–10	44.2	
Lithuania	−7.2	2008–10	38.0	
Luxembourg	−0.9		19.1	
Malta	−3.7	2008–10	69.4	2004; 2008–10
Netherlands	−5.1	2003; 2009–10	62.9	2009–10
Poland	−7.8	2004–06; 2008–10	54.8	
Portugal	−9.8	1998–2010	93.3	2005–10
Romania	−6.8	2008–10	30.5	
Slovakia	−7.7	2006; 2009–10	41.1	
Slovenia	−6.0	2009–10	38.8	
Spain	−9.3	2008–10	61.2	2010
Sweden	0.3		39.4	
United Kingdom	−10.2	2003–05; 2008–10	79.6	2009–10
Eurozone	−6.2		85.8	
EU27	−6.5		80.2	

[1] Periods covered apply only from date of countries' EU membership
Source: European Commission: General Government Data; Revenue, Expenditure, Balances and Gross Debt (Part II; Tables by Series)

breach of the fiscal deficit limit of 3 per cent of GDP. Fourteen of the EU group exceeded the limit for three or more years (eight for at least three years consecutively). The average deficit of EU countries in 2010 was 6.5 per cent of GDP, while that of the eurozone as a whole was 6.2 per cent, in both cases over twice the limit. The picture as regards government debt was almost as bad. As of 2010, average public debt of EU members amounted to over 80 per cent of GDP. The ratio for the eurozone was 86 per cent, with twelve out of seventeen members surpassing the limit. Breaches of the criteria were by no means confined to smaller 'peripheral' economies. France's budget deficit—7.1 per cent of GDP as of end-2010—was out of compliance with Maastricht in six years out of nines since 2002 (in Italy's case, 9 out of 10 years since 2001), while Germany's deficits exceeded 3 per cent of GDP in seven years between 2001 and 2010.

How was this allowed to happen? A major difficulty was that the sanctions procedures were not applied effectively. Although fines were supposed to be imposed on recalcitrant countries, no decisions to do so were ever taken by the EU's decision-making body, the EU Council of Ministers. This was particularly important where Germany and France were concerned. Despite the EU Commission recommending at one stage that fines be levied on both these countries, the Council of Ministers—a political body dominated by the larger members—rejected the proposal. In the wake of this episode, it was hard to escape the conclusion that, if the bigger countries 'can get away with it', why should smaller members bother?

Maastricht also required a commitment by any country that had strayed beyond the fiscal and debt limits to return at some point to the path of righteousness. In particular, the Excessive Deficit Procedure (EDP) required that non-compliant members establish a deadline for eliminating the portion of their budget deficit above 3 per cent of GDP. However, the EDP did not specify *ex ante* any time path for correction which usually differed across members. Moreover, the required adjustment trajectory could change frequently for the same country, in light of economic and financial developments and, it is fair to assume, political influences, including at Council of Ministers level. The correction mechanism under Maastricht thus had strong characteristics of a 'moving (and somewhat vague) target'.

More fundamentally, the fact that the process did not contain an effective means for identifying (let alone sanctioning) underlying structural deficits proved a fatal flaw. The *ex post* nature of the Maastricht exercise meant that countries could pursue underlying fiscal policies that were quite likely to lead to an excessive deficit at some stage, and indeed many did. Yet before such a deficit actually materialized, there was relatively little that could be done *ex ante* by way of effective preventative actions.[13] The discussions that countries held regularly with the EU Commission were mainly limited to aspects that had a direct bearing on the fiscal deficit, to the neglect of broader macroeconomic surveillance.[14] For example, broader discussion of issues such as property prices, the state of the banking system, or external competitiveness was discouraged.

In sum, the procedure lacked a mechanism for heading off possible looming disasters before they actually happened. Indeed, Ireland by a fairly considerable margin is the most striking example of the failure of the Maastricht 'gentleman's agreement' approach. As late as 2007, one year before the budget began to implode, Ireland was in fact deemed to be in full compliance with the

---

[13] In Ireland's case a 'warning' was issued in 2001 by the EU regarding the risks of expansionary budgetary policies. However, this did not involve any explicit sanctions or enforcement mechanism.

[14] See Agerholm, Mikklesen, and Nisen (2012) for further elaboration of this point.

convergence criteria. The problem was compounded by the lack of political will by major countries to enforce meaningful sanctions in the case of *ex post* breaches of the criteria, even when these did occur. In these circumstances, it is not too surprising that several countries, either consciously or not, succumbed to a fiscal 'free rider' enticement, thereby ending up wreaking considerable havoc for others in the system.

6.3 The Role of the Department of Finance

Various elements—internal and external—together led to Ireland's fiscal disaster. However, the role of the chief watchdog over the nation's finances, the Department of Finance (civil servants and the Minister of Finance), deserves special scrutiny. This key aspect was investigated by an expert panel chaired by Rob Wright (former Deputy Minister of Finance of Canada), which published its report in late 2010. The Wright group had access to all memoranda prepared within the Department during the period although, for reasons of confidentiality, it was decided not to publish internal material or attribute views or policy recommendations to specific individuals. Nor, for reasons of Cabinet confidentiality, could it report on or refer to discussions that took place in Cabinet between the Minister of Finance and his ministerial colleagues.

Despite these constraints, the Wright report (2010) paints an interesting picture of the broad characteristics of the Department's work throughout the period. While rejecting the accusation that the Department 'was not fit for purpose', it highlights several major features and weaknesses:

- the advice prepared by the Department 'did provide clear warnings on the risks of pro-cyclical fiscal action . . . [which were] more direct and comprehensive than concerns expressed by others in Ireland or by international agencies';
- however, by and large these warnings went unheeded. The Report therefore concludes that the Department 'should have adapted its advice in tone and urgency after a number of years of fiscal complacency';
- '[the Department] should have been more sensitive to and provided specific advice on broader macroeconomic risks'; and
- '[the Department] should have shown more initiative in making these points and in its advice on the construction sector, and tax policy generally'.

The report attributes the government's failure to react significantly to internal departmental concerns to three factors. First, there were 'the extraordinary expectations of Government . . . to create spending and tax initiatives to share the fruits of recent economic gains', expectations which were shared 'by all political parties'. Second, as the government's budgetary process 'was completely overwhelmed by two dominant processes—the Programme for Government and the Social Partnership'—the role of the budget (and by inference the Department) was relegated to 'pay the bills' for decisions already taken elsewhere. And finally, as noted already, the Department failed to press its concerns with sufficient vigour.

The report also highlighted major internal weaknesses in structure and staffing within the Department: the lack of a 'critical mass in areas where technical skills are required'; the presence of 'too many generalists'; a culture 'more numbers driven, than strategic'; insufficient 'engagement with the broader economic community'; an approach that often operated 'in silos'; 'poorly structured' internal organization; and 'poor' human resources management.

While the report rightly draws attention to these serious shortcomings, it neglected to address some important aspects which also featured in other parts of the Irish economic policy making establishment of the time. Firstly, as recognized above, 'concerns were expressed' by Department of Finance officials about the risks of pro-cyclical policies and the associated problems of excessive tax expenditures and artificial boosting of the construction sector. However, Wright does not discuss whether these were accompanied by concrete analytical work to assess the implications of major deviations from the prevailing benign assessments and outlook. It can be inferred that explicit analyses of alternative scenarios to reflect low probability, but high cost outcomes, which could have been made available for the Minister (and, if necessary, the Cabinet) were absent. The report tellingly notes that while the panel was advised of some important 'oral briefs' reinforcing the Department's concerns, these were not part of the official record.[15]

Secondly, it is disappointing that the report does not contain any assessment of the quantity, coverage, or quality of the economic output of some thirty-two economists in the Department (a far lower proportion, however, than in comparable OECD countries). It does not consider how many of this group were actually undertaking professional economic work, as opposed to other more routine tasks. The report notes that the main contribution to internal debate within the Department took place in mid-year, suggesting that afterwards the political process essentially took over. The report leaves the impression that little or no macroeconomic or financial analysis was undertaken, apart from that geared to preparation of the budget *per se*.

[15] In this regard, the Wright report established that concerns about possible access by the public to internal departmental written material under Freedom of Information legislation would have been misplaced as the relevant Act limits the release of the written record of non-consensual advice.

Third, the report did not discuss the 'culture' within the Department at the time and its openness (or lack thereof) to internal debate. It has emerged subsequently that there were at least two identified 'contrarians'—officials at middle/senior management level who expressed alternative, less benign points of view. An assistant principal, Robert Pye, raised the prospect of a crisis emanating from abroad and urged that the Department act much more forcefully to persuade politicians of 'the sheer recklessness of their policies'.[16] However, his advice appears not to have been given serious attention. A second official, Maria Mackle, in her drafting of replies to parliamentary questions on property-related topics, reportedly sought to reflect much more of a cautious tone but was instructed by her superiors 'to cease and desist', as such thinking was inconsistent with the government 'line' at the time.[17]

Both these officials submitted detailed files on their experiences to the Wright and/or Nyberg enquiries. It is regrettable that in light of this, the Wright report, while respecting personal confidentiality aspects, did not address the general question as to why the Department did not encourage analytical investigations of alternative opinions or scenarios. Analyses of low probability but high cost outcomes should have been an important and regular feature of contingency planning in the context of overall risk management.

Senior departmental officials did not take seriously the possibility of a potential disaster scenario and therefore would have been unwilling to devote resources to a more rigorous assessment of its implications. But even if they had harboured significant worries, a reluctance to be seen as challenging too forcefully perceived wisdom (especially 'for the record') would likely have been a decisive inhibiting factor. Unfortunately, many officials would have found it difficult, and very possibly counterproductive, to question consistently their political masters after the latters' minds had been made up, especially since independent bodies such as the Economic and Social Research Institute (ESRI), the IMF, and the OECD were not expressing any major concerns. Although officials could 'raise concerns', if these were ignored and an alternative course of action decided upon, what would be the gains from persisting in advocating a contrary viewpoint? As occurs in administrations elsewhere, Ministers would hardly have taken kindly to such a stance, with possible implications for career and promotion prospects. Moreover, there was

---

[16] Pye, while still in the department, sought to publicize his views in an article submitted to the *Irish Times* in 2007 but was forbidden to do so by his superiors. Following his retirement, he related his experiences in a subsequent newspaper article (Pye 2011) and provided an extensive file on the matter to the Wright Inquiry (a more extended exposition of his views at the time is provided in Cooper (2011: 361–3).

[17] Mackle's experiences were recounted in the *Sunday Independent* (22 April 2012). It was also reported that, according to Mackle, the memos referred to in the newspaper were not provided by her, although she had expressed relief that the matter had come into the open.

no precedent in Ireland for resignation by civil service officials on grounds of policy differences. It appears that such an idea would have been regarded as somewhat bizarre.

The main deficiency of civil servants in the Department of Finance may not have been that they should have critiqued 'more forcefully' policies advocated by politicians (although that would have been highly desirable). Rather, it may be that they did not equip themselves with the intellectual ammunition to ensure a more rigorous debate on key issues, especially that of 'thinking the unthinkable'. While the eventual policy decisions might or might not have ended up radically different, politicians would have faced a higher bar before discarding explicitly well-reasoned analysis and advice. Moreover, these inputs could and should have been on the written record, even if not publicly available for some years into the future.

The apparent absence of serious analytical work of this nature leaves a sense that during the boom, the Department overall was preoccupied with implementation of government policy, to the neglect of developing and presenting high-quality professional advice and policy options which could have highlighted attendant risks. Unfortunately, as a consequence, the reputation of the Department—a critical institutional element in the formulation of sound government policies—was seriously affected.

6.4 Conclusions

It is often argued that the main reason for Ireland's economic and financial collapse was the banking sector debacle and, especially, the government banking guarantee of end-September 2008. According to this view, the main blame lies with bankers, developers, the Financial Regulator, and the misguided guarantee decision. Such an interpretation allows for a more narrow search for scapegoats and diverts attention away from the size of the separate fiscal disaster and the imperative need to address it.

The above paradigm, comforting though it may appear to many, is a very partial reading of the reality. The major share of Ireland's debt burden arises from the need to continue to borrow to finance the ongoing budget deficit— the largest among the eurozone debt troubled members—for several years to come. By any standards, a budget deficit of close to 12 per cent of GDP—before taking into account the costs of the bank bailout—represented a deep and fundamental disequilibrium.

The road to Ireland's fiscal meltdown was triggered by a conscious policy decision of the government to 'spread the bounty' of the property and construction boom throughout the wider population. Although, not unnaturally, welcomed with more or less open arms, this led to a sharp erosion in the underlying tax base and the boosting of expenditures to well beyond sustainable levels. While remaining concealed almost until the very eve of the crash, once the property bubble burst, the harsh truth was revealed. Ireland Inc., and the vast majority of the Irish people, had been living well beyond their means for most of the decade.

A key component of the euro area architecture, surveillance over fiscal policies, exhibited fatal flaws. A large majority of countries flouted the limits agreed under the Stability and Growth Pact, many by wide margins and for extended periods. No fines were ever levied on errant countries, which included the two largest, Germany and France. Most fundamentally, the procedures under the Stability and Growth Pact were wholly ineffective in detecting and addressing the underlying fiscal disequilibria that could suddenly emerge and create budgetary havoc. Indeed, Ireland was probably the most prominent example of the failure of this part of the process.

Finally, the chief domestic watchdog, the Department of Finance, proved unable to stem the budgetary profligacy. Its approach has been rightly criticized as insufficiently assertive in the face of political pressures. In the final analysis, it is politicians who must be held responsible for policy decisions. Nevertheless, there is an onus on senior officials to present the best professional analysis and advice, even if this involves considering explicit consideration of unpalatable risks and almost unthinkable outcomes. Although the Wright report regrettably did not address this aspect, there is little or no evidence available (at least publicly) that the necessary analytical economic work was undertaken within the Department. The views of a few officials who raised serious concerns, rather than acting as an encouragement to dig deeper into these issues, appear, for whatever reasons, to have been largely ignored.

References

Addison-Smyth, Diarmaid, and Kieran McQuinn (2010) 'Quantifying Revenue Windfalls from the Irish Housing Market', *Economic and Social Review*, Vol. 41, No. 2, Summer, 2010.

Agerholm, Jens Bech, Uffe Mikklesesn, and Karoline Gorm Nisen (2012) 'Fiscal Policy in the EU—What Have We Learned from the Crisis?', *Danmarks National Bank, Monetary Review*, 2nd Quarter Part 1, 59–71.

Cooper, Matt (2011) *How Ireland Went Bust* (Dublin).

IMF (2007) *Ireland: Staff Report for the 2007 Article IV Consultation*, 2 August.

IMF (2009) *Ireland, Staff Report for the 2009 Article IV Consultation*, 20 May.

McArdle, Pat (2012) 'The Debt of a Nation', *Irish Times*, 25 May.

O'Brien, Dan (2012) 'Claims that Bank Debt is Source of All Woes Untrue', *Irish Times*, 23 March.

OECD (2006) *'Economic Survey of Ireland; Policy Brief'*, April 2008.

O'Toole, Fintan (2009) *Ship of Fools*, Dublin.

OECD (2008) *Economic Surveys: Ireland*, (April).

Pye, Robert (2011) 'Stop Brussels Elite from Ransacking Our Country', *Irish Times*, 6 May.

Wright, Rob (2010) *Strengthening the Capacity of the Department of Finance*, Report of the Independent Review Panel, Department of Finance, December 2010.

7

The Property-based Revenue Boom and the Accompanying Expenditure Surge

The boom times are getting even more boomer

Bertie Ahern, former Taoiseach, 2006[1]

The ATM machine is nicely stacked up. I look forward to that spitting out money in all directions...

Senator Joe O'Toole, head of the Irish National Teachers Organisation, referring to the benchmarking process in the Irish Senate, 2003[2]

The previous chapter depicted the broad elements that led to the emergence of the major fiscal crisis from 2008 onwards. The purpose of this chapter is to review in more detail the revenue and expenditure policies that caused such a damaging transformation in Irish public finances in just a few short years.

Although for most of the years preceding the crash, the budget was recording in cash terms, a balance or a small surplus, this, in reality, masked a very large underlying or 'structural' deficit. The structure of revenue had tilted dramatically towards reliance on receipts from construction and property-related activities at the expense of other sources. Simultaneously, as the Exchequer coffers filled to overflowing, government expenditures were increased commensurately, particularly in the area of public sector remuneration. When the property bubble burst and the economy fell into deep recession, the revenue base collapsed. Notwithstanding this, the inbuilt surge in expenditures could not be easily halted, let alone reversed. Massive budget deficits appeared almost overnight which, combined with the fiscal costs of recapitalizing the stricken banks, led to the full-blown financial crisis of late 2010.

---

[1] The *Irish Times*, July 14, 2006.   [2] The *Irish Times*, August 15, 2003.

7.1 The Change in Revenue Structure

The immediate cause of the budgetary nightmare that started to appear in 2008 was the collapse in fiscal receipts. Although overall revenue as a percentage of GDP had remained broadly stable during previous years, there had been a major structural shift in favour of property-related receipts. Between 2000 and 2006, the combined share of stamp duties and capital gains taxes in total tax revenues more than doubled, from 7 per cent to 15 per cent (Table 7.1). According to a broader Eurostat measure, which includes VAT on housing construction, the share of property-related tax revenue in total revenues rose from 8.4 per cent in 2002 to 18 per cent by 2006 (Table 7.2 and Figure 7.1). This figure is still an underestimate as it does not include rapidly increasing income taxes from those employed in construction. Correspondingly, in the six years ending in 2006, the contribution of personal income taxes fell dramatically, by over 6 percentage points, from 33.7 per cent to 27.2 per cent. This was mainly as a result of a reduction in marginal tax rates and upward adjustments (exceeding the rate of inflation) in the threshold above which income taxes were levied.

Just three years later, by 2009 after the crash hit with full force, total Exchequer revenue had dropped precipitously, from €46.1 billion in 2006 to €34.3 billion. The main explanatory factor was the collapse of the property sector. In 2009–10, the share of stamp duties and capital gains taxes plummeted to average only 4.3 per cent per annum while, according to the broader Eurostat measure referred to above, the share of property-related revenue declined even more sharply, to average 3 per cent, compared to 18 per cent in 2006. In absolute terms, the impact was enormous. The Exchequer faced an

Table 7.1. Ireland—Composition of Exchequer Tax Revenue by Major Category, 2000–2011 (per cent of total tax revenues)

	Income Taxes	Corporation Tax	VAT	Excise Duties	Capital Gains Tax	Stamp Duties	Capital Acquisitions Tax	Customs
2000	33.7	14.4	27.6	15.7	2.9	4.1	0.8	0.8
2001	33.5	14.9	28.4	14.5	3.2	4.4	0.6	0.6
2002	30.9	16.4	30.3	15.2	2.1	4.0	0.5	0.5
2003	28.5	16.1	30.3	14.2	4.5	5.3	0.7	0.4
2004	29.9	15.0	30.1	13.8	4.3	5.9	0.5	0.5
2005	28.7	14.0	30.8	13.3	5.0	6.9	0.6	0.6
2006	27.2	14.7	29.5	12.3	6.8	8.2	0.8	0.6
2007	28.7	13.5	30.7	12.4	6.6	6.7	0.8	0.6
2008	32.3	12.4	32.9	13.3	3.5	4.0	0.8	0.6
2009	35.8	11.8	32.3	14.2	1.6	2.8	0.8	0.6
2010	35.5	12.4	31.8	14.7	1.1	3.0	0.7	0.7
2011	40.5	10.3	28.6	13.7	1.2	4.1	0.7	0.7

Source: Department of Finance

Table 7.2. Ireland—Property-related Tax Revenues, 2002–2011

	Capital Gains Tax from Property and Land	Stamp Duty on Property and Land	VAT from Housing	Total Property-Related Tax Revenue	
	% of Total Tax Revenues			% of Total Tax Revenues	% of GDP
2002	1.2	2.3	4.9	8.4	1.9
2003	2.5	3.3	5.8	11.7	2.7
2004	2.3	4.1	6.5	13.0	3.1
2005	3.1	5.1	7.2	15.5	3.7
2006	4.3	6.6	7.1	18.0	4.6
2007	3.6	5.0	4.1	12.8	3.2
2008	1.9	2.6	2.4	6.9	1.6
2009	0.9	1.0	1.5	3.4	0.7
2010	0.6	0.9	1.1	2.6	0.5
2011	0.6	0.5	0.8	1.9	0.4

Source: European Commission

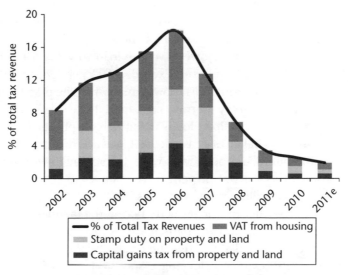

Figure 7.1 Property-related Tax Revenues
Source: European Commission

unprecedented shortfall of around €12 billion in available resources. This was before taking into consideration the unavoidable expenditure pressures arising from the deepening recession and the carry over of significant non-postponable spending commitments.

There were several factors that caused this exceptional and dangerous reliance on these so-called 'cyclical' taxes which eventually led to the Exchequer's acute problems:

(i) The shift in the composition of GDP and the associated increased dependence on the rapidly expanding tax base relating to the property sector.

(ii) The reduction in the burden of personal income tax.

(iii) The growth and proliferation of a large number of 'tax expenditures'.[3]

The first, and most important, element was the implications for taxation of the changing structure of GDP in favour of construction and property. Apart from the huge boost in tax revenues arising from capital gains tax, stamp duties, and VAT on housing, corporation tax also performed strongly throughout, bolstered by the profitability of the construction and construction-related sectors. 'Residential investment had reached nearly 13 per cent of GDP in 2006, twice its long run average, while the construction sector's contribution to employment roughly doubled between the nineties and 2007' (Regling and Watson 2010: 22).

Surging profits for those involved in property facilitated the payment of the required taxes to the Revenue. In the normal course of events, continually increasing prices might have been expected to have constrained somewhat transactors' ability to pay capital gains taxes and stamp duty, which were both levied on an *ad valorem* basis. However, rising loan to value (LTV) ratios for mortgages that approached and even exceeded 100 per cent in the boom's latter stages, alleviated potential cash flow constraints. The practice described in Chapter 4, whereby many borrowers—especially those with large tax liabilities—continuously obtained loans using (paper) profits attributable to their prior transactions in lieu of a cash deposit, was a very important factor. In the case of stamp duties, although rates were lowered by the government on several occasions, this did not prevent further surges in revenues from this source, due to ever spiralling property values.

Apart from over reliance on the property boom, the taxing method used to extract revenue from the sector was particularly unfortunate and came back to haunt governments immediately after the crash. Ireland was virtually alone among OECD countries in not levying a specific tax based on household property value. Such a tax, by definition, constitutes a more stable source of revenue than stamp duties and capital gains taxes, which dry up as soon as the unusually rapid turnover associated with a property boom ceases.

The absence of a household property tax in Ireland long predated the start of the recent boom. Its demise occurred at the time of the 1977 general election, when the promise to abolish 'domestic rates' (as household property

---

[3] 'Tax expenditures' refer to exemptions or deductions in respect of certain activities that taxpayers may avail of to reduce their tax liabilities. The term 'expenditure' is used, as such arrangements can be considered equivalent to the government providing a subsidy directly to the activity in question.

taxes had traditionally been known in Ireland) proved an irresistible lure to the campaigning Fianna Fáil party. Fine Gael (the main opposition party) also urged reform/possible abolition.

Starting from the 1980s, outside observers, including the EU, the IMF, and the OECD, as well as domestic bodies such as the first Commission on Taxation and the National Economic and Social Council, continuously advised reintroduction of a meaningful household property tax. Their recommendations were largely ignored.[4] Successive governments remained opposed to committing themselves on the issue, at least within any specific time period. Relying on cyclical taxes, given the exuberant property market and the relatively easy access to mortgages, proved politically more palatable. Nor did the government undertake any serious contingency preparations for an eventual introduction of a household property tax. This would have required substantial time and resources due to the outdatedness of the valuation mechanisms associated with the old rates regime. Introduction of a property tax also raised issues with respect to the treatment of stamp duty paid on previously acquired property.

Putting the property tax issue, as well as several other long-standing gaps in the Irish revenue system (such as the absence of water charges for domestic users), on the proverbial long finger meant that, once the easily tappable stamp duties and capital gains taxes suddenly disappeared there was nothing readily at hand to replace them. During 2012, the government, under strong pressure from the EU/IMF troika, resorted to an *ad hoc* and highly unpopular (albeit modest) regressive flat rate household charge of €100, pending the design and implementation of an appropriate and fair property tax, which was introduced finally in early 2013.

The second key factor, namely, government policies to lower the personal income tax burden, worked in tandem with the windfall from the property boom. They involved both a gradual reduction of marginal tax rates, along with a diminution in the taxable base as the minimum threshold subject to tax was increased by more than the domestic inflation rate. By 2007, as reported by Whelan (2010: 239), the income tax burden had been lightened very considerably. For example, the average income tax rate for a single-earning married couple with two children receiving the average wage was only 6.7 per cent in Ireland, compared with an EU average of 23.7 per cent and an OECD average of 21.1 per cent.

---

[4] Subsequently, in 1982 a property tax was reintroduced, applicable to houses above a certain valuation and where the householder's income exceeded a given threshold. However, the tax proved highly controversial, ensuring compliance was difficult, and only a handful of households (largely in better-off urban areas and reportedly representing less than 10 per cent of all those liable) actually paid the tax. It was abolished in 1997 for households, although rates on commercial property remained in force.

The government's thinking on income tax policies was influenced by two considerations. Firstly, there was a desire to maintain wage and salary restraint so as to avoid industrial unrest and threats to social peace, via national social partnership agreements between the government, industry, and the trade unions. Tax reductions were traded off in return for the acceptance of wage moderation. Secondly, there was a general belief that, along with a general policy of 'light regulation', low tax rates were a recipe for incentivizing growth. The Minister of Finance, Charlie McCreevy, is also thought to have favoured some income tax cuts so as to have less financial resources accumulating to the Exchequer and thus be in a better position to resist expenditure pressures. While the above objectives had a certain underlying rationale, they were based on the assumption of continuous revenue buoyancy due to uninterrupted economic expansion, if not necessarily a permanent property boom. Little attention was paid, at least publicly, to the tax revenue consequences of a stagnation in economic activity, let alone a property crash and a brutal recession.

Effectively, the changes in the income tax regime shifted the burden of personal income tax towards a smaller group of higher earning individuals. Workers on the minimum wage paid no income tax. Overall, by 2008 just under half of all income tax was paid by the top 7 per cent of taxpayers earning over €100,000 a year (OECD 2009: 60). While this change in the incidence of income tax may well have been justified on distributional and egalitarian grounds, the associated narrowing of the tax base had serious repercussions in the wake of the crash. By early 2009, the government had to introduce on an emergency basis, hastily conceived *ad hoc* measures, mainly in the form of a 'pension levy', in order to try to partially recoup revenues lost as a result of the erosion of the income tax base.

Thirdly, the structure of tax revenue was influenced significantly by the proliferation of a large number of 'tax expenditures' (i.e., through the granting of various tax reliefs and exemptions).[5] Many of these arrangements were linked to the property sector and reduced the intake from stamp duties and capital gains taxes as well as corporation and personal income taxes. These added to the pressures stemming from the cuts in tax rates and the raising of the minimum income tax threshold. According to the OECD (2009: 60), by 2005, the size of all such 'personal income-tax expenditures', at €11.5 billion (7.2 per cent of GDP), actually exceeded income tax receipts collected (€11.3 billion, or 7 per cent of GDP). Moreover, these expenditures (excluding

---

[5] The Commission on Taxation in 2009 concluded that of 245 tax relieving measures then in place, 115 were tax expenditures.

personal income tax credits) were equivalent to 18 per cent of total tax revenues, over three times the EU average at the time.[6]

As discussed in Chapter 4, many of the tax reliefs/exemptions relating to property were introduced (or, in some cases, broadened or extended) in the early 2000s, in an effort to forestall the fear of a looming sharp downturn in the sector. The scope of the various schemes was wide. They were in many cases directed to particular parts of the country, presumably partly in response to local political pressures, and often appeared to be *ad hoc* and less than fully transparent.

Even during the latter half of the decade, when the shortcomings and weaknesses of the schemes had started to attract increasing attention, opposition to their withdrawal by vested interests proved very difficult to overcome. Investors involved pleaded 'acquired rights' and pressed for extensive grandfathering. This occurred in 2004 when capital allowances scheduled for expiration were extended until 2007. Without this extension, many of the 'prize' developments such as the Ritz Carlton in Powerscourt, Co. Wicklow and Fota Island in Cork (both of which subsequently encountered major financial difficulties) would not have taken place. Despite a comprehensive external review (Department of Finance 2006) which recommended that most of the schemes be abolished, the dismantling process proceeded partially and hesitantly. On a number of occasions, the withdrawal of certain exemptions announced in Budget speeches was subsequently modified/abandoned by the time the implementing Finance Bill was published a short while later. While there was little public comment at the time, it is clear that the construction and property sector, supported by much of the public, constituted a formidable lobbying force in the corridors of power.

Apart from their fiscal and governance shortcomings, these tax expenditures also involved a significant distortion of incentives. Many of the schemes tilted resources artificially towards property acquisition in both the housing and commercial markets, thus exacerbating the length and extent of the bubble. A particularly striking effect was the legacy of abandoned 'ghost estates' in certain parts of the country, which reflects both the granting of property-related tax relief in general and its targeting at particular locations.[7] Other specific tax arrangements may also have had undesirable side effects. For example, the provision of tax incentives for private pension contributions

[6] Total income tax-related expenditures included relief in some form or another relating to personal allowances and credits, age credits and exemptions, health-related expenditures, pension contributions, interest relief, social schemes (including rent paid on private tenancies, third-level education fees, exemption of child benefits, and trade union subscriptions), and various savings and investment arrangements (OECD 2009: 60).

[7] While at the outset many property-related schemes were targeted at deprived areas, such as in the inner cities, over time they were extended throughout the country.

was criticized (see OECD 2009: 61), on the grounds that it tended to direct funds from other financial investment, rather than increase overall savings as the incentives were poorly directed at marginal savers.

Finally, it is difficult to defend many tax expenditures on equity grounds. With the exception of personal allowances, most other arrangements were regressive, that is, they were not means-tested and were usually an offset to taxpayers' marginal, as opposed to the standard, income tax rate. Nor were they subject to a cap on the total amount of relief. Those earning the most and paying the highest marginal tax rates received the greatest financial benefit. In other words, the large majority of taxpayers paying the standard rate of income tax ended up subsidizing higher income earning groups.

7.2 Unrestrained Growth in Expenditure

The overall trend in government expenditure during the boom is clear. Between 2000 and 2007 the ratio of total expenditure to GDP, which had hitherto remained fairly stable, rose steadily, from 31.2 per cent to 36.6 per cent (Table 6.1). Then, in 2008, when economic growth turned negative, the ratio jumped further, to 42.8 per cent. Nominal primary expenditure (i.e. excluding interest payments) rose 140 per cent over 2000–08 (IMF 2012: 14). In real terms (i.e. after adjusting for the change in the GDP deflator— Table 7.3), expenditure levels by 2007 were two-thirds higher than at the start of the decade (Table 7.4). Real outlays continued to surge in 2008–09 by a cumulative 21 per cent as nominal amounts rose further despite a fall of around 5 per cent in prices. This increase occurred just as the revenue base was beginning to collapse.[8]

The boost in spending, not surprisingly, appears to have been most marked in 2001–02 and 2006–07, both general election periods. Moreover, unlike in some countries where expenditure control policies may be lax in an administrative sense, there is little evidence that this was so in Ireland, at least so far as the current budget was concerned.[9] Expenditure outcomes were the result of conscious policy choices.

[8] Whelan (2010) argues that even during the boom period, the characterization of an Irish 'bloated public sector' (overall) is misleading, since the share of public spending in Ireland remained well below the EU average. While a valid observation, the issue is not so much whether Ireland's public/private output mix differs from elsewhere. Rather, it is whether, after having established a certain 'equilibrium' mix (at whatever level, depending on social preferences) at a certain point, this balance was overturned by increases in expenditure unaccompanied by sustainable revenue generation. This also holds true in the case of the growth in the public sector payroll (see subsection 7.2.1 below), where Whelan makes a similar comparative argument.

[9] The same cannot necessarily be said of the capital budget where substantial overruns occurred relative to original cost estimates. However, this may have been due largely to unforeseen increases in construction and land acquisition costs as the property boom gathered ever more steam during

Table 7.3. Ireland—Inflation Indices and Growth Rates, 2000–2011

	Inflation Indices (Base: 2000 = 100)		Growth Year-on-Year (per cent)
	Consumer Price Index	GDP Deflator	Real GDP
2000	100.0	100.0	9.3
2001	104.9	106.5	4.8
2002	109.7	111.8	5.9
2003	113.6	115.2	4.2
2004	116.1	117.8	4.5
2005	118.8	121.4	5.3
2006	123.6	125.7	5.3
2007	129.6	127.3	5.2
2008	134.7	124.4	-3.0
2009	128.8	119.3	-7.0
2010	127.5	116.4	-0.4
2011	130.8	115.9	0.7

Source: CSO

In one respect, however, actual outlays did differ from plans made earlier. A Department of Finance report (2011) noted that in almost every year during the 2000s, approved expenditures ended up exceeding the level for the budget year in question that had been projected under prior 'rolling three year' indicative plans published by the Department. Although the Department's forecasts for the three year period ahead appeared on the fairly cautious side, the projections were in no sense binding and do not appear to have had a great deal of operational content. Thus, when, as very often transpired, realized revenues ran ahead of forecasts, the earlier 'plan' was abandoned in favour of new, higher expenditure levels. Reining in this process was not made easier by a similar tendency on the part of the Department of Finance to project revenues in the annual budget conservatively, in an effort to constrain over ambitious spending pressures from government and politicians. However, once actual revenue collections showed greater buoyancy than had been officially forecasted, a perceived systematic bias in the Department's projections became a source of recurrent criticism, including by politicians, who had hoped to be able to spend more at the outset.

What were the major factors driving the acceleration in expenditure? Most of this occurred in the three high-spending sectors, education, health, and social protection, whose combined total outlays together accounted for 64 per cent of total expenditure in 2007 (Table 7.5). Between 2000 and 2007, expenditure in real terms on education rose by 58 per cent, expenditure on health by

the long gestation life of projects. Analysis of this element—and of the capital budget in general—is hampered by the absence of detailed published cost estimates and associated analyses of rates of return at the time projects were authorized.

Table 7.4. Ireland—Real General Government Expenditure by Major Function and Sector, 2000–2010 (base: 2000 = 100)[1]

| | Health | | Education | | Social Protection | Total Government | |
	Total Expenditure	...of which Compensation of Employees	Total Expenditure	...of which Compensation of Employees	Total Expenditure	Total Expenditure	...of which Compensation of Employees
2000	100.0	100.0	100.0	100.0	100.0	100.0	100.0
2001	117.2	118.9	109.8	111.3	109.5	110.9	110.3
2002	130.9	132.8	116.1	124.1	124.2	118.5	120.6
2003	142.2	146.2	123.6	140.5	128.7	122.6	130.4
2004	154.4	155.4	129.5	150.9	139.5	129.6	138.8
2005	152.6	189.6	136.3	157.8	161.3	137.7	154.7
2006	159.8	200.4	144.4	167.2	171.3	147.3	164.3
2007	176.8	217.5	158.4	179.4	192.2	165.6	177.9
2008	191.8	235.6	172.0	203.5	221.4	187.8	194.7
2009	203.0	255.2	179.3	223.9	245.5	199.0	196.4
2010	195.8	247.1	175.1	221.5	256.3	271.4	187.9

[1] Series deflated using GDP deflator

Source: Eurostat

Table 7.5. Ireland—Total General Government Expenditure by Selected Function and Sector, 1990–2010 (per cent of total Government[1])

	Health		Education		Social Protection
		...of which		...of which	
	Total Expenditure	Compensation of Employees	Total Expenditure	Compensation of Employees	Total Expenditure
1990	12.2	19.8	12.3	26.2	30.8
1991	12.6	20.0	12.3	26.0	31.2
1992	13.1	20.4	13.0	26.9	31.9
1993	13.4	21.4	13.1	26.8	31.9
1994	13.4	21.3	13.3	27.1	33.0
1995	14.3	23.5	13.1	26.8	32.7
1996	14.8	25.0	13.4	26.4	31.0
1997	15.7	26.4	13.6	26.4	30.3
1998	15.9	26.6	13.5	25.7	29.5
1999	16.5	29.5	13.2	24.7	32.4
2000	17.8	31.2	13.9	23.0	27.2
2001	18.8	33.7	13.8	23.2	26.9
2002	19.6	34.4	13.6	23.7	28.5
2003	20.6	35.0	14.0	24.8	28.6
2004	21.2	35.0	13.9	25.0	29.3
2005	19.7	38.3	13.7	23.5	31.9
2006	19.3	38.1	13.6	23.4	31.7
2007	19.0	38.2	13.3	23.2	31.6
2008	18.1	37.8	12.7	24.1	32.1
2009	18.1	40.6	12.5	26.3	33.6
2010	12.8	41.1	9.0	27.2	25.7

[1] Data are shown as per cent of total government expenditure for each overall expenditure item and as per cent of total government compensation of employees for each compensation item

Source: Eurostat

77 per cent, and expenditure on social protection by 92 per cent (Table 7.4). The major explanatory element by far, in the case of education and health, was the growth in compensation (pay and pensions), which rose by 118 per cent and 79 per cent respectively. It is instructive first, to examine the process that led to an unsustainable rise in public sector salaries, and second, to assess the outcomes (including whatever lasting benefits it is possible to identify) associated with the huge boost in expenditures that occurred in these major sectors.

7.2.1 Public Sector Pay and Pensions

The increase in the public sector pay bill was the dominating element driving government expenditures from 2000 onward. This partly reflected an expansion in personnel—the number of public servants rose by 35 per cent during

2000–08 (IMF 2012: 19). In parallel, pay rates were also rising sharply. Average earnings in the public sector (other than in the health sector) increased by 32 per cent during 2003–08, compared to cumulative consumer price inflation of 18 per cent. This surpassed by a considerable margin the increase in private sector wages during the same period of about 25 per cent (OECD 2009: 65).[10]

Throughout the boom, public sector pay rates were based on the output and recommendations of three structures whose work was ongoing during 2002–08: (i) the *Public Sector Benchmarking Body* (PSBB); (ii) the *Review Body on Higher Remuneration in the Public Service* (RHMPS); and (iii) *Social Partnership Pay Agreements*. The first two bodies dealt with public sector pay (all grades, and more senior grades only, respectively), while the partnership agreements covered all workers in the public and private sectors. Thus, a senior civil servant would typically receive a total pay increase, in addition to annual increments (except for those already at the top of the relevant pay scale), based on the cumulative effect of awards recommended by all three processes.

The exercises conducted by the PSBB and the RHMPS were initiated partly in response to a complaint that public sector workers were not benefiting sufficiently from the major boost in economic growth. Although public sector salaries in the past had tended to lag somewhat behind the private sector, the gap had been tolerated because of other benefits such as favourable pension arrangements and relative security of tenure. But the difference was considered to have become unacceptably large, given the private sector boom which many in the public sector (especially at senior policy levels) also felt they had helped create. Secondly, there was considerable dissatisfaction with the traditional approach to pay determination within the public sector which was based on cross-sectoral relativities and which had led to chains of pay claims and 'leapfrogging'. For both these reasons, the idea was borne that a comprehensive examination of the jobs, pay, and conditions of both private and public sector workers could, in principle, lead to more differentiated levels of public service pay better aligned with their private sector equivalents.

The PSBB and RHMPS processes had two fundamental problems. First, reliance on job evaluation techniques (a core element of the exercise), by its very nature, involves a high degree of subjectivity, with the conclusions inevitably influenced by intensive lobbying from interested groups. Second, especially in the first Benchmarking exercise of 2002, the recommended awards for the public sector were, in principle, tied to commitments to improve productivity and, more generally, to 'modernize' the public sector, as stipulated in the Social Partnership agreements. However, the measurement

---

[10] According to IMF data, public sector wages rose by 60 per cent between 2000 and 2008, compared to per capita GDP growth of 45 per cent (IMF 2012: 19).

of levels and changes in labour productivity in most parts of public administration is particularly difficult, both conceptually and practically.

Lane (2011) draws attention to the so-called Baumol's disease, which hypothesizes that productivity gains are the major determinant of wage gains in the private sector. But in the non-market sector, including services such as education, health, and public administration, where wages need to be competitive with the private sector, productivity gains may be difficult to measure and/or achieve. In the case of the Irish public sector, it is widely acknowledged that only lip service was paid to assessing whether the 'increases in productivity' envisaged were actually taking place.[11] In an environment of significant staff expansion and a widespread belief that there was 'enough money for all' this appears to have been a classical example of Baumol's disease in action. Indeed it was only very recently, in the context of the 2012 Budget, that the government began to tackle the issue of public sector productivity seriously.

The awards granted under the 2002 Benchmarking exercise, in particular, appear to have been largely the outcome of an exercise driven by a preordained decision to grant substantial increases to public sector employees, regardless of the economic rationale or implications. Many observers and commentators (excluding interest groups who, naturally, benefited from the process) were scathing in their criticisms. The papers by Ruane and Lyons (2002) and O'Leary (2002), who resigned from the Benchmarking body in protest in April 2002, emphasized the absence of a clear economic methodology underlying the exercise, the fact that no evidence was presented suggesting that the private/public sector pay differential had altered or that the public service overall was experiencing any difficulties in staff recruitment or retention. Critics also noted the emphasis on jobs as opposed to performance, and the failure to address the implications of the pay awards for competitiveness, despite this element having being included in the Body's terms of reference.[12]

Disturbingly, the whole exercise was carried out in secret, behind closed doors without public disclosure of the specific data underlying the analysis or recommendations. Attempts under the Freedom of Information Act (FoI) to obtain this material were denied. Based on some internal official communications that were made available, Fitzgerald (2002) observes that:

---

[11] Nor does it appear that much consideration was given to valuing the security of tenure associated with a lifelong public service appointment or the generous sizeable pension arrangements (including severance pay elements) involved. These aspects have come to the fore in the current steep recession, with a massive jump in unemployment and with many private sector workers facing sharp cuts in their originally anticipated pension levels.

[12] O'Leary surmises that this aspect was contained in the terms of reference mainly to discourage the private sector from seeking 'leapfrog' awards subsequently.

These papers [those released under FoI] are illuminating. [According to them], a senior official argues 'it would be undesirable in an industrial relations and pay determination context that any party should seek to look behind the published reports, reasonings and findings of the bodies.'

'Any party' clearly includes the Department of Finance itself. In a further memo, the official goes on to argue that it would be inappropriate for the records of the Body to revert to the Department at any subsequent date (where as records held by the Department they would be open to disclosure under FoI). In other words, the Department does not want to know, either now or in the future, the reasoning behind proposals to spend €1,000 million a year [the projected cost of the 2002 awards] in additional public money.

Charges that these records have been subsequently 'shredded' or have 'disappeared'—see Corless (2004) and Oireachtas (2003: 23)—have not been denied. Economist Jim O' Leary summarized later:

At the end of the day, the benchmarking exercise tells us a lot more about governance in this country and about the nature of social partnership in particular, than it tells us about the state of the labour market (O'Leary 2002: 13).

The end result of the combined processes was that average public sector salaries were raised to completely unsustainable levels. In particular, while the stated objective of the exercise was to bring public sector pay more in line with the private sector, the outcome went far beyond this goal. Kelly, McGuinness, and O'Connell (2009a) contains a comprehensive analysis of the extent to which the 'public sector pay premium' (the difference between average public and private salaries, after adjusting for differences in educational attainment, work experience, and other job-related characteristics), evolved in the wake of the various pay awards. Their results indicate that:

the public sector premium increased dramatically from 9.7 per cent to 21.6 per cent between 2003 and 2006. Furthermore, ... by 2006 senior public service workers earned almost 8 per cent more than their private sector counterparts, while those in lower-level grades earned between 22 and 31 per cent more (Kelly et al. 2009a: 339).[13]

A surprising feature of the 2002 Benchmarking exercise was the neglect of the more favourable pension arrangements enjoyed by the public sector.[14]

---

[13] The paper by Kelly et al. summarizes earlier studies on this subject for Ireland as well as comparative analysis undertaken for other countries. They conclude that the range of figures estimated for Ireland are much larger than those found elsewhere. Sub-sectoral analysis contained in Kelly et al. (2009b) estimated that the premium had risen from 14 per cent in 2003 to 26 per cent in 2006.

[14] This shortcoming was, however, addressed to some extent in the second Benchmarking exercise in 2007 which, partly as a result, recommended increases for only about 10 per cent of the over 100 grades analysed. However, it did not consider any 'roll back' of increases granted under the earlier (flawed, at least in this respect) 2002 exercise.

The paper by Kelly et al. (2009a) made a partial adjustment for this element by incorporating differential rates of pension coverage across the public and private sector. Due to data limitations, the adjustment could only be applied to 2003. However, it raised the estimated public sector premium from 9.7 per cent to 12.9 per cent for that year, even prior to the jump recorded between then and 2006. Moreover, the calculation understated the size of the total premium, as it did not take into account the significant difference in value between public and private sector pensions,[15] nor the much greater security of job tenure enjoyed by the public sector.[16]

Apart from underestimating the pension element, as of end-2008 the actual premium is likely to have been higher than that indicated by the calculation for end-2006. Further awards under all three pay award processes were made in 2007–08, when private sector wages and salaries may have been already feeling the effects of the deepening recession.[17] Also, civil servants, except for those at the top of the salary scale, continued to receive pay increments throughout this period. In a later update (CSO 2012), the premium (considering wages and salaries only) was estimated to have ranged from 6–19 per cent in 2010, compared to 10–26 per cent in 2007.[18]

The staggered implementation of pay increases (as well as increments) to be awarded in the future was not easily reversed. Partly as a consequence, in 2008–09 when GDP and budgetary revenue collapsed, current government expenditure in real terms increased by a cumulative 22 per cent. Real public sector pay rose by 9.4 per cent in 2008 and by 0.9 per cent in 2009, before

---

[15] They note that public sector pensions are index-linked to the pay earned by the current incumbent of the comparable position formerly held by the retiree, whereas private sector pensions are substantially less favourable.

[16] Foley and O'Callaghan (CSO 2009) analysed the public–private sector wage gap for 2007 (but did not include any adjustment for pensions). Their results suggested a much lower premium, in the range of 12–16 per cent. However, in commenting on this work, McGuinness (2009) showed, using the earlier data for 2006, that a large part of this difference was due to the inappropriate inclusion of two data series, trades union membership and organization size, as variables explaining the 'non premium-related' component of public sector pay. Both McGuinness and O'Leary (2009) also criticized the suggested exclusion by the CSO of employees from personal protective service occupations (on the grounds of lack of comparability), arguing that such a justification could equally be advanced in respect of other groups such as nurses, teachers, and university lecturers. While some disagreements on the appropriate specification of the model used in exercises such as these are to be expected, based on this interchange, one could gain a sense that the CSO's methodology was tilted in the direction of arriving at conclusions that would tend to understate the estimated size of the premium.

[17] However, the awards made during this period were of a partial, interim nature, owing to the emergence of intensified budgetary pressures and the 'inability to pay' clause of the agreements. The question can be asked as to why the government did not invoke this clause to a much greater extent during 2007–08.

[18] However, the methodology underlying the CSO's calculation was again subject to criticism by Kelly et al. (2012) who argued that the average premium in 2010 in fact was likely to have been close to 17 per cent.

Table 7.6. Benchmarking of Irish salaries by OECD (public sector)

Occupation	Ireland's Ranking	Higher
Secondary Teaching	Fifth Highest of 32 States	Luxembourg, Switzerland, Germany, Korea
Medical Consultants	Highest	
Nurses	Fourth Highest	Luxembourg, US, Australia
Central Government Senior Managers	Sixth Highest	Italy, New Zealand, UK, Austria, Belgium
Middle Ranking Senior Servants	Sixth Highest	US, Italy, UK, Netherlands, Belgium
Executive Secretaries in Civil Service	Eighth Highest	US, Netherlands, Finland, Belgium, Denmark, Austria, Brazil

Source: Laffan (2011)

falling by 4.3 per cent, in 2010 (Table 7.4). The benchmarking 'juggernaut' could not be easily halted, let alone turned around.

The end result was that even after the crash, and despite effective nominal reductions in 2009–10, public sector salaries remained at levels significantly above their average EU/OECD counterparts. Laffan (2011) summarizes the results of an OECD report, *Government at a Glance* (2011a), which, for the first time, included internationally comparable data on compensation for a number of public sector professions. The results (Table 7.6) are striking. As Laffan points out, it is especially noteworthy that no other country appears in the top eight as often as Ireland. Thus, Luxembourg pays its teachers and nurses more but not its civil servants. Belgium, the UK, and Italy pay their senior and middle civil servants generously, but not their medical consultants, teachers, and nurses. Laffan also observes that the Nordic countries and the Netherlands (with the exception of one category), are not among those who pay their public servants the most. Although these are considered 'high tax' countries, government revenues do not appear to be used to reward public sector employees disproportionately, but rather to provide a greater quantum of higher quality services.

Apart from the fiscal unsustainability (and arguably redistributive) aspects, the broader implications for external competitiveness of Ireland's approach to setting public sector pay also became more apparent. In 2009, the IMF concluded that both Irish wages and prices had risen rapidly before stabilizing (as of end-2007) at levels that were the highest and second highest, respectively, in the euro area (IMF 2009: 12). Not surprisingly, this led to a significant 'raising of eyebrows' from Ireland's EU partners from 2008 onwards, as the prospect of their having to finance Ireland's yawning fiscal gap began to loom.[19]

[19] In September 2007, the German Ambassador to Ireland, Christian Pauls, delivered a speech which, intentionally or not, made its way into the public domain shortly afterwards. The

In parallel, outlays on pensions also grew rapidly, rising in real terms by 130 per cent between 2000 and 2008. One important factor contributing to this excessive increase was the pay-parity link, whereby public servants were guaranteed pensions based on the current salary of the position they had held prior to retirement. Thus, the large pay raises awarded under benchmarking exercises were automatically translated into higher pensions for long-retired civil servants. Moreover, when current public service salaries were effectively *reduced* for the first time in early 2009 (via a pension levy), it was decided that the reduction would not affect pensions payable to those in service or who had already retired. This was a striking example of asymmetric cyclicality— when times were good, civil servants on pensions automatically benefited but when bad times arrived they were (at least initially) shielded from any adverse effect.[20]

The benchmarking described above needs to be seen in the context of successive 'social partnership' agreements, that is, comprehensive frameworks covering, in addition to pay rates in the public and private sectors, related government taxation and expenditure policies. Social partnership appears to have placed an exceptionally high premium on avoiding social tension or any outbreak of industrial strife. However, the price was excessive and the conse-quences far reaching. Apart from contributing to a loss in external competi-tiveness, the massive expansion in the public sector payroll bill contributed in a major way to the subsequent fiscal collapse.

7.2.2 Expenditures and Achievements by Sector

Public expenditure on the **education sector** increased in real terms at an average annual rate of just over 6 per cent between 2000 and 2009 (Table 7.4). As of 2007, total expenditure (private and public) per student was at or slightly above the EU/OECD average for all levels (primary, secondary and

Ambassador described Ireland as a 'coarse place', observing that junior ministers earned more than the German Chancellor, that some 20 per cent of the population were public servants, that 'chaotic' hospital waiting lists would not be tolerated anywhere else and that wage demands were too high (*The Irish Independent*, 17 September 2007). The Ambassador subsequently was officially reprimanded by the Irish Department of Foreign Affairs for remarks that were described as 'inaccurate, misinformed and inappropriate'.

[20] This decision, that the deduction via the 'pension levy' (Public Service Pension Reduction (PSRD)) introduced in early 2009 would not affect current or future pensions, may have reflected, apart from lobbying by the public service unions concerned, legal obstacles. On 1 January 2010, a public service pay cut averaging 7 per cent was announced which did not impact immediately on pensions, i.e., pensions in payment were not affected and, in the case of current employees, the cut did not impact on their pension entitlement, provided they retired during a grace period that expired on 29 February 2012—pensions coming into effect after that date reflected reduced pay rates. On 1 January 2011, an average reduction of 4 per cent (the Public Sector Pension Reduction (PSPR)) was applied to all pensions unaffected by the pay cut. In early 2013 further planned cuts in current pubic sector pay and pensions were announced, before being rejected by the trade unions.

tertiary)[21]. This very substantial increase during the boom deserves scrutiny, in order to assess what value for money may have been achieved. Higher outlays in themselves are not any guarantee of improved educational attainment, which is affected by many complex factors well beyond the scope of this book. Nevertheless, based on available evidence, some broad observations appear relevant, particularly as regards trends in student-teacher ratios, graduation rates, the composition of expenditures, evidence pertaining to educational outcomes, and issues of equity.

- A large part of the educational expenditure bill went to increasing the numbers of teachers (between 2000 and 2010, by 42 per cent and by 15 per cent, at primary and secondary level, respectively).The total increase (combining both levels) of about 13,000 was more than accounted for by a rapid expansion of some 17,000 non-classroom teachers (who mainly provide support in areas such as special needs, the disadvantaged, travellers (itinerants), and language support, as well as senior management).[22] By 2008, the number of students per teaching staff in primary and secondary schools had been reduced to 17.8 and 12.8, respectively, compared with corresponding EU averages of 14.6 and 12.0 (Newman 2011: 365).[23]

- Graduation rates in Ireland rose very sharply. Thus, the proportion of the population aged seventeen to eighteen graduating from upper-secondary level surged from 74 per cent in 2000 to 96 per cent in 2008, well above the EU average of 80 per cent. A similar trend became apparent at tertiary level (Newman 2011: 366).

- Outlays on teachers' salaries comprise almost 80 per cent of current expenditures at first and second level. Between 2000 and 2010, expenditure on pay at primary and secondary levels combined rose by 110 per cent. While partly explained by the rise in numbers, about two-thirds of this increase was accounted for by higher levels of pay.[24] By 2008, Irish teacher salaries had attained levels far higher than their EU counterparts on average, a feature which continued in 2009, even as the budgetary squeeze intensified. In 2010 the pay of Irish primary school teachers with fifteen years experience ranked fourth highest among thirty-four OECD members (OECD 2012: 465). Between 2000 and 2009,

---

[21] Newman (2011: 363). Much of the content of this section draws on this survey article.

[22] Data provided by the Department of Education.

[23] Average class size, which adjusts for the presence of special teachers, also declined significantly. The evidence on the educational impact of decreasing class size appears rather inconclusive. The broad consensus appears to be that class size is only one (and by no means the most important) factor affecting attainment rates on average, with the impact greater for children at a very young age and/or with special needs.

[24] Data provided by the Department of Education.

average salaries in real terms for primary and secondary teachers rose by 28–29 per cent, compared with an OECD-wide average increase of 19–23 per cent (OECD 2012: 468).[25]

- Despite the additional resources devoted to the primary and secondary sectors, the overall outcome in terms of educational attainment on average is disappointing. According to the most recent results of the OECD Programme for International Student Assessment (PISA), Ireland has experienced a major decline in relative ranking of reading scores, from fifth place in 2000 to seventeenth place in 2009—by far the largest fall among all OECD members—Perkins et al. (2010). Between 2003 and 2009, Ireland's mathematics ranking also fell, from twentieth to twenty-sixth place, and the fall in the absolute score was the second largest among participating countries. However, in the case of science, the results (which cover only 2006 and 2009) show a slight improvement. Methodological issues (including sampling techniques) can affect somewhat the comparability both over time and between countries of these results.[26] However, the overall evidence raises serious questions as to whether expenditures on education have been put to the best use.[27,28]

- An avowed objective of government policy was to improve access and educational achievement for students from less advantaged backgrounds. The provision of universal free post-primary education from the 1960s onwards, the abolition of university fees in 1995, and a host of programs directed at supporting specific groups (including an unprecedented expansion in the numbers of special teachers) have been the main policy instruments.

- Time and study is needed before the success of these initiatives can be assessed properly. However, the impact in terms of greater equity and improved access of one major measure, the removal of third level fees regardless of means testing is, at best, uncertain. As noted by the OECD (2009: 70), this policy is highly regressive and benefits disproportionally

[25] These data do not include various allowances paid to teachers for qualifications and other benefits.

[26] It has been suggested, for instance, that demographic changes, especially immigration, may have had an effect on Ireland's results. However, the proportion of students (15-year-olds) in the sample for whom English was not their first language spoken at home, increased relatively modestly, from 0.9 per cent in 2000 to 3.5 per cent in 2009.

[27] The National Assessment of Mathematics and English reading (carried out by the Education Research Centre of the Department of Education) show no overall change from 1993 to 2004 in the case of literacy, or from 1999 to 2994 in the case of mathematics. Due to methodological changes, assessments for later years are not comparable to these earlier results.

[28] In May 2012, Education Minister Ruairi Quinn stated that claims that Ireland had the best education system in the world were 'manure', that the system 'badly needs to be reformed' and that 'despite extra resources going in to the education system, the outcomes [had] not improved' (The *Irish Times*, 25 May 2012).

those in upper income brackets. Moreover, there is evidence that due to the 'points system' that determines access to third level education, the proportion of students who succeed in entering university from 'elite' expensive private fee-paying schools (in Dublin or other major cities) is exceptionally high.[29] Families on higher incomes will have had an incentive to reallocate funds otherwise spent on university fees and enrol their children in such establishments which themselves are subsidized as well as spend money on additional support such as 'grinds' (extra out of school hours teaching). In turn, for less well-off students, many of whom paid no tuition fees before abolition, the difficulty in actually obtaining a third level place, especially in 'high points' faculties such as medical or legal professions, may even have increased due to competition from those able to afford fee-paying schools.[30] Over the last decade, several Ministers of Education were charged with exploring the reintroduction of some form of fees/loans arrangements and commissioned reports and extensive consultations on the matter. However, in the end, due to political resistance at broader cabinet level, all these initiatives came to nought.

- The abolition of university fees has also left universities in increasingly acute financial difficulties, even before the recession. In this context, similar to primary and secondary level, the issue of salaries paid to academics may be relevant. Comparable international data on third level teachers' salaries are not published by the OECD or others. In any event, as Newman (2011) points out, cross-country, or even cross-institution, comparisons are difficult because of differing contractual arrangements regarding teaching loads and opportunities for outside earnings, the possibilities of joint appointments with more than one institution and variations in quality and reputation. Nevertheless, it is believed that Irish salaries have been pitched somewhat above the EU average, particularly at professorial level where they are linked to the Assistant Secretary pay grade in the civil service (which has benefited from benchmarking). The variance in salaries is thought to be relatively low.

- For whatever reasons (including inadequate funding arrangements), the international standing of Irish universities has suffered a sharp decline in recent year. Surveys undertaken since late 2011 have shown a dramatic fall in the rankings for most institutions. According to *The Times* (2012),

---

[29] As reported in the 2011 *Irish Times* annual school league tables, virtually every student in middle-class areas proceeds to college (100 per cent in the case of 20 fee paying schools), while the progression rate is less than 40 per cent in many working class areas (The *Irish Times*, 22 November 2011).

[30] This effect will be mitigated to the extent that (a) income related subsidies for those attending fee paying schools have been availed of and (b) third level universities accept students in special access programs outside the regular points system.

only one Irish university currently ranks in the top 100, although earlier in the decade, one (Trinity College) had been in the top 50 and another (University College Dublin) in the top 100; the QS (2012) survey indicates a similar pattern. While elements of the methodologies used can be subject to question, there is a consensus that the end of the boom has coincided with a significant reputational problem for Irish third level education.

• Finally, according to Eurostat data (O'Brien 2012), overall costs in education have increased at a particularly fast rate. Between 1999 and 2011, Irish education prices rose by 117 per cent, compared to 46 per cent across the EU on average. In the three years ended 2011, they increased by 14 per cent, over three times the average EU growth of 4 per cent.

Alongside rising outlays on education and social protection, **health sector expenditures** continued to surge during the boom, more than doubling in real terms between 2000 and 2009 (Table 7.4).[31] According to OECD data, spending rose from 7.1 per cent of Gross National Income (GNI) in 2000 to 9.3 per cent in 2008, the largest percentage point increase among comparable OECD countries during this period (Nolan 2011: 337).[32] However, despite this sustained rate of growth, perhaps more than for any other component of public expenditure, the ability of the Irish health services to deliver appropriate health care has been a source of continued heated controversy.

The issues involved in the provision of an efficient and equitable health system are even more multi-faceted and complex than in the case of education, particularly in Ireland which has an unusual public–private mix in health delivery.[33] Moreover, by their very nature, improvements in health outcomes, in many cases, can usually only be evaluated after a very substantial lag.[34] There is also the issue of rising expectations and the discrepancy between falling subjective but rising objective indicators of health status during the boom period (see Layte, Nolan, and Nolan 2007). The observations

---

[31] The discussion in this section draws heavily on the survey article by Nolan (2011).

[32] The proportion of the Irish population aged 65 and over, averaging 11.5 per cent, was the lowest among OECD countries during this period.

[33] As observed by Nolan (2011: 339), 'the literature highlights the fact that social, environmental and cultural factors such as diet, exercise, genetic inheritance, lifestyle, education, social status, income distribution, social support and housing, and their interaction, may be more important in determining the level and distribution of health outcomes than simple health expenditure.'

[34] Nevertheless positive outcomes for Ireland in two important health areas during the period should be noted: (i) the sharp drop in deaths from diseases of the circulatory system between 1995 and 2005 among older age groups in Ireland—see Layte et al. (2010); and (ii) a halving of the perinatal mortality (the number of stillbirths and early neonatal deaths) between 1984 and 2006—see Layte and Clyne (2010). Both of these papers referred to attempt to explain statistically the possible causes of these phenomena.

that follow, are therefore limited to selected aspects of the composition of expenditures.

- As in Ireland's education sector, the impact of labour costs is especially important, amounting to approximately 50 per cent of total health expenditures (in the acute hospitals sector the figure is closer to 70 per cent—Nolan (2011: 344)). Recent research indicates that the numbers of management and administrative staff in the health sector grew significantly both prior to the establishment of the Health Services Executive (HSE) in 2005 and afterwards (with some evidence to suggest that growth since 2005 was largely in the higher grades—Brick et al (2010)). The OECD (2009: 66) reports that the number of hospital staff rose by one-third in the first half of the 2000s, with a relatively high ratio of practising nursing staff to physicians.
- Nurses' pay rose very sharply.[35] In 2009, average nurses' **salaries**, at the equivalent of US$54, 000 (converted using purchasing parity exchange rates), were the third highest among comparable OECD countries, after Luxembourg and the United States (OECD 2011b: 77). The annual average real growth of just over 3 per cent in nurse's, salaries from 2000–09 was the third fastest after the Czech Republic and the Slovak Republic. Nurses' unions were among the more militant of public sector workers' groups, threatening on several occasions in earlier years to withhold services unless their demands, including those relating to work conditions, were addressed satisfactorily.[36]
- The salaries of doctors are also deserving of scrutiny. According to the OECD, between 2000 and 2009, the annual average growth in real remuneration of general practitioners in Ireland was the third highest among comparable countries, while that of consultants was the second highest. Moreover, the data do not include earnings from private practice (OECD 2011b: 67). The ratio of Irish consultant salaries to the average wage was the second highest among the group. As noted above, Laffan (2011) reported that medical consultants in Ireland were the best paid among OECD countries. Laffan also pointed out that Ireland had fewer specialists per 1000 of the population than the OECD average (1.1 compared to 1.8) and suggested that the high cost of consultant salaries undermines the ability to employ sufficient consultant numbers. The negotiation of a new contract between the government and

---

[35] One of the major issues with respect to nurses' pay is the large (and by international standards generous) non-basic components (e.g., overtime, Sunday pay—Brick et al. 2010: Table 13.8).

[36] In the run up to the 2007 election, nurses' unions engaged in several work stoppages in pursuit of a reduction in the working week from 39 to 35 hours.

consultants—finally completed in 2008—proved to be particularly protracted and at times acrimonious.[37, 38]

- Reforms introduced in 2009 sought to constrain what had been rapidly growing public expenditure on the provision of drugs, including related fees paid to health personnel under various delivery schemes. Gorecki et al. (2012: vii) noted that during the 2000s, Ireland had 'experienced one of the highest annual growth rates in pharmaceutical expenditures of any OECD country . . . In 2009 Ireland spent more on pharmaceuticals per capita than any other OECD country (with the exception of the US, Canada and Greece)'.[39] Their report observed that recent reforms had led to a significant reduction in the prices of new pharmaceuticals and those no longer subject to patent protection and that both wholesale and pharmacist mark-ups had fallen. Nevertheless, it urged that more be done to achieve better value for money.[40] The EU/IMF Memorandum of Understanding agreed with the government in late 2010 also referred to the need for further actions in the pharmacy sector.

- Finally, similar to education, in the dozen years ended 2011, according to Eurostat data, Irish health prices rose by a cumulative 85 per cent, almost triple the EU-wide increase of 30 per cent (O'Brien 2012). Despite the recession and the fall in the overall price level, health prices continued to climb during 2008–11, by 8 per cent, double the EU average.

---

[37] At one stage during the negotiations, a former president of the Irish Hospital Consultants Association (Josh Keaveney), remarked that the proposed offer by the government of a salary of €220–240,000, in the light of the possible earning capacity of Irish doctors abroad, was 'Mickey Mouse' money (*The Irish Independent*, 17 April 2007). Although this was not stated publicly, facing rising costs in Ireland, especially of housing, many consultants returning from abroad may have had difficulty enjoying a lifestyle to which their predecessors in pre-boom years had become accustomed.

[38] During the 2007 election the consultant body formally expressed a vote of 'no confidence' in then Minister of Health, Mary Harney. Disquiet at high consultant salaries has continued unabated. In March 2012, Sean McGrath, shortly after retiring as head of HSE human resources (to take up a post as Vice President of Human Resources at the World Bank) stated that up to 500 consultants were earning over €200,000 with many receiving over €250, 000 and some, over €300, 000 from the public purse. He also referred to 'resistance' to implementation of some parts of the consultants' contract (The *Irish Times*, 21 March 2012).

[39] Over the 2000s, the failure to control expenditure on drugs and related payments to doctors, which was largely demand driven, was notable, even though the proportion of the population eligible for these schemes was falling.

[40] The specific recommendations included: (i) setting the ex-factory price of new pharmaceuticals subject to patent protection with reference to the lowest comparable EU Member State ex-factory price; (ii) ensuring that lower priced parallel imports of new products not requiring patent authorization . . . be reflected in the cash prices charged to patients; (iii) reducing barriers to the full realization of benefits from the supply of products from generic competitors once patent protection expires; (iv) retaining the current wholesale competitive business model despite some falling profits and demand; (iv) expanding significantly the information supplied by pharmacists to patients regarding prices, mark-ups, and dispensing fees as well as services provided; and (v) encouraging prescribers to write a prescription in terms of a particular pharmaceutical rather than a particular supplier or brand.

Spending on **social protection**, which in 2008 accounted for one-third of all government outlays, also rose sharply in real terms during the boom, albeit from relatively low levels. By 2008, the size of the child benefit allowance had quadrupled since 1997 and both the state contributory pension and the long-term job seekers allowance had doubled by comparison with 1999 and 2001, respectively (OECD 2009: 70). The levels of benefits were high by international standards, including, in some cases, relative to those available in the United Kingdom, and reportedly encouraged some temporary 'domiciling' across the border from Northern Ireland. The period also saw the introduction of a large number of other benefits for the first time, as well as the expansion of already existing schemes. Between 2000 and 2008, the indices of short-term and long-term rates of payment for a single person increased by 112 per cent and 98 per cent, respectively, compared to a rise in the consumer price index during the same period of 42 per cent (Department of Social Protection 2008: 24).[41]

As budgetary pressures intensified from 2008 onwards, rapid adjustment of social welfare expenditures towards more sustainable levels was complicated by several socio-political as well as administrative aspects. Firstly, at the time of their introduction, many social outlays were not means tested. Proposals to introduce targeting—on grounds of fiscal constraints and equity—ran up against citizens' acquired sense of 'entitlement'.[42] Secondly, issues of social stigma, as well as some administrative complications associated with defining total 'household income', also arose.[43] Thirdly, it is often politically easier to reduce the real value of benefits (and hence their cost) by simply leaving their nominal levels unchanged in an environment of modest inflation. However, inflation was close to zero or negative in the latter half of the 2000s. For example, in the 2009 Budget, as pointed out by the OECD

[41] The range of schemes in effect as of 2008 appears exceptionally extensive and is divided into three categories (see Department of Social Protection 2008: 22). Social insurance payments comprised long-term payments (state pension, invalidity pension, widows, pension/deserted wives' benefit, guardian's payment, death benefit, and disabled benefit) and short-term payments (illness/jobseeker's benefit and carer's benefit). Social assistance payments also are classified under long-term payments (state pension, widow's pension, deserted/prisoners wives' allowance, one parent family payment, guardian's payment, carer's allowance, job seeker's allowance, pre-retirement allowance, disability allowance, and farm assist) and short-term payments (short-term jobseeker's allowance and supplementary allowance). A third category, 'other payments' comprised living alone allowance, over-80 allowance, island allowance, and child benefit (separately for the first and second child, and third and other children).

[42] A case in point was the government's announced intention in early 2009 to withdraw the automatic (non-means-tested) entitlement of all citizens to a medical card at age 70. After massive 'gray power' protests outside the Irish parliament, the government hastily withdrew the proposal.

[43] Thus, account had to be taken of the changing composition of Irish households during the previous decades where single parents and non-married partnerships had become common. Also, for some benefits, establishing the bona fide residence and eligibility of immigrants who had flocked into Ireland during the boom (some of whom had returned home) created additional complications.

(2009: 71), a reduction in welfare payments of around 4 per cent would have been needed to avoid a further increase in the real value of benefits. However, the opposite occurred—welfare payments were adjusted upward by around 3 per cent.[44]

7.3 Conclusions

The budgetary largesse associated with Ireland's property and construction boom was distributed widely and comprehensively, and few segments of the population failed to benefit significantly. Tax rates were lowered at all income levels, while tax exemptions and other special arrangements proliferated, thereby eroding the tax base. Many of these schemes, which were much more prevalent in Ireland than in other EU/OECD countries, were directed at the property sector (thus exacerbating the bubble) and benefited disproportionately those earning higher incomes.

Extending the fruits of the bubble was especially marked in the case of government expenditure policies. The various benchmarking processes and social partnership agreements that determined pay awards sent public sector salaries soaring to well beyond levels of both the Irish private sector and official counterparts abroad. There was little public transparency as regards the processes involved, in particular, those associated with the 2002 exercise. Only lip service was paid to so-called 'productivity gains' that were supposed to have been a condition for these awards. In tandem, the pension bill, partly reflecting the particular pay-parity link arrangement prevailing in Ireland, jumped.

The rise in public sector salaries was a major force driving the rapid growth in outlays on the education and health sectors. The remuneration of teachers, nurses, and hospital consultants, as well as pharmaceutical costs, rose to levels at or close to the highest prevailing in comparable countries. Outlays on social welfare also increased very rapidly, due to sharp increases in the benefit rates and coverage of existing arrangements as well as the introduction of new schemes.

It is too early to venture a judgment as to the extent to which there have been major improvements in the quantum and quality of services in the education and health sectors where, for well over a decade, prices have been rising annually at rates double or triple the EU average. However, the evidence in the case of education so far is, at best, mixed. About two-thirds of the doubling in expenditure on the primary and secondary teachers' payroll between 2000 and 2010 was accounted for by higher salaries. Although measures such as teacher/student ratios and the proportion of the population

---

[44] Furthermore, they were left unchanged in the Supplementary Budget of March 2009.

graduating at all levels have shown striking improvement, the same cannot be said of actual educational attainment. At secondary level, the most recent PISA results show a sharp drop in reading and mathematics skills, while the world rankings of Irish universities have also fallen very significantly. The failure to introduce some form of university fee or student loan scheme during the boom, apart from contributing to major funding shortfalls in third level education, also raises important issues relating to greater equity and improved access. So far as the health sector is concerned, a large part of the additional outlays was devoted to increased labour costs. An assessment of whether these will bear lasting fruit will require considerable time and further study.

References

Brick, Aoife et al. (2010) 'Resource Allocation, Financing and Sustainability in Health Care', Evidence for the Expert Group on Resource Allocation and Financing in the Health Sector, Vol.1, *The Economic and Social Research Institute*, July (Dublin).

Central Statistics Office (2012) *National Employment Survey 2009 and 2010: Supplementary Analysis*, October.

Corless, Damien (2004) 'Nice Work if You Can Get It'. *Irish Independent*, February 24.

Department of Finance (2006) 'Budget 2006, Review of Tax Schemes' Vol. 1, Indecon Review of Property-based Tax Incentive Schemes, February (Dublin).

Department of Finance (2011) *Reforming Ireland's Budgetary Framework*, March 2011.

Department of Social Protection (2008) Statistical Information on Social Welfare Services. (Dublin).

Fitzgerald, Eithne (2002) 'Social Rights and Funding' Irish Social Policy Conference, Dublin City University, September 13, 2002.

Foley, Patrick and Fiona O'Callaghan (2009) 'Investigating the Public-Private Wage Gap in Ireland Using Data from the National Employment Survey 2007', *Journal of the Statistical and Social Inquiry Society of Ireland*, Vol. XXXIX, November 2009, 23–45.

Gorecki, Paul, Anne Nolan, Aoife Brick, and Sean Lyons (2012) 'Delivery of Pharmaceuticals in Ireland: getting a Bigger Bang for the Buck', ESRI Research Series no. 24, January 2012.

IMF (2009) *Ireland: Staff Report for the 2009 Article IV Consultation*, May 20, 2009.

IMF (2012) *Ireland: Staff Report for the 2012 Article IV Consultation*, August 21, 2012.

Kelly, Elish, Seamus McGuinness, and Phillip O'Connell (2009a) 'Benchmarking, Social Partnership and Higher Remuneration: Wage Settling Institutions and the Public-Private Sector Wage Gap in Ireland', *Economic and Social Review*, Vol 40, No.3, Autumn, 2009, 339–370.

Kelly, Elish, Seamus McGuinness, and Phillip O'Connell (2009b) 'The Public-Private Sector Pay Gap in Ireland: What Lies Behind' ESRI Working Paper no 321, *The Economic and Social Research Institute*, Dublin.

Kelly, Elish, Seamus McGuinness, and Phillip O'Connell (2012) 'Comparing Public and Private Sector Pay in Ireland: Size Matters' *ESRI Quarterly Economic Commentary*, Winter 2012 (Dublin).

Laffan, Bridget (2011), *'Hard Choices Have to be Made'* in *Transforming Ireland, 2011–2016* (ed. Joe Mulholland), Dublin, 152–161.

Lane, Philip (2011) *'Role of Government: Rationale and Issue'*, in O'Hagan, John and Carol Newman, *The Economy of Ireland*, Dublin, 62–86.

Layte, Richard, Anne Nolan, and Brian Nolan (2007) *'Health and Health Care'* in *The Best of Times?: The Social Impact of the Celtic Tiger*, Foley T., Russell, H., and Whelan, C. T. (eds), Dublin, Institute of Public Administration.

Layte, Richard, Sinead O'Hara, and Kathleen Bennett (2010) *'Exploring Structural Change in Cardiovascular Mortality in Ireland 1995–2005; a Time Series Analysis'*, European Journal of Public Health, August 4, 2010, 1–6.

Layte, Richard, and Barbara Clyne (2010) 'Did the Celtic Tiger Decrease Socio-economic Differences in Perinatal Mortality in Ireland?', *Economic and Social Review*, Vol.41, no. 2, Summer 2010, 173–199.

McGuinness, Seamus (2009) *'Comments'* on Foley and O'Callaghan (2009), *Journal of the Statistical and Social Inquiry Society of Ireland*, Vol XXXIX, November, 2009, 46–50.

Newman, Carol (2011) 'Education: Market Failure and Government Intervention' in O'Hagan, John and Carol Newman, *The Economy of Ireland*, Dublin, 349–373.

Nolan, Anne (2011) 'Health: Funding, Access and Efficiency' in O'Hagan, John and Carol Newman, *The Economy of Ireland*, Gill and MacMillan, Dublin, 2011, 324–348.

Oireachtas (2003) 'Benchmarking: Motion' Seanad Eireann Debate, Vol.174, No.2.

O'Brien, Dan (2012), 'Irish Prices Fall to Fifth Dearest in EU', *Irish Times*, June 23, 2012.

O'Leary, Jim (2002) 'Benchmarking the Benchmarkers' *ESRI Quarterly Economic Commentary*, Winter, 77–91 (Dublin).

O'Leary, Jim (2009) *'Comments'* on Foley and O'Callaghan (2009), *Journal of the Statistical and Social Inquiry Society of Ireland*, Vol XXXIX, November, 2009, 51–52.

OECD (2009), *Economic Surveys, Ireland*, November 2009.

OECD (2011a), *Government at a Glance*, June 24, 2011.

OECD (2011b), *Health at a Glance*, November 23, 2011.

OECD (2012), *Education at a Glance*, OECD Indicators, OECD Publishing, September 12, 2012 (Paris).

Perkins, Rachel, Grainne Moran, Jude Cosgrove and Gerry Shields (2010) *'PISA 2009 The Performance and Progress of 15-year olds in Ireland'*, Department of Education, Research Centre (Dublin).

QS (2012) *World University Rankings*, September 11, 2012.

Regling, Klaus and Max Watson (2010) *A Preliminary Report on the Irish Banking Crisis*, May 2010.

Ruane, Frances and Ronan Lyons (2002) 'Wage Determination in the Irish Economy: an Economist's Perspective on the Benchmarking Report', ESRI Quarterly Economic Commentary, Policy Discussion Forum, Winter 2002. *The Economic and Social Research Institute*, Dublin.

The Times (2012) Higher Education Rankings, October 3, 2012.

Whelan, Karl (2010) 'Policy Lessons from Ireland's Latest Depression', *Economic and Social Review*, Vol. 41, No.2, Summer, 2010, 225–254.

8

The Climate of Public Opinion—Politicians, Economists, and the Media

The Celtic Tiger is dead

George Lee, RTE Economics Editor, June 2006[1]

Sitting on the sidelines, cribbing and moaning is a lost opportunity. I don't know how people who engage in that don't commit suicide...

former Taoiseach Bertie Ahern[2]

Chapters 5 and 6 reviewed the roles of the Central Bank, the Financial Regulator, and the Department of Finance in the lead up to the crisis. A consistent pattern emerged. Each of these institutions, to varying extents, allowed itself to be swept up in the general euphoria and neglected to carry out key risk assessment functions effectively. None of them saw any particular need to consider the possible consequences if the house of cards was to collapse.

The thinking of the key officials—and their policy actions or inactions—did not evolve in a vacuum, however. They were inevitably influenced, consciously or not, by general public perceptions and commentary at the time. This is important in order to understand the causes of the fall of the Celtic Tiger. To paraphrase the Nyberg report, if even one of the key groups in society had 'shouted stop', the bubble might have been pricked earlier on and a full scale financial crisis averted. But by and large, with a small number of exceptions, no one did. Thus, the 'blame' for what happened extends beyond traditional scapegoats such as a largely passive government, reckless banks, and greedy property developers. The climate of public opinion also played a major supportive role in the debacle.

---

[1] *Boom,* documentary presented by RTE, June 2006.
[2] 4 July 2007. Ahern subsequently apologized for the remark.

This topic, while referred to on occasion, has not been subject to much systematic examination to date. In what follows, three important dimensions are considered: the views of politicians (beyond just those of the government), the role of the Irish economist community, and the influence of the media. These three groups contributed, explicitly or implicitly, to shaping the environment in which major economic policy mistakes were made.

8.1 The Views of Politicians

Throughout most of the decade (until about 2008), political debate took place in self-congratulatory atmosphere arising from the continuing success of the 'Celtic Tiger'. Opposition parties, apart from normal partisan criticism of government personalities (including ethical issues associated with then Taoiseach Bertie Ahern), mostly criticized deficiencies in the provision of public services and infrastructure and alleged inefficiencies and 'wastage'. Politicians of all hues did not question the reduction of taxes or the expansion of the public sector payroll described in Chapter 7.

Such discussions as there were on the continuing property boom focused more on the question of housing affordability for first time buyers, including the contentious issue of the stamp duty regime.[3] The sustainability of property prices was not placed in doubt, at least publicly. Many senior politicians mingled freely with the new stars in the firmament, the major property developers, partaking of their untold riches and extravagant lifestyles. Envy was present, rather than any serious questioning of the viability of the developers' ever more grandiose projects. Their latest successes were celebrated widely as reflecting the fruits of the far-sighted policies implemented by the political leadership.

There was little or no public discussion of the policies of the Financial Regulator (even less those of the Central Bank) with respect to the banks' lending or borrowing behaviour. By contrast, the consumer protection side of the Regulator was the focus of considerable attention, as aggrieved bank customers, with politicians following hastily in their wake, pursued scandals associated with bank overcharging and the deposit retention tax (DIRT) scheme.

On the broader macroeconomic front, overall high rates of economic growth dampened worries about the major shift in the composition of economic activity away from exports towards construction and property. While the Central Bank expressed concerns about a deterioration in Ireland's

---

[3] Issues relating to the housing market were addressed extensively in the three Bacon reports commissioned by the government.

external competitiveness due to inflation that was persistently higher than the European average, these were largely ignored in political debate.[4] Despite the rising cost pressures, overflowing budgetary coffers allowed generous increases in real public sector salaries. The private sector, buoyed by the spillover effects of the construction boom, followed suit. It was generally accepted that both the public and the private labour force fully deserved the rapid increases in living standards as a reward for Ireland having discovered the 'magic potion' for lasting economic success. Even when incomes could not quite catch up with the frenzied consumer boom, lenders encouraged households to increase their personal debt as if there was no tomorrow.

Exports were also a continuing source of optimism, despite some evidence of a deceleration by the multinational sector—see Chapter 4. The slowdown that began to emerge as the decade progressed was ascribed more to a weakening of the world economy, with less attention paid (at least by the public) to the effects of increases in Irish costs. The feeling of well-being was boosted by a stream of highly favourable comments on Ireland's bright economic prospects and the surge of immigration from Eastern Europe and elsewhere.

While political debate was of course ongoing throughout the decade, the two general election campaigns (2002 and 2007) offer a helpful snapshot of the thinking of the main political parties on economic and budgetary matters.

8.1.1 *The 2002 Election*

The general election of May 2002 took place against the background of a significant deterioration (by the standards of the time) in the public finances in the two previous years. According to the manifesto of the main opposition party, Fine Gael, an Exchequer surplus of €3 billion in 2000 was set to turn into a deficit of up to €6 billion by 2004. Government spending had consistently exceeded budget projections by very large amounts, while revenue had been overestimated significantly.[5] This trend continued to be reflected in the data for the early months of the year which were released just prior to the election. However, with the partial exception of Fine Gael and some media commentary, the issue of expenditure overruns was not subjected to much critical analysis or discussion during the campaign, especially since the budget was registering a surplus and the debt to GDP ratio had fallen very sharply. Nevertheless, the various parties' election manifestos to varying degrees, did

---

[4] However, the regular reports of the National Competitiveness Council raised significant concerns on this score.

[5] Garret Fitzgerald, the former Fine Gael Taoiseach, in one of his several *Irish Times* commentaries during the campaign, observed that budgetary overruns had climbed from €200 million in 1998 to €450 million in 2000 and to €800 million in 2001.

commit themselves, at least in principle, to prudent fiscal policies in the future, including abiding by the 'rules' set by Brussels.

The election platform of the incumbent Fianna Fáil government party projected a budget deficit of 1 per cent for 2002, but undertook to maintain the deficit below this level on average during the following years. The smaller opposition party, Labour, was willing to let the deficit rise to around 1.5 per cent of GDP, while the junior Coalition Government party, the Progressive Democrats (PDs), aimed for approximate balance. On the other hand, Fine Gael, who were more critical of the outgoing government's handling of the public finances, insisted that the budget would remain in surplus throughout. These fiscal plans were broadly consistent with the perceived leanings of the different parties, apart from Fianna Fáil, which tended to be less ideological, emphasizing the virtues of a pragmatic approach.

There were significant differences in the specific taxation and expenditure proposals of the election manifestos, although the coverage of issues tended to be selective and limited. Except for Labour, who favoured a doubling of the capital gains tax and a raising of employers' social insurance contributions, the other parties all proclaimed themselves, to varying degrees, 'low tax' advocates. The PDs proposed lowering the highest marginal income tax rate from 42 to 40 per cent, while all parties appeared to endorse keeping those on the minimum wage outside the income tax net, and more generally, reducing the tax burden of lower income earning groups.

There was a broad consensus that the growth in current spending could not be maintained at the exceptionally high rates of earlier years. Labour proposed the highest annual increase (10 per cent), while the other parties envisaged curtailing growth to 8 per cent or a little more.[6] All the manifestos assumed future real economic growth of 5 per cent, while Labour projected 6.5 per cent.

Each party placed considerable emphasis on increasing capital expenditure to address major shortcomings in infrastructure. Fianna Fáil was the most ambitious and proposed the creation of a National Development Finance Agency to raise funds for investment, including via public–private partnership arrangements. Somewhat controversially, outgoing Minister of Finance McCreevy claimed that any borrowing by the state for projects generating 'an economic rate of return' would not be counted as part of the deficit by the EU and thus escape their strictures. This proposal was denounced by Fine Gael leader Michael Noonan as 'yet another Indian rope

---

[6] Several commentators (although not politicians) observed that with the public sector payroll already expected to rise (even before the results of the benchmarking exercise were taken into account), this projection could prove unrealistic. The issue was not explored during the campaign.

trick ... apparently to disguise borrowing', while Labour also denounced it as 'a big con'. All the other manifestos envisaged the possible sale of state assets (including the 'hardy annual' candidates such as the Electricity Supply Board (ESB), Aer Lingus, and An Bord Gais), as well as the use (in the case of the PDs) of 'excess resources' of the Central Bank following entry into the euro area.[7] Labour suggested that the state's ongoing contribution to the resources of the National Pension Fund be reduced, a proposal generally resisted by others.

Fine Gael was alone in criticizing the major overruns in spending under the outgoing government. Its leader, Michael Noonan, observed that '[Fianna Fáil had turned a surplus into a deficit] faster than Mandrake the Magician'. Fianna Fáil did not consider the issue worth engaging on, while the PDs (who were implicated as members of the outgoing government) and Labour generally remained silent.[8]

As for the media, the *Irish Times*, in its editorials (and some opinion pieces), did not shy away from criticism. The sharpest attacks came from former Fine Gael Taoiseach Garret Fitzgerald who observed:

> It is astonishing that the outgoing Dail [lower House of Parliament] does not seem to have been exercised about the question of how all this [expenditure overruns] came about. Nor in the run-up to this election has any party made these matters an issue, although they go to the root of the credibility of the present Government (Fitzgerald 2002a).

The pattern was similar concerning the future budgetary outlook. Some worries were noted by Fine Gael, but the most trenchant concerns were registered by the *Irish Times*, including (again) Garret Fitzgerald:

> The Minister of Finance who will have to bring in next year's budget looks like facing a multi-billion deficit that will require extremely drastic action in the form of spending cuts and/or tax increases. Listening to the political parties, reading our papers, or viewing television coverage of the election campaign, no one could possibly know that this is what now lies in store for us. This election is taking place in a dream world which is about to become a nightmare. ... For what is abundantly clear is that Charlie McCreevy is in fact the last person who should be let back into the half-wrecked china shop of our public finances (Fitzgerald 2002b).[9]

---

[7] The use of Central Bank excess funds had already been tapped the previous year by Minister McCreevy in what was viewed as an 'emergency' measure to cope with the deteriorating budgetary situation.

[8] For example, Taoiseach Bertie Ahern was dismissive of an ESRI quarterly report published during the campaign which suggested the likelihood of further expenditure overruns in 2002.

[9] It should be noted, however, that Fitzgerald's gloomy forecast proved to be quite wrong as property-based revenues continued to surge by more than expected, leaving the Exchequer in a comfortable position.

Academic economists generally seem to have contributed relatively little to whatever public debate—at least in the print media—was taking place.[10] However, the *Irish Times* posed a series of questions to a number of economists: Dan McLoughlin (Bank of Ireland), Jim O'Leary, (National University of Ireland, Maynooth), Jim Power (Friends First), and Jim Beggs (AIB). Their consensus outlook for the next five years was quite bullish regarding the short-term growth outlook and the options facing the government.

Perhaps most striking were those issues missing from the debate. For example, the reasons for, or the defensibility of, expenditure overruns, possible proposals to improve public sector efficiency, policies regarding public sector pay,[11] or issues of external competitiveness received little or no attention. Nor was taxation policy, including the best approach to take to the already overheated property sector, raised. In general, the topic of property was by and large ignored during the campaign, although issues arising from the recommendations of the various Bacon reports had been earlier debated on an ongoing basis.

The election result was clear cut. Fianna Fáil continued to be the party with the largest number of seats. However, it did not gain an overall majority and thus had to rely on the PDs in order to form a coalition. It was generally believed that voters, while supportive of Fianna Fáil's record in government, wished to place some 'constraints' on potential future excesses by insisting on a coalition government.

Fine Gael suffered a crushing defeat—the worst in its history—and shortly afterwards Michael Noonan was replaced as party leader by Enda Kenny. Personalities may have played a role in explaining Fine Gael's disaster. However, Fine Gael had portrayed its economic policy as the 'most responsible', criticizing what they termed the 'excesses' of the Ahern/McCreevy era. Voters may well have feared that a Fine Gael-led government would bring too abrupt an end to the good times. If this was believed to have been a significant factor in Fine Gael's defeat, was there a (political) lesson to be learned by the party for the next election?

8.1.2 *The 2007 Election*

The 2007 election campaign has been aptly characterized as an 'auction of politicians' promises'. Gone were the complaints about overruns in spending that had been featured to some extent by Fine Gael in the previous election.

---

[10] However, an article by academics Gerry Boyle and Jim O'Leary (2002) discussed some fundamental issues relating to how public spending could be brought under control. An attempt to agree on a panel of independent economists to assess the parties' fiscal policies collapsed.

[11] This may have partly reflected the fact that the report of the first Benchmarking Body was due to be published a month after the election.

The main issue debated was whether the sums underlying the myriad of spending commitments made by all parties 'added up'. As was the case five years earlier, topics such as a possible property bubble, the lending practices of the banks, public sector pay increases or external competitiveness, did not receive a mention.

The four main competing groupings—Fianna Fáil, Fine Gael/Labour (who ran on a joint policy platform), the Green Party, and the PDs—assumed real growth of between 4 and 5 per cent per annum (the small Sinn Féin party did not provide any macroeconomic or budgetary forecasts). A consensus formed around targeting current spending growth at 7–8 per cent per annum. In what was considered a quite reasonable and normal projection, Fianna Fáil and Fine Gael/Labour foresaw the debt to GDP ratio falling to 3 per cent, while the Greens targeted the elimination of debt 'over a 10–15 year period'.

These macroeconomic and budgetary projections were broadly in line with those of all the official institutions at the time of the preparation of the manifestos. Except for some largely unnoticed commentary they were not deemed worthy of broad media debate. Thus, election quarrels essentially were about whether the 'promises' of the different parties manifestos could be met.[12]

Arguments raged over whether undertakings to put more Gardai (policemen) on the streets, increase the number of hospital beds, or provide tax relief in support of the co-location of private and public hospitals, had or had not been properly costed. Commitments were made to increase child benefits, raise pensions, and devote more resources to improving infrastructure. Taxation proposals encompassed lowering the standard and/or higher rate of income tax, raising and/or indexing income tax bands, and reducing or abolishing stamp duty. With the exception of some suggested environmental taxes (mainly by the Green Party), the placing of limits on the benefits from tax breaks or the modification of taxation arrangements linked to pensions, virtually all the expenditure and taxation plans were in an unabashedly expansionary direction. This was doubtless favoured by the 'clientelistic' approach that many observers have used to describe the Irish political system.

Some, albeit muted, questioning of the basic assumptions underlying the major parties' economic plans did surface. In a series of articles, Marc Coleman, Economics Editor of the *Irish Times*, drew attention to the fact that just prior to the start of the formal campaign, a range of official and private forecasts indicated that real growth in 2008 was likely to be 3–4 per cent, less than the 4.5 per cent and 4.2 per cent assumed by Fianna Fáil and Fine Gael/Labour, respectively. A main reason was increasing signs of a weakening

---

[12] A consistent Fianna Fáil theme was that Fine Gael and Labour had spent their planned expenditure 'two or three times over' in the campaign.

in the property market. However, when the possibility of slower growth was put to the parties by Coleman, their responses were evasive, Fine Gael appeared to suggest that in such an eventuality, a somewhat higher budget deficit could be accommodated without any major problem.

The *Irish Times* published an insightful article by Michael Casey, former Chief Economist of the Irish Central Bank (Casey 2007). Casey discussed the likelihood of economic growth slowing to 2 per cent or less in the future, with a consequent significant jump in unemployment (to 6 or 7 per cent). He pointed to underlying adverse factors: the loss in competitiveness, the unsustainable increase in property prices, suboptimal domestic investment caused in part by excessively low interest rates; and vulnerabilities related to over-reliance on foreign direct investment. With considerable foresight, Casey observed that if such a relatively poor economic performance was to materialize, a new government would preside over a 'poisoned chalice' and would 'suffer electoral damage for a very long time to come' He concluded by lamenting the fact that 'few had looked at the deeper parameters behind the headline figures' nor 'thought through the critical issue: Plan B'. No one during the campaign addressed the issues raised by Casey.

In the event, following a leaders' debate which Taoiseach Ahern won decisively, and the party's success in 'parking' ethical issues surrounding the Taoiseach's financial affairs, Fianna Fáil scored a resounding victory. Fine Gael also performed exceptionally well, with a very sizeable increase in the number of seats won. Fianna Fáil returned to government, joined this time by the (depleted) PDs and the Green Party. However, euphoria was short lived. It was not very long before Michael Casey's 'poisoned chalice' began to wreak its deadly effect.

8.2 The Economists

Since the crisis broke, many have asked in a puzzled, in some cases, accusatory, tone: 'where (with a few notable exceptions) were all the economists?' How could such an economic and financial catastrophe not have been foreseen—and warned of—by the 'experts'? Ireland did not suffer from a shortage of economists in academia, the Economic and Social Research Institute (the ESRI), official bodies such as the Central Bank, the Department of Finance, and the National Treasury Management Agency (NTMA), or in private sector circles (among the banks, stockbrokers, real estate companies, and the media). Moreover, outside financial experts, including those of the IMF, the EU, and the OECD, as well as representatives of foreign banks and multinationals engaged in massive lending or direct investment, were far from thin on the ground.

There was some debate among economists at the time as to the appropriate approach to fiscal policy, although none identified the size of the underlying structural budgetary deficit discussed in Chapter 6.[13] However, to date there has been only limited systematic discussion of the more serious failure to foresee the possibility of a broader banking and financial crisis. Some of the explanations are of general applicability and arise partly from Ireland's membership of the euro area, while others appear to relate to incentive structures and institutional features (including 'cultural' aspects) of the professional environment at the time.

Economists undertook relatively little research on Irish macroeconomic/monetary or 'financial' policies in the years leading up to the crisis. To some extent, this seemed perfectly reasonable as, by definition, there was no meaning attached to the concept of 'Irish monetary policy' within a common currency area. Monetary policy analysis perforce would have to be carried out at the aggregate euro area level. That said, arguably some macroeconomic issues could have received more prominence, for instance, the fact that Ireland was experiencing inflation consistently higher than the European average. The logic of a common monetary policy suggested that this would be temporary as prices and costs (adjusted for productivity differences, location aspects, and incomplete factor mobility) would tend to converge across eurozone member states. However, Ireland's experience, both before and after the crash, suggests that this cost and price convergence process is slow and hesitant, and would thus have merited greater investigation.

Another topic worthy of greater attention might have been the growing current account deficits of the balance of payments experienced by Ireland in the years prior to 2008, which partly reflected the declining export performance. On the other hand, it was believed by many at the time that the balance of payments of an individual member of a currency union is not very relevant, as only the aggregate external payments deficit or surplus of all the members affects the common exchange rate.[14]

However, the most important shortcoming in the work of Irish economists (other than of a small number in the Central Bank), was the neglect of what has come to be called 'macro-prudential' issues. These refer to the implications of lending and funding decisions by banks or other financial institutions for the stability of the financial system and the overall health of the economy. Chapter 2 discussed the ideological reasons that help explain the general lack of emphasis on the topic worldwide, a tendency reflected in turn in the

---

[13] See, for example, Lane (2003).

[14] See Fitzgerald (2011) for a discussion of this issue. The topic had been raised in the ESRI's Quarterly Economic Commentary of Winter 2006 and was subsequently taken up in the *Irish Times* article by Barrett (2006).

priorities of the Irish economist community. Ever since traditional Keynesian 'fine tuning' had become discredited, the importance of macroeconomics as a discipline had been downplayed. Monetary policy was assigned to an independent central bank charged with implementing a fairly straightforward set of rules. In parallel, adherents of New Classical Economics and the Efficient Markets Hypothesis saw little role for investigating the inner workings of the financial system since, ultimately, markets could be largely trusted to self-regulate.

These intellectual strands of thinking were fairly pervasive in Ireland, as elsewhere, and were reflected in the research priorities in **academia** where macroeconomics in general and financial stability issues in particular received progressively less attention. Moreover, academic economists would have had little or no opportunity to access and use data on individual financial institutions. On the other hand, there had been a significant increase in the quantum of microeconomic data for Ireland pertaining to a wide range of topics, while comparative aggregate macroeconomic data across EU countries had become more available. From a practical perspective, this affected the research priorities of economists.

There were additional contributing elements present within the **Central Bank.** As described in Chapter 5, the results of aggregate stress testing of banks were presented in the Bank's Financial Stability Reports (FSRs). However, for a number of reasons, the great majority of the Bank's economist resources were devoted to topics other than macro-prudential issues. Firstly, as in academia and research institutes such as the ESRI, career advancement was determined largely by publications in professional journals, particularly those of international repute. Such journals would not have been particularly interested in research pertaining only to a small, (presumed) non-systemically important corner of the wider euro area. Secondly, since financial stability issues were likely to prove sensitive, there was a clear risk that research related to this topic might be 'censored' or even withheld from publication altogether—as indeed occurred. Thus, in order to maximize publication potential, the Central Bank research community had a strong incentive to devote their energies elsewhere.[15] Finally, even if Bank economists had wanted to explore financial stability issues, they were hampered by the lack of easy access to the Financial Regulator's data for individual financial institutions and confidentiality restrictions preventing their use for publication.

The **ESRI** had published very extensively on the broad macroeconomic impact of developments in the housing market—see Fitzgerald (2011).

---

[15] Agreement had been reached at European Central Bank (ECB) level that national central banks would specialize in different research areas. In Ireland's case it was decided that this would be the topic of productivity.

However, its research agenda did not encompass macro-financial issues. One reason was the absence of expertise in this area from late in the decade of the nineties, following a move by the (current) Governor of the Central Bank, Patrick Honohan, from the ESRI to an academic post in Trinity College, Dublin. This gap is strikingly illustrated by the extensive (almost 200 pages) detailed report on Medium Term Economic Perspectives (2008–2015) (Fitzgerald et al. 2008) published in June 2008, just a few months before the crisis began. The Report does not contain any references to the financial system or to banking topics.[16]

The ESRI's Quarterly Economic Commentary (QEC) assessed recent macro-developments and the short-term (including one- to two-year ahead) economic and financial prospects. The QEC was prepared independently by a small team of ESRI economists. Given its mandate, the QEC could not have been expected to delve deeply into macro-prudential issues. However, as significant banking problems began to emerge around 2008, QECs could have drawn greater attention to the potential for sizeable associated fiscal costs (for example, by describing experiences in other countries that had faced similar problems). Prior to publication, the draft QEC was shown to the Department of Finance. It is quite possible that the Department would have expressed concerns to the ESRI, lest any statements or views expressed in the QEC cast doubt on the sanguine official assessment of the Department at the time.[17] It is a matter for conjecture as to how the ESRI might have reacted to any such interventions.

The **Department of Finance** had about thirty qualified economists on its staff at the time of the crash although, as discussed in Chapter 6, the macro-economic analysis they undertook was limited in scope and devoted largely to preparing the aggregate forecasts underpinning the budget. The Department had no specific mandate or expertise to delve into macro-prudential issues. Indeed, any such move likely would have been resisted by the Financial Regulator and the Central Bank whose sole prerogative this was at the time. Only in 2009, was a decision taken to recruit banking expertise within the Department.

---

[16] It should be pointed out, however, that owing to the complex and extensive nature of the report, much of the work underpinning the report needed to be completed several months prior to publication. This shortcoming was recognized explicitly by Fitzgerald himself (2011: 9) 'the wider economics community, and myself in particular, did not devote adequate attention to the topic of financial stability in the years preceding the crash. Of course, these comments also apply to the economics profession in many other countries.'

[17] Although the ESRI is an independent body, unlike the situation in many other state bodies, the Secretary General of the Department of Finance is an *ex officio* member of the ESRI Council which oversees its operations. As in the case of the Board of the Central Bank (see Chapter 5), formally, the Secretary General is a member of the Council on a personal basis.

A significant number of individual economists were employed in the **Irish private financial sector** throughout this period. Usually representatives of banks, other financial institutions, or property firms, many became quite well-known media personalities. Their views featured prominently in public discussions on short-term prospects for economic growth and the outlook for the property and stock markets. The media tended to pay considerable attention to the forecasts for property prices of economists from the banks or mortgage institutions or real estate agents. This group sometimes cited their own (proprietary) models as a source for their predictions and, almost without exception, remained bullish until very close to the end. Even when the plummeting of bank shares (or stock prices more broadly) could not be denied, share prices were generally expected to level out and recover 'soon'. Opinions on property prices were usually couched in terms of how much the rate of growth might slow, rarely that prices could conceivably fall significantly, let alone collapse entirely. Their misplaced sense of confidence was hardly surprising. Although many involved may have put their best abilities to work, this group by and large had everything to gain—including in a personal financial sense—by acting as cheerleaders 'talking up' the market.

Apart from incentive aspects, a structural element, namely, a distinct compartmentalization of tasks, affected official or semi-official entities. Thus, the Central Bank was the only institution dealing, in principle, with macro-financial stability matters. However, only a small number of Bank staff were concerned with Financial Stability Reports (FSRs), and the other economists at the Bank pursued their differing research and analytical activities diligently, but with relatively little interaction. In turn, the ESRI's macroeconomic work dealt largely with the real economy and did not analyse linkages between the real and financial sectors. As noted already, the Department of Finance's involvement in macroeconomic matters was mainly in support of budget preparation.

This 'division of labour' may have been due to a desire to avoid duplication of effort among institutions, despite the fact that broadly speaking, budgetary constraints had never been looser than during the boom period. The 'economizing on economists' may also have reflected a sense that the contribution of this group (especially on macroeconomic matters) was no longer that important, now that only fair weather lay ahead. Indeed, as seen below, those few economists who did raise questions were denounced as 'cribbers' and harbingers of 'gloom and doom'. The 'silo tendencies' within and across institutions did not encourage cross-fertilization of ideas or questioning of easily accepted beliefs. Some overlap of responsibilities among different entities would have helped avoid the emergence of the 'consensus approach' that was, as the Nyberg report observed, a recurring feature underlying the Irish policy failure. It appears that over time, the extent of interchanges between these institutions (as well as between them and academics) tended to diminish. However, greater interaction on analytic work (including, for instance, joint research) would not have compromised the role of each institution in drawing its own policy conclusions.

The prevailing consensus was shared (explicitly or implicitly) by many, but not all. Concerns were raised by a small number of dissenting economists. Morgan Kelly, a Professor of Economics at University College Dublin, was by far the most 'contrarian' of this group. He was drawn to analysing the Irish property boom almost out of curiosity, after examining data on house price cycles for all OECD countries since 1970. Kelly first published his findings in a celebrated newspaper article in the *Irish Times* (Kelly 2006) in December 2006 which attracted widespread public attention as well as considerable criticism—see section 8.3. At the initiative of the ESRI, the paper containing his detailed analysis was published subsequently as a 'special article' in the ESRI QEC (Kelly 2007).

Kelly's econometric analysis led to a striking and simple (or so it seemed) conclusion, namely, that the size of the initial property boom was a strong predictor of the size and duration of the subsequent bust. According to what he described as a remarkably robust relationship, during a crash real house prices typically lose 70 per cent of what they had gained beforehand. Assuming Ireland was to experience the same housing dynamics as every other OECD economy except Spain in the early 1990s, the predicted fall in real prices would be 40–60 per cent, over a period of eight to nine years.

Kelly's article cast ice cold water on the widely accepted belief at the time that the house price boom merely reflected strong 'fundamentals', such as rising income and increased household formation, declining household size, rising employment, and immigration. He pointed out that were this a valid argument, one would have expected to observe an associated rise in rents. However, rents had stagnated relative to income since 2000. This fact, together with the large number of recently built housing units lying empty, led him to conclude that the Irish housing market 'had left the dull world of fundamentals far behind it'. Kelly speculated on the macroeconomic implications of such a house price fall, in particular for economic growth and employment, and foresaw 'considerable economic dislocation.' Although he did not consider the impact on the commercial and development segment of the market—let alone the disastrous consequences for the budget and the banks—his contribution on this particular topic was remarkably prescient.[18]

Kelly's conclusions were widely derided by many commentators and were not taken seriously by the senior levels of the Central Bank which devoted just

[18] While Kelly certainly identified before others a looming property crash, several of his subsequent 'gloom and doom' predictions, referring to the 'vaporization' of the Irish economy, a 'run on Irish banks' and 'mass mortgage default' have proven, so far, unfounded.

a few dismissive lines to his work in its 2007 Financial Stability Report. But as the collapse unfolded and his earlier predictions started to come all too true, Kelly began to acquire a 'guru'-like reputation, as the one person in Ireland who had experienced much public opprobrium by daring to suggest that 'the emperor might have no clothes'.

Alan Ahearne was also a contrarian voice, although not to quite the same extent as Kelly. Ahearne, a graduate of the University of Limerick and Carnegie Mellon University in Pittsburgh, worked as an economist with the US Federal Reserve System from 1998 to 2005, before returning to an academic position with the National University of Ireland (Galway) in 2005. Between July 2007 and February 2009, he contributed a weekly column to the *Sunday Independent*, mainly discussing property and property-related topics. In March 2009, Ahearne was appointed as special Advisor to then Minister of Finance Brian Lenihan where he served until the change of government in early 2011.

At a time when most commentators were downplaying any concerns, Ahearne's assessments, similar to those of Kelly, reflected a healthy realism as to the likely extent and duration of a possible property downturn. Drawing on his own research published by the US Federal Reserve, in mid-2007 he took issue with the rosy predictions for continued price increases made by most Irish real estate firms. He argued that the interest rate hikes that had started in late 2005 would lead to a significant drop in values from early 2007 onwards. Ahearne drew attention to the results of a US Federal Reserve study of forty-four house price booms and busts in industrial countries since 1970 which showed that in real, that is, inflation adjusted terms, house prices typically declined for almost five years after a peak. He also observed that the size of Ireland's housing boom had dwarfed each of the other forty-four cases studied.

Ahearne's writings emphasized several interrelated themes. He criticized widespread calls to lower stamp duties as interfering artificially in the natural process of allowing a vastly overheated market to adjust and representing a shift of losses from developers to taxpayers. Similarly to Kelly, he stressed the sharp decline in housing rents and hence in yields which mirrored a worldwide trend. Unless 'mysterious factors' were at play, this was further *prima facie* evidence of excessively high property values. Ahearne foresaw that many Irish buy-to-let 'amateur' investors who had bid up house prices to 'ludicrous' levels would 'drop like flies'.

After examining underlying demand factors, Ahearne rejected the optimistic projections for the numbers of likely housing starts. He stressed the risks associated with increased use of 100 per cent and/or 35-year mortgages and cited the Scandinavian property bust, where banks had relied too heavily on collateral rather than underlying project viability. Finally, he warned against Irish investors' continued purchases of foreign properties, citing his own research—Ahearne et al. (2005)—that showed significant positive correlation (in Ireland and abroad) between different segments of the property markets in downturns across countries.

Ahearne reserved his strongest criticism for, as he put it, the 'guff' heard from many commentators and vested interests who were continuing (largely in vain) to try to 'talk up' the property market. These included estate agents who were not publishing accurate figures on the true prices achieved in private sales, as well as stockbrokers and lending institutions. He concluded that much of the advice of so-called 'economic experts', who regularly featured in the media, was 'at odds with basic economic reasoning and evidence' and that, in short, their views were 'nothing but dangerous nonsense'.

In retrospect, as with Morgan Kelly, Ahearne turned out to have been a 'prophet before his time'. However, even his clear cut and logical analysis did not go so far as to conceive of the extent of the property disaster or the impact on the banking system.[19] Ahearne's assessments were not welcomed by many vested interests (the Central Bank's FSRs made no reference to the studies he cited). Ahearne himself doubted that 'pessimistic' media commentary was playing much of a role in depressing the market. As he put it, using a sporting analogy, many observers had expressed pessimism about the Irish team's prospects prior to the Rugby World Cup. Did these gloomy pundits talk down the Irish team into putting in a somewhat indifferent performance? In Ahearne's words, 'of course not'.[20]

Finally, both Kelly and Ahearne's writings, largely speaking, dealt only with the property market and the implications for the real sector. Patrick Honohan (2006) was the first to consider the issue of the major reliance by Irish banks on wholesale funding from abroad. His analysis, also prescient, raised the spectre that a cut off in such funding—for whatever reason—could have major consequences for the stability of the Irish banking system.

8.3 The Media

The role of the media has received relatively little attention in the outpouring of public commentary debate as to the myriad causes of Ireland's crisis.[21] Although by no means the main institution responsible, it nonetheless

---

[19] Nor did he, of course, foresee the Lehman Brothers collapse and hence the timing of a possible Irish crisis.

[20] In one column, Ahearne welcomed an earlier RTE Prime Time special presented by George Lee that had gone some distance to explore the possible serious consequences of a property crash. The programme was criticized heavily. But, as Ahearne remarked, 'it makes as much sense to blame George Lee, known as a less than sanguine pundit, for housing misfortunes as to blame George Hook [a leading critic of the Irish rugby team] for our rugby misfortunes'.

[21] An exception is the thoughtful overview of some issues by Whelan (2012).

exercised an important influence by the choice of events deemed to be news-worthy and by helping define the agenda of public debate. The days when media content simply reflected a record of contemporaneous happenings had long passed.

That said, the media naturally took their cue to some extent from the broader economic and financial environment of the time. The population at large was heavily caught up in the property boom and the associated soaring personal (albeit largely paper) wealth. Many newspapers and television and radio programmes were an outgrowth of an apparently insatiable interest in a subject that seemed to be daily on almost everyone's mind. Also, the media, in particular, the newspapers, were deriving very large amounts of revenues from property advertising. Moreover, many working in media were enjoying the financial fruits of the Celtic Tiger and, no more than anyone else, might have resisted, consciously or unconsciously, 'blowing the whistle'.

Two broad questions seem relevant. Firstly, to what extent did commercial or financial pressures influence—directly or indirectly—the substance or 'tone' of editorial content? Secondly, did the media pursue uncomfortable topics that ran against the grain of prevailing public and political opinions sufficiently actively? Comprehensive answers to these questions would require a separate in-depth study. However, discussions between the authors and some prominent figures in the print and television media may provide some, albeit selective, insight as to the climate of the times.[22] It is apparent that the topic remains quite sensitive personally for some who were involved.

Among the print media, the *Irish Times* was the flagship title, so far as coverage of property matters was concerned. Its weekly property supplement was the most prestigious and contributed a great deal of revenue to the newspaper's overall finances. The supplement, which included much adver-tising of foreign properties and of weekend 'property fairs' aimed at luring eager Irish buyers to part with their funds abroad, began to resemble a tele-phone directory in size—see Chapter 4. The content of the supplement (i.e., the write ups by the *Irish Times* staff of the various properties for sale) was subject, in principle, to the newspaper's overall editorial control. However, in practice, it was difficult to enforce quality standards so as to avoid embellished or exaggerated descriptions. It was also necessary to ensure (on occasion not without difficulty) that journalists whose own properties or those of their relatives (known collectively as 'Irish Times houses') were described only if accompanied by full disclosure of the personal interest involved.

---

[22] No attempt has been made to analyse the content of the very many radio programmes and talk shows that dealt daily with a wide variety of economic and financial topics.

The purchase by the *Irish Times* in mid-2006 for reportedly €50 million of the property website myhome.ie also created complications,[23] including the appearance, if not necessarily the reality, of a conflict of interest. It proved difficult at times to maintain an appropriate 'fire wall' between the commercial and editorial interests of the newspaper. As myhome.ie 'crashed and burnt' in the wake of the bursting of the property bubble, the proposal was made (but not approved) that the operation of the website move closer to the editorial wing of the newspaper in order to save on expenses.

However, the *Irish Times* did seek to maintain overall a strong independent stance as regards editorial matters. It did not hesitate to publish the path-breaking, highly controversial article by Morgan Kelly referred to in section 8.2. There was no attempt to 'tone down' the article to take account of any sensitivities. After the article appeared, many aggrieved bodies, presumably reflecting commercial and property interests, made their unhappiness known to the newspaper. In a farewell speech on her retirement in 24 June 2011, the then Editor, Geraldine Kennedy, noted that she had been 'severely criticized for damaging the national interest of the State and the commercial interests of [the] newspaper'.[24] Such criticisms had been rejected by Kennedy, who was aware of Kelly's senior academic status in University College Dublin and that he represented an alternative to the prevailing orthodoxy among economists regarding a likely 'soft landing'. Kennedy emphasized that it was the paper's policy to present a wide range of arguments and views. Indeed, the *Irish Times* subsequently published several more articles by Kelly dealing with similar controversial topics.

The *Sunday Independent* (the paper with the largest weekend circulation) had a somewhat mixed record with its coverage of property-related issues. It led the charge to denounce controversial RTE documentaries of George Lee and Richard Curran. However, the business editor, then Senator, Shane Ross, successfully resisted two specific attempts to interfere with the editorial content of the business section. First, the regular commentaries by Alan Ahearne, described in section 8.2, elicited strong criticism from various property and related interest groups (undoubtedly linked to advertisers), including urgings that the paper cease to carry his contributions. These were conveyed to Ross but ignored by him. Ahearne's regular columns continued appearing until his appointment as advisor to Minister of Finance Lenihan in early 2009. The second controversy arose from an extended campaign by Ross denouncing the practices of the Irish Auctioneers and Valuers Institute (IAVI), in particular, their use of highly misleading 'guide prices' in property sales. Ross, although he was attacked repeatedly by IAVI representatives (who also made

[23] The *Irish Times*, 27 July 2006.
[24] The *Irish Times*, 24 June 2011.

threatening noises concerning a possible withdrawal of advertising), stood his ground.

These examples suggest that commercial pressures could be, and were, successfully withstood. However, the two newspapers in question were highly profitable at the time (in the case of the *Sunday Independent* for broader reasons than property advertising revenue). Some observers have suggested that other elements of the print media that were not in such a strong financial position (including local titles) may have been more vulnerable to interference.

A somewhat different picture seems to emerge in the case of the national television station, RTE. There is a sense that RTE did not shrink from controversy in its reporting and interviews, providing that different perspectives on a sensitive issue were represented. Thus care was taken that, documentaries, which tended to reflect the overall views of the presenter, were sufficiently balanced.

RTE broadcast several documentaries in the middle of the decade which generated major controversy. RTE's Economics Editor George Lee (well known for his sceptical and relentless questioning of politicians on economic issues) concluded in *Boom* (June 2006), that by then 'the Celtic Tiger was dead'. Lee outlined the fall in foreign investment, eroding competitiveness, soaring household debt financed from abroad, and, above all, the enormous dependence of the economy on the artificial and unsustainable property boom. A second documentary by Lee in March 2009, *How We Blew the Boom*, traced the effects of the property implosion on growth and unemployment and the catastrophic impact on the budget. The only element that Lee did not foresee in these two documentaries was the serious threat to the solvency of the banks. He commented later:

> I did not experience any editorial pressures within RTE during the making of these two programmes. RTE was naturally anxious to ensure an appropriate 'balance' in their tone and content—they knew that especially the 2009 programme was likely to provoke strong public reactions. I think that by that time, people had become seriously frightened at the prospect of what a crash might mean for them personally. However, RTE (perhaps more than in the case of the print media generally) had a culture which prided itself on being resistant to political pressures. The Director General of RTE told me at one stage he was well aware of such pressures, but had dismissed them. I recall receiving a phone call from a person in the Department of Finance following a broadcast in 2008, intimating that such 'negative' programming could impact on RTE's ability to secure an increase in the television and radio license fee. Taoiseach Bertie Ahern had made his infamous 'suicide' remark the previous July which, many believed, was aimed at people such as Morgan Kelly and myself.[25]

[25] Interview with the authors, August 2012.

Another highly controversial RTE programme, *Property Crash*, presented by Richard Curran, Deputy Editor of the *Sunday Business Post*, was broadcast in April 2007. Six months earlier, in an RTE Prime Time interview, Curran had taken strong issue with the popular assumption of a 'soft landing' for the property market, exemplified by the confident predictions of economists such as Austin Hughes of KBC Bank in Dublin and Dan McLaughlin, the chief economist of the Bank of Ireland, who forecast a house price rise of 3 per cent for 2007. Curran later recalled what was an unprecedented experience for him:

The morning after the *Property Crash* programme broadcast, I met an elderly gentleman outside my house who congratulated me for saying what had to be said. But I was collectively annihilated by a torrent of criticism from most of the media, the estate agents, the IAVI and the Construction Industry Federation. One well known estate agent (Ken McDonald of Hooke and McDonald), after seeing the advance promos for the broadcast, emailed and phoned me to convey his outrage at what he called a "property horror show", before actually having viewed the programme! In fairness, the banks stayed silent and the *Irish Times* adopted a fairly neutral posture. But I kept hearing back some of the things being said about me around Dublin by prominent estate agents, property consultants and others. The most vitriolic criticism came from estate agents who I had high-lighted in the programme as having sold their businesses at the height of the boom in the summer of 2006 and I had asked what that might have meant. But politicians, including Bertie Ahern, joined in denouncing the broadcast as 'irresponsible' or worse. A number of private sector economists had pulled out of the programme on the morning they were due to be interviewed as rumours spread in banking circles that I was making a programme about a crash, as opposed to simply one about the property market. One person I knew accused me personally of having wrecked the attempted sale of her own property.

I sensed that people who had a greater awareness of what had happened in Ireland during the eighties and earlier, or who had emigrated to London back then, reacted more positively. I received a good deal of personal encouragement from RTE staff who tended to be somewhat older and more questioning of business and political agendas than those in the print media. However, younger people were more upset, perhaps because they had so much to lose financially, were the bubble to burst. In any event, there was little or no support from the newspapers, except for a few individual commentators. I have no doubt that advertising pressures played a role in the almost hysterical reaction. I did not participate in the controversies following the broadcast. In the end, so as to avoid complicating matters further, I decided that I would no longer write on property-related issues for the *Sunday Business Post* for some time.

Looking back on this rather extraordinary episode, I suppose it was a net gain for me professionally since, as time went on, my name came to be associated with that particular programme more than with anything else I did. On a personal level, I learned a lot about group think and the lies people tell themselves and to others.

I remember Sean, the man who ran our local post office, telling me at one stage in the middle of the fall out from the programme, to 'stick to my guns'. I casually said to him that sometimes people didn't like to hear that there might not be a happy ending. He replied 'No—what really annoys people is when you tell them something that deep down they know is true...'[26]

These RTE programmes and the willingness of the *Irish Times* and the *Sunday Independent* to publish unpopular views are important instances of the unbiased role of some of the media. But should they and others have gone further and probed difficult issues more aggressively and insistently?

Many younger newspaper journalists tended to focus on 'business stories' describing the latest Irish financial successes, especially those associated with property. Whelan (2012) observed that 'the question "where is all this money coming from?" was not put with sufficient consistency, nor was there sufficient tenacity in seeking an answer to this question'. Perhaps it was assumed that foreigners could not be engaged in foolish lending activities to Ireland.

The economist and journalist, David McWilliams, however, represented a major contrarian view from the earlier part of the decade, especially with respect to stressing the dangers of a property boom. Author of several best-selling books and a frequent participant in media events, he was also a prolific writer, including as a regular columnist for the *Sunday Business Post*. Cliff Taylor, Editor of the *Sunday Business Post* from 2000 onwards later remarked:

> No one was 'banging on doors' to try to influence our editorial content. One of our prominent columnists—David McWilliams—had clearly identified the issues. I remember one particular piece where he looked at the rental yield on properties and forecast how much their prices were overvalued—the figures were so striking that I rang him to make sure they were right.
>
> In general, we certainly missed out on the scale of the crisis that was going to hit. Media organizations made money from the boom for sure—particularly from advertising—but I don't think that was the primary reason. It was more a failure to anticipate the extent of the risks—in fairness very few did, even among expert economists. While the media picked up some of the threads of the problems, very few—with the exception of McWilliams or Richard Curran's TV programme—actually came close to tying it all together.[27]

Brendan Keenan, Economics Editor of the *Irish Independent*, has voiced similar sentiments:

> I would reject the charge that the print media 'puffed up' the property bubble. There was no shortage of warnings of danger and, generally speaking, we would have been pretty resistant to any attempts to interfere with our content. But we

---

[26] Interview with the authors, July 2012.
[27] Interview with the authors, July 2012.

could plead guilty to the accusation of not having done enough to investigate what was going on. Looking back, one problem, from my own perspective, was that the views of, say, a Morgan Kelly, George Lee, or a David McWilliams, were considered very much those of 'eccentric outliers' at the time and were directly contrary to the assessments of others such as the ESRI, the Central Bank, the OECD and so on. There simply wasn't a story one could settle on to report. Again, we are primarily journalists, not economists. Also, the subject of the banks was traditionally considered rather boring and we didn't have enough expertise or experience to probe sufficiently into what might be really happening.[28]

There were several experienced economists among the print media such as the late Paul Tansey, Economics Editor of the *Irish Times* for a period and who wrote frequently about competitiveness concerns and the shift in composition of output from exports to construction. However, despite indications that some were encouraged to do so, they did not dig deeper to try to assess what lay beneath the banks' activities. This would probably have required significant investment in acquiring the expertise necessary to explore the issues properly. Also, as with so many other groups in Irish society at the time, concerns at being cast publicly in the villain's role of a Morgan Kelly or Richard Curran might have played some part, if only subconsciously.

8.4 Conclusions

Most analysis of the 'home grown' causes of Ireland's economic and financial collapse has focused on the reckless behaviour of the banks and developers, the ineffectiveness of the Central Bank and the Financial Regulator, and the irresponsible fiscal policies of the Fianna Fáil-led governments. However, this paints too limited a canvas. Politicians across the spectrum influence the agenda for debate on economic and financial matters. Professional economists can bring their expertise to bear in highlighting what may appear to be complex, but important, policy issues. Finally, the media have a significant role in actively questioning received wisdom. This chapter has considered the impact of each of these groups in helping to shape public opinion in the years prior to the crash. This is important for a fuller understanding of why, as Nyberg (2011: 95) put it, a collective 'mania' took hold.

Politicians both influence and reflect the thinking of the day. Elected governments can execute their mandate effectively, only if their policies are endorsed explicitly or implicitly by large sections of the population (as was largely the case in Ireland until 2007–08). The record of the two general

---

[28] Interview with the authors, July 2012.

election campaigns confirms that the government's expansionary budgetary policies received overwhelming approval. The main opposition party, Fine Gael, had raised some concerns regarding overruns in government spending in 2002 but suffered its worst electoral defeat ever. By the time of the 2007 campaign, any articulation by Fine Gael of such concerns had been decisively cast aside.

All parties sought to out compete each other in the 2007 election with promises to continue to lower taxation and boost expenditure. The only issue was which party's sums seemed to most credibly add up. Neither in 2002 or 2007 did topics such as the sustainability of the property boom, the state of the banking system, or the effects of public and private sector pay increases on competitiveness, merit mention. Although (especially in 2007) some solitary voices queried the assumptions underlying the parties' plans, these were drowned in a sea of political and popular good feeling and group think.

The economics profession, with a small number of notable exceptions, also failed to question the consensus. Although some attention was paid within the Central Bank to analysing the property market, macro-prudential issues were given limited attention, apart from the work of a small number of Bank economists. This prioritization, generally shared by academic economists, reflected a worldwide intellectual disinterest in the nuts and bolts of financial markets. The view was also held that it made little professional sense to devote time to macroeconomic/monetary policy issues, given Ireland's membership of the euro area.

There were also some Ireland-specific factors at work. Because of perceived sensitivities, many Central Bank economists choose to stay away from research on financial stability issues that might not be publishable, quite apart from confidentiality restrictions relating to the use of financial data. In addition, something of a 'silo' mentality prevailed. Key institutions such as the Central Bank, the ESRI, and the Department of Finance, tended to work separately in their respective areas with little overlap. This militated against cross-fertilization of ideas and healthy intellectual competition and questioning of received wisdom.

The role of the media appears to have been mixed as between the print and broadcast media and within the newspaper industry itself. Advertising and commercial pressures were constant throughout, but manifested themselves in different ways. In the case of the *Irish Times*, while these did cause complications, broad editorial independence appears to have been maintained. The *Sunday Independent*, although an early cheerleader of the property excesses, also resisted some specific pressures. However, smaller titles and/or those in a weaker financial position, may have been more vulnerable.

RTE, the national radio and television station, does not appear to have been exposed to commercial pressures, although political complaints about certain broadcasts could have had some subconscious impact. Nevertheless, RTE placed no restrictions on a number of highly controversial programmes dealing with the deteriorating state of the economy and the strong possibility of a collapse in the property bubble. The presenters of these programmes, George Lee and Richard Curran, regrettably, were subject to sustained attacks from a wide range of the media, public, and politicians.

Although some in the media did raise their 'head above the parapet', the general public atmosphere, especially as the bubble was about to burst in 2006–07 and many stood to lose a great deal, had a chilling effect. In common with most of Irish society at the time, a readiness to accept group think and avoid confronting unpleasant realities by and large dominated. But as the next chapter describes, from mid-2007 onwards as the situation started to unravel, the emerging crisis started to slowly permeate the public consciousness.

References

Ahearne, Alan et al. (2005) 'Monetary Policy and House Prices: A Cross-Country Study', *International Finance Discussion Papers* 841, Washington D.C., Board of Governors of the Federal Reserve System.

Barrett, Alan (2006) 'Price of Increase in the Deficit Not Clear', *Irish Times,* 21 December.

Boyle, Gerry and Jim O'Leary (2002) 'System to Control Spending Needed', *Irish Times*, 9 May.

Casey, Michael (2007) 'Inevitable Recession Awaits Poll Winners', *Irish Times*, 14 May.

Fitzgerald, Garret (2002a),'Giant Financial Headache is in Store for Next Government', *Irish Times*, 27 April.

Fitzgerald, Garret (2002b) 'We Need a Tough Minister of Finance to Sort Out Our Financial Mess', *Irish Times*, 11 May.

Fitzgerald John, et al, (2008) *Medium Term Economic Review, 2008–2015*, Economic and Social Research Institute, Dublin.

Fitzgerald, John (2011) 'The Irish Economy Today: Albatross or Phoenix', Economic and Social Research Institute, Working Paper no 384.

Honohan, Patrick (2006) 'To What Extent Has Foreign Finance Been a Driver of Ireland's Economic Success?', *ESRI Quarterly Economic Commentary*, December, pp. 59–72 (Dublin).

Kelly, Morgan (2006) 'How the Housing Corner Stones of Our Economy Could Go Into a Rapid Freefall' *Irish Times*, 28 December.

Kelly, Morgan (2007) 'On the Likely Extent of Falls in Irish House Prices', *ESRI Quarterly Economic Commentary*, Summer, pp. 42–54 (Dublin).

Lane, Philip (2003) 'Assessing Ireland's Strategy: Recent Experience and Future Plans', Budget Perspectives, *Economic and Social Research Institute*.

Nyberg, Peter (2011) *Misjudging Risk: Causes of the Systemic Banking Crisis in Ireland*: Report of the Commission of Investigation into the Banking Sector in Ireland, Government Publications, Dublin, March 2011.

Whelan, Sean (2012) 'Catastrophe: Irish Media and the Financial Crisis', Presentation to a University of Limerick Workshop, 28 March.

Part III
The Crash

9

The Storm Clouds Gather

You only find out who's swimming naked when the tide goes out

Financier Warren Buffet, 2001[1]

Everyone failed to appreciate...our sophisticated, hypermodern, highly
hedged, derivatives-based financial system—how ultimately fragile it really
was

Federal Reserve Chairman Ben Bernanke, 2012[2]

From 2005–06 onwards, although unrecognized (with a few exceptions) by
hardly anyone at the time, the Irish economy was beginning its final lurch
towards disaster. The property boom, fuelled by massive bank lending largely
funded from abroad, gathered steam for a last throw of the dice before peaking
at end-2006/early 2007. The Financial Regulator was able to enjoy the laud-
atory observations of the IMF's 2006 Financial Assessment report. The Central
Bank's Financial Stability Report issued in mid-2007, strengthened the general
conviction that a soft landing was in store for the property market and that, in
any case, the banks were in a strong position to weather any possible shocks.
On the fiscal front, all seemed well. Both the 2006 and 2007 budgets registered
surpluses of 2.9 per cent and 0.1 per cent of GDP, respectively, the debt to GDP
ratio had fallen to below 25 per cent, around that of Luxembourg, and the
Irish authorities continued to receive congratulations for their commitment to
sound fiscal policies.

Despite the apparent calm on the surface, storm clouds had started to
appear on the horizon. From 2007 onwards, the US housing market
commenced a downward spiral. In parallel, the nature and extent of the US
sub-prime mortgage problem—and its potential for spillover into the broader

---

[1] Buffett (2001). The material is copyrighted and used with permission of the author.
[2] Lowenstein (2012: 54).

domestic and worldwide financial system—had begun to emerge more clearly. Financial markets were beginning to show signs of serious jitters and their appetite for maintaining exposures, particularly where property-related lending was an issue, was called increasingly into question.

The Irish authorities had started to become aware of the deteriorating external environment and the impact that this could have on Ireland's small open economy. However, they were very far from realizing the extent to which the banking sector, as well as the budget, were vulnerable. Nevertheless, following the collapse of UK Northern Rock in August 2007 and the intensification of the US sub-prime problem, from early 2008 they started to consider how best to cope with any difficulties that might emerge.

During September 2008 the accelerating drop in international market confidence was reflected in government intervention in a number of troubled European institutions. This turbulence quickly washed over Irish shores. By the end of that month, an unprecedented crisis involving the possible imminent collapse of the Irish banking system was looming, culminating in the granting of the comprehensive state guarantee in respect of the financial liabilities of all six domestic banks.

The decision by the government to provide this guarantee arguably has proved to be the single most controversial action in Ireland's short economic and financial history. Despite receiving widespread domestic support at the time, for many, partly with the benefit of hindsight, it has come to represent the source of much of the enormous financial difficulties the country has faced in the years since.

The next chapter considers in detail the guarantee decision itself and, especially, whether better alternatives were available to the government at the time. However, in order to assess that decision in a reasoned and balanced fashion, it is essential to examine carefully the background. This chapter throws light on the official thinking and preparations as the international and (increasingly) domestic environment began to unravel in the 12 months after the collapse of UK Northern Rock in mid-2007.

This chapter first discusses the guiding principles adopted at an early stage by Irish officials and which are crucial to understanding the approach eventually taken. The preparations from mid-2007 onwards by staff within the concerned official institutions are then assessed. The 'warning signals' raised by the episode of the placement of National Treasury Management Agency (NTMA) deposits with Anglo Irish Bank (Anglo) in 2007 are worthy of special attention. Finally, the international and domestic developments that played a key role throughout 2008, especially in the months and weeks leading up to end-September, are described.

9.1 Guiding Principles

In early 2007, when the tectonic plates in the international financial environment started to shift, the inherent weaknesses of the Irish banking system and the perilous underlying state of the budgetary finances had not been perceived by the government or Irish officials. In the US, there were increasing intimations of emerging difficulties in its financial system. The growth of sub-prime mortgages had spawned a wide range of financial derivatives, in the form of securitized loans, called Collateralized Debt Obligations (CDOs), and Credit Default Swaps (CDSs—see Chapter 3). In February, New Century Financial Corporation, a major sub-prime mortgage broker in the US, was forced to file for bankruptcy. On 6 July 2007, Bear Stearns, one of Wall Street's most prestigious investment banks, suspended redemptions for its so-called 'High-Grade Structured Credit Strategies Enhanced Leverage Fund'.

On 7 August 2007, the international linkages between the US sub-prime market and allied derivative markets first appeared when the French bank, BNP Paribas, was obliged to suspend the redemption of shares in three money-market funds. It soon became evident that the French bank's involvement in sub-prime lending was part of a broader pattern of systemic links between the US financial system and its international counterparts. Barely a month later, the British financial system experienced its first banking run since the 19th century, when crowds queued outside the offices of Northern Rock (including in Dublin) to withdraw their deposits. The sight of such queues in a country priding itself on the calibre of its financial institutions suggested that depositors were starting to lose that vital ingredient central to all financial transactions, namely, confidence.

The collapse of Northern Rock sounded the first alarm bells closer to home that a difficult road could lie ahead for Ireland. During the following twelve months, anticipating that the increasing international turbulence might spill over domestically, the Irish authorities took some, albeit halting, preventative steps. The degree of awareness of the pending danger varied between and, to some extent, within key institutions. However, thinking—and hence preparations for possible difficulties—was guided by a consensus on two key principles which early on were implicitly or explicitly taken as 'given'. These elements, which were never revisited prior to end-September 2008, are the key to understanding why, once international and domestic events began to spin out of control, the decision to grant some form of a comprehensive government guarantee can be viewed as almost inevitable.

9.1.1 'No Bank can be Allowed to Fail'

The first fundamental principle was that 'no Irish bank can be allowed to fail', in the sense of closing its doors to depositors or other creditors such as bondholders. There is no evidence to suggest that in the twelve months or so prior to end-September 2008, this principle was ever subjected to critical analysis. The commitment to prevent any bank failure was never stated publicly, lest it encourage reckless behaviour by banks or convey any sense of disquiet that the question had ever even thought. However, there can be no doubt that behind closed doors this position was accepted as unambiguous government policy by all concerned, including the Department of Finance, the Central Bank, and the Financial Regulator—see Honohan (2010: 119–120) and Nyberg (2011: 78). Although the European Central Bank (ECB) may not have communicated its views explicitly,[3] the Irish side took this to be its clear stance also. In addition, experience with UK Northern Rock served to reinforce the perception that the 'no bank can fail' principle was shared by the non-euro-area EU authorities.

The fact that this was *the* principle—adopted, it seems, without little or any debate—does not necessarily mean that it was ill thought out or wrong. There was no precedent for allowing a eurozone bank to fail before 2008.[4] The choice was between a policy of refusal to allow banks to fail so as to prevent contagion effects and a policy of letting banks collapse so as to avoid the moral hazard that would arise if inefficient insolvent banks were bailed out. The euro area was, relatively speaking, still in its infancy and it appears that the first principle, that of avoiding contagion that could result from bank failures, was uppermost in the mindset of those charged with the maintenance of the currency's fledgling reputation.

This attitude contrasts somewhat with the situation in the United States where bank failures are by no means uncommon. However, as a result of the experience of the 1930s, the US authorities introduced a system of federal

---

[3] However, the policy was made explicit later, in October 2009, by the European Council of Ministers.

[4] Prior to Ireland's entry to the euro area, some smaller bank failures had occurred. In 1976, Irish Trust Bank run by Ken Bates (subsequently the owner of Chelsea Football Club) was put into liquidation with IR£4 million in debts. When the Fianna Fáil party was returned to power in 1977, it reimbursed fully the bank's depositors at a cost to taxpayers of IR£500,000. The Central Bank opposed this move. In 1982, Merchant Banking, owned by businessman Patrick Gallagher, collapsed. Depositors in the Republic were not paid but those depositors in its Northern Ireland subsidiary, MERBRO Financial, received 75 pence in the pound up to a maximum of £10,000 via the Bank of England's Deposit Protection Fund. No charges were brought in the Republic against Gallagher but he was jailed for two years in Northern Ireland for the provision of false accounts and theft. In 1985 the Insurance Corporation of Ireland (ICI), a fully owned insurance subsidiary of Allied Irish Bank (AIB) collapsed with losses of IR£200 million due to poor underwriting and the provision of inadequate reserves. The government, along with the Irish banks (including AIB), provided a bailout package. This action appears to have been at the insistence of the Central Bank which feared that failure to do so would lead to a run on AIB itself.

deposit insurance which effectively stopped runs on most major banks. Banks who do not participate in this voluntary federal insurance scheme are generally small in size and their possible failure is viewed as an acceptable and manageable risk. In Ireland, the government operated a guarantee scheme for depositors of all the six covered banks which provided coverage up to €20,000 per depositor per bank (in September 2008, in an unsuccessful attempt to stem the erosion of confidence, this limit was raised to €100,000). However, the size of the Irish guarantee fund, which was financed by contributions from the financial institutions themselves, was only a tiny fraction of the total amount of deposits. Like most such arrangements, the scheme was designed in principle to handle the possible failure of a 'small' institution, rather than cope with a generalized bank run.

In Europe, however, a more risk averse approach appears to have prevailed, together with a greater appetite for protecting national banking structures from systemic disturbances. At the time of the crisis in 2007–08, allowing a significant financial entity to close its doors was thought to entail unacceptable risks of contagion spreading elsewhere. The European authorities firmly believed that if generalized panic was allowed to take hold, the collateral damage would be very difficult and costly to contain, irrespective of the underlying financial strength of other institutions.

This issue lies at the heart of the debate about the Irish guarantee decision and cannot be dismissed lightly. History is replete with instances where widespread fear led to a run on the banks, a dramatic erosion of financial confidence, and a breakdown in the payments system, often accompanied by major social disturbances and political upheaval. In practical terms, the collapse of the payments system is likely to cause an immediate emptying of ATM machines and an inability to cash cheques. This tends to result in the use of 'scrip money' or IOUs as an alternative means of payment. Such 'money' usually starts to trade at a discount, reflecting holders' fears that it will not be redeemable at par later and its issuance is often a precursor to a devaluation of the currency towards an equilibrium level. Moreover, apart from the breakdown in the payments system, in extreme cases a freezing of bank deposits may result in a 'de facto' confiscation of part of them held by more vulnerable groups, with devastating welfare and political effects. Needless to say, from an external reputational perspective, the overall costs of a generalized bank failure for the country concerned are enormous and long-lasting.

Two well known instances of bank runs and associated financial crises are those of Argentina (2001–02) and Indonesia (1997). In Argentina's case, the problem was part of a broader economic and financial malaise associated with excessive borrowing by the government and an overvalued exchange rate which caused a steady erosion of financial confidence. Because of a cash shortage, the central and provincial governments increasingly resorted to issuing their own 'quasi money' in the form of IOUs. Following an intensification of capital flight and widespread panic that led to a run on the banks, on 1 December 2001, the government froze all bank accounts for up to 12 months, permitting weekly withdrawals not exceeding pesos 250–300 (about US$60–75). Apart from the paralysing effects on the payments system (many transactions were normally conducted in cash), violent riots ensued with businesses and banks forced to protect themselves with metal barriers to avoid physical and arson attacks. After one such round of riots in late December 2001 when several died, the President was forced to flee the Presidential Palace by helicopter. The financial consequences for many savers were very painful as some financial assets were subject to forced conversion to pesos at exchange rates that differed considerably from the market peso/US$ exchange rate (which itself had depreciated from 1:1 to 4:1 as a result of the collapse in confidence). The social damage was also immense. Between May 2001 and October 2002, the proportion of the population living in extreme poverty and below the poverty line rose from 12 to 28 per cent and from 36 to 58 per cent, respectively.

The experience of Indonesia involved the initial closure of some sixteen banks which were known to have serious financial and governance problems. However, this caused panic and a run on the entire banking system (a good part of which was, in fact, financially sound) and was accompanied by ethnic riots and disturbances. To prevent a collapse, the Central Bank was forced to inject massive liquidity into the banks which in turn led to a serious threat of hyperinflation. Of particular relevance for Ireland's experience, the government shortly thereafter was forced to introduce a blanket guarantee covering all domestic Indonesian banks, in order to try to restore confidence.

A much more recent instance of a collapse in confidence in the banking system is the Cypriot financial crisis that came to a head in March 2013. Faced with an imminent cut of funds by the ECB due to the the overhanging insolvency of the banking system, the Cypriot authorities, in the context of discussions on an emergency bail out by the EU/IMF troika, opted initially to impose a very sizeable "confiscatory tax" on all bank deposits, including those deposits under €100,000 that were, in principle, guaranteed by the government. The authorities 'plan was rejected outright by the Cypriot Parliament, financial panic ensued, and the government had no option but to close the banks for a period of over a week; access to ATMS was severely restricted and the payments system began to grind to a halt. In the interim, an alternative plan was hurriedly adopted that involved the effective loss of (at least 50 per cent) for most deposits over €100,000. The banks finally reopened but, in the face of a continued risk of a bank run, the authorities were forced to impose severe capital controls limiting the outward transfer of funds held in the financial system as well as restrictions on the amount of permissible deposit withdrawals and the use of credit cards and cheques.

There were special circumstances present in the Cyprus case, including the fact that a large part of bank deposits were held by Russians who had over the years moved funds to what was considered a "low regulation" banking system (partly, it is widely believed, to escape taxes and other domestic constraints). Also, there appeared to be no readily available alternative to the tax as a means of closing the major financing gap in order to secure agreement from the troika. Nevertheless, both the initial and revised plan were criticized as potentially opening a "Pandora's box", in the sense of undermining confidence in the integrity of the banking and payments system throughout the euro area. At this point, it seems clear that Cyprus' financial reputation – both domestically and internationally – has been very severely, if not fatally damaged. While it is far too soon to judge, history may very well not look kindly on an episode that had such potentially devastating effects, as a minimum for Cyprus itself, on financial confidence.

It is not difficult to imagine the huge reputational damage that Ireland would suffer if a situation such as happened in Cyprus, was allowed to occur in the domestic banking system. Ireland somehow 'managed' a closure of the banks during the bank strikes of 1966, 1970, and 1976—see Murphy (1978). However, at no stage in the Irish bank strikes was it suggested that the banks themselves were in any financial difficulty. Moreover, the costs associated with even a temporary bank closure would be far higher in the current, more highly sophisticated, domestic and international payments environment.

The critical issue is whether the failure of an individual bank causes, or is likely to cause, a priori a 'bank run' via a generalized loss of confidence. As the experience in the US (and elsewhere) shows, the possibility of permitting any single entity to go to the wall should not be excluded *a priori*. The merits of the 'no failure' position of the Irish and euro area authorities throughout (and following) the 2007–08 crisis thus depended on the conclusion that an institution at risk is of 'systemic 'importance'. In the context of Anglo, Honohan (2010: 131) noted that the systemic importance of a bank does not necessarily require that it be of a certain size relative to other banks or that its activities be considered somehow unique. A particular institution could well be 'done without' in that whatever was left of its worthwhile operations could be taken over by others.[5] However, even if this was so, the closure of the bank

---

[5] This point is sometimes made in the Irish context that it was not necessary to maintain the banking activities of Anglo and Irish Nationwide Building Society (INBS) once the property bubble began to burst. This is certainly valid but is not the relevant question in considering Anglo/INBS' systemic importance at the time.

in question could, in many circumstances such as those prevailng in Argentine, Indonesia and, more recently, Cyprus), trigger panic and cause depositors to rush to withdraw their funds from other institutions. Honohan concluded unequivocally that 'in this sense, the systemic importance of Anglo at that time cannot seriously be disputed'.

9.1.2 'The Only Issue is a Temporary Shortage of Liquidity'

The second fundamental principle in the run up to the crisis was the firm and unwavering conviction that whatever difficulties might lie in store for the banks were of a liquidity, rather than a solvency nature. This view prevailed up to and including the night of 29 September. Indeed, as will be seen in Chapter 11, it continued to hold sway for several months afterwards, even after the first 'outside' inspection of the banks' situation was completed by PricewaterhouseCoopers (PwC) in late 2008/early 2009.

The main basis for this fundamentally erroneous belief was the assumed 'soft landing' for the Irish property market and the assessment that whatever fall in prices was envisaged (15 per cent or so for residential property and an unspecified drop for commercial real estate) could be managed by the banks. As discussed in Chapter 5, a scenario of a much greater fall in prices involving potential insolvency for the banks (as well as a collapse of budgetary tax receipts) was simply never considered. Furthermore, this sanguine view was echoed in international assessments. Neither the continuing precipitous decline in the market values of Irish bank shares or negative commentary, including from several rating agencies and economists such as Morgan Kelly, that had started to appear from 2007 onwards gave rise to significant questioning of the proposition that the situation could be handled without major problems.

This conviction also helped alleviate possible concerns about the banks' overreliance on shorter term external wholesale funding sources. While it was realized that this could cause disturbances—stemming from exogenous international developments—it was not thought to be a fundamental worry. It was believed that, once the dust settled, lenders would be able to recognize the underlying strengths of Irish financial institutions and not take any precipitous action to cut off their funding.

The range of scenarios and the policy options contemplated in the months prior to September 2008 thus were limited to handling the banks' temporary liquidity difficulties. Combined with the first overarching principle, namely, that no bank should be allowed to fail, it implied that right up to the decision to grant the guarantee, the only real issue for the authorities was how to generate sufficient confidence so that all the six Irish domestic banks could continue their apparently profitable activities.

9.2 Pre-crisis Preparations by the Central Bank/Financial Regulator and the Department of Finance

Notwithstanding this underlying sense of confidence, from August 2007 onward officials stepped up their preparations, realizing the distinct possibility that some (assumed temporary) problems could emerge. Unfortunately, the scope and urgency of these activities were constrained by their underlying positive view of the world.

The newly constituted Domestic Standing Group (DSG), composed of senior officials of the Department of Finance, the Central Bank, and the Regulator, was the main forum for ongoing activity. During 2008, the NTMA also became a regular participant. The establishment of the DSG was in line with the requirements of an EU-driven mandate that suitable institutional arrangements be in place to deal with possible financial crises. The DSG met on several occasions between late 2007 and mid-2008, at a level below that of 'principals'. In the event of a crisis, it was intended that participation would comprise the most senior officials of the Central Bank, the Regulator, and the Department of Finance. However, when the actual crisis began to unfold, the DSG structure fell into abeyance, replaced by frequent informal, *ad hoc* contacts between the key highest-level decision makers.

Although earlier meetings of the DSG involved some written record-keeping, the subsequent reliance on informal structures involved a major drawback, from the perspective of *ex post* assessment and accountability. The Honohan and Nyberg reports emphasized the significant shortage of written documentation relating to developments as the crisis unfolded. Both had to rely largely on oral recollections, supplemented in some instances by informal and limited note-taking not publicly available. While in the midst of a crisis, record-keeping may not receive the highest priority, it could also be inferred that at least some participants in the discussions may not have wished to express their views explicitly for the record. This has hindered significantly the process of detailed *ex post* evaluation and accountability.

The DSG also spent time updating the so-called 'Black Book', intended to serve as an operational guide in the event of a crisis. However, this compendium, consisting mainly of procedural and logistical information (such as how to contact relevant officials), was more of an address book than a road map dealing with substantive issues. There was no reference to the Black Book during the actual crisis so that the updating exercise proved largely futile.

Some internal analysis was undertaken by DSG members to consider options for handling an institution 'in trouble' (i.e., where sufficient liquidity would not be forthcoming). A paper written by Department of Finance officials (later made public via the Oireachtas Public Accounts Committee and summarized in Nyberg (2011: 75)) outlined general principles for dealing with a troubled financial institution. In its initial draft of February 2008, the Department strongly resisted the notion that public monies should be placed at risk in the context of any rescue effort:

> ...as a matter of public policy, to protect the interests of taxpayers any requirement to provide an open-end/legally binding State guarantee which would expose the Exchequer to the risk of very significant costs [is] not regarded as part of the toolkit for successful crisis management and resolution.

However, in a later version dated April 2008, the above conclusion was subject to an important modification/addition:

> ...there are circumstances where such guarantees may be unavoidable to maintain confidence in the overall financial system.

This amendment suggests that the possibility that public financial support might prove to be necessary was already beginning to emerge, albeit tentatively.

At around the same time, other related work was undertaken within the Central Bank/Department of Finance. Although not publicly available, their content was summarized by Nyberg (2011: 75) as follows:

> ...[The Central Bank staff document] outlined, in fairly general terms, the options available if an individual institution were to encounter difficulties (*the possibility of a systemic crisis was not considered* [present authors' emphasis]). Information on Anglo was provided as a backdrop to the discussion, although the quantitative implications for Anglo of alternative approaches were not explored.
>
> [The Department of Finance's scoping paper] examined three cases: (i) an institution that is illiquid but solvent; (ii) an institution that is insolvent or is approaching insolvency; and (iii) a scenario in which it is unclear whether the institution is illiquid or insolvent. A number of possible solutions were identified for each of these scenarios.

Judging by both the Honohan and Nyberg reports, there is considerable doubt whether the specific analysis or recommendations contained in the above body of work was followed up or factored into later crisis decision-making. Their reports did not identify any summaries, points for action or tentative conclusions among the official record. Thus, while some Central Bank and Department of Finance staff had given thought to crisis resolution issues, the work seems to have been considered a largely hypothetical exercise of limited relevance, at least so far as senior levels were concerned.

However, the DSG and the subsequent informal structures did undertake, on a highly confidential basis, groundwork for draft legislation providing for the possible nationalization at some point of 'an institution'. This initiative seems to have been partly an outgrowth of the experience with the UK

Northern Rock; it was felt that the absence of nationalization legislation in Ireland was a *lacuna* in the authorities' 'tool kit'.

The possibility of legislation to enable implementation of a 'special resolution regime' for a financial institution was also explored. Existing Irish company law provisions were not suitable for 'seizing control' (i.e., action short of nationalization) of a troubled institution. An appropriate resolution regime for financial institutions would have needed to involve distinct features such as separate and possibly differentiated treatment of creditors that were not addressed in the then prevailing legislative framework.

In the event, this matter was unfortunately not pursued further at the time. It appears that the legislation would have been quite complex and taken considerable time to prepare. It would also have required consultations with a host of concerned entities, both inside and outside government, involving fears of a leak. There would have been concern that media reports that they were considering plans to permit a (hypothetical) 'take over' of a distressed financial institution could have led to heightened market instability. This was an eventuality that the authorities were anxious to avoid at almost all cost, even if it meant that when the crisis broke, causing far more turmoil than could have been imagined, they were far from adequately prepared. Officials were more concerned about the potential damage that could arise from leaks about appropriate contingency planning than the benefits that such planning could entail.

The absence of a special resolution regime at the time of the crisis was unfortunate, as it prevented using a possible 'intermediate' option short of outright nationalization or closure to deal with a troubled bank. Such a regime might have broadened the menu of options beyond that of the eventual guarantee.[6] On the other hand, as noted by Nyberg (2011: 76), for this to have made a difference it would have required agreement on burden sharing among creditors which was by no means assured. In the event, legislation dealing with the issue was eventually passed only in early 2011, as part of undertakings in the EU/IMF agreement.

9.3 Maximizing Liquidity Availability and the NTMA Deposit Episode

Consistent with the view that the banks' problems were temporary, starting in late 2007, much effort was devoted to intensifying work on monitoring and

---

[6] It should be noted that in the case of Cyprus, legislation introducing a special resolution regime was passed on an emergency basis prior to the finalisation of the bail out agreement with the troika.

overseeing their evolving liquidity positions. The Central Bank established a special group aimed at obtaining more up-to-date and comprehensive information on payments falling due. The banks also tried to adjust the composition of their assets in order to maximize the 'ECB-eligible collateral' that could be used to obtain liquidity assistance from the ECB in an emergency. Extensive background work was undertaken on the legal aspects and decision-making involved in the provision of Emergency Liquidity Assistance (ELA) by the Central Bank, including a decision by the CBFSAI Board in November 2007 to approve the delegation of powers to the Governor with respect to the granting of ELA (Honohan 2010: 116).

Apart from access to liquidity from Central Bank/ECB sources, towards the end of 2007 a broader 'green jersey' agenda began to surface explicitly or implicitly. The objective was to try to generate liquidity support from 'domestic' sources for the banks. One such source was the NTMA. When subsequently, in late 2010, the NTMA's role in providing deposits to Anglo came to light, considerable controversy ensued, involving the head of the NTMA, Michael Somers, during this 2007–08 period.[7]

The NTMA, as part of its regular Treasury operations, maintained deposits with Irish financial institutions. The placement of these deposits was subject to regular review and renewal (or not, as the case might be). From summer 2007 onwards, according to Somers, the NTMA started to switch deposits from Irish commercial banks to the Central Bank as a precaution, due to increasing international fears about pressures on banks generally and the NTMA's risk assessments of problems facing the Irish banking system. In the case of a €40 million deposit placed with Anglo in August 2007, the NTMA considered taking out insurance in respect of the deposit but decided against doing so on grounds of expense.

Following this switch in deposits, the NTMA experienced, in Somers' words, a 'fair bit of pressure at official level' from the Department of Finance/the Central Bank. In December 2007, Somers decided to seek a legal opinion and was advised that he should obtain a written 'direction' from the Minister of Finance with regard to the placement of deposits. On 21 December 2007, then Finance Minister Brian Cowen issued such an instruction which led to the placement of deposits of €200 million each in AIB and BoI, €50 million in Irish Life and Permanent, and €40 million each in Anglo and EBS. In July 2008, a further direction was issued by the newly appointed Minister of Finance, Brian

---

[7] The account of the NTMA controversy which follows is based on numerous media interventions by Michael Somers during 2010–11. See, for instance, the *Marian Finucane Show*, RTE, 16 May 2010; the *Irish Times*, 15 and 17 September 2010; *the Irish Examiner*, 15 January 2011; *the Irish Independent*, 11 January 2011; and *the Sunday Business Post*, 16 January 2011.

Lenihan, to roll over these deposits, including the earlier one-year deposit with Anglo.[8]

The NTMA deposit episode and the subsequent controversy raised two issues of governance and public policy. First, to what extent were pressures—inappropriate or otherwise—exercised by official quarters on the 'independent' NTMA to override its professional financial judgment and help prop up the ailing banks? Second, to the extent that senior NTMA officials and, in particular, Michael Somers, had formed from 2007 onwards a much less sanguine assessment of the prospects of the weakest bank, Anglo, should they, as the institution charged with managing the overall financial resources of the state, have sought to press their view at appropriately high official and political levels?

These issues are important. With respect to the first, the role of the Taoiseach came into question. According to David Drumm, then Chief Executive of Anglo, at an Anglo Board dinner in April 2008 to which Taoiseach Brian Cowen was invited (an occurrence which itself raised some eyebrows later), the subject of Anglo's financial difficulties and, in particular, the placement of NTMA deposits with the bank was discussed. Drumm indicated that at the dinner the Taoiseach promised intervention, a statement subsequently denied by the Taoiseach.[9]

Somers was asked later for his reactions to these statements by Drumm. He stated that he had no recollection of any order from the Taoiseach to deposit state funds specifically with Anglo. He confirmed that if the Minister of Finance wanted him to do something that went against his judgment, the appropriate procedure was for the Minister to convey his position in writing to the NTMA (which in fact occurred). He reiterated that there was a 'bit of heat' from Department of Finance officials, in terms of the maintenance of deposit levels in general.[10]

The second question is whether the doubts the NTMA had about the placement of funds with Anglo should have been conveyed directly to the Minister of Finance. The nature of the concerns regarding Anglo was mainly,

---

[8] A statement issued by the Department of Finance subsequent to the outbreak of the controversy noted that the direction had set out that it remained open to the NTMA to deposit money elsewhere if better [interest] rates were available.

[9] According to Drumm, Cowen reportedly said 'I told those f***ers' (*Irish Examiner*, 15 January 2011).

[10] Somers' attitude to all this was that 'it wasn't the [NTMA's] job to deal with the problems of the banking system. There was a big entity down on Dame Street [the Central Bank/Financial Regulator] supposed to do that and there was another banking unit in the Department of Finance'. In describing the pressure from official sources, he remarked that it had been 'very carefully worded because they were not going to be blamed. If anything went wrong, the blame would have been ours'. He added that the NTMA had 'swallowed hard' in placing the €40 million but this amount was one of the lowest amounts that the agency would have put with any bank—'it was only €40 million and we reckoned they were a huge outfit and should be good for €40 million'.

according to Somers, that Anglo's business model seemed 'odd', in that it was raising and lending a lot of money but seemed to be paying and charging 'over the odds.' The then Finance Director of the NTMA (and Somers' replacement as NTMA head), Brendan McDonagh, remarked later that the NTMA had become concerned at the explosive growth in Anglo's balance sheet in the early 2000s and that 'they didn't understand the business model at Anglo.' On several occasions, afterwards, Somers has stressed that although he had a 'gut feeling' something was amiss at Anglo, he had not possessed any special knowledge regarding the bank's situation other than that generally available in the market.

Even if Somers had serious concerns, an initiative on his part to go to see officials in Dame Street and/or Merrion Street (headquarters of the Central Bank and the Department of Finance, respectively) and deliver unasked for opinions regarding a bank on which he did not have detailed information would hardly have been welcomed or considered appropriate. Given the regrettably compartmentalized structure of responsibilities at the time, such a step would most likely have been denounced by the Financial Regulator, who was giving Anglo and all the others a clean bill of health as unacceptable NTMA meddling. Nor would it have been greeted enthusiastically by Department of Finance officials whose relations with Somers during his earlier period at the Department and his subsequent tenure at the NTMA had never been very comfortable.[11] As Somers later put it, ' . . . If I had [raised concerns] they would have said: Would you ever go and mind your own business? This is a very successful institution—what are you on about?' On another occasion, he wondered, if he had said something about the bank, 'God knows what would have happened to me?'.

The pressures and constraints perceived by Somers, regrettable as they may seem now, strike a chord with the broader official desire at the time to avoid any questioning of the 'consensus'. It is nevertheless instructive to conjecture as to what might have happened if, given Anglo's systemic importance, Somers and senior NTMA staff had decided at some stage to go beyond their formal brief and used their extensive experience and standing to try to investigate and assess what might really going on in the bank. Indeed, the authorities might have been somewhat better prepared for the events of late 2008 if, in the latter part of 2007, the NTMA and Somers had chosen to leave aside bureaucratic and institutional constraints and to convey their misgivings directly at sufficiently high levels. On the other hand, given Somers'

[11] The NTMA was established by then Taoiseach Charles Haughey as a separate entity which reported directly to the Minister of Finance rather than to Department officials. Somers was in charge of the NTMA until mid-2009. The compensation of senior NTMA staff, although a closely guarded secret until information was later made available under the Freedom of Information Act, was a sizeable multiple of regular civil service levels.

relationship with the Department of Finance, such warnings might well have been ignored.

During the weeks leading up to 29 September 2008, thought was also given to establishing a specific, more comprehensive domestic 'fighting fund' (sometimes referred to as a Secured Lending Scheme) to provide additional emergency liquidity to the banks, in the event of other sources drying up. Such a fund could have involved drawing on the resources of the Central Bank itself, the NTMA (where Treasury balances were maintained), and the National Pension Reserve Fund (also managed by the NTMA).

It is not clear how far this idea went and what were the reactions of the NTMA. Given earlier NTMA views on the placement of deposits with Anglo, it is likely that the NTMA would have been very sceptical. Pursuing the option seriously would doubtless have necessitated a written direction from the Minister to the NTMA. Given the very large sums potentially involved— much greater than in the earlier matter of the deposits[12]—this might well have turned out to be a bridge too far for senior NTMA management, including Somers, to cross. In any event, although the views of possible participants in the 'fighting fund' are not publicly available, the proposal remained, at least in principle, 'on the table' until close to 29 September.

9.4 2008—The Crisis Worsens

9.4.1 Mounting Domestic Worries

From mid-2007 onwards, Irish bank share prices began to fall steadily (Figure 9.1). However, no serious thought was given to the possibility that markets were beginning to conclude (correctly, as it turned out) that something fundamental might be seriously amiss. The official mantra was first, that Irish banks were fundamentally sound (as confirmed by stress tests and adherence to all regulatory requirements) and second, that the property market was headed for a 'soft landing.' The official caveat that the 'situation was being watched carefully', was explained in the context of a deteriorating external financing environment, rather than as implying that any in-depth assessment of the situation of the banks was necessary.

These comforting statements did not reassure markets or some observers. The newspaper articles by economist Morgan Kelly in late 2006 and July and September 2007 predicting a house price crash and consequent problems for the banks (see Chapter 8) had not gone unnoticed. John McManus, Business

---

[12] According to Honohan (2010: 122), a total of about €20 billion was mentioned, with about half of that to come from the CBFSAI and the remainder, possibly, from NTMA and/or the National Pension Reserve Fund.

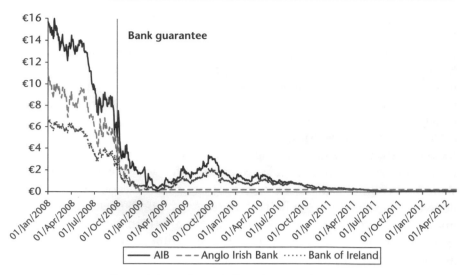

Figure 9.1   Irish Bank Share Prices, 2008–2012
Source: Irish Stock Exchange

Editor of the *Irish Times*, drew attention in November 2007 to Anglo's exceptional reliance on wholesale international funding. In early March 2008, *the Daily Telegraph* published a quote from Morgan Kelly that 'we are going to see banks on life support with very big bail-outs'. For some time, an influential advisor within Davy stockbrokers had been communicating a less than positive assessment of Anglo to his clients. Also in March 2008, Merrill Lynch issued a report highly critical of Anglo's lending activities in the UK (by then a major part of its overall exposure), citing it as the bank with the highest credit risk in the commercial property market. After an angry response by Anglo, the report was withdrawn from circulation.

Despite efforts by Anglo to counteract these negative assessments, the share prices of the banks and especially that of Anglo continued to decline. A particularly negative point was reached on 17 March 2008 (the so-called 'St Patrick's Day Massacre') when share prices of all the Irish banks fell very sharply; in the case of Anglo the price dropped 23 per cent at one stage before ending the day down 15 per cent. Part of the trigger for the sell-off was the earlier near collapse of Bear Stearns, one of the largest US investment banks (the rescue of which the US authorities had arranged with JP Morgan), and rumours about the vulnerability of other large financial institutions. In Ireland's case, negative sentiment was fuelled by a newspaper article in *the Financial Times* singling out Anglo as a bank with commercial property exposure that 'no one wants anything to do with'.

Within official circles, blame was generally placed for the 'St Patrick's Day Massacre' on uninformed assessments as well as possible market manipulation.[13] However, some believed that an important contributing factor might have been leaking of the true state of the Quinn 'Contracts for Difference' (CFD) affair. In brief, since 2005 Sean Quinn, head of the Quinn Group and reputed to be the richest businessman in Ireland, had started to gamble very heavily by secretly purchasing up to 25 per cent or more of Anglo shares via CFDs.[14] The CFD mechanism required the purchaser to put up cash for only a fraction of the price of the shares, similar to a margin purchase (except that the CFDs were held by brokers), with the remaining payment borrowed. If the share price continued to rise, the buyer would be able to pocket the difference between it and the acquisition price of the CFD and would not incur any immediate financial obligation.[15] But the approach is highly risky since, if the share price falls, the purchaser faces a 'margin call' (i.e. cash to make up the prospective loss). Moreover, the brokers holding the CFDs may choose to sell them, creating further downward pressure on the share price, aggravating the financial squeeze on the purchaser.

As Anglo's share price continued to spiral downwards (probably due to other underlying factors), Quinn came under major financial pressure and Anglo began to lend him very large amounts so that the required margin calls could be satisfied. Anglo itself realized that the situation was untenable. At some point, Quinn would have little choice but to sell his shares so as to 'cut his losses', an action that had the potential to push Anglo's share price down even further. Moreover, if the true size of the Quinn stake in Anglo became known to the market, other investors, aware of the extent of Quinn's predicament, would have been presented with a golden opportunity to short sell the shares, adding to the price pressures. Both Anglo and the Regulator feared that another collapse in Anglo's shares similar to the St Patrick's Day Massacre could cause a 'run' on Anglo, which in turn would create major knock-on effects for other financial institutions. The Regulator was also concerned that the size of the loans extended by Anglo to Quinn would start to exceed the regulatory limit of the percentage of a bank's capital that can be lent to any one client.

The Quinn CFD problem, necessarily managed in the utmost secrecy, given the risk of market destabilization, appears to have occupied much time and

---

[13] The Financial Regulator's subsequent investigation into allegations that Anglo had been the victim of the spreading of false rumours rejected such claims.

[14] Sean Quinn was described in *The Sunday Times* (23 October 2005) as 'the man with the Midas touch'.

[15] Quinn continued to acquire shares via CFDs even after Anglo's share price started to fall, in the apparent belief that this would be reversed. The scale of transactions involving CFDs was encouraged by a decision by the government, following intense lobbying, to reverse a plan by the Revenue Commissioners, announced in March 2006, to apply a tax to CFD transactions.

effort of the Regulator and the Central Bank during 2008. Alerted to looming difficulties, no foreign investors could be found with an interest in acquiring Anglo shares. The eventual unwinding of the CFD transaction involved the purchase of about 15 per cent of the shares by Quinn family members—financed by loans from Anglo—and 10 per cent by ten individuals (including some Anglo directors and major clients) also funded by Anglo.[16] The latter, so-called 'Maple 10' affair, later proved to be highly controversial. Following extensive investigations, in July 2012, three former Anglo officials, including the ex-Chairman, Sean Fitzpatrick, were charged with criminal breaches of company law with respect to the transaction. Earlier, some former Anglo officials stated that the Financial Regulator—and, possibly, by inference the Central Bank—were aware of the transactions involved and were supportive throughout.

Apart from the considerable distraction, the Quinn episode might also have encouraged a belief by some in the Central Bank and the Regulator that the continuous fall in Anglo's share price was due to market speculation—including that arising from the CFD affair—rather than to more deep-rooted concerns about Anglo's viability. Anglo officials stressed, presumably with the support of the Regulator, that the 'fundamentals' of the bank were sound and that uninformed judgments and/or 'speculators' were at work to push down share prices. However, these optimistic conclusions delayed undertaking the necessary analysis to identify and confront the underlying problems. Regrettably, in attempting to shore up Anglo, officials lost sight of the rapidly deteriorating underlying market sentiment towards much of the Irish banking system from mid-2007 onwards.

A second 'market-related shock' occurred in early September 2008. Following an adverse rating by Moodys which cited the Irish Nationwide Building Society's (INBS) commercial property exposure, Reuters published, on 7 September, a report stating that INBS had entered talks with its lenders aimed at avoiding insolvency. The Central Bank and the Regulator reacted with alarm and Reuters retracted the report and issued an apology. The liquidity position of INBS began to stabilize and the possibility of having to nationalize it (using the draft contingency legislation described earlier in this chapter (Section 9.3) receded, at least temporarily. However, although the Reuters report was factually wrong, as with Anglo, too hasty and complacent conclusions were drawn with respect to the underlying soundness of INBS.

---

[16] The arrangement involved provision of a personal guarantee, but only up to 25 per cent of the loan amount.

9.4.2 Banks Worldwide Under Mounting Pressures

Developments in Ireland during the fifteen months or so prior to end-September 2008 unfolded against a steadily deteriorating external financial environment. A gradually emerging shortage of international liquidity caused serious pressures on several key institutions worldwide, and led to major, in some cases unprecedented, policy initiatives. It is difficult to know the extent to which the Irish authorities, preoccupied with their own mounting domestic concerns, were influenced by events elsewhere. However, the decisions they eventually took have to be seen in the context of those of others encountering similar difficulties.

As noted earlier, the initial trigger—especially from an Irish perspective—was the run on the UK bank, Northern Rock in September 2007, an experience which appears to have played an important role in influencing subsequent Irish thinking. Following a drying up of wholesale lending, the Bank of England extended unprecedented amounts of ELA to Northern Rock. However, when this became publicly known, panic ensued among retail depositors and long queues formed outside Northern Rock's bank branches, including in Dublin. The UK Government introduced a guarantee covering all deposits and uncollateralized wholesale borrowing. The bank was eventually nationalized in February 2008 and the guarantee was withdrawn in May 2010.

Across the Atlantic, the financial pressures that had started to first emerge in early 2007 became more acute. In October 2007 Citibank began to implement a series of major write-downs due to losses on sub-prime mortgages and obtained a special loan from the Abu Dhabi Investment Authority the following month. Countrywide Financial, a troubled institution specializing in sub-prime lending, was purchased by Bank of America in January 2008. In March 2008, the US investment firm Bear Stearns, after reporting a massive fall in its liquid assets, collapsed. However, it was considered 'too big to fail' and was rescued by the US Federal Reserve via an emergency loan, before being purchased by JP Morgan.

During the summer of 2008, attention remained focused on the US. In early September, the two pillars of the US mortgage market, Fannie May and Freddie Mac, were put into conservatorship. At around the same time, concerns were mounting about Lehman Brothers. Following reports of increasing losses and threatened downgrades, and despite pressures on the US authorities to provide another bail out similar to that for Bear Stearns, Lehman Brothers was allowed to fail, filing for bankruptcy on 15 September.

The Lehmans bankruptcy—the largest in Wall Street's history—sent shock waves throughout the entire world financial system. The next day, the giant insurance company AIG, which had written over $400 billion of credit default swaps on sub-prime loans, was forced to avail of an $85 billion loan from the

US Federal Reserve. One day later, following a run by depositors, the net asset value of a major money-market fund, Reserve Primary, fell below US $1 (termed 'breaking the buck'), precipitating runs on other similar funds. Fearing a financial meltdown, the US authorities introduced an emergency insurance program which succeeded in stabilizing the money-market fund sector. On 19 September, a major initiative, subsequently called TARP (the Troubled Assets Relief Program), designed to stabilize the banking system was submitted for approval to the US Congress. However, the plan was rejected by Congress on 28 September, which destabilized markets further.[17]

The collapse of Lehman Brothers had enormous domestic and international implications. It had borrowed heavily on international markets and there was fear of a domino effect on other Wall Street investment banks.[18] The realization that liquidity was near frozen in US financial markets raised questions as to the viability of financial institutions worldwide. An inability to borrow implies an inability to lend. Moreover, as the collateral institutions had provided began to fall in value, those who lent to them began to demand a greater amount of margin in the form of cash. As a consequence, institutions came under pressure to dispose of their assets under fire sale conditions, lowering the value of collateral further and intensifying the downward financial spiral.[19]

Turmoil in the US spread quickly to Europe as financial problems sprang up across the continent. In the last week of September, a series of dramatic interventions occurred. The Dutch bank Fortis had to be rescued over the weekend of 27–28 September via a joint capital injection from the Belgian, Dutch, and Luxembourg governments, together with authorization of ELA (which was not, however, announced).[20] On 29 September, the German bank Hypo RE, which had acquired Irish-based DepFa in 2007, had to receive a

---

[17] Other notable events in the US during this time included intervention on 19 September by the Federal Reserve *vis-à-vis* Washington Mutual (the 7th largest US bank—eventually sold to JP Morgan) and intervention by the FDIC to help rescue Wachovia (the 6th largest US bank—sold initially to CitiGroup).

[18] Even Goldman Sachs, the doyen of US investment banks, needed emergency lines of credit, including from the financier Warren Buffett.

[19] What happened in the US in the first half of September was a run on the 'shadow banking system' rather than a classic bank run (see Gorton and Metrick 2009). In this system, institutions borrowed short by means of repos (repurchase agreements) collateralized by longer-term assets such as mortgages. As the value of mortgages declined, more collateral had to be posted. Mishkin describes the process as follows:

As the value of mortgage-backed securities fell and uncertainty about their future value increased, haircuts [on collateral] rose to levels as high as 50 per cent. The result was that the same amount of collateral would now support less borrowing, leading to deleveraging in which financial institutions had to sell off assets. The resulting 'fire sale' dynamic . . . led to an adverse feedback loop in which the decline in asset values lowered the collateral's value, while further raising uncertainty, causing haircuts to rise further, forcing financial institutions to deleverage and sell more assets, and so on (Mishkin 2010: 2).

[20] Jean Claude Trichet, President of the ECB, participated in these emergency talks.

massive bail out from the German authorities and a consortium of banks.[21] Also on 29 September, Dexia Bank suffered a major downgrading which led to a rescue package comprising capital injections, a partial government guarantee, and ELA. In Iceland, the banking system, led by its three largest banks, Glitnir, Kaupting, and Landesbanki, was self-destructing with significant implications for the British banking system.

The crisis crept ever closer to Irish shores. On 26 September, the Governor of the Bank of England, Mervyn King, informed the Chancellor of the Exchequer, Alistair Darling, that 'unless the banking system as a whole was recapitalized, further failures were inevitable' (Darling 2011: 145). The same day, the UK Financial Services Authority (FSA) withdrew permission for the building society Bradford and Bingley, to take new deposits. After intense discussions, the institution was nationalized on 29 September, with the Spanish bank, Santander, agreeing to a partial purchase. It subsequently emerged that two of Britain's biggest banks, Royal Bank of Scotland and Halifax Bank of Scotland (which had become part of Lloyds Group), were in considerable difficulties.[22]

9.4.3 September 2008—The Wave Crests

The decision by the US authorities to let Lehmans fail brought matters to an abrupt head so far as the Irish and indeed many other banks were concerned. It caused a massive wave of uncertainty, if not quasi panic, with a good number of institutions, and especially those heavily exposed to property lending, coming under sudden intense scrutiny. Ireland had become acutely vulnerable.

The liquidity position of Anglo was quickly becoming untenable and efforts to seek foreign funding had failed. Anglo management explored all avenues to see if a domestic 'rescue' could be arranged, all the while stressing that the bank remained fundamentally strong. On 18 September a meeting took place

---

[21] DepFa was a very large institution specializing in the financing of public and public–private partnership activities. In 2007, DepFa was acquired by the German bank Hypoverein which specialized in property lending. A drying up of funding affected adversely the activities undertaken by the former DepFa, while Hypo suffered on account of the property downturn. It has been suggested that since DepFa was a major factor in Hypo's downfall, earlier lax Irish financial supervision may have been partly responsible. When Hypo's takeover of DepFa was under consideration, the German financial regulatory authority sent a large team to Ireland to assess its financial position. No evidence has been made available suggesting that at the time significant concerns were raised by the German side with respect to DepFa. On 2 January 2010 the *Irish Times* reported that German lawyers investigating the near collapse of Hypo RE were considering legal action against the former directors of Depfa.

[22] According to Darling, Fred Goodwin [the CEO of Royal Bank of Scotland] had been in touch...to say that the banks were increasingly worried about both liquidity and capital (Darling 2011: 145).

with Finance Minister Lenihan to discuss, as a possible solution, a merger of Anglo and INBS, an idea that was met with official incredulity.[23] Anglo approached Irish Life & Permanent regarding a merger but was rejected. Finally, contact was made with the Bank of Ireland and Allied Irish Bank to see if emergency liquidity support could be arranged. This too was rejected, although, as will be seen in the following chapter, the idea remained alive, resurfacing at the time of the discussions on the granting of the guarantee.

Informal contacts between the key official parties intensified throughout September. The Central Bank (under the leadership of Governor John Hurley who had returned in mid-September from medical leave) worked very closely with the Financial Regulator, Patrick Neary, and his staff and Department of Finance officials led by David Doyle, Secretary General, and Kevin Cardiff, Assistant Secretary.[24] The Irish financial system was now facing considerable difficulties and a major initiative was necessary. But the question remained as to what to do? Given the 'thinness' of the paper trail that is publicly available, the precise positions advocated by the principal participants during the crisis-filled days prior to 29 September are not clear. It can be inferred from both the Honohan and Nyberg reports that the lack of documentation on the public record reflected more the absence of such material rather than any official reluctance to release whatever exists.

Six days after the collapse of Lehmans, the Board of the Central Bank convened on Thursday, 24 September—the last meeting prior to 29 September. Some options were discussed, without, however, any decision taken as to the recommendations the Central Bank should make to the government. Nevertheless, Governor Hurley was requested by the Secretary General of the Department of Finance, an *ex officio* member of the Board, to convey the Bank's views in writing on the situation in advance of an anticipated tense and decisive weekend. However, this did not occur.[25] At some point around this time, as will be taken up in the next chapter, there were discussions with the senior echelons of the ECB.

On Sunday, 28 September, the Cabinet met and, according to the Green Party leader John Gormley, Ministers were briefed on the overall situation. However, it is unclear as to whether the Cabinet discussed possible specific proposed actions such as the idea of a comprehensive government guarantee.

Although internal official discussions had intensified, so far as key Anglo management was concerned, they had not yielded any positive outcome. The

---

[23] As the economist Colm McCarthy quoted in Carswell (2011: 198) succinctly stated: 'you tie two stones together—they'll still sink to the bottom'.

[24] The onset of the crisis appears to have led to much closer cooperation between the Central Bank and the Financial Regulator than had occurred up to then (see Chapter 5).

[25] On 18 October, the Governor provided in writing his (retroactive) support for the government decision of 29 September.

Chairman of Anglo, Sean Fitzpatrick, who had been in fairly close informal contact with the Regulator throughout, unexpectedly appeared with David Drumm, the CEO of Anglo, around midday on 29 September at the offices of the economic consultancy company run by Alan Gray with whom they had already met in early September. Gray, a non-Executive Director of the Central Bank, was known to have had direct interaction with Taoiseach Brian Cowen on other matters.[26] According to a statement issued by Gray in January 2011, after the earlier meeting came to light, as well as the description contained in Carswell (2011), the Anglo representatives explained that the bank was experiencing extremely serious liquidity difficulties. However, according to Gray, they did not ask him (Gray) to take any action on the matter. Gray suggested that they should discuss the issue with the Central Bank to which they responded that they already had done so.

Anglo's motive in meeting with Gray presumably was to see if he could be of any assistance in conveying directly to government its concerns which by then had reached a critical point. In the event, Gray did not contact the Taoiseach nor, somewhat surprisingly, in view of his membership of the Board of the Central Bank, did he inform Governor Hurley of the visit. The incident became known two and a half years later, following 'revelations' of earlier encounters between the Taoiseach and Anglo representatives, one of which Gray had attended. Gray may not have wished to give prominence to the Fitzpatrick initiative of 29 September by reporting it to the Central Bank.[27]

Media reports on the morning of Monday, 29 September were fairly low key, indicating (limited, in the case of the *Irish Times,* to only the business pages) that discussions were taking place to deal with the growing liquidity difficulties facing the banks. However, the gravity of the situation had started to reach the ears of the public. Ten days earlier, an RTE afternoon radio programme with Joe Duffy ('Talk to Joe') had featured a flood of calls from listeners who had withdrawn their funds from Irish banks. Although on 20 September, Minister Lenihan had announced an increase in the limit covered by the normal state guarantee scheme for deposits, from €20,000 to €100,000 (as well as an increase in the percentage of the deposit covered from 90 to 100 per cent), this had had little overall positive effect. Anecdotal evidence suggests that there was a definite whiff of panic and fear in financial circles in Dublin

[26] In 2008 Gray had attended a dinner, following a golf game involving the Taoiseach and some Anglo figures, at which Gray presented some views and suggestions regarding the overall economic situation and prospects.

[27] In a phone call with the Taoiseach later that night during the meeting on the guarantee, according to Gray's statement, the Taoiseach asked him for his views, as a director of the Central Bank, on the market reaction to a possible government guarantee. Gray raised the question of possible state aid issues and also recommended that the guarantee be charged for through the banks and be time bound.

that day as some major Irish corporates began to withdraw deposits from Irish banks.

As Monday progressed, it was clear that Anglo's share price and liquidity position was worsening further by the hour. Since, in the absence of action, it would not be in a position to make sizeable payments falling due the following day, Anglo would, in effect, be forced to default and close its doors. Bank of Ireland and AIB, while not facing such extreme pressures immediately, also concluded that were Anglo to fail, very shortly they too could face an unsustainable situation. The Chairmen and CEOs of both banks (Richard Burrows and Brian Goggin of Bank of Ireland, and Dermot Gleeson and Eugene Sheehy of AIB) requested a joint meeting with the Taoiseach and Minister Lenihan to apprise them of their fears. It was agreed that they would come to Merrion Street later that evening, where the Taoiseach, the Minister of Finance and his senior officials had already gathered in crisis mode. The stage was set for the longest and most controversial night in Ireland's economic and financial history.

9.5 Conclusions

In reviewing the events of 2008, it has often been emphasized that the Irish authorities were completely unprepared for the shock wave which hit the financial system in late 2008. While this is beyond dispute, it would not be correct to conclude that they were entirely complacent about the situation. Officials were aware of the deteriorating international and domestic financial environment. However, there were two critical problems. Firstly, they had underestimated, along with virtually everyone else, the extent of the looming world financial 'tsunami'. But secondly, and more fundamentally, they had totally misdiagnosed the nature of the problem that Irish banks were facing.

The thinking throughout 2008 was that the difficulties spilling over from abroad were almost entirely due to external factors for which they were not responsible or could influence. The possibility that these represented a world-wide bursting of a credit-fuelled asset bubble, which might end up producing particularly damaging consequences for the Irish banks, was not thought about seriously. There appeared to be an unshakeable confidence in official circles that, despite the massive expansion in lending in support of soaring property prices, Irish banks were fundamentally sound and all that was in prospect was a mild property correction that could be safely managed. Thus, the approach was to batten down the hatches and try to ride out the storm as best as one could.

No consideration was given to the possibility of letting any of the six domestic banks fail. Preventing this happening was a given throughout the

EU (including in the UK, as demonstrated by the experience with Northern Rock) and, more importantly, the eurozone. The scale and frequency of European emergency rescues in the weeks and days prior to end-September confirmed the Irish view that, from a national and a European perspective, allowing one institution to close its doors could not be tolerated, as it could very well lead to the collapse of the entire system.

It needs to be emphasized that this stance, that no bank in the eurozone could be permitted to fail, was not seriously questioned by governments or the public until the Cypriot crisis in March 2013. It was not a decision that was lightly taken, since the costs to the public purse of preventing a bank collapse can be, and often are, exceptionally high. As evidenced by the experiences of Argentine, Indonesia and Cyprus, bank runs and breakdowns of the payments systems are very likely to end up having huge economic and financial, as well as social and political, repercussions. The risks and dangers involved would have been quite apparent to Irish officials, as they were to those in Europe. Their concerns cannot be simply brushed aside by critics of the actions of the Irish government.

However, this fundamental line of thinking seriously constrained the Irish authorities' preparations from mid-2007 onwards. The Irish property market had peaked in mid-2006. Particularly after the alarm bells raised by the US sub-prime crisis in the United States in August 2007, it became evident that collapsing prices would create significant problems for financial institutions that had over-lent into the property sector. Even a casual perusal by the Central Bank and the Regulator of the Irish banks' balance sheets in late 2007 would have and should have highlighted their massive over-dependence on property lending and their vulnerability.

Although some internal staff work was done on possible ways to handle troubled institutions, this does not appear to have featured significantly in discussions during the actual crisis. A 'green jersey' agenda emerged, with all hands called on deck to try to maximize liquidity availability for the banks. However, this served only to patch up a fatally leaking ship and distracted attention from the more fundamental problem of the banks' potential insolvency. It also led to some, at a minimum questionable, pressures on the NTMA to act against its best professional judgment. The NTMA reluctantly complied with explicit government instructions. However, one can conjecture as to what might have happened if the NTMA, given its considerable professional experience and standing, had sought to press at high levels its significant misgivings with respect to Anglo.

In fairness to Irish officials, there were few indications from abroad that the Irish problem could in fact be much more serious. Throughout Europe, the common emphasis was on firefighting in order to somehow muddle through what was regarded as a short-term crisis. Similar to Ireland, no potential solvency alarm bells were ringing. The ECB's stance was that there was no problem requiring a pan-European solution and Ireland, together with others, could be left to fend for themselves as best as they could.

This does not excuse the short-sightedness of officials both in Ireland as well as in Europe that had led to this erroneous assessment. As discussed in Chapter 5, the ECB was still focused largely on the objective of controlling inflation and, in the absence of a mandate with respect to pan-European financial regulation, was ineffective in ensuring macro-prudential financial stability. Thus, at this juncture, neither Irish nor European officials were able to analyse or appreciate the potentially enormous scale of the damaging financial developments that were starting to occur daily before their eyes. Critically, they had developed few, if any, contingency plans to deal with them.

Thus began the countdown to the fateful decision taken on the night of 29 September. Ireland was in a bind. The markets, sensing that Anglo (and possibly others) might be facing serious problems, reacted predictably by making a rush for the exit. There was no prospect for any European assistance. The consensus—shared by Irish and European officials alike—was that a bank failure leading to a possible collapse of the banking system had to be prevented. Indeed, even before the weekend prior to 29 September, the noose had begun to tighten and the options facing Taoiseach Brian Cowen and his Minister of Finance, Brian Lenihan, had already narrowed sharply. Given the intensified pressures and growing sense of panic throughout the following Monday, by that evening the government had very little room left for manoeuvre.

References

Buffet, Warren (2001) *Chairman's Letter*, Berkshire Hathaway <http://www.berkshire-hathaway.com/2001ar/2001letter.html>, accessed 3 Feb 2013.

Carswell, Simon (2011) *Anglo Republic: Inside the Bank that Broke Ireland* (Ireland).

Darling, Alistair (2011) *Back From the Brink* (London).

Gordon, Gary and Andrew Metrick (2009) 'Securitized Banking and the Run on the Repo', Yale School of Management, Working Paper AMZ 2358 (Yale).

Honohan, Patrick (2010) *The Irish Banking Crisis: Regulatory and Financial Stability Policy, 2003–2008*, A Report to the Minister of Finance, by the Governor of the Central Bank (Dublin).

Lowenstein, Roger (2012) 'The Villain', I, April 2012, 49–60.

Mishkin, Frederic S. (2010) 'Over the Cliff: From the Subprime to the Global Financial Crisis' NBER Working Paper 16609, December.

Murphy, Antoin (1978) 'Money in an Economy without Banks' Manchester School, Vol. 46 (Manchester).

Nyberg, Peter (2011) *Misjudging Risk: Causes of the Systemic Banking Crisis in Ireland*, Report of the Commission of Investigation into the Banking Sector in Ireland, Government Publications (Dublin).

10

The Guarantee Decision
of 29 September 2008

This was the cheapest bail out in the world so far

Brian Lenihan, Minister of Finance, October 2008[1]

[The Guarantee] decision is an act of economic treason for which this country is now paying very dearly

Eamon Gilmore, leader of the Labour Party, March 2010[2]

Seldom in the economic and financial history of a country has one single action proved as controversial as the decision on the night of 29 September 2008 to provide a comprehensive government guarantee in respect of nearly all the financial liabilities of the domestic Irish banking system. This decision, despite receiving broad domestic support at the time, later came to represent for many, the source of much of the enormous financial difficulties the State has faced in the four and a half years since that fateful night.

The reasons for the controversy are clear. The guarantee implied that a dishonouring of its obligations to creditors covered by the guarantee by any of the six domestic financial institutions would represent, in effect, a default by the sovereign Irish Government. At the time of the decision, of course, this was generally not considered relevant. The benefits of the guarantee in terms of helping to increase confidence in the domestic banking system and thereby addressing the temporary liquidity problem were emphasized. However, once the collapse of much of the property-related asset side of their balance sheets emerged, the banks were faced with massive losses. These losses would have been less to the extent that the liabilities owed to creditors could have been written down. But given the existence of the guarantee, such a course of action

---

[1] The *Irish Times*, 24 October 2008.   [2] The *Irish Times*, 1 April 2010.

was effectively precluded by the need to prevent any damage to the sovereign creditworthiness of the State.[3]

In these circumstances, the eventual outcome became inevitable, despite being, at the time of the guarantee, unthinkable. As the banks' losses mounted, the government had little or no alternative but to make good the continually growing holes in their balance sheets by injecting capital during 2010–12. As of end-2012, public funds provided to recapitalize the banks amounted to €64 billion, equivalent to 40 per cent of 2012 GDP.

The debate about the decision taken on the night of 29 September 2008 has been justifiably intense. Politically, this in part has reflected attempts by the then opposition parties (now in government) to pin the blame on the ruling Fianna Fáil-led Government that was responsible for granting the guarantee. Former Taoiseach Brian Cowen, as well as his late Finance Minister, Brian Lenihan, have stoutly defended their actions, arguing that, in the circumstances of the time, it was the only feasible and least worst option available. They have accused critics of second guessing with the benefit of hindsight. At times, suggestions—strongly denied by leading Fianna Fáil politicians—have been made that the decision was influenced by pressures from groups such as property developers and certain bankers alleged to have had close links to elements of the Fianna Fáil party.

The Honohan (2010) and Nyberg (2011) reports, which contain an extensive narrative of the events leading up and including 29 September 2008, reviewed several aspects of the guarantee decision itself. These reports offer broad, albeit not unqualified, support for the decision, while presenting possible variations of it that, in the views of the reports' authors, might have merited further consideration.[4]

A theme common to both the Honohan and Nyberg reports is the relative absence of official records outlining the specific views of participants and the options considered during and leading up to the 29 September discussions. The absence of a paper trail has meant that these reports had to rely to a significant extent on the oral testimony provided by those involved who could not be mentioned by name, because of confidentiality restrictions. This shortage of written documentation is disturbing and complicates attempts to provide an accurate historical assessment of these key events. Furthermore, it appears that Oireachtas committees, in the absence of a

---

[3] Moreover, the Governor of the Central Bank, Patrick Honohan stated in mid-2011 that, according to legal advice received by the Central Bank subsequently, once granted, the guarantee could not easily be revoked prior to its expiration date.

[4] Some commentators have suggested that the reports' conclusions are not unequivocal. For example, in a televised exchange with then Taoiseach Brian Cowen in early 2011, Miriam O'Callaghan, the RTE interviewer, quoted from the Honohan report to argue that Honohan did not support the guarantee. However, the Taoiseach, employing different quotes, claimed the opposite.

modification to the Irish constitution, are constrained with respect to the scope of hearings on matters such as this. Legislative changes may be required even for the Oireachtas to compel witnesses to attend hearings and give evidence. However, during 2011, the Department of Finance provided some documentation to the Oireachtas Public Accounts Committee relating to relevant internal policy discussions during 2007–08. This publicly available material provides some insights into certain aspects of official thinking at the time.

This chapter takes a fresh look at the guarantee decision. Following a recapitulation of the setting and the broad state of the authorities' thinking leading up to end-September 2008, key issues that have featured in subsequent debate are considered, including: (i) were there realistic and feasible alternatives to a broad guarantee, including not taking or delaying action; (ii) should the coverage by institution, instrument type, or by time period have been different; (iii) was Anglo a special case that merited a different approach (perhaps including nationalization); (iv) did Merrill Lynch (the Department of Finance's external advisers) support the granting of a guarantee and, if so, of what type; (v) is there evidence to support the assertion that the government was 'rolled' by the banks into the guarantee; and (vi) given the lack of accurate information then available, would or should a similar decision have been taken if, for the sake of argument, more had been known about the true insolvency of the banks at the time? Finally, the contemporaneous reactions of foreign partners (EU governments and the ECB), domestic politicians, and the media and commentators to the decision are discussed.

10.1 The Setting

Present in Government Buildings on Merrion Street on the night of 29 September were the Taoiseach, Brian Cowen; the Minister of Finance, Brian Lenihan; the Secretary General of the Department of Finance, David Doyle; his Assistant Secretary, Kevin Cardiff; the Attorney General, Paul Gallagher; and the Secretary General to the Taoiseach, Dermot McCarthy. The Central Bank and the Financial Regulator were represented mainly by Central Bank Governor, John Hurley; the Director General of the Central Bank, Tony Grimes; and the Financial Regulator, Patrick Neary. Senior National Treasury Management Agency (NTMA) officials also furnished advice. Merrill Lynch representatives were in the background, providing views (including in writing) to Department of Finance officials. The discussions took place in several different rooms, with the main focus on the gatherings chaired by the Taoiseach in which officials took part at various stages.

There appear to have been no official minutes kept of the discussions (or at least none that have been made available to the public). However, from a close reading of the Honohan report, some hints can be gleaned as to which institutions or individuals may have favoured certain courses of action. While presumably the decision taken by the incorporeal Cabinet meeting by telephone in the early hours of 30 September has been recorded,[5] issues of confidentiality are likely to apply as regards the Cabinet meeting itself (as well as whatever legal advice the Attorney General may have given). Most participants (save for the Taoiseach and Minister of Finance Lenihan) have not yet indicated publicly their views on what transpired, except, in some cases, to convey that they 'joined in the consensus'. It seems that the guarantee commanded widespread support from all who were present.

The decision provided a comprehensive government guarantee in respect of the financial obligations of the six domestic institutions—Allied Irish Banks (AIB), Anglo Irish Bank (Anglo), Bank of Ireland, Educational Building Society, Irish Life & Permanent, and Irish Nationwide Building Society (INBS)— falling due over the following two years.[6] Nearly all financial liabilities were covered, including (dated) subordinated debt. As Honohan (2010: 11) stated, the scope of the Irish guarantee was exceptionally broad.

The participants in this decision were aware of the contingent financial liability—put at some €440 billion at the time—that the Irish government (and thus the Irish taxpayer) was exposed to by the guarantee. This amounted to 287 per cent of Irish GNP in 2008, although it would have been far-fetched to have assumed that the Irish financial institutions had no assets to cover their liabilities.

The two principles discussed in the previous chapter, namely, that a bank run had to be avoided at all costs and that the problem was only one of liquidity, continued to hold unquestioned dominance at the meeting. An unswerving conviction on these key points appears to have been sufficient to dispel—or at least to reduce sufficiently—any worries or misgivings that anyone may have had about the true situation of the banks.

Against the background of very considerable turmoil throughout the euro area at the time, all necessary official initiatives had been geared to ensure that no eurozone bank would have to close its doors and default. Despite the volatile environment, there was no reason to believe that Irish officials or the ECB were experiencing any change of heart on this critical issue, especially since the earlier failure of Lehman Brothers had wrought such financial havoc.

---

[5] The meeting held in the Taoiseach's office on 29 September was not a meeting of the Cabinet. Therefore, an 'incorporeal' meeting (i.e. one where Cabinet ministers were not physically present) needed to be conducted by telephone in order to inform ministers and seek their assent. Several of the ministers contacted in this way have said subsequently that no substantive discussions took place during the process.

[6] Foreign banks operating in Ireland subsequently were offered the option of availing of the guarantee for a fee similar to that levied on domestic Irish institutions. However, in the end, they decided not to participate.

The sense of worldwide panic was heightened by news of the rejection by the US Congress of the US administration's proposed Troubled Assets Relief Programme (TARP), a development that intensified the conviction that an Irish bank closure had to be avoided at all costs.

According to Honohan (2010:121), 'it became apparent from informal contacts that notwithstanding the general turbulence, there was at that stage no European-wide effort underway to mount an initiative to help distressed institutions.' At the same time, the ECB would have emphasized the potential contagion effects arising from a banking collapse in Ireland (or indeed anywhere else within the euro area). Honohan concluded (a view later confirmed publicly by the former Taoiseach (Cowen 2012)) that the message from the ECB was clear, namely, that 'each national authority would have to take whatever measures might prove necessary to deal with its own situation'. Given the crucial issues at stake, there can be little doubt but that such 'informal contacts' would have involved communications at an appropriately high level, most probably between ECB President, Jean Claude Trichet and Central Bank Governor, John Hurley. The message would have been that the ECB, while not prepared at the time to embark on any specific rescue package for a country in difficulties, opposed strongly any suggestion of the country in question allowing its banking system to default.

While details of the timing and precise content of the interaction with the ECB have not been made public, once a message along the above lines had been conveyed from Frankfurt, the options became quite limited. Assuming there was such a communication before the weekend preceding 29 September, for the Irish government, in effect, the die had been largely cast at that stage. Although the dam finally burst only on the following Monday, 29 September, and there was no rethink from Frankfurt, it appears most probable that some form of major state commitment was already uppermost in the authorities' minds. This is important to emphasize, as some commentators have suggested that the events of 29 September that led to state support in the form of a guarantee, were a 'bolt from the blue' for the officials concerned. Based on the available evidence regarding the activities that are likely to have taken place during the preceding days and weekend, this is unlikely to have been the case.[7]

The second principle held to firmly was the diagnosis of the difficulties facing the banks. The Financial Regulator, Patrick Neary, confirmed to the meeting that all institutions were solvent as of end-September. Such a certification was required if the option of extending Emergency Liquidity Assistance

---

[7] The well-known economic journalist, David McWilliams, in a newspaper article the previous weekend, had explicitly urged that some form of government guarantee be provided.

(ELA) was to be pursued, since the provision of ELA to an insolvent institution was prohibited explicitly.

Financial Regulator Neary's conclusion underscores the 'static' nature of official thinking at the time. The fact that the banks were formally meeting the solvency test as of a certain date, while important, left aside entirely the much more critical question—would they remain solvent in the future, that is, under various assumptions about property prices and the quality of their lending portfolio? This was the key economic, as opposed to accounting, issue. It is not known whether the Regulator's opinion was sought on this question. Presumably, if asked, he would have deferred to the judgment of Central Bank Governor Hurley, namely, that based on the standard stress testing of the banks and assuming (more or less as an article of faith) that a 'soft landing' for the property market was in prospect, there was no cause for any fundamental worry.

10.2 Alternatives to the Guarantee

The appropriateness of various elements of the guarantee can be examined from two distinct perspectives. First, given the Irish authorities' assessment of the banks' financial situation ('what they knew at the time'), were there alternatives that might have ended up limiting significantly the ultimate exposure to the taxpayer? This is the issue most commonly debated. However, a second hypothetical, but nonetheless intriguing, issue is also worth considering. Suppose that by late September 2008, the Regulator (and/or other officials) belatedly had somehow formed a much more negative impression of the banks' capacity to withstand a far sharper downturn in the property market. In such a scenario ('if only they had known'), would or should the decision taken have been radically different? This question is also discussed in what follows.

Given the authorities' state of knowledge at the time, what alternatives to the decision were available?

10.2.1 'Do Nothing and Let the Chips Fall Where They Lie'

It was argued in Chapter 9 that, faced with a looming crisis, it would not have been responsible for any government to simply let Anglo close its doors the following morning. The collateral damage, while impossible to predict accurately, would have been enormous, both for Anglo and, very probably, the other banks who were known to be heavily exposed to the property market and who had significant interbank financial claims on Anglo. Furthermore, as suggested earlier, if Anglo had been allowed to collapse, after a period of some considerable financial chaos, the government most probably would have ended up taking action similar to the guarantee, but only after having suffered major reputational damage in the meantime. Also, although not necessarily uppermost in officials' minds, Ireland would have been held responsible and blamed by their European partners for whatever contagion-related damage that might have arisen elsewhere.

10.2.2 'Provide Emergency Liquidity Assistance in Various Forms, Rather Than a Guarantee'

Various ideas along these lines that had surfaced prior to 29 September were rejected (or in the end proved unnecessary). The provision of ELA by the Central Bank to keep the banks afloat for a while might have been an option. However, there were major drawbacks. First, at that time ELA was intended to deal with a single, solvent but temporarily illiquid, institution, rather than a possible systemic crisis. Since the problems experienced by Anglo would very likely have ended up spreading to other Irish banks (some capital flight from Ireland reportedly was already taking place), this criterion could not have been satisfied with any confidence. Secondly, ELA in principle was supposed to be extended more or less secretly, so as to avoid the risk of further market destabilization. Prior experience with the run on UK Northern Rock had demonstrated that public awareness of the deployment of ELA could increase, rather than diminish possible panic. Given Anglo's increasingly publicized fragile position, there were serious doubts that such secrecy could have been maintained. Thirdly, provision of ELA would have most likely involved an open-ended commitment of uncertain magnitude and duration. While the Central Bank bore the immediate financial risk, the extension of the ELA required a 'letter of comfort', indicating that the Irish government would 'stand behind' the Bank in the event of repayment difficulties. Finally, the use of ELA was subject to approval on a 'no objection' basis by the ECB, although there was no reason to believe that if a request had been put to the ECB (which it was not), support would not have been forthcoming. Nevertheless, use of ELA would simply have shifted the burden on the Irish State to a different location (the Central Bank of Ireland), without affecting the ultimate outcome. For all of what seemed to be good reasons, the ELA option was discarded early on.[8]

A second possibility (perhaps combined with some element of ELA) involved gathering emergency liquidity from other domestic sources. The

---

[8] However, following the guarantee decision a modest amount of ELA was made available as a back up, in case the guarantee failed to restore confidence sufficiently. In the end it was not necessary to avail of this funding at that time.

main components of such a domestic 'fighting fund' would have been cash and other liquid balances maintained by the Exchequer and the National Pension Reserve Fund (NPRF), both managed by the NTMA, as well as some assets of the Central Bank itself. It is not clear to what extent such a proposal (akin to 'raiding the piggy bank') gained traction, particularly as it shared several of the drawbacks associated with the use of ELA already described. Moreover, for the reasons discussed in Chapter 9, such an approach would likely have been resisted by the NTMA. In the event, the 'fighting fund' avenue was not pursued.

The Bank of Ireland and AIB, who were both believed (at the time) to be in relatively strong financial health, were approached to contribute—perhaps as part of a broader liquidity package—short-term assistance to help shore up Anglo. They agreed and a fund of €5 billion was hastily established around 29 September. However, the use of these resources turned out to be unnecessary, following the immediate success of the guarantee in stemming outflows. AIB and Bank of Ireland's willingness to make funds available was made contingent on their receipt of a government guarantee in the event of non-repayment by Anglo.

The above proposals all implied a major commitment of public monies (directly, in the case of the first two possibilities and in the form of a contingent liability under the third). When comparing these proposals to the guarantee, it is unlikely that the financial implications for the taxpayer would have ended up being fundamentally different. Most probably, resources to support liquidity needs would have been expended immediately, as opposed to much later when, notwithstanding the guarantee, public funding was required to make up for the banks' financial shortfall.

10.2.3 'Time Should Have Been Sought to Persuade the ECB to Implement Some (Unspecified) Pan-European Solution, (perhaps even Involving Some Relaxation of the "No Bank Should Fail" Principle)'

This possibility was put forward by both the Nyberg and Honohan reports. It presumably would have entailed some injection of liquidity (perhaps only for a few days), using a combination of the options discussed above. Although a sudden shift in the ECB's position was not impossible to imagine, there is no evidence to suggest that it would have adopted a more flexible or proactive approach, at least in the immediate future. While the interactions between the ECB and the Central Bank have not been disclosed publicly, neither institution has provided indications that a short delay might have led to a change in the ECB's attitude.[9] Although a direct appeal by Ireland to the euro area political leadership conceivably could have had some effect, this remains highly speculative. The costs of waiting would have been substantial as, barring a sustained return of financial confidence, funds expended on liquidity support would likely have proven to be unrecoverable. The pursuit of this option, as acknowledged by the Nyberg report, would have been highly risky, entailing immediate and major financial risk and unknown and uncertain benefits.

10.2.4 'The Time Period of the Guarantee Could Have Been Shorter Than Two Years so as to Provide More Flexibility to Take Advantage of Unfolding Events'

Flexibility involves advantages, but it also creates uncertainty. If the underlying situation had not significantly improved as the expiration date of an (assumed to be shorter) guarantee period approached, pressures from creditors to withdraw funds would have reignited. In fact, this occurred later on, during August–September 2010, when the Irish banks experienced a haemorrhaging of deposits as the termination date of the initial guarantee came closer. On the other hand, if developments had turned out more favourably, the length of the guarantee would have been largely irrelevant. From this perspective, and given the major inherent uncertainties, it is difficult to quarrel with the period chosen. That said, in retrospect, the time period did prove to be a constraint in one important sense. It was not possible to embark on any restructuring of the Irish banking system while the guarantee was in force as this could have prompted bondholders to declare an 'event of default', and seek immediate repayment under the guarantee.

10.2.5 'The Coverage was Excessive'

There has been considerable controversy as regards this aspect of the guarantee. Although no suggestions have been made that deposits should not have been included (the Cypriot alternative described in Chapter 9 was never considered), the debate has focused on whether the coverage should have excluded certain other classes of liabilities, such as bonds. Particular attention has focused on whether 'junior' (sometimes called 'subordinated'), as opposed to 'senior', bonds should not have been included.

Liabilities of a financial institution are ranked in a hierarchy according to which creditors are prioritized in the event of the institution experiencing financial stress, including, in the limit, insolvency. Typically, deposits rank at

---

[9] Indeed, key elements of the ECB stance, namely that no bank could be allowed to fail and that bondholders (other than some junior debt holders—see Section 10.2.5) could not be 'burned', did not change until the financial crises of Greece in 2011–12 and Cyprus in 2013.

or close to the top behind, for example, claims by the tax authorities, while shareholders' equity is at the bottom. In between, various 'senior' and 'junior' or 'subordinated' bond categories are distinguished. The interest paid on junior bonds is usually higher in order to compensate for the lower degree of protection that they typically enjoy.[10]

In the case of a default on senior bonds, there was a widespread fear that this could have generated international contagion effects for the euro area financial system, such as had occurred when Lehmans was allowed to fail in the US. Such a concern was likely to have been uppermost in the thinking of the ECB and 'informally' communicated to the Central Bank of Ireland. This message undoubtedly was passed on—see Cowen (2012)—to those attending the 29 September meeting. The fact that Ireland respected this constraint and did not 'burn' senior bondholders had major consequences, in terms of the costs to be borne later by Irish taxpayers. While Ireland's action was mainly directed at safeguarding the Irish financial system, it also provided protection for European financial institutions' senior bondholders who had imprudently lent to Ireland. As indicated in Chapter 11, this has had important implications for the discussions at eurozone level aimed at addressing Ireland's current very high debt burden.

There was a second constraint to burning the holders of senior bonds which arose from their legal status. Both the Taoiseach and Minister of Finance Lenihan, a skilled senior counsel barrister, argued later that, according to legal advice, under Irish law depositors and (senior) bondholders had equal protected status, thus impeding any differential treatment. Legal opinions that may have been provided by the Attorney General at the time on this matter have not been revealed publicly, presumably on confidentiality grounds. Nor, to the authors' knowledge, has the issue been tested so far in the courts. However, despite all the controversy surrounding different aspects of the guarantee, no legal opinions contradicting Minister Lenihan's view appears to have been thus far surfaced. A default on senior bonds might even have been challenged on constitutional grounds. Moreover, apart from foreign bondholders, some of the senior bonds in questions were believed to have been held by Irish institutions, such as pension funds or credit unions.

In the case of subordinated (junior) debt, however, the Honohan report concluded that the inclusion of junior bondholders in the guarantee was unnecessary and undesirable.[11] There are arguments on both sides of this issue. Advocates of the exclusion of this debt category rightly stress that

---

[10] See Honohan (2010: Annex 4) for a more detailed discussion of this topic.

[11] The Honohan report also suggested that it would have been sufficient to only cover debt falling due. However, if the objective was to seek to maintain a given level of financial exposure to the banks, this would have required that new debt also be guaranteed. It is not clear that such an approach in the end would have reduced the total contingent liability involved.

subordinated debt is closer in nature to share capital and earns a high return commensurate with the associated risk. Consequently, as with share capital, creditors holding such debt should have been exposed to incur substantial financial losses.

The positions of those who have defended the inclusion of junior debt are somewhat vague. It has been suggested that, given the high degree of uncertainty, if not panic, prevailing, attempts to fine-tune the coverage of the guarantee might not have been well understood by markets the following morning and could have derailed the overriding objective of restoring confidence in the Irish banks.[12] There may also have been a concern that, given cross default clauses, reneging on subordinated debt might have had repercussions for some other liabilities covered by the guarantee, including, possibly, rendering them immediately payable.

The arguments on the issue are not conclusive. Minister Lenihan, in a subsequent concession (his only concession with respect to the guarantee decision), accepted that inclusion of subordinated debt may have been a mistake. While subordinated debt at the time comprised only 3 per cent of debt covered by the guarantee (around €13 billion), the savings from exclusion could have been considerable, as all this amount could be subject to a subsequent large-scale 'burning' operation. Nevertheless, an important point—see Cowen (2012)—is that after the expiration of the guarantee at end-September 2010, very large 'haircuts' in fact were imposed on holders of subordinated debt of AIB and Bank of Ireland, as well as of the two 'dead' banks Anglo and INBS.

In March 2012, former Taoiseach Brian Cowen, in his first major speech since leaving office, provided a robust defence of the overall coverage of the guarantee, including the inclusion of senior and subordinated debt:

> It is the case that no discounts were applied to senior bonds, which raises the question as to whether the State could have reduced the bill for the banks by excluding senior bonds from the guarantee, either at the beginning or subsequently. The extent to which losses could be imposed on senior bonds of European banks is limited by the legal framework that requires equal treatment of all senior bank creditors, including senior bondholders and depositors. This state of affairs is very different from the US, where senior bonds and depositors can be treated differently...
>
> Notwithstanding these legal issues, what the passage of time has shown is that, in reality, as a member of the euro area, the senior bonds of Irish banks had to be repaid in full, even if there had been no guarantee. At no stage in the crisis would the European authorities, especially the European Central Bank, have

---

[12] As against this, Honohan (2010: 128) notes that the guarantee did in fact entail some fine-tuning as certain other categories of liabilities apart from share capital were also excluded.

countenanced the dishonouring of senior bank bonds. The euro area policy of 'no bank failures and no burning of senior bank creditors' has been a constant during the crisis. And as a member of the euro area, Ireland must play by the rules....

Regarding the scope of the guarantee, it is true that some types of bonds were included in the scheme. However, it is important to note that we set a limited duration of two years on this broad guarantee. That scheme expired in September 2010 and junior bonds were no longer guaranteed by the State after that date. Critically, the bulk of the junior bonds covered by the guarantee were scheduled to mature, that is, to be repaid, after September 2010. They did not mature during the period of the guarantee. Their inclusion in the scheme did not preclude the bonds eventually sharing in the burden of the banks' losses. And in the event, when the true scale of bank losses had been revealed, these junior bonds did take their share of the losses. There was about €20 billion of junior bonds outstanding in September 2008 and average discounts of between 80–90 per cent were eventually applied to these bonds under legislation introduced by my government (Cowen 2012).

This is an important statement by the former Taoiseach who has been accused by many of making a fatal mistake by guaranteeing all the senior and junior bonds of the covered Irish banks. It highlights the very real constraints the government that he led faced at the time, arising both from Irish legislation and euro area policies.

10.2.6 'Specific Actions Should Have Been Taken With Respect to Anglo'

Although from the perspective of the Financial Regulator, Anglo's financial position at end-September 2008 was certified as sound, some in official circles may have held misgivings about the bank's underlying situation. This may have reflected unease regarding Anglo's unorthodox, even aggressive, approach, exemplified by the style of its leadership under Sean Fitzpatrick. Moreover, on the night the crisis broke, it was the institution under the greatest pressure, threatening to 'take the other banks down'.

According to both the Honohan and Nyberg reports, the possibility of nationalizing Anglo surfaced at some stage on 29 September, although it is not clear how seriously this was pursued.[13] While, in principle, legislation was—or could have been rapidly made—available to nationalize any of the covered institutions (see Chapter 9), the reasons that might have justified such drastic action in the case of Anglo were by no means obvious at the time. Later in 2008 (after the guarantee decision), the government stated that it would intervene if Anglo could not raise sufficient capital (see Chapter 11) and in

---

[13] Media reports that have never been confirmed suggested that early on in the deliberations the Taoiseach personally and quite bluntly vetoed nationalization of any financial institution.

January 2009 Anglo was nationalized. However, throughout 2008, Anglo was in compliance with all regulatory norms, including those relating to capital adequacy. Suspicions—even bordering on dislike—of an institution's style of operations would hardly have been sufficient to justify publicly the radical step of nationalization. And, unfortunately, a possible 'halfway house', namely, appointment of a receiver under a special bank resolution regime, was not available since, as noted already, the required legislation had earlier been put on the back burner.

This aspect aside, from the taxpayers' point of view, a takeover of Anglo, as opposed to only a guarantee of its liabilities, might have constituted an even greater contingent burden for the taxpayer. By putting its full weight behind Anglo, the government would not necessarily have signalled the institution's strength but rather its possible underlying weakness.[14] Furthermore, if Anglo had been quickly nationalized, and for reasons that were not immediately obvious to the public, the government could have come under pressure to nationalize other institutions, causing the process to spin out of control.[15]

Apart from these elements, the Honohan report remarks that governance aspects could, in principle, have been a relevant consideration pointing in the direction of nationalization. Nationalization of Anglo, presumably, would have led to a replacement of the bank's senior personnel. To the extent that in the short period following the guarantee but preceding eventual nationalization in early 2009, inappropriate financial practices might have been engaged in, the delay in taking the nationalization approach—while understandable at the time—would have entailed some costs.[16]

10.2.7 'Merrill Lynch Did Not Support the Guarantee'

Various commentators have suggested that Merrill Lynch, the consultants engaged a few days prior to 29 September to advise the Irish authorities and who were present in Government Buildings that night, opposed the guarantee, while others have argued the opposite. Although Merrill Lynch has chosen not to comment publicly on its role in the 29 September discussions, two documents that they prepared for the Department of Finance at the time

---

[14] This line of argument assumes that a nationalized Anglo would remain under no less pressure to meet its obligations for the broader 'contagion' considerations already alluded to. There appears to be no reason to believe otherwise.

[15] Honohan (2010: fn 162) discusses one theoretical option, namely, the closure of Anglo and the provision of the guarantee to all the other five banks. However, he concludes that given the systemic importance of Anglo, as well as the lack of knowledge as to its underlying situation, such a possibility was 'of academic interest only'.

[16] This aspect has been raised in the context of legal proceedings between the current Anglo—now IBRC—management and the former Chief Executive of Anglo at the time, David Drumm.

have been submitted to the Oireachtas Public Accounts Committee and made public.

The first document, dated 29 September 2008 (PAC 2010a), was transmitted that same evening to Assistant Secretary of the Department of Finance Kevin Cardiff. At the outset, Merrill stressed that: (i) 'liquidity concerns aside, all of the Irish banks are profitable and well capitalized'; and (ii) after consideration, 'one outcome, allowing an Irish bank to fail and go into liquidation without any government intervention [should be discounted] . . . we strongly advocate a more controlled interventionist approach.'

Although the memorandum discussed various options, it is difficult to discern a clear hierarchy of preferences, perhaps because it was written under considerable time pressure. Support was voiced for the provision of immediate liquidity by the ECB (and, if that was not possible, by the Central Bank), as well as for 'state protective custody' (which could have implied some form of nationalization), in the case of Anglo and INBS. The memorandum also favoured creation of a 'Secured Lending Scheme' (SLS), very similar to the proposal of a 'Fighting Fund' referred to above, of about €20 billion, but with potential funding reaching €100 billion. The feasibility (in legal, financial, or political terms) of these schemes was not spelled out.

The document stated that the alternative to a SLS facility was to offer a 'complete state guarantee' to the six domestic institutions. It recognized that although this should 'be sufficient to stem outflows and encourage inflows . . . the scale of such a guarantee could be over €500 billion . . . [which] would almost certainly negatively impact the State's sovereign credit rating and raise issues as to its credibility', concerns likely to have been shared by some of the participating officials. Overall, the memorandum stops short of expressing a clear preference for one single approach over others.

The memorandum was ambiguous in relation to the appropriate treatment of subordinated debt. In discussing the state protective custody option for Anglo and INBS, it stated that 'a State guarantee would be given to all depositors and senior creditors *as well as dated subordinated debt holders* (given the cross over between these two holders) which would again send a strong implicit message to the investor community that *this level of protection would be afforded to all other Irish banks* (authors' italics)'. However, later on, Merrill urged that a complete state guarantee 'be given to all depositors and *senior creditors* (authors' italics)'. This apparent contradiction is somewhat puzzling. It is difficult to comprehend why one would exclude junior debt from a general guarantee applicable to all banks, but include it in the case of the two banks (Anglo and INBS) which were in worst shape and hence most likely to incur the largest potential losses. It may well have reflected hurried drafting.

A second document, a Merrill PowerPoint presentation to officials only three days earlier, on 26 September 2008—further evidence that some preparatory work had taken place prior to 29 September—adds to the sense of a lack of clarity (PAC 2010b). Under a listing of the features of a 'Guarantee for 6 primary regulated Irish Banks', reference is made to the fact that this would protect 'senior *and subordinated creditors*' (authors' italics).

Overall, based on the record, the advice of Merrill Lynch, while opposed to allowing any Irish bank to default, did not express a clear view in favour or against the guarantee plan. As with other options, pros and cons were noted, although these did not comprise an exhaustive list nor were they subject to a comprehensive analysis. The evidence regarding the treatment advocated for subordinated debt is somewhat ambiguous.[17]

10.2.8 'The Government Was "Rolled" by the Banks into Giving the Guarantee'

The arrival (at their request) of the leadership of Bank of Ireland and AIB at the meeting early in the evening of 29 September has contributed to the accusation that the guarantee decision was due to pressures exerted by the major banks. However, in a situation where the government was facing the possible imminent collapse of the banking system, it was reasonable to assume that the two largest banks would be included in the consultations, especially since they had been asked to provide emergency liquidity to Anglo. But is there evidence that the banks' role went further?

The Bank of Ireland and AIB representatives confirmed to the Taoiseach and his colleagues that Anglo was facing a crisis and that, if nothing was done, they too would shortly face severe and quite possibly unsustainable pressures. There has been no suggestion that any issues were raised as to the financial soundness of Bank of Ireland or AIB themselves. This was hardly surprising, since apparently no such discussion occurred even in the case of Anglo, about which some may have harboured suspicions. The two banks supported the idea of a guarantee. They reportedly also took the opportunity to urge unspecified 'action' with respect to Anglo. From their perspective, Anglo's reputation was causing adverse contagion effects for Irish banks in general, and their own apparently more 'respectable' institutions, in particular. Of course, the banks' motivation could well be viewed as self-serving, stemming from competitive considerations. In any event, assuming Anglo was to be allowed to survive, as noted above, the two banks agreed to a request to make available, as part of an overall package, short-term funding backed by a government guarantee.

---

[17] This view differs from that expressed by Honohan (2010: 125) and Carswell (2011: 216), which both argue that Merrill Lynch opposed the inclusion of subordinated debt. However, careful analysis of both documents does not lend support to their unequivocal conclusion.

The two banks themselves—in common with virtually everyone else—had little or no idea of their own underlying financial vulnerability.[18] It was natural that they would join the growing chorus in favour of a guarantee, viewing the problem as merely one of liquidity. One can conjecture that the banks would not have been against proposals such as the 'fighting fund' or the provision of ELA, provided that these somehow succeeded in injecting liquidity into their institutions sufficiently quickly. Certainly, the bankers wanted their banks rescued from their temporary liquidity problems, but at that stage who did not?

The guarantee had two effects: first, it 'bailed out' the banks' creditors; and second, it kept the major banks open for business and their management and staff employed, at least for some time. There is a common misperception that the guarantee in and of itself provided protection to the banks' shareholders. This is far from the case—shareholder write-downs for the six covered banks ended up exceeding €29 billion (Honohan 2012). At the time of the guarantee (and indeed for quite some period afterwards), the two major banks were not held responsible for serious managerial errors. Nor were they believed to be in fundamental difficulties. A call for 'heads to roll' at that stage would not have been well-founded. However, once the banks' problems began to unfold, failure to do so became less defensible as changes in bank directors and senior personnel were slow and hesitant. But such a criticism is logically separate from issues associated with the guarantee *per se*.

Apart from a very temporary boost, neither the guarantee nor other subsequent initiatives, including government injection of capital, put a brake on a further collapse of the banks' share prices and stockholders' massive losses. The sense that these two banks were conveying at the time of the guarantee, namely, that they did not wish to be associated with the 'buccaneering' bad bank of Anglo, turned out to be misplaced. Soon the truth began to emerge. Anglo and INBS were not just the 'bad apples' in a good fruit cart—AIB, in particular, turned out to be in almost as disastrous a condition.

10.2.9 'What If on 29 September the Authorities Had Had a Much Better Appreciation of the Underlying Weaknesses of the Banks?'

It has often been stressed that the guarantee was provided on the basis of an entirely false and rose-coloured view of the banks' vulnerability. This is incontrovertible. But one may well conjecture as to what might have happened if

---

[18] In this respect, the oft heard accusation that the banks 'lied' to the authorities at the time of the guarantee is misplaced. It is far more likely that they themselves, through negligence, had equally little appreciation of their true situation. In July 2008 the rating agency Standard and Poors reported 'The ratings on Bank of Ireland reflect its very strong market position in Ireland, good business diversity, and sound track record'.

the starting point had been different. For the sake of argument, suppose that the Central Bank and the Financial Regulator, in the weeks leading up to the crisis, had come to a sudden belated conclusion that most of the banks were, after all, staring at huge losses, and that to stave off a default, massive recapitalization from the State would be required. In other words, what if the scenario that later actually emerged had already been anticipated to some extent at end-September 2008?

An immediate answer might be that in that case, the guarantee, which was to end up condemning taxpayers to foot an enormous bill, should either not have been provided, or should have been provided only in a much more restrictive form. But such a response still raises the question—what should have been done instead? It could be argued that, under the assumed scenario, whichever of the banks that were known to be 'bad' should have been allowed to go to the wall and a guarantee given only to whatever 'good' banks remained. One can speculate as to whether such an approach would have succeeded in addressing satisfactorily the 'run on the banks' problem. But, more fundamentally, assuming one somehow knew then what is known now, it would have been clear that in fact *all* the banks were facing huge difficulties (Bank of Ireland less so). Anglo was not just the 'bad apple in the cart'—the entire cart was contaminated. In such circumstances, logic might have dictated that none of the banks, including Bank of Ireland and AIB, deserved a rescue via a guarantee. However, it is hardly conceivable that all of the Irish banks would have been allowed to fail in the interest of saving taxpayer money. Political imperatives surely would have required that Ireland still possessed a functioning domestic banking system.[19]

Putting it differently, under this scenario, assuming that preservation of a domestic banking system was considered essential and that picking between 'good' and 'bad' banks was somewhat illusory, it is difficult to see how a comprehensive guarantee of some sort covering all domestic institutions could have been avoided.

That said, one can conjecture further and ask whether the ECB would have taken up a different stance, under a scenario where the true state of the Irish banks had been known at that stage. For instance, might the ECB have accepted that some form of European support was necessary to prevent an intolerable financial burden for the Irish government? The likelihood of this happening would perhaps have been greater if it was thought at the time that many European banks, and not just those of Ireland, were facing similar problems. But it took several years—from 2008 to 2012—before this began

---

[19] That said, the takeover of all domestic banks by foreign interests at some stage could have remained a logical possibility, although the price likely to have been offered by foreign buyers, in the absence of a guarantee, presumably would have been very low.

to dawn. Of course, a true appreciation of the extent of the Irish problem at end-2008 could have prompted earlier and more intensive investigations of banking system difficulties elsewhere. However, unless that had happened, it seems unlikely that a special scheme or exception to the generally prevailing approach would have been put in place at end-September 2008. The Irish problem, including its magnitude, would have been interpreted as a more or less isolated case.

In early 2009, the IMF (2009: 16) noted correctly that 'the [Irish] guarantee, covering over 200 per cent of Irish GDP, [was] much larger than in other countries'. Its report (IMF 2009: Text Table 1) also contained information on the coverage of six other 'blanket guarantees' extended in recent decades (Finland, 1993–98; Indonesia, 1993–2007; Japan, 1998–2005; Korea, 1997–2000; Sweden, 1992–96; Turkey, 1997–2004). The scope of all these guarantees was broad, although, generally speaking, not quite as all encompassing as in the Irish example. Although, as in Ireland, shareholders' equity was omitted in every case, only three of the six schemes appear to have specifically excluded subordinated debt; depending on the country, certain other particular categories of deposits were not covered. Thus, contrary to what has been claimed by some commentators, the concept of a comprehensive guarantee was by no means unique to Ireland. The problem was not so much the principle of the Irish scheme or perhaps even its coverage, but the sheer size of the underlying losses of the Irish banks. These turned out to far exceed expectations when the guarantee was issued, as well as experiences in other countries.

In the end, whatever mechanisms or fine-tuning might have been employed, the ultimate burden on taxpayers could only have been lessened significantly if the Irish government was willing and able to impose significant losses on senior bank creditors. But the reality is that, apart from subordinated debt, in the almost four years since the guarantee, the government has not pursued such an approach. This partly reflects concerns about the potential reputational costs for Ireland. But it also reflects pressures from the ECB and elsewhere owing to fears about contagion (within both Ireland and the euro area) and, relatedly, the creation of unacceptable precedents. Irish consideration of the burning of bondholders option undoubtedly has also had to take into account the willingness of the ECB to continue to provide low cost funding to Irish banks. While reasonable people may differ as to the merits of these various arguments, the fact remains that no losses have yet been imposed.

10.3 Contemporaneous Reactions to the Guarantee

10.3.1 *The ECB and Other Governments*

The ECB and (selected) other EU governments were informed of the Irish government's decision in the early hours of 30 September, before financial markets opened. The initial ECB reaction is not known, while the public response from ECB President Trichet was somewhat noncommittal. The ECB may well not have been informed beforehand of all the elements of the guarantee; there has been no suggestion that prior explicit ECB approval of the plan was sought or obtained.[20]

However, the guarantee provoked anger within UK government circles, who feared, correctly, that it would encourage capital flight across the Irish Sea. Tense telephone conversations took place between Chancellor of the Exchequer, Alistair Darling and Finance Minister Brian Lenihan. Two points are relevant in this context. First, any initiatives, such as a guarantee, that affect capital markets tend to cause abrupt movements of funds. However, the action taken by Ireland was not forbidden under the relevant EU agreements.[21] There is no evidence that the UK or other governments had raised principled concerns regarding the concept of countries granting a guarantee during the days or weeks before the Irish decision. EU governments generally (including the UK itself, in the case of Northern Rock) wanted to retain the flexibility to implement drastic measures if they were to find themselves in an unfortunate position similar to Ireland's. It would be stretching matters to suggest, as some have, that the Irish measure in any sense pressurized other countries into following a similar approach. Indeed, as described in Chapter 8, in the period immediately before and after the Irish guarantee, several 'support arrangements' were put in place by governments across Europe.

Second, although it might have been more 'diplomatic' for the Irish authorities to have consulted with their European colleagues before taking the decision, in the world of financial *realpolitik*, this would have been somewhat naïve. Had the government followed such a strategy, major pressures might well have been exerted to desist or to delay the decision—pressures that might have proved hard to resist, especially at the political level. In the meantime, serious damage would have occurred. No domestic Irish politician could have defended a potentially calamitous delay by explaining that 'permission was being sought' before Ireland took action to protect its vital interests.

---

[20] That said, it is quite clear—and confirmed by former Taoiseach Cowen's statement quoted in Section 10.2.5—that the ECB would have opposed any attempt to burn senior bondholders.

[21] Nevertheless, issues were raised by the EU as to whether the guarantee conflicted with restrictions on the provision of state aid. After lengthy discussions the EU later gave it a 'green light'.

Sometimes, as in the case of a currency devaluation, secrecy prior to a *fait accompli* may be the only workable approach.

10.3.2 *Other Reactions*

The initial public reaction to the announcement was fairly positive overall. The main opposition party, Fine Gael, while critical of the government in general, supported the guarantee in parliament and was praised for having adopted a 'statesman like' attitude in a crisis situation. Sinn Féin also took the government and the banks to task, but ended up voting for the measure. The Green Party announced its support, but 'with gritted teeth'. On the other hand, from the outset, the Labour Party consistently opposed the guarantee, citing the lack of details as to how the scheme would work and emphasizing the nature of the 'blank cheque' that the taxpayers might end up paying.

Markets, at least in the short run, gave what one analyst termed a resounding 'thumbs up'. Banks' share prices, after plummeting to an historic low on 29 September, shot up dramatically with jumps of 68 per cent, 21 per cent, and 18 per cent recorded for Anglo, Bank of Ireland, and AIB, respectively, in the immediate aftermath. The rating agencies Moodys and Finch issued very positive statements.

The foreign media highlighted prominently the Irish decision which they described variously as 'dramatic' and 'extraordinary', but tended to refrain from direct criticism. Not surprisingly, the UK media complained about the unilateral nature of the decision, referring to the 'angry' interchanges between the Irish and UK governments in the days after 29 September and criticizing the blatant efforts by Michael Fingleton Jnr., son of INBS head, Michael Fingleton, to entice UK funds to INBS following the guarantee.

Domestic commentators were, on the whole, positive. The government was praised for taking a clear position and for sticking with it—in contrast to the inept and indecisive handling of the US administration's bank rescue package—and, as one writer put it, 'buying that most precious commodity, time'. Economists overall had relatively little to say, probably reflecting their general lack of focus at the time on financial stability issues.

There were exceptions, however. Not surprisingly, economist Morgan Kelly (2008), writing on 2 October, presciently asserted that the real reason foreign banks had started to shun Irish banks was that international investors had gradually come to realize the full extent of their lending to builders and property speculators. Kelly did not pull any punches, stating: 'It [the guarantee] has put the taxpayer at risk of considerable losses... Irish banks were facing potential losses of the order of €10 billion to €20 billion ... at one stroke it looks as if it will be you, rather than bank shareholders, who will be taking the loss'.[22] And in shades of matters to come, future Central Bank Governor Patrick Honohan, then Professor of Economics at Trinity College Dublin, writing on 4 October, worried that

> official statements continue to rule out any possibility that the banks might require any additional capital...True, the authorities have access to somewhat more information than the market but are they processing that information through rose-tinted spectacles of denial? (Honohan 2008)

10.4 Conclusions

The guarantee decision of 29 September 2008 has provoked, and will continue to provoke, controversy for years to come. This is understandable, since, to many, it has condemned Irish taxpayers to pay an enormous bill arising from the reckless activities of domestic and foreign banks and those who reaped rich rewards from the property bubble. However, the issues involved are complex. In order to arrive at a balanced overall assessment of the decision, one must examine clinically and in some detail the options available at that time. The key question is not whether the guarantee was a 'good' decision, but whether, given the circumstances and constraints at the time, it was 'the least worse' option available.

The main justification for the guarantee was, and remains, the need to prevent any Irish bank from failing thus to avoid the reputational cost and financial chaos that could have ensued otherwise. This position was strongly supported by the ECB, who at some stage prior to 29 September also made clear that 'Ireland was on its own'. Not letting a bank fail was also the position of Irish officials at the time. Given this policy, it became inevitable that some form of major state commitment would be required. Matters came to a head on 29 September in the wake of intolerable market pressures. However, they had been building for some time and an inference that the authorities were hit by a 'bolt from the blue' on that day and only at that point began to think of possibilities such as a guarantee is not correct.

As discussed in the previous chapter, the shared view at the time that no bank could be allowed to fail was not adopted without good reason. Indeed, neither European nor Irish positions (including those of politicians and opinion makers) on this fundamental point changed in the four and a half years since the guarantee, with the exceptional (and possibly questionable) recent case of Cyprus. Against this background, given other unpalatable approaches,

---

[22] Kelly misspoke. In fact, bank shareholders did end up being almost entirely wiped out—what the guarantee did was ensure that lenders to the banks were bailed out by the Irish taxpayer.

which would, in any event, have implied very large and open-ended commitments of Irish taxpayers' money, there was no better alternative to the provision of some sort of comprehensive guarantee. Both the Honohan and Nyberg reports, as well as Irish politicians across the spectrum (except for the Labour Party), came to this conclusion. While a few economists and media commentators rightly raised concerns at the time, none advocated either inaction or specific alternative courses of action.

Nevertheless, the burden placed on the taxpayer has led to much heated discussion as to whether specific elements of the guarantee could or should have been different. This chapter has examined carefully all of the various options that, at one time or another, have been mentioned in the course of the debate. Given the crisis atmosphere and the real fears of Irish officials, delaying action was not a viable option in view of the attendant risks and uncertainties. In terms of coverage (by period or instrument type), there does not appear to have been a clear cut *a priori* case in favour of a different approach. While there is a legitimate question mark over the inclusion of subordinated debt, the balance of the argumentation is not conclusive. It would also have been difficult to justify what would have appeared to be unfounded and precipitous action in the case of Anglo and INBS, on the basis of the information then available. Finally, a close inspection of the record does not support unequivocally the contention that the government's advisers, Merrill Lynch, either opposed the guarantee or the inclusion of subordinated debt.

That said, the real (and devastating) criticism of all involved was that they were operating at the time under the gravely mistaken impression that the only problem facing the banks was a temporary liquidity shortage. Of course, this quickly turned out to be far from the case. However, even if the authorities had somehow become aware of the real solvency issues of the banks at the time, it would not have avoided the dilemma that, in order to maintain some semblance of a domestic banking system, significant support from the State was inevitable. Nor, under such a scenario can it be asserted with confidence that at the time (as opposed to four years later), Europe would have been willing to help manage what would have been perceived as a very bad, but uniquely Irish, situation.

The cost of the guarantee also needs to be assessed against the losses that would likely have been incurred in its absence. One measure of the gross cost is the €64 billion in capital injections that was required subsequently to keep the six domestic banks afloat. However, in the case of Bank of Ireland and AIB—especially the former—the stake of the government has some significant value, currently estimated at around €10 billion, which, if and when it is realized, will accrue to the taxpayer. How does a (net) expenditure of some €54 billion (about 30 per cent of GDP) arising from the guarantee compare with the cumulative costs of a hypothetical collapse of the Irish banking system otherwise? These costs, while impossible to quantify, need to take into account severe economic dislocation and, especially important in Ireland's case, the incalculable reputational damage *vis-à-vis* foreign investors consequent upon a default. Moreover, over €60 billion at the time would have been required to compensate individual depositors of less than €100,000 under the normal deposit guarantee scheme, had the government been obliged to intervene in order to prevent a default on these obligations also.

In the end, the possibility of reducing the burden on taxpayers depended on the Irish government's ability to impose significant losses on senior bank creditors. However, both in September 2008 and during the four years subsequently, for a variety of reasons (including the dependence of the sovereign and Irish banks on external financing from the EU/IMF and the ECB), this has not proved possible.

Current euro area and ECB policies are in the process of review and possible change. However, from an historical perspective, policymakers' decisions have to be judged in light of contemporaneous events and the domestic and external constraints they faced at the time. Moreover, the recent Cypriot experience should give pause for thought to those critics who have condemned the guarantee despite the fact that it maintained the stability of the banking and payments system. Taking into account the very substantial (but unknown) costs that would otherwise have been incurred, the guarantee decision of 29 September 2008, despite its huge cost consequences, nonetheless may have been the 'least worse' solution available. The granting of the guarantee was not the 'big mistake' that caused Ireland's financial crisis—the crisis was due to very serious errors of judgment made by many institutions and individuals long before end-September 2008.

References

Carswell, Simon (2011) *Anglo Republic: Inside the Bank that Broke Ireland* (Dublin).

Cowen, Brian (2012) 'The Euro: From Crisis to Resolution? Some Reflections from Ireland on the Road Thus Far', Georgetown University, Washington, D.C., 21 March.

Honohan Patrick (2008) 'Outcome of Bank Guarantees Abroad May Worry Taxpayers', *Irish Times*, 4 October 4, 2008.

Honohan, Patrick (2010) *The Irish Banking Crisis: Regulatory and Financial Stability Policy, 2003–2008*, A Report to the Minister of Finance by the Governor of the Central Bank (Dublin).

Honohan, Patrick (2012) 'Recapitalisation of Failed Banks: Some Lessons from the Irish Experience', Address at the 44th Annual Money, Macro and Finance Conference, Trinity College, Dublin, 7 September.

International Monetary Fund (2009) *Ireland: Staff Report for the Article IV Consultation.*

Kelly, Morgan (2008) 'Bailout Inept and Potentially Dangerous', *Irish Times*, 2 October.

Nyberg, Peter (2011) *Misjudging Risk: Causes of the Systemic Banking Crisis in Ireland.* Report of the Commission of Investigation into the Banking Sector in Ireland, Government Publications (Dublin).

Public Accounts Committee (2010a), *Memorandum from Merrill Lynch*, dated 28 September 2008, made public 16 July 2010.

Public Accounts Committee (2010b), *Presentation by Merrill Lynch* to the National Treasury Management Agency dated 26 September 2009, made public 16 July 2010.

11

From the Guarantee to the Bailout

There has been no question of a negotiation for a bailout.

Taoiseach Brian Cowen, 17 November 2010

The end-September 2008 banking guarantee was broadly (but not universally) welcomed as a bold and decisive initiative by the government. There were some concerns raised as to the extent of the potential financial liability of the State. However, these were muted by a feeling that some lost confidence had been restored, as there was an initial reflow of deposits into the Irish banking system. Thus, although budgetary pressures were starting to become more serious—and the external economic environment was far from favourable—there was considerable hope that the worst might be over. With luck, Ireland could weather the storm reasonably well. The possibility of having to seek some outside financial assistance—let alone a bailout from the 'infamous IMF'—was far from almost anyone's mind.

Yet just over two years later, the unimaginable came to pass. In the early morning of 18 November 2010, the Irish people awoke to be told, via a live RTE Morning Ireland radio interview from Frankfurt, the humiliating truth by the Governor of the Irish Central Bank, Patrick Honohan. He informed listeners that an IMF team, together with officials from the EU and the European Central Bank (ECB), were arriving in Dublin shortly to discuss a major financial rescue package for Ireland.[1] In an editorial the following day, the *Irish Times* asked whether the men of 1916 had died for 'a bailout from the German Chancellor with a few shillings of sympathy from the British Chancellor on the side... the shame of it all.'[2] The loss of sovereignty was palpable—in the words of economist Morgan Kelly (2011) a few months later, Ireland had now become 'dependent on the kindness of strangers'.

---

[1] The full text of the interview is reproduced in Appendix B.
[2] The *Irish Times*, 19 November 2010. The reference to the UK reflected the announcement that its government would contribute a supplementary amount to the bailout for Ireland organized by eurozone members.

The respite following the guarantee of end-September 2008 indeed proved short lived. Soon afterwards, bank share prices resumed their fall, while the outflow of funds from the banking system also recommenced, reaching a peak in early 2009. The question can thus be asked—between then and the late autumn of 2010, could anything have been done differently to avoid the final outcome? Or was the eventual recourse to the bailout, in a sense, largely inevitable?

This chapter considers this issue by critically examining events during the tumultuous two years following the guarantee. The erosion of confidence in the Irish banks as the estimates of their losses rose steadily, together with the intense, but in the end largely unsuccessful, efforts of the government to arrest the rapidly deteriorating budgetary position, are first described. The (at times controversial) roles of the key Irish and foreign officials in the weeks prior to the final arrival of the bailout team in Dublin in mid-November 2010 are then discussed. This is followed by an assessment of the substance of the bailout agreement itself.

11.1 The Mounting Losses of the Banking System

Immediately following the 29 September 2008 guarantee, funds began to reflow to the domestic banking system. Although the weakest bank, Anglo, did not secure all the deposits lost in the run up to September 2008, it was still able to meet ongoing obligations without serious difficulty. Nevertheless, in a somewhat ominous sign, the share prices of all the Irish banks continued to fall steadily (Figure 9.1). Moreover, before long the net outflows of funds resumed, attaining their highest level in March–April 2009 (Figure 11.1).[3]

Despite the strong positive assurances by the Financial Regulator at end-September 2008, soon thereafter, unease began to emerge among some senior officials—especially in the Department of Finance—that this might not be an accurate depiction of the banks' true situation. The sober 'morning after' realization of the enormous potential liability of the Irish State undoubtedly helped concentrate the minds of many. Indeed, even before the guarantee, in early September 2008, PricewaterhouseCoopers (PwC) had been called in to undertake a more thorough investigation of some key elements, in particular, the banks' exposures to large property developers.

This was the first of four attempts during the following two and a half years to obtain a clear picture of the financial implications of the banks' meltdown

---

[3] See McQuinn and Woods (2012) for a discussion of the net movements in deposits from early 2009 onwards.

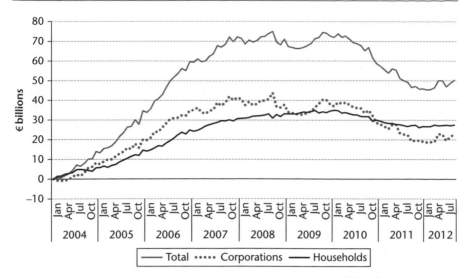

Figure 11.1 Cumulative Irish Private Sector Deposit Flows, 2004–2012[1]
[1] Indexed to January 2004 = €0
Source: Central Bank, Money and Banking Statistics and ESRI calculations

and their consequent needs for recapitalization.[4] The estimates of a second assessment—the Prudential Capital Assessment Requirements (PCAR)—exercise undertaken in March 2010 were subsequently revised upwards in September 2010. The last of the four exercises was completed in March 2011, as part of commitments under the bailout agreement with the EU/IMF troika. On each of the three earlier occasions, it was announced with some confidence that an accurate assessment of the real capitalization needs of the banks had been arrived at. However, for various reasons described below, this turned out to be optimistic. The revisions were generally in one direction only and the 'bill for the banks' continued to mount. Although other important factors were at work (see Section 11.2), the periodic upward revisions of the extent of the banking disaster contributed to an underlying erosion of market confidence, especially from late summer 2010 onwards. Together with major concerns of the ECB relating to the rapidly rising levels of the Irish banks' indebtedness to the ECB and the Irish Central Bank, it was a catalyst for the eventual insistence by external partners that Ireland seek a bailout from the EU/IMF.

Several factors help explain the long, drawn-out nature of the process of estimating the prospective losses for the banks (a process not dissimilar to that experienced by other countries such as the US and Spain, where official cost estimates ballooned over the course of a year). First, the exceptionally severe recession and the unique scale of the problem facing the banks made it very

---

[4] A comprehensive and detailed review of the process is provided in Honohan (2012).

difficult to narrow the extremely wide range of uncertainty associated with any central estimate, including the ultimate extent of the fall in property prices. Second, the initial investigation by PwC did not involve intensive 'drilling down' at the micro level.[5] This aspect began to be addressed after the National Asset Management Agency (NAMA, which commenced operating in mid-2009)[6] undertook a transaction-by-transaction evaluation of major development loans to be transferred to it. Such an approach, mandated by the requirements of the Competition Directorate General of the EU Commission, was possible because the individual loan exposures involved were very large. On the other hand, prior to the March 2011 exercise, the Central Bank's estimates relating to non-NAMA-destined loans (which were much more numerous and smaller in magnitude) were based on broad categories of exposures. Third, the specialized staff recruited from 2009 onwards to try to assess accurately the current situation and prospects for loan recovery did not have any real hands-on experience dealing with such an unprecedentedly large and complex problem, nor were there sufficient data or information to be able to satisfactorily 'parametrize' suitable models that might be employed. Finally, in the case of larger borrowers, unravelling the true nature of the maze of loan transactions typically involved enormous expenditure of time and effort.[7]

The parallel nature of the exercise, which entailed NAMA and the Central Bank assessing two different sets of loans throughout 2009–10, also led to complications.[8] Because of the nature of the work involved, the valuation and transfer of loans to NAMA was undertaken in tranches on a phased basis. At the same time, the creation of a new, complex, and little-understood entity for which the taxpayer would be ultimately responsible provoked unfavourable

---

[5] The study by PwC at end-2008 had concluded that while some losses were likely, the banks were all expected to remain solvent through end-2011, even under (what were regarded at the time) reasonably demanding stress tests. However, PwC, took as a starting point information provided by the banks themselves, including their assumptions regarding future profitability and the extent of possible loan impairment. Thus, the exercise appears to have been more of an elaborate accounting and arithmetical nature, as opposed to a questioning of the underlying quality and reliability of the banks' own assessments.

[6] In a formal sense NAMA was established only at end-2009.

[7] Detailed investigations by armies of accountants and legal experts of key elements such as the extent of cross-collateralization (the same property pledged against more than one loan), the enforceability of personal guarantees (including complex legal issues relating to the transfer of properties into the names of family members), and often simply major deficiencies in documentation, including title veracity, were required. The banks themselves may not have been fully knowledgeable as regards all these aspects, especially the quality of the collateral they held.

[8] Whether justifiably or not, since its inception NAMA has been the subject of considerable public controversy, including issues of insufficient transparency, high salaries paid to NAMA staff and consultants, and the employment of former property owners/developers to manage their properties under NAMA's control. Many of these aspects are dealt with by Cooper (2011: 253–342). This book considers only the role of NAMA in arriving at the estimated likely overall losses of the banks and their consequent need for recapitalization.

Table 11.1. Increasing Recapitalization Requirements for Irish Banks, 2009–2011

€ billion	BOI	AIB	Anglo	INBS	EBS	ILP	Reason
Phase 1: Early 2009	3.5	3.5	4.0				Initial global estimate.
Phase 2A: March 2010 (PCAR)	2.7	7.4	18.0	2.6	0.9		First NAMA tranche haircuts applied; top-down PCAR (non-NAMA) estimates for 3 banks (BOI, AIB, EBS).
Phase 2B: September 2010	0.0	3.0	7.3	2.8		0.1	Losses projected on wind-down basis for Anglo, INBS.
Phase 3: March 2011 (PCAR)	5.2	13.3			1.5	4.0	Higher capital ratio target; deleveraging costs; bottom-up PCAR (non-NAMA) loan-loss estimates using BlackRock methodology.

Source: Reproduced from Honohan (2012)

public and political reaction. It was suggested by some that NAMA would be pressurized by what was (still) viewed as a powerful and influential banking lobby to buy bank assets at too high a price with eventual losses for the taxpayer. NAMA may well have sought to make doubly sure that they could not be accused of accepting a rosy picture proffered by the banks. The banks also complained that the asset transfer process was not an arms-length transaction, since ultimately they had little option but to accept the valuations decided upon by NAMA. However, in the final analysis, from an overall economic and financial perspective, the issue of NAMA's asset valuations had little lasting effect since both NAMA and, in large measure, the banks ended up owned by the government.[9]

The successive estimates of the recapitalization needs of the banks from end-2008 are summarized in Table 11.1. In early 2009, the government decided that because of increasingly uncertain market environment, €3.5 billion would need to be injected into Allied Irish Banks (AIB) and Bank of Ireland, followed (in June) by €4 billion into Anglo (which had been nationalized in January). The Central Bank, preoccupied with other matters deemed more pressing (legislative changes, reorganization and recruitment of new staff, including some with credit management experience), does not appear to have revisited the recapitalization issue in any depth during most of 2009. However, in September 2009, a new Governor of the Central Bank, Patrick Honohan, formerly a Professor of Economics at Trinity College Dublin, was appointed and in January 2010, Matthew Elderfield took over as Financial Regulator. At this point the Central Bank, under new leadership, moved

---

[9] However, during the discussions between NAMA and the banks at the time, this issue did matter as the size of the eventual discount would determine the banks' losses and hence the financial outcome for private shareholders.

quickly to undertake the first major assessment of the true financial state of the banks.

This exercise was completed under a very tight deadline of end-March 2010 with limited resources. The Central Bank/Regulator, still lacking sufficient staff with the necessary expertise in this area, worked with the banks who, in some cases had developed in-house quantitative techniques, and with the rating agency, Standard and Poors, who had prepared some projected three-year loan loss rates. The methodology was not ideal and reflected a somewhat broad brush approach to examining different classes of assets across institutions. It also reflected a judgment as to the appropriate level of capital the banks required (set at 8 per cent Tier 1 capital). The Central Bank concluded that additional capital of €32 billion was required by the banks. This calculation took into account the average discount of 50 per cent per cent (the discount differed between banks) set by NAMA on the first tranche of loans that had been transferred to it. The Bank's estimate was based on an important assumption that each bank would suffer the same discount on future loan tranches still to be assessed, as it did for the first tranche.

However, by the summer of 2010, it became alarmingly evident that the prospective discount on the remaining tranches of NAMA loans would end up significantly higher than had been assumed. The reasons are not entirely clear. Perhaps the initial large developer loans were associated with many foreign properties that were not declining as sharply in value. Also, the initial loan dossiers may have been more complete and of better quality.

For this, and other reasons, the original end-March estimates were no longer credible. After intense and detailed exchanges involving the Central Bank, NAMA, and Anglo, it was announced at end-September 2010 that due to a combination of factors (larger discounts on further tranches of NAMA-destined loans relating to Anglo, INBS, and Bank of Ireland,[10] as well as higher estimates of non-NAMA loan losses for Anglo), an additional amount of €13 billion was required. The news was greeted with dismay by a disillusioned public, especially given the size of the losses facing Anglo, although several market commentators had been predicting a major upward revision for some time beforehand.

The major difference between the conclusions of the March and September 2010 exercises undertaken under the new Central Bank management team has been the subject of some questioning. In retrospect, the provisional nature

[10] The increase in AIB losses was of particular concern as it had passed a CEBS (Committee of European Bank Supervisors) stress test only a few weeks beforehand. Overall, the average discount for all the NAMA loans (€74 billion) ended up as 57 per cent, compared to the discount of 50 per cent applied to the first tranche of €16 billion. In the case of Anglo, the discount rose from 55 per cent applied to the first tranche of €9 billion to 61 per cent applied to the total loans transferred of €34 billion.

of the end-March exercise and the large margin of uncertainty surrounding the entire process, should have been conveyed more clearly to the public at the time. Another possibility would have been for the Central Bank to have added to its March estimate an extra amount as a 'contingency' to take account of this uncertainty and the preliminary nature of the previous estimate. Although the banks would have reacted very negatively, as they naturally resisted demands for what they argued were 'excessive' capital requirements, that would in itself not have been a significant deterrent.

More important, however, a 'topping up' in March 2010 of any amount close to that which eventually proved to be necessary would have been—and seen to have been—an insupportable financial burden for the state to bear at that time.[11] It would likely have had an immediate and negative impact on market lenders' sentiments towards Ireland (especially since the Greek crisis was starting to intensify around this time). Honohan (2012) argued that 'it [such an approach] would have undermined the State's already precarious finances and tipped it into an immediate need for a programme of assistance from the IMF and EU partners', several months before this actually happened.

In March 2011, as part of the bailout agreement, a further comprehensive and sophisticated analysis was undertaken under the auspices of external consultants BlackRock Solutions. The approach, which relied heavily on models and extensive databases to estimate likely probabilities of loan default,[12] required a computerized and rigorous examination of every individual bank loan. Most of the total increase of €24 billion in bank recapitalization needs resulted from greater losses associated with the rapid asset deleveraging required under the bailout programme, the imposition of a higher capital ratio, and the inclusion of a buffer to reflect possible life-time (as opposed to three-year) losses, derived using the BlackRock methodology. The NAMA discount issue had already been settled at that point and the loan transfer to NAMA completed.

During the assessments of the banks' recapitalization requirements from late 2008 onwards, serious governance issues at Anglo came to light, culminating in the departure of Sean Fitzpatrick and David Drumm as Chairman and Chief Executive, respectively, in December 2008. Following nationalization in January 2009, the new management team (consisting of Alan Dukes and Mike Aynsley as Chairman and Chief Executive, respectively), with the encouragement of the Minister of Finance, prepared a plan to split Anglo into a 'good'

---

[11] That is not to suggest that the Central Bank was under pressure from the Department of Finance to come up with 'low' numbers—by all accounts the Bank was free to employ whatever assumptions it chose, including, for example, the capital ratio to be required of the banks.

[12] For residential mortgages, for example, BlackRock assumed that bank forbearance would not be successful in avoiding foreclosures and that negative equity would be a driving force underlying bank losses.

and 'bad' bank. The 'bad bank' would gradually dispose of impaired assets,[13] while the 'good bank' would begin operations anew. However, many felt that the proposal was impractical and based on overly optimistic assumptions. The EU also raised a large number of issues that would have to be addressed. An important element was the 'smell factor', that is, hostility by the market to the idea of Anglo's continued existence in any meaningful operational form. In the event, the proposal was abandoned and a decision taken to wind down Anglo in September 2010. Anglo's sole mission would be to secure an orderly recovery and rundown of assets while meeting inherited obligations to depositors and bond holders.

11.2 The Budgetary Collapse Intensifies

The attempts to assess the true bill for the banks and to decide on the future of Anglo, while critically important, were perceived, fairly or otherwise, as somewhat reactive and piecemeal and did not dispel the increasing sense of public and market unease. Taken together with the rapidly accelerating fiscal crisis, there were emerging worries that the situation was beginning to spin out of Ireland's control. The bursting of the property bubble and the collapse of the construction sector, combined with the worldwide economic slowdown, was producing the sharpest recession in Ireland's economic history and causing Exchequer revenue to plummet. Severe expenditure pressures associated with the surge in unemployment were exacerbated by the spillover of earlier public sector pay awards (see Chapter 7). While part of these increases was deferred and eventually cancelled, the government concluded that it could not abrogate adjustments already in place. Despite the gravity of the revenue shortfall, the public sector payroll bill rose in real terms rose by 9.4 per cent in 2008 and by a further 0.9 per cent in 2009. Moreover, the increase in 2009 occurred despite a nominal salary and wage cut via a 'pension levy' averaging 8 per cent announced in March of that year.

Although the government in mid-July 2008 already implemented expenditure cuts totalling €1 billion, this did little to stem the widening tide of fiscal red ink. In a dramatic shift, the 2008 budget moved from a small surplus only one year earlier to a deficit of 7.3 per cent of GDP. The 2009 budget (announced in October 2008) contained €2 billion of new revenue measures. In February 2009, further expenditure cuts amounting to €2.1 billion were ordered. But there was worse to come. Two months later, in April 2009 the

---

[13] Although not given much publicity at the time, a by product of this plan was that it could facilitate a possible 'burning ' of senior bondholders as the quarantining into a 'bad bank' might dampen possible contagion concerns (see Section 11.5 below).

government had to introduce a full-scale supplementary budget, with a combined revenue and expenditure package aimed at further savings of €5.4 billion. These emergency measures were insufficient to halt, let alone turn around, the fiscal deterioration. Thus, the deficit for 2009 (excluding banking assistance measures) turned out be 11.8 per cent of GDP, three percentage points of GDP higher than in 2008.

Clearly more—a lot more—had to be done as a budget deficit of almost 12 per cent of GDP was not sustainable in any sense. The budget for 2010 included further expenditure cuts and (minor) revenue-raising measures amounting to €4.1 billion, which finally succeeded in slightly reducing the deficit to just under 11 per cent of GDP. Nevertheless, despite the unprecedented cumulative budgetary adjustment between 2008–10 of almost €15 billion (roughly 10 per cent of 2010 GDP), the state of the public finances remained perilous.

Preparations for the 2011 budget were dominated by the extent of the additional measures that inevitably would be required. Department of Finance officials prepared various scenarios, involving an adjustment package ranging from €3 billion to €6 billion. The possibility of increasing the savings to €8 billion was raised informally by EU and ECB officials but was rejected. According to a senior ECB official, Lorenzo Bini Smaghi, it was also suggested (but denied later by Minister of Finance Lenihan) that, in order to try to dispel uncertainty and boost confidence, the announcement of the budget be brought forward from the planned end-December 2010 date.

The attempts to regain budgetary control took place against the background of the ongoing requirement by the EU Commission to commit to reduce the deficit towards the maximum level of 3 per cent of GDP permitted under the Stability and Growth Pact. The time-frame agreed to reach this target was modified on several occasions, always in the direction of extending it as the full extent of the government's acute fiscal difficulties became more apparent. The medium-term adjustment path underlying the 2010 budget, after taking into account bank bailout-related costs, implied a sharp and sudden jump in Ireland's debt to GDP ratio, from 25 per cent per cent in 2007 to well over 100 per cent by 2013–14. Given increasing euro area-wide concerns about the fragile outlook for sovereign debt in general, such a trajectory was bound to be a source of growing worry to external observers, including the market.

11.3 2010—The Noose Begins to Tighten

In a narrow financial sense, 2010 began relatively well for Ireland. Although the economy was mired at the bottom of an extraordinarily deep recession, the NTMA continued to borrow at rates which, although slightly higher than normal, were still well within an acceptable range. By end-April, the government could state that the budget was fully funded until mid-2011. In January, ECB President Trichet made some positive public remarks in support of Irish adjustment efforts.

These favourable developments were counterbalanced by some negative news. Eurostat (the statistical agency of the European Commission) announced in April that the transactions involving the recapitalization of Anglo would have to be included in the measurement of both the government budget deficit and debt. Irish officials emphasized that this was largely a matter of statistical classification with no underlying financial impact. However, the optics were highly negative as it boosted the prospective budget deficit for 2010 to an unheard-of 32 per cent of GDP, albeit on a one-off basis. Such a gigantic number was quoted in circles abroad that were not necessarily fully informed or well disposed to view Ireland's situation benignly.

At around the same time, a crisis was intensifying at the far end of the eurozone that would have far reaching implications for Ireland. It had become increasingly clear for some time that Greece would no longer be able to retain the confidence of market lenders. The Greek economy, while not experiencing a property bubble such as that of Ireland, nonetheless suffered from long-standing structural problems and large budget deficits. These persistent deficits, combined with low growth, had set public debt on a clearly unsustainable trajectory. Given Greece's deep rooted weaknesses (including a highly regulated economy, an inhospitable climate for domestic and foreign private investment, a culture of tax evasion, and an exchange rate thought to be overvalued by at least 25–30 per cent), the short-term prospects offered no hope for a speedy recovery. External perceptions were not helped by a consistent pattern of Greece falsifying data it had provided to the EU and other international bodies.

By the spring of 2010, it was clear that Greece would require emergency external assistance. Greek government bond yields had soared to over 15 per cent and the government could not borrow any further. To stave off default, a bailout, together with a stringent adjustment program, was inevitable, although, in a precursor of the Irish situation to come, the Greek government remained in denial almost to the end.

Once the principle of a Greek bailout (applied for formally in April 2010) could not be avoided, the question as to the source of the bailout funds became important. The IMF had taken the lead in bailing out Iceland in November 2008 (the first IMF loan to an industrial country since the Italian and UK crises in the mid-1970s). However, lending to a euro area country represented a major departure. Some legal issues had to be considered,[14] but the main issue was political. The involvement of the IMF (especially given its poor image, at least in the eyes of much of the public) could be portrayed as a serious admission of Europe's inability to handle problems 'within the family'. This concern may have been felt especially by the ECB which feared a loss in prestige and reputation if the IMF was to intervene as part of the rescue.[15]

The debate on this aspect intensified as the Greek crisis accelerated. In the end, Chancellor Merkel was the driving force behind the decision to involve the IMF, for several reasons. First, the IMF would contribute one-third of the funding, thereby lessening the financial and risk burden for European (and especially German) taxpayers. Secondly, it had vast experience developed over more than half a century in dealing with financial and debt crises. By contrast, the EU, facing such a situation for the first time, did not possess the same technical expertise and its slow and cumbersome bureaucratic style was thought unsuited for efficient handling of fast-moving crises. Thirdly, decisions by the EU inevitably would be perceived as reflecting a strong political element which could cause significant stresses between donor and recipient countries.[16] From this perspective, involvement by a seemingly more 'neutral' and 'technocratic' agency such as the IMF would have certain advantages. Finally, the IMF has a very strong, albeit not entirely unblemished, record in ensuring that countries do not default on IMF loans, which may have given some comfort to those doubting Greece's capacity and willingness to repay.

Before the Greek bailout, it was hoped that any external assistance that might be needed by Ireland could be obtained from within the EU family. The government (and much of the media) frequently invoked the spectre of hypothetical IMF intervention to argue for preventative austerity measures. However, after the agreement with Greece, it had to be reluctantly accepted that the scenario of the 'IMF descending on Ireland' could by no means be ruled out. Privately, within some official circles, such a possibility had already

[14] This was because the IMF is formally empowered only to provide balance of payments support, as opposed to budgetary financing for governments, and the euro area as a whole was not experiencing a balance of payments problem, However, a precedent in this area had already been set several decades earlier when the IMF began to lend extensively to individual members of the West and Central African currency unions and the local currency proceeds of these loans were permitted to finance their governments' budgets. The IMF is generally regarded as a fairly pragmatic institution. Once the IMF's major shareholders take a policy decision (in this case to finance individual members of the euro area), supporting legal justifications are usually identified without too much difficulty.

[15] Personalities may also have played some role.

[16] Since the bailout with Greece began, relations between Germany and Greece appeared to reach an all-time post-war low, with continual references to the Second World War and alleged German intentions to buy up Greek islands. These were matched by charges by the German media, for example, that their taxpayers were being asked to finance a lowering of the Greek retirement age while their own was being raised in Germany. Similar strains, albeit not to the same extent, have surfaced in some domestic media coverage of Ireland's bailout.

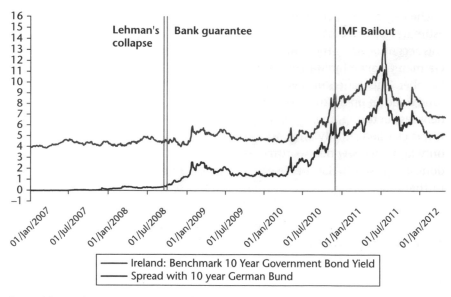

Figure 11.2 Irish Bond Yields, Jan 2007–May 2012
Source: Datastream—Thompson Reuters

begun to be contemplated. Indeed, quite some time before, in early 2009, outside advice had been informally provided to Minister Lenihan's newly appointed special economic adviser, Alan Ahearne, that sketched out the circumstances in which an IMF bailout might end up as a necessity as well as its likely content and *modus operandi*.[17]

Around the time of the Greek crisis, Irish government bond yields rose in April–May before falling back. However, following the issuance by Standard and Poors of a very unfavourable rating assessment for Ireland in August, yields—both in absolute terms and relative to benchmark German bonds—increased very sharply (Figure 11.2). The erosion in Ireland's creditworthiness was mirrored in upward movement in another indicator, the interest rate on Credit Default Swaps (CDSs) for Irish sovereign debt. Moreover, the rise in yields had occurred despite some discreet market intervention by the ECB to buy sovereign Irish debt. At end-September, the government announced its intention to withdraw from the market. While portrayed as a tactical move—officials stressed that the budget was already fully funded until mid-2011—the decision sharpened the focus of the market on an assessment of Irish sovereign risk.

---

[17] This hitherto unpublished document—Donovan (2009)—by one of the co-authors of this book is reproduced as Appendix C.

The negative impact of the Standard and Poors downgrading and the higher estimates of the cost of bank recapitalization announced at end-September was accentuated by the statement issued following a bilateral summit between German Chancellor Merkel and French President Sarkozy in Deauville in mid-October. The leaders declared that a new permanent euro area financial rescue fund to be set up by 2013 would require private sector creditors to accept some debt restructuring, that is, losses. This caused further market jitters. Although it was clarified shortly afterwards that the debt restructuring provision would only apply to new debt contracted after 2013, the damage had already been done and Irish officials made little secret of their dismay. Bond yields jumped further.

11.4 The Final *Dénouement*

Many of the events from mid-2010 onwards (summarized in Box 11.1) have been described elsewhere.[18] The various twists and turns included denials and

---

Box 11.1 THE ROAD TO THE EU/IMF BAILOUT, APRIL–NOVEMBER 2010

April
After intensive market and political pressure (yields on Greek two-year bonds had reached 15.3 per cent), Greece requests a bailout from the IMF and EU.

EUROSTAT announces a significant upward adjustment in the measurement of the Irish budget deficit and government debt for 2009 to reflect the Government's commitment to inject funds to recapitalize the banks.

The *Daily Telegraph* of London voices support for Minister Lenihan's efforts.

Nobel prize winning economist Paul Krugman criticizes Irish policies as likely to deepen the economic slump.

After falling somewhat in March the spread between Irish and German ten-year bonds widens to 2.27 per cent (29 April).

May
The EU decides to establish a 'fighting fund', the European Financial Stability Facility (EFSF), supported by financing from the IMF.

EU Council President Van Rompuy announces plans to increase surveillance exercised by EU peers over individual countries' budget plans; multi-year budgetary plans called for.

continues

---

[18] Cooper (2011) contains an extensive description of much of what transpired, especially the unfolding political drama and the actions of key personalities (the Taoiseach, Finance Minister Lenihan, and Central Bank Governor Honohan). The accounts by Beesley (2011a and 2011b) may reflect additional information provided by participants. A BBC radio interview with Minister Lenihan in May 2011 (shortly before his death) contains further elements (O'Brien (2011).

Box 11.1 (Continued)

Finance Minister Lenihan states that he is under no pressure from the EU to accelerate his austerity plans nor does he envisage Ireland having to seek help from the IMF.

Morgan Kelly writing in the *Irish Times* predicts a worsening debt and borrowing crisis as lenders will decide to flee Irish banks. The Department of Finance describes article as 'extremely pessimistic' and containing 'very serious inaccuracies'.

August

24 August Standard and Poors, arguing that the costs of recapitalizing Irish banks would reach up to €50 billion (compared to previous estimates of €35 billion)—a figure denied by Irish officials—downgrades Ireland's debt rating from AA to AA-.

Large outflows of deposits from Irish banks start to accelerate, especially in the weeks preceding the expiration of the original guarantee at end-September; major increase in ECB lending exposure to Ireland.

September

8 September Minister of Finance Lenihan announces that the original proposal by Anglo management to split the bank into a good and bad bank (which reportedly was criticized by, among others, the EU Commission) has been rejected. Anglo is to be progressively wound down.

Irish borrowing costs reach new high of 6.1 per cent; spread between Irish ten-year bond yields and those on corresponding German bonds reaches 3.8 per cent.

Rates on CDSs for Ireland rise sharply.

Finance Minister Lenihan claims there is a 'concerted attack' on eurozone members and urges the media to provide more balanced reporting.

29 September Irish borrowing costs rise to 6.7 per cent.

30 September ('Black Thursday') Irish authorities announce upward revision of cost of bank recapitalization to €50 billion.

Finance Minister Lenihan announces that Ireland will withdraw from borrowing on the international markets for the time being.

Four-year recovery plan is to be unveiled in early November.

October

1 October A team of EU officials arrives in Dublin for 'talks' on the four-year plan: EU spokesperson denies any participation by the team in the drafting of the plan.

4 October A confidential letter received by Minister Lenihan from ECB President Trichet expresses concerns about the situation of the Irish banks.

8 October Finance Minister Lenihan attends IMF Annual Meetings in Washington. Although this is described as 'routine' by the Department of Finance, it is the first such attendance by an Irish Minister in several years.

18 October At a summit in Deauville, Chancellor Merkel and President Sarkozy announce the proposed creation of a new permanent financial rescue fund which also involves possible debt restructuring by the private sector.

29 October Chancellor Merkel clarifies that the proposed debt restructuring would apply only to bonds issued after 2013.

Spread between Irish and German ten-year bond yields reaches 4.3 per cent.

continues

Box 11.1 (Continued)

November

3 November Four-year budgetary plan is announced which reflects agreement with EU Commission to extend deadline for reducing the budget deficit to 3 per cent of GDP from 2013 to 2014.

4 November A second letter is received by Minister Lenihan from ECB President Trichet reiterating concerns regarding Irish banks.

8 November EU Commissioner Rehn visits Dublin and expresses support for Irish efforts; refuses to speculate on possible EU financial assistance.

9 November Finance Minister Lenihan denies 'absolutely' any need for a bailout.

10 November Irish ten-year bond yield closes at 8.5 per cent (spread *vis-á-vis* German bonds reaches 6 per cent) against background of media reports that that the ECB had purchased substantial quantities of Irish bonds.

11 November Ten-year bond yield rises to 8.6 per cent.

Although Irish representatives are not present, Irish crisis is high on the agenda of G-7 Finance Ministers meeting in Seoul, South Korea.

Central Bank Governor Honohan suggests that Irish bond yields would fall to more sustainable levels if the planned fiscal adjustment is implemented.

12 November ECB Governing Council decides via teleconference that it could not sustain its very large exposure to Irish banks and calls for significant deleveraging by the banks; some ECB Council members stress to Governor Honohan that the Irish government needs to apply for financial help immediately.

ECB/EU 'sources' commence off the record media briefings. Leads to Reuters and other media reports that Ireland will need a bailout and that 'discussions' are under way.

A further communication (precise nature unknown) takes place between Minister Lenihan and ECB President Trichet, followed by a phone call between the two men.

13 November Intensive internal discussions involving the Taoiseach, Finance Minister Lenihan, and key officials.

Government Ministers Ahern, Dempsey, Hanafin, and Roche all deny forcefully that any talks on a bailout are taking place.

14 November Large Irish delegation travels by government jet to Brussels to commence, by prior agreement, technical discussions with EU Commission officials on measures that might be taken under a bailout.

15 November Taoiseach continues to deny on RTE News that there is any question of Ireland applying for a bailout.

Lobbying on Irish side to see if a rescue could be portrayed as a rescue of the banking system as opposed to a bailout of the Government.

16 November Taoiseach informs Cabinet colleagues for the first time of the position of the ECB and the discussions with the EU Commission the previous weekend. Insists to Fianna Fáil party colleagues that there is no question of a bailout.

At ECOFIN meeting in Brussels, Finance Minister Lenihan is pressurized strongly by eurozone colleagues (especially Germany) to announce that Ireland is applying for a bailout; compromise reached via EU announcement that an EU delegation, together with IMF staff, would travel to Dublin forthwith.

17 November In radio interview Finance Minister Lenihan refers circumspectly to working with the EU/IMF team in order to address banking system issues.

Taoiseach denies in Dáil any involvement in negotiations on a bailout and criticizes media reports and commentary.

continues

Box 11.1 (Continued)

18 November In early morning radio interview from Frankfurt, Governor Honohan announces that the EU/IMF team arriving in Ireland would work out arrangements to provide Ireland with a 'large loan'.

IMF/EU/ECB team officially begins work in Dublin.

19 November ECB President Trichet sends letter to Finance Minister Lenihan which, according to the Minister's subsequent interpretation, threatens withdrawal of ECB support in the absence of a bailout request.

21 November Government announces intention to request assistance from the EU and the IMF. Letter sent by Minister Lenihan to ECB President Trichet to this effect.

28 November An agreement with the troika is announced and Ireland applies formally for emergency financial assistance.

increasingly frantic attempts by the authorities to stave off external financial intervention, in the end, to no avail. On the morning of Thursday, 18 November, in a live radio interview from Frankfurt, Central Bank Governor Honohan, who was attending a meeting of the ECB Governing Council, informed the nation of what many feared but thought could never happen—the imminent arrival of a large EU/ECB/IMF team to negotiate a 'very substantial' loan to Ireland. This was a major disappointment to the many Irish officials who had fought hard for over a year to try to prevent this happening.

Could the final outcome somehow have been averted? Consideration of this question requires a careful assessment of the roles of the key domestic and external institutions and individuals involved. What can be inferred about their actions and motivations? Were options available that might have succeeded in forestalling what finally transpired?

Media commentary during much of 2010 conveyed mixed messages. Ever since the guarantee decision in late 2008, Ireland's economic and financial predicament had attracted considerable foreign media attention—if only because of a fascination with success stories that end tragically and the UK media's increasingly europhobic approach. Earlier harsh budgetary adjustment measures had won some praise (notably from *the Daily Telegraph* in April 2009 followed by *the Wall Street Journal* in June 2010), tempered by caution that austerity might prove self-defeating and unsustainable. An article by economist Morgan Kelly in May, which saw little prospect of avoiding a crisis, was criticized by the Department of Finance, partly on the grounds that certain of Kelly's debt data were considered inaccurate and misleading. Nevertheless, Kelly's gloomy prognosis fuelled the pessimism of those who felt that the 'guru' had turned out to have been correct in the past. In any event, whatever praise was on offer stopped well short of concluding that Ireland would soon be 'out of the woods'. Well-publicized foreign commentaries by Nobel Prize winning economist and *New York Times* columnist Paul Krugman (entitled 'Erin go Broke') and *Vanity Fair* articles of Michael Lewis in mid-April depicted Ireland as a country that had 'gone far off the rails'. Although Irish officials sought to play up the positive assessments, this seemed to have had little impact on underlying market sentiment.

The **EU Commission** played a somewhat opaque role throughout. It regularly praised Irish adjustment efforts (including the commitment to prepare a four year budgetary plan), culminating in what was perceived as a relatively positive public assessment by EU Commissioner, Ollie Rehn, during his visit to Dublin in early November. The Commission sent a team to Dublin around that time to 'discuss' the government's draft plan, but stressed that officials were in no way 'involved in the drafting of this plan.'[19] Consistent with its generally collegial approach, the Commission did not wish to take the lead role in pressuring the Irish authorities publicly. However, while offering soothing words, it was careful never to imply that the measures being undertaken by Ireland would be 'enough' or sufficient to ward off any possible bailout request—a subject judiciously sidestepped whenever it arose publicly.

Irrespective of the public rhetoric, Commissioner Rehn would later state that 'I would say that latest, from mid-September in my thinking, the probability of Ireland avoiding a rescue package was very small. For some time then [before my visit to Dublin] we had known that we had to move to a programme' (Beesley 2011a and Beesley 2011b). It is not known publicly whether such a tough message was delivered privately by Rehn to Irish officials, in particular, during his 'final days' visit to Dublin in early November. In any event, when the call came to launch the bailout operation, the EU team was more than adequately prepared.

The **European Central Bank (ECB)** also followed a somewhat guarded approach, although it seems that it was the 'orchestrator' of the final initiative to push Ireland into the bailout.[20] On several occasions, ECB President Trichet strongly encouraged the Irish authorities to persevere with their budgetary adjustment. He dismissed the characterization of Ireland as the 'weakest link' in the eurozone, saying that there was no such thing as a 'weakest link'. Trichet addressed to an even lesser extent than the EU Commission the question of whether Ireland was doing 'enough'. However, the most pressing

---

[19] The careful wording should be noted. It is quite consistent with the EU team making forceful suggestions as to what would be acceptable for inclusion in the plan, without ever participating in actual drafting.

[20] ECB Vice President, Lorenzo Bini-Smaghi gave an interview to the *Irish Times* in early 2011 which was very critical of Ireland on budgetary and external competitiveness grounds. His intervention was criticized widely and helped create the impression that the ECB was fundamentally unsympathetic to Ireland (see discussion later in this section of Minister Lenihan's subsequent reactions). This charge has been denied vigorously by Trichet and other ECB officials sources.

source of his and the ECB's concern, was the extent of the ECB's financial exposure to Irish banks.

The ECB engaged in direct lending to Irish banks secured against eligible collateral. Once this collateral was exhausted, the banks could seek Emergency Liquidity Assistance (ELA) from the Irish Central Bank (see Chapter 9) which required approval (on a 'no objection basis') from the ECB.[21] Both these components rose sharply, especially from August 2010 onwards, reaching around €120 billion by end-October 2010, of which around €35 billion is estimated to have been accounted for by ELA (Figure 11.3).[22,23]

This was equivalent to about 25 per cent of the ECB's total lending, an unprecedented level of exposure to a country such as Ireland whose share in the capital of the ECB was less than 1 per cent. Should the ECB, for whatever

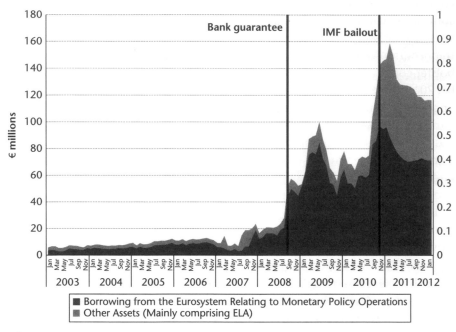

Figure 11.3 Central Bank of Ireland Liquidity Operations, 2003–2012
Source: Central Bank of Ireland, Money and Banking Statistics

[21] The extension of ELA is collateralized, in some cases by government paper, supplemented, as necessary, by 'letters of comfort' from the government to the Central Bank.

[22] This figure of €35 billion is a slight overestimate as it refers to the figure for total 'other assets' published by the Central Bank. It is understood that this series contains a small amount of assets that do not correspond to ELA.

[23] By end-February 2011, this had soared to its peak level of €159 billion, of which the ELA component was estimated at around €70 billion. By end-December, 2011, it had fallen to €116 billion.

reason, end up incurring financial losses relating to this exposure, these would end up being distributed among the central banks in proportion to members' share capital which reflected their relative economic weights in the euro area. In such an eventuality, the German central bank, the Bundesbank, would incur a financial burden about seventeen times that of Ireland and, in principle, German taxpayers could end up with the bill.

The surge in exposure to the ECB during August–September, which became publicly known only with some lag, was in response to accelerated outflows from the banks. The original two-year government guarantee was scheduled to expire at end-September. Although the EU most likely would approve an extension, the market could not be confident that the government would have the capacity to honour fully any further guarantee, especially if the ECB was to move to limit its financial exposure to Ireland. More generally, the combination of a sharply deteriorating economy, rising Irish bond yields, and continuing bad news regarding the banks' financial losses, contributed to a sense that it was time for creditors 'to get out' of Ireland, before becoming trapped. Ironically, the ECB's pressure proved counterproductive to efforts to bolster confidence. Thus, the statement by ECB President Trichet in September 2010 expressed concern about the amount of ELA outstanding to Anglo, as opposed to conveying some reassurances that this exposure would be maintained. This alone would have caused depositors to take flight as quickly as possible before the ECB might decide to 'turn off the tap'.

In any event, regardless of the impact on the market, the ECB started to ratchet up pressure on Ireland, probably in the first instance via concerns conveyed to Governor Honohan during the fortnightly meetings of the ECB's Governing Council. The campaign was intensified by means of letters from ECB President Trichet to Minister Lenihan in mid-October and early November. While not officially released, the content of the letters has been reported and involved strong urgings to 'act' so as to address the ECB's perception of a serious threat to the integrity of the system.[24] An additional communication (the precise nature of which is not known) appears to have been received on 12 November, followed by a phone call between Lenihan and Trichet (and a subsequent letter on 19 November).[25] Minister Lenihan

[24] See Collins (2012).
[25] According to Beesley (2011a), Minister Lenihan recalled receiving an actual letter on 12 November from Trichet. However, it now seems clear that the letter in question was in fact sent on 19 November. This was explicitly confirmed by a response from current ECB President, Mario Draghi, explaining the ECB's refusal to release this letter. Draghi's reply stated that the 19 November letter had expressed 'the ECB's Governing Council's concerns about the extraordinarily severe and difficult situation of the Irish financial sector and ... invited the Irish Government to take swift and bold action to address these concerns ... [adding] ... with this letter, the ECB aimed at protecting the integrity of its monetary policy and the stability of the Irish financial system in the interest of euro area citizens'. It should be noted that this letter dated 19

recalled subsequently that so far as he was concerned, irrespective of the diplomatic tone, these various communications raised 'the question about whether Ireland would be participating in a programme at that stage', with an implicit threat that ECB support for Ireland's banks was at risk (Beesley 2011b).

Additionally, in early November, the ECB decided to require a programme of 'deleveraging' the Irish banks (i.e. divesting assets) with the aim of using the proceeds to reduce their exposure. Finally, in mid-November, the ECB began to lobby the international media aggressively, quoting 'informed ECB sources' that Ireland had to take action to apply for a bailout. Reports to this effect appeared immediately in the world media, several of whom then decided to come to Dublin to witness the final *dénouement*. It was a highly unprecedented move for a central bank to take such direct action by using the media (and thus financial markets) so as to force a member country to conform to its wishes.

The ECB's determination to move decisively resonated quickly within the other European institutions. The EU, which up to then had adopted a somewhat lower key public posture, 'moved off the fence' and events started to pick up speed. Upon instructions of Minister Lenihan, on the weekend of 13–14 November, unbeknownst to the general public, a large Irish official delegation travelled by government jet to Brussels to conduct 'technical discussions' on the content of a possible programme, although no application for a bailout had been made.[26] Matters moved rapidly to the political level. At the ECOFIN meeting the following Tuesday, 16 November, Minister Lenihan encountered aggressive insistence, most notably from German Minister of Finance Schauble, supported by some (but not all) other European Ministers, that Ireland seek a bailout forthwith.

Reportedly, the Taoiseach and his colleagues spent much of the weekend of 13–14 November trying to shore up Ireland's fast-deteriorating negotiating position. While details have not been divulged, since at the euro level the position seemed beyond retrieval, one can only speculate whether thought was given to casting the net further afield by seeking some intervention by others (for example, the US). This would not have proved fruitful. **The G-7 Finance Ministers,** meeting the previous Friday in Seoul, Korea, had conveyed a clear message that Ireland had to apply quickly for a bailout. US Secretary of the Treasury, Timothy Geithner, believed that in the absence of a bailout, an

November was received *after* the decision had already been taken to commence negotiations with the troika team that arrived in Dublin on 18 November.

[26] Cooper (2011: 94) suggests that an Irish delegation that had visited Brussels the previous Friday for what they had assumed were routine discussions was shocked by EU officials' insistence on raising the subject of a bailout. In any event, the purpose and content of the subsequent weekend meetings (which at the request of the Irish side took place in Brussels rather than in Dublin) was arranged beforehand.

Irish collapse could have major repercussions on confidence worldwide, including via the effects on the CDS market. Thus, if the Taoiseach had sought to play 'the green card', in all probability, the White House, on the advice of US Treasury officials, would have politely but firmly indicated that the best course of action was for Ireland to bow to European demands forthwith.

The **Central Bank of Ireland**, and especially Governor Patrick Honohan, had a difficult and complex role to play throughout. Honohan himself, partly because of his prior extensive experience at the World Bank dealing with various financial crises, had an earlier sense than most that an EU/IMF bailout might be unavoidable. Moreover, the Governor met fortnightly with his colleagues on the Governing Council of the ECB where concerns were constantly raised, especially with respect to the ECB's very large exposure to Ireland. These would, as a matter of course, have been conveyed, either formally or informally by the Governor to Minister Lenihan, who presumably would have passed them on, as he saw fit, to Taoiseach Brian Cowen. The extent of any direct contact between the Governor and the Taoiseach on these matters is not known. However, irrespective of Honohan's personal views, it remained the decision solely of the government as to whether and when to accelerate a move towards a bailout.

It has been implied in some quarters (including by the Taoiseach shortly thereafter)[27] that the Governor's announcement from Frankfurt early on the morning of 18 November undercut the government's attempts to seek an alternative to a full-scale bailout. Such a criticism does not stand up to careful scrutiny. It is quite evident that over the previous several days—if not weeks—the views of all of Ireland's external partners, as well as senior officials in the Department of Finance and the Central Bank, had converged to the position that there was no acceptable feasible alternative than to start discussions on a possible bailout. However, it also clear that prior to 18 November, the Taoiseach and his Finance Minister were unable or unwilling to accept this reality.[28]

The Governor indicated subsequently that his decision to undertake the radio interview from Frankfurt on 18 November was precipitated by learning, late the previous night, of the content of an editorial that was published the next morning by the *Financial Times*. The editorial painted an alarming picture, referring to the 'explosive instability' of the Irish banking system and the

---

[27] On the afternoon of 18 November, the Taoiseach stated in the Dáil (Irish Lower House of Parliament): 'The Governor is part of the Governing Council of the ECB, and it is a matter of public knowledge what the ECB general view has been.... we understand all that...The Governor gave his view. He is entitled to give his view'.

[28] Former Taoiseach Garret Fitzgerald, writing in the *Irish Times* on 20 November referred to the 'naïve, week long attempt by the Government to disguise the reality of discussions taking place with the [troika] [and to a] foolish and transparent ploy [which] achieved nothing positive but...had several damaging consequences.'

possibility that 'if Irish banks collapse—and if one fails it will not fail alone—it may well trigger bank failures across a continent. Preparations must now be made for dealing with a run on banks . . . '. This apocalyptic vision was consistent with accelerating deposit withdrawals from Irish banks in the preceding days—the largest ever one-day outflow of retail deposits, around €1 billion, had occurred on 17 November (Figure 11.3). In such circumstances, the Governor's action could be considered an appropriate and responsible step aimed at calming markets and warding off possibly even more catastrophic damage to the Irish financial system. The Governor would also probably have felt that, unlike civil servants who are statutorily dependent on their Minister, as an independent central bank governor, he could not, nor should not conceal the true reality of what was happening from the public for no apparent good reason.

That said, Governor Honohan's statement, via the interview, on a matter of great public importance, was unprecedented from a governance viewpoint.[29] Ireland had never before been involved in a financial bailout and to reach such a point would have been virtually unthinkable even a few months earlier. It is very regrettable that the Taoiseach and/or the Minister of Finance, rather than the Governor, did not take the lead in informing the nation of the factual matter of the arrival of the troika and its presumed purpose.[30] Undoubtedly, as and when further details come into the public domain, the appropriateness of the Governor's action will be subject to reassessment by future historians.

It has also been suggested that the position of the Governor of the Central Bank entails 'divided loyalties', in that the occupant is also a member of the ECB's Governing Council.[31] However, this claim is based on a misunderstanding

---

[29] In her memoirs, Mary O'Rourke, a former Fianna Fáil Minister and then a Senator, remembered dining with Minister Lenihan, her nephew, on the evening of 17 November in the Dáil canteen. Sometime after 9 p.m. the Minister's Private Secretary, Dermot Moylan, came into the canteen and told the Minister that Governor Patrick Honohan was on the phone and wished to talk urgently with him. According to his aunt, the Minister, when he returned some twenty minutes later, 'was quietly fulminating'. She added:

It appeared that Honohan had wanted him to call a Cabinet meeting that night, in order to say that we were going to accept help from the IMF. Brian had replied that it was not he who called Cabinet meetings—that this was only within the remit of the Taoiseach—and that therefore he couldn't do it. Clearly, he had no desire for his hand to be forced in such a way. (O'Rourke 2012: 200)

It appears that neither the Minister of Finance nor the Taoiseach were made aware in advance of the Governor's statement to be made the following morning. If they had been they might well have urged him not to proceed with the interview - this would have placed the Governor in a very difficult position.

[30] The Governor's interview (see Appendix B) did not foreclose the possibility of some funding agreement other than that which finally transpired. However, such alternative options (which were later disclosed by Minister Lenihan—see Section 11.4) had already been rejected by troika representatives some days earlier.

[31] This charge was specifically levelled by economist Morgan Kelly who wrote on 7 May 2011 that 'he [Honohan] also plays for the opposing team as a member of the council of the European

of the governance arrangements relating to international organizations. It is good general practice that the governing bodies of these entities comprise official representatives of member countries, as is also the case for the IMF and the World Bank. This duality of roles, rather than a drawback, ensures that Irish interests are fully reflected in the decision-making process.

What of the beleaguered **Taoiseach and his Minister of Finance**, who steadfastly rejected any suggestions in the months, weeks, and days prior to 18 November of a possible bailout? The true state of affairs was also concealed from other Cabinet Ministers, who, even during that fateful weekend prior to 18 November, joined in the collective chorus of denial. Immediately after the Honohan announcement, Cowen and Lenihan faced the anger of their party colleagues and other Ministers.[32] Although the Taoiseach argued subsequently that his statements were factually correct—Ireland did not apply formally for financial assistance until 21 November after the negotiations with the EU/IMF team were well under way—this cut little ice with the media or the public.[33]

Internal communications within the government had been clearly defective and public pronouncements seriously misleading. However, the Taoiseach's subsequent defence should not be dismissed completely. So long as there was any possibility, albeit slim (especially in hindsight), the Taoiseach and his Finance Minister would have felt it their duty to try to pursue a solution other than a bailout for as long as possible. The history of similar crises in other countries involving a request for an IMF loan suggests a common pattern. Governments will often resist to the very end, hoping against hope that some other solution might somehow emerge, before capitulating.

The government, perhaps because of inexperience, miscalculated the huge odds it was up against. For example, prior to 18 November, reportedly there were efforts to arrange a bailout that could be portrayed as financing the banks rather than funding the government and thus somehow escape the stigma of 'IMF conditionality'. This was naïve—a loan from the IMF is always extended to a sovereign government, irrespective of the uses to which it will be put (for example, to finance the regular budget or bank recapitalization).[34] The

---

Central Bank, whose decisions he is bound to carry out.... rarely has a finance minister been so deftly sliced off at the ankles by his central bank governor' (Kelly 2011).

[32] One Minister, Dermot Ahern, later stated that he had specifically sought assurances from the Department of Finance before denying to the media that weekend that there was any question of talks on a possible bailout.

[33] Such a procedure is often followed in that a formal letter requesting a loan from the IMF or EU is transmitted only after substantive negotiations are well in train or have concluded. The request to hold discussions is often handled informally, as in Ireland's case. However, in fact, the crucial substantive decision to commence negotiations had already been taken.

[34] It is true that in the case of EU (but not IMF) assistance to the Spanish banks, this possibility was discussed actively during 2012 (despite German reluctance). However, in 2010, such an idea was far from anyone's mind.

government also brought some of the wrath upon itself beforehand by portraying any recourse to the IMF as placing Ireland on a par with countries such as Zimbabwe or Argentina.[35] Government leaders thus magnified the sense of humiliation associated with acceding to the demands of Washington, Frankfurt, and Brussels.

In the event, the government's gamble did not pay off and charges of deception were added to the substantive failure. The Green Party promptly decided to withdraw from government and in early 2011, the ruling Fianna Fáil party suffered electoral meltdown. From a political viewpoint, the bungled handling of the entire affair was an unmitigated disaster. That said, one cannot dismiss completely the government's motivation in seeking somehow to avoid the bailout. Many other governments might well have tried to continue the struggle for as long as possible, knowing full well that failure would have even more politically catastrophic consequences.

In April 2011, shortly before succumbing to cancer, Brian Lenihan (by then in Opposition) provided for the record (O'Brien 2011) personal thoughts on the events leading up to the November 2010 bailout, many of which have been discussed in this chapter. He was especially critical of what he referred to as 'betrayal' by some senior officials of the ECB who had 'briefed against Ireland'—he undoubtedly had in mind the negative newspaper interview with ECB Vice President, Bini Smaghi, and the highly damaging ECB 'leaks' to the media around mid-November. According to Lenihan's recollections, the EU Commission had at no stage raised the necessity of a bailout. In somewhat puzzling remarks, he also stated that he had not had the impression until late in the day (for example, around the time of the receipt of the letter from ECB President Trichet in mid-November) that the ECB had serious problems with the extent of the financial exposure of the Irish banks. However, already in mid-October, Trichet had written to Lenihan expressing his concerns (Collins 2012). Moreover, it is also reasonable to assume that Governor Honohan briefed his Minister fully on the broad thrust of the regular ECB Governing Council discussions concerning Ireland.

It is possible that the expression of such ECB 'concerns' may not have been viewed as a serious direct threat to actually withhold ECB funding. Indeed, even if such a threat was made (or implied), the Irish side may well have concluded that it was not credible. A refusal to approve continuation of ELA would have triggered a default by Irish banks, an outcome that the ECB was at all costs anxious to avoid. Therefore it used its considerable clout to

---

[35] However, Governor Honohan, in a speech on 11 November, had stated that measures that the IMF would want Ireland to take were those that the government was planning to implement anyway. These remarks appear to have been the first oblique 'official' references to the idea of IMF involvement and contained the important inference that, at least from an economic point of view, this might not be the worst outcome.

orchestrate the broader external insistence that Ireland accept the bailout route. Moreover, even if some officials were discounting a specific ECB ultimatum involving a cut-off of funds, many had already come to the conclusion that, for broader reasons, applying for emergency assistance was the only feasible approach to follow.

Lenihan, who showed remarkable bravery in coping with the final stages of terminal illness at the time, also defended the decision to delay any public acknowledgement of a looming bailout. He disclosed for the first time that, apart from seeking a possible 'bank financing only' loan, he had raised the idea of a 'precautionary' financing agreement. Under such an arrangement, which could have been portrayed as not constituting a full 'bailout', Ireland would only draw on external official funds if market access was not regained quickly. For this to have been feasible, the ECB would have had to commit to the maintenance of its exposure to Irish banks while simultaneously intervening, if necessary, in the markets to prevent any further increase in Irish sovereign bond yields. Lenihan also argued that, before entering into any negotiations, it was essential that discussion of Ireland's contentious corporate tax regime (see Chapter 12) be excluded from the agenda.

Apart from the corporate tax issue—where the decision by the EU not to press Ireland appears to have been taken some time earlier—the other options Lenihan referred to had in fact been rejected by the weekend of 11–12 November.[36] A definitive judgment as to how vigorously these possibilities were pursued will have to await release of the documentation relating to the formal and informal contacts between the parties. For now—apart from some of Lenihan's remarks—the record that is available suggests that for quite some time before 18 November, Ireland's external partners had already made up their mind that a full-blown bailout was the only way forward.

11.5 The Bailout Agreement

The final act proved to be the least dramatic, involving no real surprises. The arrival of the EU/IMF team, while fascinating to the public and domestic and foreign media, did not lead to immediate savage expenditure cuts and massive job layoffs, as some had predicted. Unlike in many situations involving the IMF, the discussions proceeded smoothly and were concluded ahead of schedule, partly due to international pressure, especially from the US.[37] At the

---

[36] Again, as in the case of the possible direct financing of the banking sector, although such ideas were raised in mid-2012, they were not an option two years earlier.

[37] The cliff-hanger nature of much of the discussions with Greece is a good example of the opposite, with IMF teams often departing peremptorily from Athens citing insufficient progress

technical level, the parties to the negotiations had discussed already many key aspects of the Irish case in Washington, Brussels, and Frankfurt. Many officials knew each other well, as a result of earlier interaction in various international fora.

It is also very likely that the major elements of the government's Four-Year Programme had already been largely agreed with the EU/IMF before finalization. While the question 'would this be a satisfactory basis for a (purely hypothetical) bailout application' may not have been put directly, it could not have been far from the minds of many officials. The macroeconomic and budgetary targets in the Memorandum of Understanding (MOU) agreed with the troika, not surprisingly, were essentially the same as those in the government's Programme. They included the path for the reduction of the budget deficit, the total size of planned budgetary adjustments, and the broad breakdown between expenditure and taxation measures.

Many of the individual measures outlined in the MOU had been identified by the government over a period of several years for possible action. However, the MOU included precise timetables (often by month or quarter) relating to individual policy actions. For some, this represented an unacceptable and intrusive micromanagement of sovereign decision-making. Others, however, welcomed the pressures placed on the government to commit finally to taking necessary measures, many of which had been delayed for a long time. The MOU did contain significantly more detailed and comprehensive measures for restructuring the banking system and strengthening the financial regulatory framework than had been previously outlined, at least publicly. As noted above, a key element was the commitment to undertake a more comprehensive assessment of the capital requirements of the banks which also took into account the ECB's insistence on a plan for asset deleveraging by the banks.

One important contentious topic was the treatment of unsecured senior bondholders that were not covered by the government guarantee (see Chapter 10). The ECB reiterated its opposition to any burning of these bondholders on the grounds of contagion.[38] By all accounts, the IMF team was open to such a possibility, although it has avoided explicit public comment on the matter.[39] Possible reasons for the IMF's flexibility include: a greater

---

and conditions being set for their return. None of these have featured in either the initial or subsequent negotiations with Ireland.

[38] It is not entirely clear whether the 'contagion' concerns of the ECB referred only to Ireland or were (implicitly or explicitly) taken as including the effects on the euro area. Both elements were probably somewhat intertwined.

[39] At press conferences held by the troika during their regular visits to Dublin, whenever the question of the treatment of senior bondholders was raised, it was referred to the representative of the ECB who has repeated the ECB's opposition to any burning initiative. However, since 2012 the IMF has indicated strong support for a restructuring of Ireland's banking sector debt which is, in large measure, the counterpart of the previous decision to honour all senior bond obligations. The IMF has not commented publicly on what happened during the November 2010 discussions on this issue.

readiness in principle to accept debt restructuring as part of a viable package (as has happened in several other IMF programmes); less concern about contagion (although the ECB might argue that, as a central bank, it is the ECB, rather than the IMF, that would have to bear the consequences of a mistaken assessment); and a view that if a restructuring is quite likely eventually, it is better to bear the associated costs sooner rather than later. This thinking underlay the IMF's insistence from mid-2011 onwards, in the face of some strong European opposition, on a major restructuring of Greek sovereign debt.

While the details are not on the public record, it is known that, with the support of Irish officials, the IMF team developed, separately from the EU/ECB members of the troika, a possible approach to dealing with senior bondholders. However, as the discussions in Dublin were proceeding, US Treasury Secretary Timothy Geithner, backed by several European Finance Ministers, intervened to register US opposition, mainly because of feared adverse effects on the CDS market. The views of the US, the most influential member of the Executive Board of the IMF, could not be taken lightly. In any event, agreement by the Irish side to take the issue off the table was necessary in order to finalize the MOU. However, the implications of continued payments to senior unsecured Anglo bondholders for the State's indebtedness resurfaced continuously throughout 2011–2013 (see Chapter 12).

Irrespective of the substance of the agreement, being forced to apply for a bailout from the IMF with its reputation (deserved or not) for overruling national sovereignty was a major blow to public pride, at least initially. The arrival every three months of teams from the IMF and EU to swarm over the accounts and hold the government to task for all aspects of its financial activities was an indignity for many, although it was welcomed by others (and not only long-standing critics of the government). The IMF stationed a permanent 'resident representative' in the Central Bank. Central Bank officials were required, as is normal practice, to provide detailed data—initially on a weekly basis—on all budgetary and banking transactions. This was designed to avoid a recurrence of a Greek-type situation where the government furnished, at least to the EU, inaccurate and misleading statistical data for several years.[40]

---

[40] Several IMF bailout cases have been encountered where governments had knowingly and deliberately supplied false and misleading information on the basis of which the IMF had agreed to disburse funding. The organization is especially sensitive to criticism on this score and as a result of these experiences, instituted quite rigorous and detailed reporting systems. In the interests of uniformity of treatment and to avoid accusations of biases, these procedures were applied to all countries requesting bailouts, irrespective of their reputation for probity or technical expertise.

11.6 Conclusions

The respite offered by the (apparently) successful guarantee granted at end-September 2008 turned out to be short lived. Although initially there were some reflows to the banking system, during 2009–10, market pressures intensified, leading eventually to a semi-collapse of confidence in the late summer and early autumn of 2010. As of early November 2010 (at the latest), the government faced increasingly strident and insistent calls from external official partners, apparently increasingly orchestrated by the ECB, for a radical solution. By the middle of the month, the message was uncompromisingly direct—Ireland had to swallow its pride and seek immediately emergency assistance from the EU and the IMF. There was no way out for the government.

Could anything have been done differently in the preceding two years that might have avoided such a disappointing outcome? Even with the benefit of hindsight, this seems unlikely. The collapse of the budget was already well in train by 2008 and the successive waves of emergency remedial measures from mid-2008 onwards could not stem the tide. By late 2010, Ireland's budgetary deficit remained, by a very large margin, unsustainable, and the debt/GDP ratio was set to soar towards 120 per cent, almost a quintupling in a few short years.

The other collapsing leg of the edifice arose from the escalating costs of the rescue of the banking system. Between early 2009 and March 2011, four successive estimates of the funds necessary to recapitalize the banks were announced, each of a higher amount. This did not instil confidence in either market or official circles or among the public that a definitive upper limit on the enormous financial burden to the taxpayer had been established. There are several reasons—not uncommon in other similar cases—why the process took so long and involved continuous upward revision: a lack of urgency on the part of the Central Bank during 2009; a shortage of suitable expertise and well-established methodologies to handle an unprecedented challenge; the enormous range of uncertainties present; and the fact that a good part of the overall exercise was being undertaken by NAMA, with its own constraints and *modus operandi*.

The Central Bank could and should have emphasized more to the general public the preliminary nature of some of the estimates (particularly those of March 2010). Arguably, given that work was still ongoing and the consequent uncertainty (including that relating to the NAMA-destined loans), an additional 'margin' could have been built into the March 2010 calculations. However, for this to have been meaningful, the adjustment factor (for example, the eventual difference between the March and September 2010 estimates) would have had to be so large as to, quite likely, imply a rapid collapse in the sovereign's creditworthiness. From this perspective, the delay in arriving at a more accurate assessment of the ultimate bill for the banks may have extended by some months the day of final reckoning. But it did not alter the outcome, namely, that Ireland could not finance the true costs of the banking (and fiscal) collapse without an external bailout.

As the summer of 2010 came to an end, the die was essentially already largely cast. This was known to key figures in the EU and the ECB and recognized increasingly by many senior Irish officials. However, despite increasingly overwhelming odds, the political leadership decided to fight on and possibly attempt to find other solutions. The EU played a customary low-key 'diplomatic' role, offering soothing encouragement publicly while all the while preparing for the inevitable. The ECB also stayed largely silent publicly but, in fact, was already beginning to enlist support from others for the bailout option. The worries expressed publicly in September by ECB President Trichet regarding the amount of ELA outstanding to Anglo only served to exacerbate the loss in market confidence. The ECB's direct campaign, which began with several private communications to Minister Lenihan, culminated in unprecedented media briefings that created a momentum such that Ireland in the end had no real choice. Finance Minister Lenihan spoke bitterly later of 'betrayal' on the part of some senior ECB members, although the latter might argue that their actions had been necessary to bring the reality home to the Irish political leadership. Nevertheless, from the viewpoint of the evolving monetary union, it was certainly a major development that the ECB would feel obliged to orchestrate events in the particular way they did.

The ECB was deeply worried by the danger to the banking system (in Ireland and elsewhere) posed by the unprecedented exposure of the Irish banks, including the financial implications for the ECB itself. Details of the tripartite interaction between Governor Honohan, ECB President Trichet, and Minister Lenihan have not been made public and it is not known to what extent a possible ECB threat to withdraw funding was spelled out and/or taken seriously by Irish officials. Somewhat surprisingly, Minister Lenihan has indicated that he had not been aware of major ECB concerns until around mid-November. However he also stated that, by that point, he was in no doubt regarding the ECB's message—Ireland needed to move to a programme.

Given Governor Honohan's position as a member of the ECB's Governing Council, some may have thought that his responsibilities involved a potential conflict of interest. However, it is evident that even before the weekend preceding 18 November, a consensus had already emerged among key Central Bank and Department of Finance officials that the bailout being urged on them by European (and US) partners was unavoidable. This was reflected in the decision to send (unbeknownst to the public at the time) a large team of officials that weekend to Brussels for 'technical discussions' on the content of a possible programme. Nevertheless, the Taoiseach and Finance Minister chose to conceal these developments, not only from Parliament and the public, but also from the Cabinet and party members.

It was highly irregular that by default it fell to the Governor of the Central Bank, rather than the Taoiseach or Minister Lenihan, to announce to the Irish people on 18 November that the troika was arriving in Dublin that same day. The Governor's unprecedented action was motivated by a desire to limit any further possible damage to the Irish banking system and probably also reflected what was considered to be the appropriate role for an independent central bank governor in such a unique situation. Nevertheless, in the days leading up to 18 November, it was the responsibility of the government, while retaining the responsibility to negotiate the best terms they could, to have acknowledged publicly the reality that was apparent to most other external observers.

By contrast with the drama that heralded the arrival of the troika, the actual negotiations on the content of the bailout were not difficult. This was due not so much to a weak negotiating position of the Irish side as to the fact that for most elements of the programme, all that remained was to agree on the precise details of numbers and timetables. Partly under pressure from the US (supported strongly by the ECB), the MOU could not be finalized without a commitment by the Irish side not to pursue the contentious issue of the possible burning of some senior bondholders at that particular time. Nevertheless, as discussed in the next chapter, the issue remained very much on the table subsequently.

There was some public anger, tempered in some quarters with resignation, at the thought that Ireland's economic and financial sovereignty had been delivered into the hands of the IMF. Others pointed out, however, that the prior budgetary excesses and the massive foreign borrowing by the domestic banks were the real causes of the loss of control over Ireland's economic destiny some time earlier. Ireland would be the recipient of €64.5 billion from the EU/IMF troika in the years ahead, most of which would fund the very large ongoing budget deficit. Nevertheless, the fact that Ireland was now formally part of a group of IMF programme countries dominated by many poor and/or financially irresponsible developing countries, was a source of deep unease.

References

Beesley, Arthur (2011a) 'Irish Bail out Resisted for Months by Lenihan and Cowen', *Irish Times*, 19 November.

Beesley, Arthur (2011b) 'Dark Days Behind the Bailout', *Irish Times,* November.

Cooper, Matt (2011) *How Ireland Went Bust* (Dublin).

Collins, Stephen (2012) 'Letters Show Extent of Pressure Put on Lenihan for Bail Out', *Irish Times*, 1 September.

Donovan, Donal (2009) 'IMF Assistance to Ireland- a Hypothetical Scenario', Paper provided informally to the Department of Finance (March).

Honohan, Patrick (2012) 'Recapitalisation of Failed Banks: Some Lessons from the Irish Experience', Address at the 44th Annual Money, Macro and Finance Conference, Trinity College, Dublin, 7 September.

Kelly, Morgan (2011) 'Ireland's Future Depends on Breaking Free From Bailout', *Irish Times,* 7 May.

McQuinn, Kieran and Moira Woods (2012) 'Modelling the Corporate Deposits of Irish Financial Institutions 2009–2010' Research Technical Papers 02/RT/12, Central Bank of Ireland.

O'Brien, Dan (2011) 'Ireland was Forced by ECB to Take Bailout, says Lenihan', *Irish Times,* 23 April.

O'Rourke, Mary (2012) *Just Mary: A Memoir* (Dublin).

Part IV
After the Crash

12

Coping with the Future

Tough times never last. Tough people do
Robert Schuller[1]

The traumatic events surrounding the fall of the Celtic Tiger have left a deep scar on the Irish psyche. After enjoying undreamt-of new wealth in the first half of the 2000s, along with many international accolades for its performance, the image of the Irish economy changed dramatically to that approaching a 'ward of court.' Few, if any, industrial countries have succumbed so quickly and so sharply to a financial crisis. Many commentators began to depict an Armageddon-like future scenario of an Ireland shackled by crushing debt and under the yoke of foreign paymasters.

This sense of extreme pessimism has dissipated somewhat as the worst fears associated with the bailout were not realized. Unlike in many countries experiencing a similar financial catastrophe, there have been no massive public sector layoffs, nor were the streets full of people waiting in line for soup kitchens. Total employment, at over 1.6 million, exceeds the levels of the early years of the decade. The currency was not devalued, inflation remains at historically low levels, most of the external competitiveness lost in the preceding years has been recouped, and the value of financial savings has been kept broadly intact.

Nevertheless, real incomes have fallen sharply, albeit from unsustainably high levels, while soaring unemployment has been accompanied by the reappearance of large-scale net emigration. Many households are trapped in negative equity for the foreseeable future, and social tensions, although by no means as acute as in, say, Greece, undoubtedly have increased.

Ireland's capacity so far to implement a very severe adjustment programme has been, in many ways, remarkable. Six successive budgets since 2008 have contained cumulative tax hikes and expenditure cuts totalling around

---

[1] Summersdale (2012).

20 per cent of GDP. Although the ruling Fianna Fáil party suffered an unprecedented collapse in the 2011 elections, over 80 per cent of the electorate favoured parties committed to the broad elements of the bailout programme.

The reasons for this support may ultimately be better analysed by sociologists or political scientists. It may be the case that the Irish people are realists at heart, and recognize that very many of them benefited from the fruits of an artificial boom. Justifiably, there continues to be much controversy as to who (including foreign lenders to the Irish banks) should pay precisely which part of the cost. Nevertheless, there appears to be broad acceptance that much of the cost of the excesses has to be borne by Irish citizens, particularly given Ireland's small open economy and its dependence on key external partners. However, there is also a strong belief that Europe should accept some part of the costs that arose from imprudent European lending.

Against a background of major uncertainty—both of external and domestic origins—this chapter considers four selected issues that are likely to have an important bearing on the future outlook: (i) the short- and medium-term growth prospects; (ii) the euro-debt problem in general and the debt burden facing Ireland, in particular; (iii) Ireland's evolving relationship with Europe, in the context of pending major reforms of the euro area's architecture; and (iv) changes in income and wealth in the wake of the crisis.

12.1 The Prospects for Recovery

Since the crisis broke, most of the public debate has focused on achieving the necessary and unavoidable major correction of the public finances outlined in the bailout agreement with the EU/ECB/IMF troika. This agreement detailed a quantitative path for the budget until 2014–15 on the basis of assumptions for key macroeconomic variables, such as GDP/GNP, unemployment, and inflation.

However, starting from 2008, official projections for real economic growth (including those in the later bailout programme) have been successively revised downwards, highlighting the exceptionally high degree of uncertainty prevailing. The absence of any significant GDP growth has rendered the achievement of deficit/GDP and debt/GDP targets that much more difficult. Against this background, it is useful to consider some of the main factors that will help determine the timing and extent of economic recovery.

Assessment of future growth scenarios needs to take into account: (i) the international environment; (ii) the domestic economic climate; and (iii) the continued prospects for multinationals investing in Ireland. As a small, exceptionally open economy, economic recovery in the rest of the world is critical for Ireland. However, a rapid return to the high worldwide growth rates that preceded the recession appears highly uncertain. The euro area debt crisis has cast a long shadow, seriously constraining European governments' ability to pursue countercyclical stimulative measures, while the United States, the traditional 'engine of growth', also faces a major long-term fiscal challenge. Although emerging economies could, over time, become the new 'locomotive', growth in some of these, such as China, has begun to show signs of a slow down.

Two factors appear to be crucial for domestic demand. First, in the short- to medium-term, that is over a two- to three-year period, much will depend on a rebound in confidence. The series of traumatic shocks that have hit the Irish economy since 2008 have badly dented consumer and investment sentiment, in some cases added to by the 'gloom and doom' predictions of several commentators whose dire predictions of doomsday scenarios, however, have not come to pass. Thus far, household consumption has been held back by stagnant incomes and high levels of both negative equity and leverage (debt relative to income). Uncertainty, especially as to the incidence and timing of further budgetary measures required over the years to come, has also been a significant factor in inhibiting expenditure decisions.

Second, risk averse lending behaviour by the banks has compounded the problem. Given their weak financial state and the fact that they are to a considerable extent owned by the State (i.e. the taxpayers), the banks have assigned a high priority to improving profitability and building up their capital reserves. However, this appears to have been at the expense of limiting credit to existing or potentially successful smaller 'indigenous' companies. The problem has been accentuated by the inadequate skill-base of the banks to engage in such lending, given that for much of the last decade a very high proportion of their financing activities was directed to the property sector.

Although the Irish economy rebounded fairly quickly after the fiscal crisis of the 1980s, the current range of problems—the euro-debt crisis, the damaged capacity of the banks to perform lending functions effectively, the degree of household indebtedness—is more extensive and severe than earlier.[2] Overall, the possibility of an 'L-shaped' recession extending for some time further can by no means be ruled out.[3]

On the third front, foreign direct investment (FDI) will continue to be a crucial element. Chapter 1 described the importance of the multinational corporations (MNCs) in driving the Celtic Tiger in the latter part of the 1990s. Despite all the recent problems, the MNCs have shown considerable robustness in continuing to increase their exports from Ireland, albeit at a slower rate

---

[2] Also, the rapid reduction in the budget deficit in the 1980s was greatly helped by the success of two tax amnesties.

[3] This issue is explored more fully in IFAC (2012b).

than before. Their future performance will be influenced by developments in the global economy and also by domestic factors such as cost competitiveness, the provision of high-quality infrastructure, the availability of a suitably skilled labour force, and the continued maintenance of the corporate tax regime.

A good part of the external competitiveness loss experienced since 2000 has been recovered. However, recent IMF estimates (IMF 2012) of trends in the real effective exchange rate (movements in the euro exchange rate *vis-à-vis* major trading partners adjusted for changes in relative costs) suggest that a gap of 8 to 12 per cent may still exist. Factors impeding a further reduction in costs include relatively high salary and wage levels that feed into the costs of public services and the need for further deregulation and improved efficiency in sectors such as the provision of legal, health, and pharmaceutical services. Although several important planned infrastructural projects have had to be postponed because of budgetary constraints, the major improvement in the principal road network and airport facilities is a significant legacy of the boom. In the area of labour skills, the drop recorded in second level educational standards and the recent downgrading of Irish universities (see Chapter 7) could pose significant problems, while the continued linguistic inadequacies of Irish students is also a hindrance.

Ireland's more favourable corporate tax regime, which has played a key role in encouraging FDI, continues to be a sensitive issue for some European partners, especially France and Germany. There has been little public debate on the topic, partly perhaps because of fears of accusations of not 'wearing the green jersey'.[4] Successive Irish governments, arguing that the policy is the cornerstone of economic recovery efforts, have emphasized the potential use of the veto by individual EU members faced with changes in national tax regimes.

There are several complex issues involved here. First, it has been claimed, although not necessarily backed up by comprehensive supporting evidence, that, after taking into account detailed tax provisions, Ireland's 'effective' corporate tax rate may not be very different from that prevailing elsewhere. Second, the policy has helped create many jobs in Ireland (although considerably less per unit of output than in the past, due to a switch to less labour intensive service sectors). However, some European critics have suggested that the tax regime has instead succeeded in 'diverting' jobs, together with associated budgetary revenue, to Ireland from elsewhere. Nevertheless, this

---

[4] For many years Sinn Féin, a significantly left of centre party, called for an increase in Ireland's corporate tax rate. However, perhaps in recognition of the current changed circumstances and the prevailing political climate, this policy plank was quietly dropped from the party's platform in recent years.

argument would not hold if, say, an increase in the Irish corporate tax rate was to cause a shift in FDI away from Ireland to non-European locations specializing in high-tech investments such as Israel or Singapore. Third, there may be complex legal and taxation issues associated with so called 'transfer pricing.' This arises when profits of multinationals are boosted artificially by means of accounting arrangements so as to take advantage of low cost tax locations such as Ireland—see Keena (2012) and Stewart (2011).

Ireland's corporate tax regime is ultimately a political issue that was successfully kept 'off the table' during the bailout negotiations with the EU.[5] Several US administrations have urged measures to dissuade American companies from locating abroad and avoiding US taxes. So far the US corporate sector has successfully resisted such proposals, by citing *inter alia* the broader geopolitical and strategic benefits of US FDI. However, continuing US budgetary pressures may make opposition difficult to sustain, especially in view of the publicized very low effective tax rates, in some cases around 5 per cent, paid by companies such as Google, and the surge in entities establishing their 'accounting headquarters' in Ireland.[6] Finally, an undue emphasis on the importance of the corporate tax regime for Ireland's recovery risks diverting attention away from the non-multinational indigenous export sector, including agriculture. The relative importance of these sectors declined during the property boom as resources were shifted towards construction. However, their future success is essential to achieve an appropriate balance between the MNCs and indigenous sectors.

12.2 Dealing with the Debt

The large public sector debt burden is a key immediate issue for many euro area members. The ratios of Ireland's debt to GDP and GNP are currently projected to peak at around 120 per cent and 150 per cent of GDP, respectively.[7] The debt to GDP ratio is the second highest in the euro area (alongside Italy and after Greece where it is over 150 per cent). The debt ratio of other debt distressed countries, such as Portugal, Spain, and France, is currently

---

[5] The Irish government has also opposed an alternative approach, namely, the introduction of a Common Consolidated Tax Base (CCTB) which in certain circumstances would achieve largely the same effect as a harmonization of the tax rates themselves. Under the CCTB proposals, the profits tax base to which tax rates would apply would take into account tax rates of countries other than where production occurs, but where sales have taken place. As an illustration, if a firm based in Ireland sold 10 per cent of its total output on the Irish market and 90 per cent to Germany, taxes paid on total profits (p) would be computed as : 0.1p (x Irish tax rate) + 0.9p (x German tax rate).

[6] In early 2012 President Obama unveiled the latest proposals to require foreign-based US companies to pay a minimum rate of profits tax.

[7] The appropriate choice between GDP and GNP as a scale variable is discussed in IFAC (2012b).

anticipated to peak at under 100 per cent (that of Cyprus is likely to be much higher. Debt burdens at, or exceeding 100 per cent are often considered on the borderline of sustainability (although there are significant exceptions such as Japan which relies heavily on domestic savings to finance its public debt).

Although Ireland earlier succeeded in reducing its debt from over 110 per cent to under 40 per cent of GDP in a twelve-year period, this occurred at a time of unprecedented economic growth. Some Irish commentators have called for a radical approach to dealing with Ireland's current debt burden, including, in some cases, urging a partial debt default. Against this background, it is useful to consider the various approaches that can, in principle, be used to address a potentially unsustainable debt problem.

The first and most costless way of reducing the burden of the debt is through **economic growth.** Faster growth tends to automatically reduce the debt to GDP ratio by increasing the denominator while leaving the numerator largely unchanged. In addition, rising living standards make it less difficult to achieve budgetary surpluses in order to repay debt. Economic growth increases the tax take, while real expenditures can also be compressed due to reduced social protection outlays and the fact that expenditure growth can be more easily constrained to less than the increase in GDP.

Debt **'write-downs'** do not make the debt 'disappear' as the financial burden is shifted from debtors to others. When in early 2012 the Greek debt owed to the private sector was written down by over 70 per cent, the cost was borne mainly by Greek and foreign banks. If banks suffer major losses, in order to avert insolvency, they are likely to require a combination of central bank funding (either from national central banks or the ECB) and injection of capital, which, given current market constraints, may have to come from official sources. On the other hand, allowing the affected banks to default implies that their creditors (such as households, enterprises, or individuals) will end up bearing the losses. Thus, debt default is a zero sum gain for the system as a whole.

Financial bailouts such as those from the EU/IMF/ECB troika provide temporary financing that buys time to reduce budgetary imbalances at a more politically acceptable pace. However, they involve the substitution of debt to official creditors such as the EU and IMF for debt that, given persistent deficits, would have had to be incurred elsewhere. Although official bailouts improve the cost and maturity structure of debt, and hence creditworthiness,[8] they involve an implicit subsidy, since the terms are less onerous than the market would require to compensate for risk.

---

[8] They may, however, affect creditworthiness as viewed by private financial markets since debt owed to the IMF has always had 'senior' status as it has first claim on being repaid. The funds provided under the EFSF and the ESM (except for possible direct ESM loans to Spanish banks) now have the same status as those of the IMF. However, it is not clear what might happen if the funds available ended up insufficient to pay both sets of 'privileged' creditors.

The current approach has also required major 'belt tightening', mainly in order to reduce unsustainable budget deficits. Could such an approach depress growth to such an extent that revenues would fall and expenditure rise, leading ultimately to no actual reduction in the budget deficit? Undoubtedly, fiscal consolidation will affect domestic demand, although the impact on growth will be less, to the extent that this is translated into lower imports. However, there is little evidence from Ireland or elsewhere to support the extreme conclusion that the budget deficit will not be reduced, although the fall in the deficit will be smaller than if growth was unaffected.[9]

Bailouts, together with reductions in unsustainable budgetary deficits as well as *inter alia* policy actions to address structural obstacles to growth, are the main elements in the approaches taken to date to deal with the debt crises facing individual euro area countries (only the agreements with Greece and Cyprus have effectively involved debt default).[10] In all these cases, sizeable budget deficits will persist, causing the debt to continue to increase. Some have argued that the prospective debt ratios are unsustainably high, while simultaneously urging a slower reduction in the budget deficit. This is logical only if either the bailout is in the form of a grant, rather than a loan, or the default option is invoked. Others, arguing that the planned deficit reductions have led to sharp reductions in living standards, neglect the fact that the reductions would have been even more severe without the emergency financing provided by the EU/IMF troika in late 2010.

Nevertheless, the current approach assumes that in the end, citizens will accept whatever adjustment measures are necessary to reach a sustainable debt position, even if this implies major fiscal retrenchment for a lengthy period. However, an 'austerity agenda' cannot be enforced from outside. It can only be strongly urged, albeit backed up by the threat of a possible withdrawal of funding which would also run the risk of major reputational loss for the debtor.

The force *per se* of a threat to cut off funding is lessened if the country is no longer incurring a primary budget deficit balance (i.e. if the government's revenues equal or exceed expenditures excluding interest payments on debt). Thus, the government is no longer required to borrow to maintain day-to-day expenditures and could consider defaulting on its debt obligations. More likely, in such a situation, it might see itself better placed to be able to persuade creditors to agree to some form of debt restructuring.

---

[9] IFAC (2012a: Box C) concluded that, although some part of Ireland's announced budgetary adjustments since the crisis hit has been offset by lower growth, the deficit would have reached almost 20 per cent of GDP, in the absence of these measures.

[10] Technically the approach followed for Greece did not involve a default but a 'voluntary writedown' approved by a high majority of creditors after the exertion of considerable political pressure. The recent bailout agreement with Cyprus involves in essence a default on a substantial part of banking sector debt.

However, it must be emphasized that any move towards actual non-payment of debt entails high risks as the costs of default can be extremely high—as illustrated by the examples referred to in Chapter 8. In Ireland's case, they would be particularly damaging, given its extremely open economy, its very high dependence on private capital inflows and the potential risk of capital flight. While default may appear superficially attractive to some, it is a wholly unrealistic option for a country in Ireland's circumstances.

It cannot be ruled out that at some point, debtors' political tolerance for further adjustment will reach a limit. If this was to happen, apart from default, a further approach would be to agree to write down some part of the current outstanding stock of sovereign debt owed to some official creditors, such as, for example, the debt incurred to the EU as a result of the bailouts. While in principle debts owed to the IMF could also be included, this is rather unlikely, given the IMF's historically acquired role as the most senior of creditors.

Another alternative involves allowing **inflation** to rise significantly so as to erode the real value of the debt. Over the centuries, many governments, including those of France, Germany, and the United States, have resorted to the printing press to help tackle large and insurmountable debt problems. Moreover, in an inflationary environment, revenues will rise faster than nominal GDP if tax brackets are not adjusted commensurately. If there are constraints preventing nominal wage reductions, real public sector pay can be reduced by granting wage increases that lag behind inflation.

Suggestions to inflate away part of the debt can evoke an almost visceral reaction in many quarters.[11] Letting inflation rise lies within the prerogative of central banks who do not have to seek parliamentary approval for their actions. Sometimes referred to as 'the cruellest tax of all', inflation affects disproportionately vulnerable groups such as those on fixed incomes, while benefiting owners of fixed assets such as property. It also penalizes financial savers. Finally, there can be fears that a sharp jump in inflation will lead to a wage–price spiral.[12]

Countries such as Germany, with an extreme historical aversion to inflation, would resist very strongly such an approach, as would the ECB. Nevertheless, the ECB, if it so wished, could decide not to treat the current inflation target of 2 per cent as cast in stone. If growth proves inadequate, the limits to fiscal adjustment are reached, and possible debt restructuring from either private or official creditors countries proves unacceptable and/or insufficient, the quiet

[11] However, the possibility has been actively discussed by some, including Nobel Prize winning economist Paul Krugman and Kenneth Rogoff, former Chief Economist of the IMF.

[12] In practical terms, higher inflation could eventually result if the substantial cash reserves held by banks with the US Federal Reserve and the ECB were withdrawn and added to liquidity without an offsetting tightening of monetary policy.

encouragement of higher inflation, despite its adverse side effects, might end up as part of the solution.

Addressing Ireland's debt problem involves the particular issue of the debt incurred by the State to recapitalize the banking system. Two possible approaches were explored in the wake of the EU Summit of June 2012. First, the European Stability Mechanism (ESM) may, at some stage, be in a position to purchase the government's current equity position in the 'going concern 'banks (i.e. those other than Anglo and INBS), without the Irish government incurring any financial obligation *vis-à-vis* the ESM. This could involve retroactive applicability of a similar approach under consideration for Spanish banks. According to the Summit declaration, it might only be implemented following the establishment of a new pan-European financial regulatory system which is not likely to occur until at least 2014. In October 2012, the German authorities (supported by the Netherlands and Finland), including Chancellor Merkel, stated that any recapitalization exercise involving the ESM would not apply to ' legacy debt' but only to possible new recapitalization needs arising after the new pan-European regulatory system has been put in place. This was interpreted by many as excluding the availability of this approach for Ireland. A joint *communiqué* was subsequently issued by Chancellor Merkel and Taoiseach Enda Kenny stating (without providing any details) that Ireland's 'unique circumstances' would be taken into account.

The second approach sought to improve the terms of the promissory notes. These promissory notes had been issued by the Irish government in 2010 in order to permit the two terminally indebted financial institutions, Anglo Irish and the Irish Nationwide Building Society (INBS) (subsequently merged into the Irish Bank Resolution Corporation (IBRC)), to obtain the necessary funds for recapitalization.[13] The notes were a device to enable the Central Bank of Ireland, in essence, to borrow from the ECB the funds necessary for IBRC to repay obligations to depositors and bondholders as they fell due in subsequent years. However, the arrangement committed the Irish government to pay in cash the amounts due under the promissory notes, together with interest, over a ten-year period at an annual rate of over €3 billion. These payments, which had the effect of reducing the amount of financing outstanding to the ECB, were perceived as creating an unsustainable annual payment burden on the Irish Exchequer.

In the extended negotiations surrounding the promissory notes the ECB had shown some reluctance to engage on the issue, partly reflecting a fear of setting precedents that could endanger the financial integrity of the ECB,

---

[13] For a fuller description of the promissory note arrangement, see IFAC (2012a).

including the contravention of its prohibition on the extension of monetary financing to governments. ECB representatives had also rejected publicly the suggestion that the ECB has been unhelpful to Ireland, rightly stressing the unprecedented levels of direct ECB financing that it had provided to the Irish banking system at very low interest rates over and above that which was obtained through the Emergency Liquidity Assistance (ELA) mechanism.

In discussing both the issue of the promissory note and that of possible bank recapitalization by the ESM, the Irish authorities emphasized the extent to which the national debt had been greatly expanded by the sovereignization of the banking debt resulting from the September 2008 government guarantee of obligations owed by Irish banks. Since this guarantee decision helped avoid a collapse of the Irish banking system that could have caused very damaging contagion effects throughout the eurozone, the Irish authorities urged that European authorities adjust their policies as needed so as to make allowances for the implicit European dimension entailed by the granting of the Irish guarantee. Moreover, it was argued that if Ireland, which has scrupulously followed all the terms of the bailout agreement, is to return successfully to the market and avoid the need for a second bailout programme, the debt outlook needed to be improved significantly.

As in many debt-related controversies, there is merit on both sides. The Irish case was strong, given the history of the debt in question and the benefits to the euro area of Ireland emerging as a 'successful bail out story'. In the discussions it was also recognized that the concerns of the ECB and some of the European creditor countries could not be lightly dismissed.

In the event, after lengthy and complex negotiations, an agreement was reached in early February 2013 relating to a restructuring of the promissory notes. Under the arrangement, the IBRC was liquidated, and the ELA extended to it extinguished. The promissory notes were replaced by a series of long-term government bonds to be held by the Central Bank. Although the agreement left the total nominal amount of the debt in question unchanged, the greatly extended bond repayment schedule, as well as the associated net interest savings on the public debt represent significant economic and financial gains for the economy and the budget.[14]

This final agreement ultimately obtained the *de facto* unanimous support of the members of the ECB's Governing Council, including, reluctantly, that of the German Bundesbank (Central Bank). Although some critics argued that the Irish authorities could have obtained a better deal by threatening a default, the broad reaction, from commentators and market analysts alike was that

---

[14] See Donovan (2013a and 2013b) and IFAC(2013) for a fuller analysis of the terms of the agreement and the issues that were involved.

it represented close to the best possible outcome, given the constraints faced by the ECB.

12.3 The Future of the Euro Area and Ireland–EU Relations

Unfolding events in Europe, especially the proposed improvements in the architecture of the euro area, will impact Ireland's economic future to a degree that could barely have been imagined even five years ago. Ireland's relations with Europe thus will matter far more than ever before.

12.3.1 *Architectural Reforms of the Euro Area*

As discussed in Chapter 5, the successful functioning of a currency union requires, as a minimum, three elements; a common monetary policy; an effective financial regulatory system; and a mechanism to prevent irresponsible fiscal policies. The current crisis revealed that, while the common monetary policy has worked quite successfully,[15] major initiatives were necessary to address fundamental weaknesses with regards to the second two aspects.

The Fiscal Compact Treaty, which followed the 'six pack' agreement in November 2011, provides for an explicit limit on countries' 'structural' budget deficits (see Chapter 6), as well as a 'debt brake' aimed at reducing the debt to GDP ratio towards 60 per cent. These provisions are to be enshrined in domestic law and, in many cases, the monitoring of compliance will involve an independent body, such as, in Ireland, the Fiscal Advisory Council. Nevertheless, the effectiveness of the Treaty's provisions will be dependent on sufficient expertise and political will to ensure compliance.

The June 2012 EU Summit decision to expedite establishment of a pan-European system of financial supervision complements the earlier setting up of a European Financial Stability Board with enhanced powers for the ECB. Some have urged that further steps be taken in the direction of a banking union, specifically, the setting up of a pan-European deposit insurance scheme and a bank resolution mechanism. At first sight, these might be viewed as increasing creditor country fears of pressures to bail out distressed banks. However, they could reinforce the determination and authority of a pan-European regulator to take actions to ensure that such situations do not arise. There have also some calls for the collectivization of debt (including

---

[15] However, the common monetary policy aspect should not be taken entirely for granted. One of the major (economic) reasons why the common currency rouble area broke up following the collapse of the Soviet Union in the early nineties lay in the refusal of the Russian Federation to follow an anti-inflationary monetary policy, against the wishes of several of the newly independent ex-Soviet Union states.

via the issuance of euro bonds) or a permanent system of fiscal transfers, perhaps leading eventually to political union. While the desirability, on broader grounds, of these steps can be debated, they do not appear, in themselves, essential for a successful currency area.

In mid-2012, the President of the ECB, Mario Draghi, announced that the ECB was prepared 'to do whatever it takes', via a bond buying programme on the secondary market, to prevent yields on sovereign debt from rising to excessive levels. Countries availing of such ECB support would be required to commit to a programme to be monitored by the EU Commission and, possibly, the IMF. Although the ECB mechanism has not yet been activated, the Draghi announcement appears to have had a salutary effect on potential speculative activity, with sovereign bond yields declining very sharply in the nine months subsequently.

Finally, the discussion in this chapter has assumed that the euro area will continue in existence. However, the possibility of a break up, involving the voluntary or enforced exit of one or a group of countries, cannot be ruled out. The Cypriot bailout in early 2013 has raised financial jitters anew. Various scenarios could be envisaged—an exit by Greece, the departure of other debt-distressed counties, or a decision by one or more creditor countries to adopt a revalued currency outside the euro. Each of these possibilities involves a host of complex economic, financial, and political issues well beyond the scope of this book.[16]

12.3.2 Ireland's Relations with Europe

In early 2011 the late eminent Europhile, former Taoiseach, Garret Fitzgerald, lamented that Irish–EU relations were at their lowest point since EU accession in 1972. The atmosphere may have improved somewhat subsequently. However, since the start of the bailout the general level of anti-European rhetoric appears to have risen, despite the provision by the EU of two-thirds of the budgetary bailout funds and unprecedented financing by the ECB of the banking system. Of course, a good part of this funding not only assisted Ireland but was also in Europe's self-interest.

From a broader historical perspective, the Irish decision to join the EU in 1972 occasioned much vigorous debate at the time. However, as discussed in Chapter 1, the outcome, at least on economic grounds, was never in serious doubt. By contrast, joining the European Monetary System (EMS) and subsequently the European Monetary Union (EMU) occasioned much less domestic controversy. Remaining in the Sterling Area was not thought of by Ireland as

---

[16] A comprehensive assessment of the relevant economic and financial considerations at play from Germany's perspective is contained in *The Economist* (2012).

a serious political option, while greatly reduced transactions costs, removal of exchange rate risk, and access to virtually unlimited financial liquidity were viewed as clear benefits.

Less public attention appears to have been paid to the obligations attached to membership of the currency union. The Maastricht Treaty provisions were thought sufficient to ensure responsible budgetary policies, perhaps reinforced by a sense that the lessons had been learnt from the fiscal excesses of the 1980s. The absence of an independent exchange rate policy or the potential for external competitiveness problems were not a source of undue worry, nor was the devolution of financial supervision to the national level. It seems to have been largely taken for granted that Ireland would be able to meet the requirements of eurozone membership and (implicitly) that any unforeseen problems could be taken care of within the 'European family'.

Some have suggested that, especially during the Celtic Tiger boom, the participation of Ireland in broader discussions of EU/euro area issues was rather limited. There is a natural tendency for smaller countries to attach highest priority to their own national interests and future historians will judge whether Ireland's approach differed from others. However, the initial rejection of the Nice and Lisbon referenda added to an impression, that the Irish, particularly during the boom years, had become 'half-hearted Europeans'. Such a perception is unlikely to have helped when the crisis led to the request for emergency bailout assistance from Europe.

Apart from the sensitive issue of Ireland's banking-related debt discussed in Section 12.2, the interest rate charged on the EU portion of the bailout funds proved contentious. Following intensification of the Greek crisis in mid-2011, the interest rate was set at the cost of raising the funds with no margin for risk. This approach, although involving a major subsidy, given market risk perceptions, tended to be viewed within Ireland not as a concession, but rather as an 'entitlement'. More recently, in April 2013, an extension in the maturity profile of EU financing to Ireland and Portugal was approved, in the wake of concessions provided earlier to Greece.

The degree of success in addressing the debt problem will affect future Irish attitudes towards Europe significantly. However, the debate in Ireland on possible solutions should take into account their broader implications for the euro area, recognizing that the financial stability of the euro area is first and foremost in Ireland's own self-interest.[17] During the 2012 referendum in Ireland on the Fiscal Compact Treaty, the No side, as to be expected, focused

---

[17] Since the crisis began, most of the public pronouncements by Irish politicians and officials on European issues have tended to focus on their implications for Ireland. However, some other small European countries are perceived to be more involved in, and have a greater impact on, broader EU or euro area policy matters.

on a broad anti-government, anti-austerity message. The Yes side emphasized that failure to ratify the Treaty would imperil Ireland's access to a possible second bailout. However, supporters also pointed out that the Treaty's provisions were essential to protect Ireland in the future from other countries pursuing policies similar to some of those adopted by Ireland itself in the recent past. The positive outcome of the referendum suggests that within Ireland there is a better appreciation of the necessity to address such euro area architectural issues.

Nevertheless, borrowing money from close neighbours such as the EU, can lead to strains in a relationship as special preferential treatment may be sought which, if not sufficiently forthcoming, can lead to resentment. Thus, in the short run, while the bailout lasts and until and unless the overall debt issue is addressed in a sufficiently satisfactory manner, the relationship can be expected to remain somewhat stressful.

12.4 Changes in Income and Wealth

The sharp decline in average *real incomes* since 2008 has meant that Ireland is no longer well above the average of real EU income per capita rankings (Whelan 2010). However, Irish living standards would still be positioned around where they were in the mid to late nineties (around the EU average) and would reflect enormous progress since joining the EU forty years ago as its then poorest member. While this may be recognized by older people, it is of little consolation to a generation who grew up in the boom years, broadly oblivious to the major economic difficulties of the 1980s, let alone the bleak decades of the 1950s, 1960s, and 1970s.

Some important distributional shifts in *wealth* have occurred which may affect future consumption and investment decisions. Firstly, total net wealth (financial and non-financial) has fallen sharply, by €281 billion between late 2008 and end-2010, equivalent to about 1.8 times GNP. The decline in household net wealth accounts for almost half of this change, mainly due to the collapse in property prices (Cussen and Phelan 2011).[18] This fall followed a sharp *increase* between 2003 and 2007 during the bubble. Moreover, the aggregate data conceal important compositional differences, partly reflecting the age profile of property owners and the acquisition dates of their property.

In the case of property that did not change hands during this period, owners experienced an initial rise in paper wealth, which was then eroded during the crash. However, as typically happens with the bursting of any asset

---

[18] The net worth of Irish households as a percentage of disposal income fell by 164 percentage points between 2007 and 2010 (Cussen et al. 2012).

bubble, those who sold property at or close to the peak of the boom gained significantly, at the expense of those who bought. Apart from maintaining their funds in Irish liquid assets, sellers could have spent their profits on increased consumption (or investment), acquired property abroad or purchased foreign financial assets.[19] Increases in foreign financial or real wealth should be captured in official data on total household wealth. However, these are compiled partly by self-reporting and surveys and may not reflect accurately all holdings of foreign assets, perhaps to some extent because of fears of the possible future imposition of a wealth tax. Nevertheless, at some stage, after confidence has returned sufficiently, the holders of such potentially substantial overseas wealth could re-invest their funds in Ireland, including in property.

Secondly, the crisis and its aftermath is likely to have seen a significant shift in resources in favour of public sector employees, as compared to those in the private sector. The public sector 'premium', that is the difference between average public and private sector pay (adjusted for factors such as education and skills), remains high (see Chapter 7). Moreover, current private sector pay levels have been partially maintained artificially by the fact that the excess labour supply, which normally would have driven wages down further, has been reflected in unemployment and/or emigration and by significantly high social welfare assistance. In addition, up to now, public sector workers have retained complete job security while having the option of availing of generous early retirement compensation packages.

Retirees across the public sector remain assured of a defined benefit pension, ultimately financed by the taxpayer. The level of public sector pensions was only partially adjusted and with a delay when salaries for current incumbents were reduced in early 2009.[20] By contrast, most of the private sector has switched to a defined contribution scheme and the future value of their pensions has eroded sharply following the financial collapse. Additionally, the increased uncertainty facing private sector employees leads to the accumulation of higher levels of precautionary savings than would be otherwise necessary.

Third, although difficult to quantify, there appears to have been a significant shift in both income and wealth towards the older generation. According to the recent Survey of Income and Living Conditions (CSO 2012), although average incomes of those over sixty-five fell by 6 per cent during 2010, this

---

[19] It is sometimes suggested that successful sellers of property reinvested their funds in Irish bank shares which subsequently collapsed and that this is how the money ' disappeared'. However, this is only true to the extent that the sellers from whom the shares were bought were non-residents. Otherwise, as in the case of property, the funds would remain, at least in the first instance, in the hands of Irish residents.

[20] As as noted in Chapter 7, according to an agreement reached in early 2013 (that was rejected subsequently by the trade unions) in the case of higher paid public sector workers, both pay and pensions were to be reduced significantly.

followed an increase of 48 per cent in the preceding five years, compared to a corresponding rise of 20 per cent of the population at large.[21]

From a wealth perspective, negative equity is concentrated more in younger groups who, in their anxiety to somehow obtain a foothold on the property ladder, took out high loan to value (LTV) mortgages at the height of the boom. Many older people simply saw their paper wealth rise and subsequently fall. However, in some cases, parents re-mortgaged their own properties to provide support for their children's acquisition of a first home. A number of these older people also now find themselves in negative equity.

Overall, people at or close to retirement from the public sector will enjoy generous pensions and lump sum retirement allowances, based, in some cases, on pre-crash salary levels. Younger entrants to the labour market (including those starting in the public sector) face lower salaries net of taxes, longer periods of service before retirement, and increased pension contribution rates. They are likely to face further charges, in the form of additional fees, for third level education. That said, real living standards of the younger generation will remain significantly higher than those of their parents during the bleak 1970s and 1980s.

12.5 Conclusions

Ireland's economic crisis, while exceptionally severe, needs to be viewed in some historical and comparative perspective. Although living standards have fallen very sharply over the last few years, the decline is from an artificially high level associated with the property bubble and unsustainable fiscal policies. A return of the economy to a somewhat higher-than-average position within the EU would still represent an enormous improvement compared to the 1970s and 1980s. Despite the acute stresses, Irish society so far has shown remarkable resilience, unlike many other countries that have experienced similar, or even less traumatic shocks. However, this is of little consolation to those unemployed or forced to emigrate, irrespective of their degree of awareness of the hardships of earlier years.

The timing and extent of recovery continue to depend very heavily on the external economic environment. In the near term, the prospects for a rapid and sustained boost in the overall world economy are unclear, especially give the continuing euro area uncertainties. At the domestic level, consumer and investment demand has been sapped by a lack of confidence, which in

[21] By 2010, the consistent poverty rate for this group had fallen to 1 per cent, compared to 4 per cent a decade earlier and 6 per cent for the population as a whole.

turn reflects fears about the timing and nature of continuing budgetary retrenchment, accentuated by high levels of household debt and the risk averse lending behaviour of the banks.

From a longer-term perspective, notwithstanding the prolonged recession, the Irish multinational sector has so far held up very well. Despite the fact that its direct impact on employment has become somewhat more limited, the sector continues to have very sizeable indirect effects on employment in support activities. Ireland's corporate tax regime remains an important factor helping to compensate for other less favourable competitiveness features— such as somewhat higher relative costs, evidence of weakening educational attainment, and gaps in infrastructure. However, given the continued external pressure, it may be unwise to assume that the current corporate tax regime will not be subject to modification at some stage.

While the current approach to resolving the euro-debt problem has shown some progress (including in Ireland's case), a greater direct contribution from the creditor countries is considered by most analysts to be necessary. Otherwise, there is a risk that the problem could end up by distributing the pain more widely, including, possibly, in the form of an acceptance of the need for higher inflation. The promissory note agreement has lessened significantly the short- to medium-term pressures associated with the Irish debt profile. This, together with the recent maturity extension of EU financing and the commitment of the ECB to help prevent speculation against sovereign euro area bonds, has increased the possibility of a sufficiently successful return of Ireland to the bond market by end-2013 so as to avoid some form of supplementary bailout. The fact that Ireland appears to be in a position to regain market access within less than three years of the start of the bailout by the troika in November 2010 suggests that a significant underlying improvement in financial prospects, both at Irish and eurozone levels, has begun to occur.

The Fiscal Compact, together with the July 2012 agreement to establish an effective pan-European banking regulator, are the minima needed to ensure a sound euro area architecture. Additional steps towards a banking union (although not necessarily towards a fiscal union) would also help. However, as the last decade has amply demonstrated, rules by themselves are ineffective in the absence of sufficient political will to enforce compliance.

Once the immediate crisis fades, as it surely will, it is important for Ireland to enhance its credibility as a 'committed European'. This means participating more actively in debates and discussions on broader European-wide issues and going beyond the perspective of Ireland's immediate interests.

The crisis has tilted the distribution of income and wealth towards older generations (especially those associated with the public sector) who enjoy greater job security and better pensions and who are less likely to be trapped in negative equity. 'Winners'—those who benefit whenever an asset bubble bursts—are most likely to be found within this group.

References

CSO (Central Statistics Office) (2012) *Survey of Income and Living Standards*.

Cussen, Mary and Gillian Phelan (2011) 'The Rise and Fall of Sectoral Net Wealth in Ireland', *Central Bank of Ireland, Quarterly Bulletin*, 03, July, pp.71–82.

Cussen, Mary, Bridie O'Leary, and Donal Smith (2012) 'The Impact of the Financial Turmoil on Households: A Cross Country Comparison', Central Bank of Ireland, Quarterly Bulletin, 02, April, pp.79–98.

Donovan, Donal (2013a) 'Promissory Note Deal a Step in the Right Direction', *Irish Times*, 11 February.

Donovan, Donal (2013b) 'The Devil was in Detail of Promissory Note Deal', *Sunday Business Post*, 17 February.

IFAC (2012a) *Fiscal Assessment Report*, Irish Fiscal Advisory Council, March.

IFAC (2012b) *Fiscal Assessment Report*, Irish Fiscal Advisory Council, September.

IFAC (2013) Fiscal *Assessment Report*, Irish Fiscal Advisory Council, April.

IMF (International Monetary Fund) (2012) Ireland: Staff Report for the Article IV Consultation.

Keena, Colm (2012) 'Irish Subsidiaries helped Microsoft Reduce US Tax Bill by euro 1.87 billion in 2011', *Irish Times*, 22 September.

Stewart, Jim (2011) 'How Important is the Corporation Tax in Ireland?' Institute of International Integration Studies, Discussion Paper No. 375, September.

Summersdale Publishers Ltd (2012) *Keep Calm Sure It'll Be Grand* (Chichester).

The Economist (2012) 'The Merkel Memorandum', *The Economist*, 11 August, 19–22.

Whelan, Karl (2010) 'Policy Lessons from Ireland's Latest Depression', *Economic and Social Review*, Vol. 41, No. 2, Summer, pp.225–54.

13

Conclusions

The broad contours of the economic and financial catastrophe that befell Ireland from late 2008 onwards are by now well known. The years leading up to the new millennium saw the extraordinary export-driven rise of the Celtic Tiger, a phenomenon widely admired the world over. But then, something happened. Soon after the golden year of 2000, the growth rate of the multinational export sector started to falter, replaced by a property boom that gradually became a classic bubble. The boom had been ignited partly by a government decision in December 2001 to introduce a wide range of fiscal incentives to forestall a possible abrupt decline in the property market. It was fuelled into an eventual frenzy of Ponzi-style financing by the banks lending virtually limitless sums for property, especially to developers, using access to wholesale foreign borrowing to bypass their traditional reliance on domestic deposit growth. The Financial Regulator and the Central Bank presided over these developments but failed to intervene to stop them.

When in 2007 the bubble started to burst, as all bubbles inevitably do, the property crisis created a banking crisis. While initially misunderstood as a liquidity crisis, the reality was that most of the banks suddenly faced insolvency as the value of collateral backing their property lending started to plummet. The Irish government, following a path trodden by many others, had little choice but to keep the banks afloat, using the comprehensive bank guarantee of September 2008. This guarantee effectively sovereignized the banks' debt and necessitated the later injection of enormous sums of taxpayers' money.

But the property and banking crises were by no means the whole story. During the acceleration of the boom and the creation of new-found paper wealth, a public and political consensus emerged that all segments of society deserved to benefit. The government spread the largesse of the Celtic Tiger period much more broadly. Continuing rapid economic growth driven by the construction boom provided the resources to ramp up public expenditures, especially on health, education, and social protection, and to increase public sector salaries to levels that eventually surpassed considerably those earned in the Irish private sector and most foreign comparators. However, once the property market and economic growth came to a shuddering halt, the bottom fell out of government receipts, as revenue from the property sector started to evaporate almost overnight. But the momentum of expenditures could not be halted easily, let alone reversed. Ireland's budget deficit quickly began to soar, even before the fiscal costs of the banking system meltdown had been taken into account.

The combination of the banking and fiscal crises proved to be a deadly mix. During 2009–2010, despite various emergency measures, the full scale of the twin problems became apparent to the market and Ireland's external partners. The final act, the full-blown financial crisis, came in late 2010 when Ireland had to cede to inexorable international pressures. For the first time in the nation's short history, economic sovereignty, via the bailout, was *de facto* transferred to the IMF and the EU.

It is not uncommon now to hear in Ireland the comment that 'we lost the run of ourselves'. But this broad brush explanation is not, in itself, helpful. It encourages the idea that since everyone was involved, the role played by any specific institution, let alone any individual, should not be singled out. Neither is such a mindset conducive to learning the necessary lessons so as to reduce the chances of something similar happening again.

This concluding chapter seeks to draw together four interrelated themes referred to in the Introduction to this book. First, who or what was to blame for what happened? Second, from the moment that the crisis began to emerge around mid-2007, was there anything that could or should have been done differently to reduce the massive costs to the Irish taxpayers or to avert the arrival of the EU/IMF troika in late 2010? Third, what can be said, albeit tentatively, about the economic and financial outlook after the bailout eventually comes to an end? And finally, what are some of the key lessons that could be drawn from the crisis?

13.1 The Assignment of Responsibility

The cast of people and institutions to whom 'blame' could be apportioned is vast and continues to be a heated topic throughout Irish society. This is to be expected, given the resentment and anger of those who lost out in the bubble and of the taxpayers who face painful adjustments necessary to right the financial ship of state. Two aspects are particularly relevant. First, the process of accountability, including the question of assessing the differences between errors of judgement and civil (and, possibly, criminal) wrongdoing. Second, there is a need to distinguish between the relative roles of international and domestic factors in the attribution of responsibility and, within a domestic context, to consider alternative ways of interpreting the concept of 'blame'.

13.1.1 The Process of Accountability

The desire to 'hang the scoundrels' is a common, and understandable response throughout history after a major financial catastrophe. For example, shortly after the death of Louis XIV in 1715, France discovered it was a bankrupt state, due to massive borrowing to finance the Crown's extravagant expenditure. To appease the public outrage, a Chamber of Justice—a type of public enquiry—was established which could sentence financiers to death, the galleys, or prison for their misdeeds. Large financiers, however, escaped lightly, as they employed the cream of the French legal system to defend themselves. Interestingly, this investigative Chamber did not have the power to investigate the activities of the late King himself or his retinue.

Many among the Irish public have called for a full public enquiry into the financial disaster. While the four official reports so far (Regling/Watson, Honohan, Nyberg, and Wright), which were all conducted out of the public eye, have together provided an illuminating and extensive assessment of the events, they did not name specific individuals. The Nyberg and Honohan reports both pointed out that the confidentiality of their enquiries greatly facilitated individuals' freedom to speak candidly, without fear of direct public opprobrium or potential legal action. Although a valid point, this has not allayed the calls for a public forum aimed at bringing specific individuals to account.

However, in Ireland, the ability of public enquiries to analyse issues of public importance in a cost-effective manner faces two constraints. First, several tribunals into various corruption-related matters in the past lasted many years—in some cases over a decade—and involved enormous legal expense, mostly paid for by the taxpayer. Second, the possibility of Oireachtas (Dáil and Senate) committees investigating such issues publicly may have been circumscribed by a recent Supreme Court judgement. The Court has ruled that the protection currently afforded to citizens under the current Irish constitution places significant constraints on the scope of hearings by such committees. The government's attempts to modify the Irish constitution via a referendum in early 2012 so as to permit the establishment of an Oireachtas inquiry into the banking crisis were rejected, reflecting doubts by the electorate that the parliamentarians could conduct such an exercise in a sufficiently impartial manner.[1] Thus, there is no easy solution to the

---

[1] Apart from a possible rerun of the referendum, there are proposals to enable an Oireachtas investigation to carry out a more limited approach. Even this, however, is likely to require enabling

dilemma of balancing public accountability, on the one hand, and ensuring appropriate protection of individual rights, on the other.

In parallel with the calls for public enquiries, there have been ongoing lengthy investigations into possible criminal wrongdoing. In July 2012, three former executives of Anglo Irish Bank (Anglo) were charged in connection with the 'Maple 10' affair (see Chapter 9). However, this episode and others still under investigation relate to specific banking-sector-related transactions. They do not, for example, address the issue of the banks' broader responsibilities. The limited scope of the prosecutorial enquiries to date suggests that, frustrating as it is to many, the disaster was the result of avarice, short-sightedness, stupidity, and insufficient professional competence, rather than criminal culpability. Indeed, many of the bankers involved believed so much in the future of their banks right up to the end that they continued to buy bank shares even as the catastrophe was starting to unfold. Some of these bankers face financial ruin.

13.1.2 The International Dimension

The philosophy prevailed that financial markets can be largely left to self regulate, subject to certain overall capital adequacy constraints and limited governance requirements. This exercised a subtle, but pervasive influence on Irish policy-thinking. Arguably, it might have been too much to expect that Ireland, especially given its proximity to the UK, would have adopted a different overall approach to financial regulation than many others subject to similar influences. In any event, ideological forces undoubtedly were an underlying contributory factor to Ireland's crisis.

However, while broad adherence to a 'light regulation' approach was an important element, the uncritical widespread acceptance of the notion that the events in Ireland did not constitute a property bubble, is a different matter. There was a further element at play in Ireland, namely, the accentuation of the traditional fixation of the Irish psyche on property—a fixation brilliantly analysed in John B. Keane's play and later film, *The Field*. During the 2000s, a feeling developed on the part of many that, after the relative poverty of the previous decades, it was time to become rich and property appeared to constitute the quickest route to wealth. Many other countries in Europe, with access to the same pool of international liquidity, did not experience property

---

legislation to compel, for example, persons to attend and give evidence. The Irish situation differs from that of the United States where traditionally, the US Senate (a body considerably more powerful and independent than either the lower or upper houses of the Irish parliament) has conducted public hearings. These US enquiries have attracted extensive media attention but have necessitated batteries of expensive lawyers representing both the committees and witnesses.

bubbles. It seems that people in Ireland lacked the common sense or willingness to be aware of and learn from the history of bubbles elsewhere.

There was a clear failure within Ireland and in Europe to give more serious attention to underlying budgetary issues and to financial stability. The Maastricht process and the Stability and Growth Pact failed to identify or prevent the emergence of Ireland's major budgetary problem and indeed, those of several other countries. A further key architectural weakness was the decision to delegate responsibility for financial regulation (and, in practice, more broadly, financial stability) to the national level, to a large extent reflecting political resistance to interference by the EU or the ECB that might affect the competitiveness of their national financial systems. As late as mid-2007, the ECB's financial stability report for the euro area as a whole, concluded that there was no cause for significant concern. Ireland, along with other countries, does not appear to have supported any strengthened pan-European surveillance of either budgetary or regulatory or financial stability issues. On the other hand, one cannot be at all certain that, even if there had been more centralized European involvement in financial regulation, it would have made a major difference.

The inherent flaws of the architecture of the euro area were not recognized, either by Ireland or others. Other influential outside organizations such as the OECD and the IMF must also shoulder blame. It was especially difficult for the opinions of 'contrarians' within Ireland to have an impact, when these prestigious institutions (especially the IMF) by and large gave a 'clean bill of health' to the government's fiscal policies as well as the approach of the Regulator and the state of the Irish banking system. These organizations' judgements, of course, turned out to be fatally in error.

13.1.3 *Responsibility at the Domestic Level*

The extent to which Europe, or other outsiders, should be held responsible for not 'saving the Irish from their own follies' can surely be debated. But at the domestic level, there is no shortage of scapegoats. Was it the fault of the people generally, the bankers, the government, or the Regulator/Central Bank? It was suggested in the Introduction that 'blame' is a complex, multidimensional concept. There are those who 'benefited' from the boom and associated government policies, those who took or influenced certain decisions at a more general level, and a third group, the 'experts', who had a particular mandate or professional responsibility in their specialized spheres of activity.

There is little doubt but that a considerable majority of Irish people benefited very significantly while the boom lasted. The public sector enjoyed the fruits of an unprecedented inflow of budgetary resources stemming from property sector driven growth. Salaries and wages, as well as social protection outlays, soared, with a knock-on effect on living standards throughout the economy. Those involved directly in property and construction or in the highly profitable expanding financial sector—including bankers in receipt of sales-based bonuses—also enjoyed rapid increases in income. Among many others, the media experienced a boom in profitability associated with rapidly rising property-related advertising revenues.

A large number of households saw their wealth surge due to soaring property valuations on property owned for a long while. Others became 'rich' quickly by acquiring investment property at home or abroad. Many people bought bank shares or other financial assets, including those of pension funds. Of course, except for those who sold their assets at the peak of the boom (an unknown but perhaps sizeable number), this paper wealth later collapsed. But during the boom, very many people felt better off, in most cases, with much higher levels of consumption than ever before. The fact that their financial liabilities were rising in tandem was downplayed, especially given prevailing low interest rates. So long as asset prices did not show signs of decelerating (let alone falling) and real incomes continued to grow, the party could seemingly last for ever. In Nyberg's phrase, a collective 'mania' seemed to have taken hold. Irish people were no different from many others before them—they enjoyed the fruits of an asset bubble while they lasted but faced a rude awakening when it collapsed.

Some have suggested that the property boom was somehow 'thrust' on Irish people by reckless avaricious banks abetted by greedy foreign lenders. Clearly, lenders at all levels behaved irresponsibly. However, as Nyberg also noted, no one was forcing either the population to accept loans from domestic banks or domestic banks to borrow funds from abroad. Renting, often misleadingly termed the payment of 'dead money,' to satisfy accommodation needs was displaced by the prospect of the acquisition of assets that would surely continue to increase in value. Unfortunately, many people sought somehow to gain a foothold on the property ladder just as the ladder collapsed.

Those who benefited had little reason to have concluded by themselves that all could end in disaster. They probably assumed that those who supposedly were in a position to question or to know better (for example, politicians, the media, or economists) would have alerted them to any inherent dangers. However, these groups (with some limited exceptions) were 'acquiescers', joining enthusiastically the general benign consensus. The two election campaigns, in 2002 and especially that of 2007, illustrated the absence of any appetite by politicians of all parties and most commentators to raise doubts that the era of new-found riches might not continue. Even the mild criticisms of government over-spending voiced by the principal opposition party, Fine Gael, in 2002 (when it suffered a crushing electoral defeat), had disappeared from the party's rhetoric five years later. The 2007 election campaign was essentially an auction of spending promises. Instances are rare, if indeed any, where, in the midst of a boom, a party wins an election by predicting that the good times were about to stop.

If politicians could not be relied on to raise warning flags, what of the media, who arguably have a particular responsibility to pose the searching questions behind the 'latest news'? Some specific pressures (financial and otherwise) from lobby groups associated with the property sector were resisted by a number of the print media. RTE, the publicly subsidized Irish radio and television station, did not hesitate to broadcast several controversial programmes that cautioned against property excesses and that elicited strong criticism, including from politicians. At the same time, much newspaper coverage dealt with the latest coup of ever more successful property developer 'stars' and there was some reluctance by specialized print journalists to probe deeper into the boom, including by assessing the risks for the banks and the budget. The relative inexperience of younger journalists (many of whom were themselves personally caught up in the boom) with little knowledge of earlier difficult times may have been a factor, while others may have been concerned at becoming typecast as a Morgan Kelly 'harbinger of doom'.

Politicians and the media would in all fairness argue that they took their cue from the third group, the 'experts'. The Central Bank and the Financial Regulator were the key specialized institutions charged with overseeing the stability of the financial system, while the Department of Finance, although not empowered to take policy decisions, was responsible for the provision to the government of high-quality professional analysis and advice, including necessary warnings with respect to risks and dangers. Given their specific responsibilities, a large part of the cause of the overall failure rests on the shoulders of these three institutions.

The Financial Regulator was the first immediate line of defence that failed to hold. Banks ultimately are responsible to their shareholders for their financial well-being. However, no different from others, bankers are rational and if there is money to be made—and there surely was—from ramping up lending and enjoying higher salaries and bonuses, profits, and share prices, they will seek to take advantage. The bubble brought together eager lenders (domestic banks and foreign lenders) and eager borrowers (the domestic banks and households and developers), to everyone's perceived mutual benefit. The particular mandate of the Regulator and the Central Bank was precisely to curb such short-sighted behaviour which, if unchecked, can predictably cause major economic damage. Yes, the banks were culpable, but so also were the institutions that did not intervene effectively to stop them.

Heavily influenced by a preference for 'principles based' regulation, the Financial Regulator emphasized process over substance, was wary of aggressive action even when 'procedural/governance' problems were identified, and appeared to have been excessively worried about placing domestic Irish banks at a competitive disadvantage or hurting the attractiveness of the International Financial Services Centre (IFSC). The Regulator ended up with little appreciation of the overall scale and true nature of lending by the banks (including that undertaken by their foreign subsidiaries), especially to property developers. Although more staff resources would have helped, a possible image of a suspicious and worried Regulator eager to intervene aggressively but thwarted by budgetary restrictions, does not bear close scrutiny. Nor does it appear that the increased focus by the Regulator on consumer protection was a hindrance *per se* to effective supervision.

The Central Bank of Ireland, in 'contributing to financial stability', was required to assess overall trends in the financial system, work closely with the Regulator to ensure that the situations of systemically important individual banks was properly scrutinized, and take preventative action as needed. There were significant failures on all three fronts. First, the Bank's annual reports on financial stability, although expressing 'concerns' at various times, fell well short of a comprehensive analysis of possible risks. No work was undertaken—even confidentially—to examine the implications of far more negative scenarios than the 'soft landing' hypothesis, despite increasing external evidence to the contrary, including by some internal Bank staff. The 2007 Financial Stability Report effectively 'froze out' internal suggestions that the property market and hence the banks could be at serious risk.

Second, the Bank failed to insist that the Regulator investigate more deeply the disquieting trends apparent from aggregate data on credit and loan growth. The suggestion that it was not appropriate for the Bank to intervene *vis-à-vis* the independent Financial Regulator in this area was decisively rejected by the Nyberg report. Nyberg concluded that, on the basis of aggregate evidence available for all to see (the growth and concentration in bank lending, and, especially, the unprecedented rapid expansion of Anglo), it should have been obvious to any seasoned trained observer that there was a problem which required far more intensive investigation, including on the part of the Regulator.

Third, even if the Bank and the Regulator had somehow thought it warranted, it is questionable whether they would have mustered the necessary will to take decisive action. The only measure, namely to raise modestly capital requirements for certain forms of property lending, was fully implemented in 2007 with a delay after extensive consultation with the affected banks, and appears to have had little or no impact on the outcome. While understandably any central bank may be reluctant to voice concerns publicly, lest this bring on a crash, there is no reason not to have done so privately. Adopting a position contrary to the mainstream prevailing 'view' would not have been popular. Nevertheless, this is the responsibility of the leadership if they are to fulfil the mandate entrusted to them as a truly independent central bank. After the crisis broke, a decision was taken to break with tradition and appoint a new Central Bank Governor from outside, as opposed to more or less automatically offering the position to the retiring Secretary General of Finance. This practice should never have been allowed to continue for as long as it did.

The Department of Finance, as in some sense the 'guardian' of the nation's finances, also bears considerable responsibility. Although ultimately, ministers are democratically accountable for all decisions, departmental officials should have pursued more aggressively concerns about the expansionary fiscal policies of successive governments throughout the boom and the heavy dependence of revenues on the property sector. There is an onus on officials to analyse thoroughly the possible implications of proposed policies under different adverse scenarios. The professional environment for economic work, together with a 'culture of conformity', were far from conducive to contingency planning. The Department had little expertise in banking matters, leaving this topic entirely to the Regulator and the Central Bank. However, as in many countries elsewhere, the Department of Finance must ensure that it has the knowledge and ability to raise issues as needed. The fact that the Regulator was independent and autonomous does not mean that it should not have been accountable and subject to questioning by the Department of Finance. Even after the Regulator was strengthened in a major way in the wake of the crash, it was rightly regarded as vital that the Department develop its own banking sector expertise. This should have been done far earlier.

The economics profession also could and should have done more to identify potential problems. Many, if not most economists had some exposure to macroeconomic and financial crises, including the lessons learned in the 1980s in Ireland. Explanations for the failure include a general shift in interest away from macroeconomics, itself a reflection of the rise of New Classical Economics ideology, reinforced by a disinterest in Irish macro/monetary issues following the adoption of the euro. There were further elements such as career advancement considerations influencing research priorities, a compartmentalization of responsibilities within and across official or semi-official agencies that discouraged cross-fertilization and encouraged 'silo' tendencies, and the internal cultures of entities such as the Central Bank and the Department of Finance that did not promote the extensive analytical macroeconomic work that should have been expected. In addition, the public did not want to hear economists expressing negative sentiments about the economy although, given their independence, this should not have acted as a deterrent to academics. All these factors, while plausible, have some parallels in the explanations provided by other professions for their own shortcomings. Clearly, the economics profession—on whom ordinary people might have come to rely for key professional and objective input on such important issues—was not fundamentally different.

The boards of the commercial banks, encouraged by institutional investors and parts of the media, and seemingly obsessed by the desire to maximize short-term earnings, supported ever increasing lending into the vastly over-heated property market. There is little or no evidence to suggest that the members of these boards attempted to question seriously, let alone stop the process.

The auditing and accountancy professions also have many questions to answer. How could international accounting firms present audits giving clean bills of health for the Irish financial institutions up to 2009? These companies essentially relied on the information provided by the banks' senior management rather than undertaking their own forensic evaluation of the true and accurate state of the banks' balance sheets. Consultancy reports on several leading Irish financial institutions indicated that they faced no major problems. Unfortunately, fiction took over from fact in audit and consultancy reports. This part of the protective belt that could have helped prevent the huge costs, initially to the shareholders and ultimately the taxpayers of Ireland, failed to function.

13.2 Could the Cost of the Banking Crisis have been Reduced Significantly and the Eventual Bailout Avoided?

A second important question is often raised in the debate. Once the crisis began to emerge, could actions have been taken to lessen the impact of the banking debacle and the bailout from the troika in late 2010? By early 2007 at the latest, nearly all the property-related loans had been extended and all that remained in essence was for the true scale of the collapse and the implications for the banks to eventually come to light. At that stage, it was impossible to turn the clock back.

That said, many argue that the eventual bill could have been significantly less if the government had not issued the comprehensive bank guarantee at end-September 2008. The detailed assessment in Chapter 11 concluded that for a variety of reasons, including the ECB's reluctance at the time to consider a pan-European intervention, the Irish authorities had no practical alternative at the time but to intervene decisively to avert a run on the domestic banking system. Preventing any bank failure was the unambiguous policy of both the Irish authorities and the ECB. This overarching priority has remained the same ever since. While the costs of state intervention are usually very substantial, the costs of a bank run would also have been extremely high. Risking the collapse of the banking system is a decision that any responsible government—in Ireland or elsewhere—would want to avoid at all costs and for good reason.

Of course, at the time of the decision, a soft landing for the property market was confidently predicted without any inkling of what really lay ahead for the banks. However, even if the reality had started to dawn before end-September 2008, the government would still have faced a similar dilemma. Many governments throughout history have used taxpayers, money to keep their banking system afloat rather than permitting a collapse. The present authors thus share the conclusions of both the Honohan and Nyberg reports that, in the circumstances, some form of comprehensive state support was unavoidable.

However, the question must be asked as to whether there were alternative approaches/modifications to the guarantee as granted that might have lessened the costs to the taxpayer? With the possible exception of the treatment of subordinated debt, Chapter 11 concluded that options such as delaying any decision, availing of Emergency Liquidity Assistance (ELA), the nationalization and/or closure of Anglo, or the restriction of the guarantee to deposits only (as opposed to bonds), were inferior alternatives less likely to have achieved the desired outcome. It is by no means obvious that any of these possibilities would have been less costly ultimately, in economic terms or in relation to the burden imposed on taxpayers. Nor does the sometimes stated view that the two major banks 'pushed' the government into the decision, or that outside advisers, Merrill Lynch, opposed major elements of the guarantee, hold up under close scrutiny.

In the end, the decision, despite all its costly consequences, appears to have been the least worst alternative facing the government. What might have happened in the absence of a guarantee can be subject to endless conjecture. However, a government's actions should be judged, not only with the benefit of hindsight, but in the circumstances and constraints of the time and via an objective assessment of the feasibility and implications of alternative courses of action. The heated debate in Ireland on the guarantee over the past four years has too often lacked these key elements.

While the guarantee was successful initially, as the property market collapse intensified, already by early 2009 deposit outflows from the banking system started to accelerate. Worries grew as to the magnitude of the banking losses to be borne by taxpayers, while the deepening recession highlighted the perilous state of the public finances. Although the clock could not be turned back, the priority was to try to get a firm assessment of the scale of the problem.

After delays throughout 2009, at end-year the task of assessing the banks' true financial state was given fresh momentum and urgency, following the appointment of a new Central Bank Governor and Financial Regulator.

The first comprehensive exercise, completed by March 2010 under severe time and resource pressures, called for larger capital injections than previously foreseen. However, given certain constraints these estimates were preliminary, based, among other things, on an assessment of the discounts to be applied to the remainder of the bank loans yet to be transferred to the National Asset Management Agency (NAMA). By late summer, it became apparent that the earlier assessment had been far too optimistic (especially in the case of Anglo) and at end-September an even higher estimate of bank recapitalization was announced.

The successive upward revisions of the banks' recapitalization requirements, coupled with a further deterioration in the budget (despite several rounds of emergency measures), contributed to a sense that the authorities still had no firm grasp of the enormity of the problem. Following a major rating agency downgrading, bond yields soared, leading to a decision to withdraw from the international bond market. In Frankfurt there was growing alarm at the rapid increase in the dependence of Irish banks on financing from the ECB and the Central Bank as capital flight, including the movement of corporate deposits out of Ireland, started to intensify. By November 2010, the amount borrowed either directly or indirectly from the ECB was about three-quarters of Irish GDP and led to highly negative leaks from the ECB to the international media to the effect that Ireland's financial position had become unsustainable. Paralleling these developments, the EU had already quietly moved to the position that an emergency bailout would be necessary.

From early autumn onwards the pressure from Europe intensified. There are (conflicting) reports as to whether the EU urged the government to accelerate announcement of the 2011 budget. In any event, during the first half of November, it became clear to most of those involved that the situation was not salvageable. In the early morning of 18 November, the Governor of the Central Bank, Patrick Honohan, announced from Frankfurt the imminent arrival of a large team from the EU/IMF, and ECB to discuss a 'large loan' for Ireland. The Governor's action, of which neither the Taoiseach or the Minister of Finance apparently had been made aware of beforehand, was a highly unusual and unprecedented decision and shows the extent to which the Irish situation had become untenable.

It is difficult to envisage how the eventual recourse to the troika bailout could have been avoided. An early announcement of the 2011 budget would hardly have made a fundamental difference. Although the continuous upward revisions of the recapitalization bill for the banks undermined external market and or official confidence, the prolongation of the process did not alter the underlying reality as regards the true cost involved. The Central Bank could have decided to add a large 'topping up' amount to the March 2010 estimate to take account of the uncertainty surrounding bank loans destined for

NAMA. However, given the effect this would have had on sovereign credit-worthiness, in all likelihood this would have simply brought forward—by six months or so—the subsequent need for a bailout.

By the autumn of 2010, the die was already cast. This was realized by many senior Irish officials but slow to be accepted by the political leadership. Right to the bitter end, the Taoiseach and the Minister of Finance, to their ultimate political cost, believed that a bailout could somehow be avoided. When this no longer proved possible, there were recriminations on the part of the Minister that the ECB had unfairly and suddenly pressurized Ireland into a bailout. The Taoiseach also implied, following the Governor of the Central Bank's November 18 interview from Frankfurt, that the Governor might have had some hand in this. Such criticisms do not stand up to objective scrutiny. Although the ECB was at the forefront in precipitating the bail out application, most notably through its unprecedented leaks to the media, the other external partners had already made up their minds. Indeed during the weekend preceding 18 November, unbeknown to the public at large, a large team of Irish officials had flown to Brussels, by prior agreement, specifically to begin discussions on the content of a possible programme. Governor Honohan was well aware of the mounting external pressures and, presumably, kept the Minister of Finance fully abreast of developments *vis-à-vis* the ECB. It was the government's choice not to inform the rest of the Cabinet or members of the governing party, let alone the public, of the true state of affairs. That said, highly important issues of governance were raised by the fact that the Central Bank Governor felt obliged to say what should have been said by the Taoiseach or his Minister of Finance.

13.3 Coping with the Future

Much recent commentary has tended to concentrate on the causes of the crash and the implementation of the bailout programme, as well as the prospects for returning to the market and regaining economic and financial sovereignty. Many have swung too far from a state of high euphoria during the boom to an attitude of extreme gloom and pessimism. True, major adjustment from the artificially high living standards and wealth in the pre-crash years is inevitable. Yet who would have predicted at the time of the bailout that less than two years later, Ireland would have succeeded in re-entering the international bond markets by mid-2012?

The Irish growth outlook will continue to depend, as always given the small size and open nature of the economy, on a major sustained improvement in the external economic environment, the prospects for which, at this juncture, remain uncertain. Nevertheless, whenever the world economy picks up,

Ireland can take advantage of it as it did in the second half of the 1990s. A key element is the ability to continue to attract foreign multinational companies. This in turn depends on several factors, including the full restoration of external competiveness lost during the boom and the availability of a sufficiently skilled labour force. Although the corporate tax regime also plays an important role, it may be unwise to take for granted that it will forever remain unchanged, as pressures from some euro area partners and elsewhere (especially the United States) should not be ignored. This also suggests the need for greater emphasis on the development of indigenous export potential, including in sectors such as agriculture and tourism.

The ECB's stated commitment in mid-2012 to be willing to intervene in bond markets to prevent unwarranted increases in sovereign bond yields has lessened considerably market worries surrounding the future of the euro area, although the Cypriot crisis has raised renewed concerns. However, against the backdrop of continued high public debt burdens, uncertainty about the prospects for a rapid eurozone recovery as well as the incidence of future budgetary measures, weighs heavily on overall Irish domestic confidence and affects consumer and investment spending decisions. The banks appear to have moved from a posture of excessive lending to undue caution, an issue linked to the needed restructuring of the banking system and the requirement for a more resolute and systematic approach to the growing problem of mortgage arrears. Without credit, it will be extremely difficult for small and medium-sized Irish enterprises to develop and grow. In curtailing the excesses of credit to the property market the problem should not be compounded by restricting access to credit for companies that have a strong history of creditworthiness.

The resolution of the debt problem of the euro area in general and that of Ireland in particular remains high on the agenda. At the European level, the bill for the excesses of the past decade, which is reflected in the unsustainable debt burden of many countries, will have to be somehow paid. Given some limits to the extent of fiscal adjustment that can be insisted upon, a combination of measures such as one time fiscal transfers, extended bailouts, large-scale intervention in sovereign bond markets and even some debt write-downs may prove necessary. If taxpayers in creditor countries are unwilling to explicitly foot the bill in this manner, higher inflation could end up as part of the solution. Ireland's own debt problem has special characteristics relating to the granting of the guarantee which was aimed not only at 'saving' the Irish banking system but also at preventing contagion affecting the European financial system. Although, to date, the idea of 'special treatment' for Ireland has encountered opposition, there were encouraging signs of a significant rethink on this front, following the EU Summit in July 2012. The agreements reached in early 2013 on a replacement of the Anglo promissory notes and the maturity extension of EU financing are significant positive steps.

Irrespective of how the euro debt problem is resolved, Ireland's relationship with Europe is in the process of changing significantly, reflecting the far-reaching architectural euro area reforms under active consideration. The Fiscal Compact Treaty will involve greater external involvement in Irish budgetary affairs, as will establishment of a pan-European financial regulatory system. However, as Ireland's own example has strikingly shown, these are indispensable, if the euro area is to survive and prosper in the future. In addition, in order to achieve a lasting improvement in the relationship with the EU, more proactive Irish involvement is needed in the broader European debates. Irish representatives, in addition to seeking to safeguard Irish interests, should place greater emphasis to considering issues from the wider perspective of the long run well being of the currency union from which Ireland will itself ultimately benefit.

Finally, the crisis and its aftermath has had important effects on the distribution of income and wealth in favour of older generations, in particular, those associated with the public sector. The broader implications of this trend will take some time to assess properly.

13.4 Lessons to be Learned

Most of this book has been devoted to the analysis of the Irish financial crisis and its consequences. This is the second time in the last twenty-five years that Ireland has faced major financial difficulties that were largely of its own making. Given the most recent painful experience, it may be quite some time before the emergence of another property bubble, reckless lending by the banks, or a return of fiscal profligacy. But the possibility of another crisis in the future—from whatever currently unknown source—cannot be excluded. What lessons may be drawn that might help prevent a repetition of the previous two major failures in Irish economic policy-making?

First, there is a clear need to pay more attention to learning both from history and experiences elsewhere—something that could be facilitated further through more educational emphasis on economic history and the history of economic thought, including at third level. The 1980s' problem was a classical example of the dangers, for a small open economy, of reliance on a major expansionary fiscal policy, financed by foreign borrowing, to boost growth. The risky nature of this approach had been well documented via countless examples elsewhere, yet it did not seem to have acted as a deterrent to policy-makers at the time. Similarly, Ireland's property bubble was extraordinarily similar in nature to those seen elsewhere across countries and through history. That said, the Irish crisis was exceptional because of its greater scale and the way in which the property crisis combined with the banking crisis and the fiscal crisis and then metamorphosed into a full-blown financial crisis. Unfortunately, Irish policymakers did not take the past into consideration, preferring to ignore the lessons of history and strongly believing that Ireland was somehow 'different this time'. Many members of the public also appear to have clung to the traditional notion—some have called it an Irish obsession—that investment in 'bricks and mortar' was the best, if not the only way to acquire financial security and wealth. As the bubble gathered strength, many forgot the principle of '*caveat emptor*' as they herded together on the apparent road to riches.

The absence of sufficient self-questioning lies at the heart of the underlying causes of the Irish crisis. Each of the key official entities seemed to have thought it was carrying out its responsibilities, taking into account the constraints it faced. Thus, successive Ministers of Finance (and their Cabinet colleagues) may have believed that given the vast inflow of resources related to the property bubble, there was simply no alternative but to ramp up spending—the political tolerance for increasing budget surpluses did not exist. For them, the boom was a given. But the problem was that they relied unquestioningly on the judgements of the 'experts' in the Central Bank and the Regulator who asserted with confidence that there was no bubble or potential banking sector problem. Each component of the policy-making structure took solace from the fact that the other parts must be doing a good job and there was therefore no cause for worry. It appears that it was simply not 'done' for, say, the Department of Finance, to engage in serious debate with the Central Bank/Financial Regulator on whether they had the expertise and experience to form sound judgements based on historical lessons. It appears to have been assumed that so long as all was prospering, whoever was in charge must be fully on top of matters in their respective area of responsibility. As another instance, it would probably have been considered unusual (if, not indeed, somewhat unacceptable) for, say, the Economic and Social Research Institute, to ask searching questions relating to financial and banking matters (for example, the history of bank runs or the broader macroeconomic consequences of potential bank insolvencies), as these were taken to be essentially the sole prerogative of Dame Street.

Greater questioning is relevant, not only within the domestic context, but also when it comes to considering the assessments of outsiders. In the pre-crisis period, considerable comfort seems to have drawn from the fact that all the official international agencies were lavishing high praise on the state of the Irish economy, especially as regards budgetary performance and the financial regulatory system. These judgements, which turned out to have been spectacularly wrong, were essentially accepted without question. There is a need to have both the capacity and willingness to subject the judgements of the outside 'experts' to close scrutiny, especially when they convey an excessively rosy assessment.

Second, and following on from the previous observation, as in any small country, especially one at the periphery, explicit effort is needed to ensure that domestic policy analysis does not become isolated from international developments. This in turn requires that key decision makers bring to the table sufficient technical expertise—essential in today's highly sophisticated financial environment—and the broad range of experience that is necessary for thorough professional analysis and sound, informed judgements. It is striking that in the years before the crisis broke, there does not appear to have been a single official within the upper echelons of the Central Bank, the Regulator, or the Department of Finance who had professional experience working outside Ireland. That is not to suggest that the views of 'outside experts' necessarily prove more reliable—indeed, as just noted, the inadequacy of the pre-crisis assessments provided by the IMF, the EU, and the OECD confirm that the opposite may be true.

Nevertheless, the presence of those with outside experience can help create a more open climate and encourage a greater degree of self-questioning. It also helps prevent the concentration of attention on 'fighting the last war'—a very common phenomenon in many organizations—as opposed to creative thinking about the new problems that might arise at some point. In this context, the recent decision to depart from tradition and appoint persons with extensive prior experience abroad to leadership posts in the Central Bank, the Financial Regulator, and the Department of Finance is a very welcome step. But it is essential that this not be seen as a temporary short-term reaction to the crisis but becomes embedded as ongoing practice.

Third, a recurrent theme throughout this book (and one stressed also in the Honohan and, especially, Nyberg reports) was the tendency in the policy-making system to dismiss or give very little weight to 'contrarian' views of those who were often portrayed as purveyors of 'gloom and doom'. This was evident in the self-censorship during the drafting of the Financial Stability Reports of the Central Bank and the Regulator and the lack of follow up within the Department of Finance to unsettling issues raised by some officials. The media also displayed a reluctance to question received wisdom, partly due to a concern that they might be typecast as 'doomsdayers'. Indeed, those who did raise serious and unpleasant issues (such as George Lee and Richard Curran in the media, or Morgan Kelly among economists) encountered considerable opprobrium and even derision from the public—including the rest of the media—lobby groups, and politicians. This attitude extended to the highest levels, with former Taoiseach Bertie Ahern, in an extreme reaction (for which he later apologized), denouncing those who held pessimistic views on the economy and wondering why they did not consider committing suicide.

Apart from the government, politicians of all parties did not seem to feel that it was their job to independently analyse or question the generally accepted 'view'. Changing this would require a fundamental shift in the Irish political system away from the current, largely 'clientelistic' approach whereby the principal role of ordinary parliamentarians is to reflect the wishes and aspirations of the voters in their constituencies. It would involve an expectation that public representatives possess greater specialized expertise in order to contribute more substantively to the policy debate. The media, likewise, needs to ensure that it invests sufficiently in acquiring a sufficient skill-set so as to be able to probe authoritatively complex issues and contribute effectively to improving public understanding and the quality of the debate.

A 'comfortable consensus' among policymakers precludes serious analysis of alternative, less benign states of the world and stifles proper risk management which must include contingency plans to deal with perceived low probability, but high cost outcomes. While the bursting of a property bubble is a prime example, more generally, consideration of major downside scenarios seems to have been almost entirely absent from mainstream policy-making by official institutions as well as by auditing and consultancy firms involved in assessing the true state of the financial institutions.

Fourth, there also seems to have been a reluctance to commit views explicitly for the record in advance of a policy discussion, pending the emergence of the consensus. Among other factors, this may help explain, for example, the absence of detailed documentation outlining alternative options or policy recommendations at the time of the controversial bank guarantee decision. Apart from anything else, this does not promote accountability, essential for good decision-making processes.

Finally, it could be suggested that some of the above tendencies are inevitable by-products of a small country where personal and professional relationships are built up over many years and sharp disagreements may cause friction and upset the smooth functioning of the system. However, the record of a number of other small countries does not suggest that this is inevitable. Indeed, a constructive and important step would be for Ireland to study closely the policy- and decision-making processes of countries similar in size in order to try to identify what lessons might be drawn.

****

The traumatic experience of the fall of the Celtic Tiger will doubtless reverberate throughout Irish society for many years and decades to come. It is a complex story which has affected every Irish person, in one way or another, both when all seemed to be very positive and when everything began to fall apart. Although the main elements are by now well known, the debate has too often been characterized by finger pointing and a hasty rush to judgement. It is hoped that this book may contribute to a balanced assessment of all of the domestic and international forces—ideological, historical, and institutional—

that help explain the fall of the Celtic Tiger, as well as indicating ways to avoid the problems experienced in the future.

Despite all the handwringing that has occurred, it is important to keep matters in perspective. Although the crash has caused much damage, the costs, including for the overall fabric of society, have not been as devastating as in a good number of other countries who have experienced similar, or even greater catastrophes. Ireland still ranks highly in terms of per capita GDP in the global economy. The MNC sector, which was central to driving the growth of the Celtic Tiger in the second half of the 1990s is still robust and has shown further recent signs of growth in areas such as social media technology. Experience in the high-tech sector is encouraging a new generation of young Irish entrepreneurs to compete globally in this area. Faced with changing global demand the potential for the agricultural sector is very considerable. Many positive elements of the Celtic Tiger period remain intact. The Irish economy and Irish people have proved resilient to misfortune before and there is every likelihood that they can and will do so again.

The Views of the IMF and the OECD in the Period Leading Up to Ireland's Financial Crisis

Aside from discussions with the EU in the context of the Stability and Growth Pact, Ireland's fiscal policies were the subject of regular review, often on an annual basis, by other outside organizations, in particular the IMF and the OECD. It is difficult to judge the extent to which some of the (limited) concerns raised in these reviews may have registered with the Irish authorities. Their impact is likely to have been fairly minor, given that Ireland was receiving substantial praise (including from these two institutions) for what was regarded as an exceptional economic performance overall. Indeed *ex post,* defenders of governmental policies at the time have emphasized the absence of any serious questioning of them by such 'prestigious' organizations.

The IMF

Teams from the IMF visited Dublin every year during 2003–07 for a regular 'consultation', that is, a review of the main aspects of macroeconomic policies. No annual visit took place in 2008. This was due to overall cuts in IMF staffing and an earlier decision to focus priorities on more problematic or systemically important cases. Somewhat ironically, at the time of that decision Ireland was not considered part of the latter group.

The team's analysis, together with a report on the Irish authorities' reactions to their conclusions/recommendations, were contained in a document (the 'staff report' for the consultation) which was published within a couple of months of the visit to Dublin.[1] It was also customary for the Department of Finance to publish a short 'preliminary' version of the staff team's views immediately following the visit. The content of these reports provide a useful glimpse into what were (and were not) the main fiscal policy issues of interest to both the IMF and the Irish authorities as well as some insights into the official line on certain, somewhat sensitive issues.

---

[1] The published version also contained a summary of the IMF Executive Board's assessment of the staff report that generally followed very closely the main elements of the report itself.

All the IMF reports lauded the exceptional overall economic performance of Ireland over many years and did not stint from heaping praise on the government for pursuing appropriate policies. Some notes of caution were sounded throughout, notably in relation to the over exuberant property market and the erosion of external competitiveness. However, with respect to budgetary policies, phrases such as 'the public finances remain strong', and 'the authorities have followed a prudent fiscal policy', occur repeatedly. The reports' messages were clear—overall there appeared to be no cause for significant concern.

The IMF were not, however, wholly uncritical of the Irish budgetary stance. In particular, a recurring and repeated (fairly relentlessly) recommendation was to pursue a less pro-cyclical budgetary stance. The 2004 report urged 'a modest tightening in the structural fiscal balance... in order to avoid a pro-cyclical fiscal policy'(IMF 2004:4) while in 2005, although it was conceded that the 'public finances are strong' the authors observed that the '2005 budget implies a significant fiscal stimulus which is ill advised' (IMF 2005: 3).

It would not have escaped the IMF staff's attention that this aspect was closely related to the political cycle, in particular the election years of 2002 and 2007. Thus, the 2003 report commented that 'fiscal policies were expansionary in 2000–2002, contrary to Fund advice' (IMF 2003: 9). In 2006, the staff recommended a 'modest fiscal tightening' in contrast to the 'substantial loosening implicit in the authorities' projections' (IMF 2006: 12). In an interestingly candid response, the Irish side is recorded as having stated that 'pressures would be especially intense in the period up to the general elections ' (IMF 2006: 14). The staff argued in the 2007 report that 'given inflationary pressures, eroding competitiveness and a widening current account deficit, substantial fiscal stimulus is unfortunate... but the authorities pointed to the need to achieve social objectives' (IMF 2007: 11).

The reports also contained observations regarding specific policy issues. There were (fairly mild) references to the desirability of an overhaul of property-related taxes and the suggestion to consider a property tax (also urged by the OECD—see Section 'The OECD') appeared in almost every annual report, although this gained little traction or received much reaction from the authorities. However, on one occasion (2007), the Irish side pointed to the political sensitivity of property-related taxes and user fees (such as water charges) (IMF 2007: 13). Benchmarking did come in for somewhat stronger criticism, particularly the 2002 exercise.[2] The staff also questioned whether the undeniable need to address public concerns about the poor quality of education, health, and other social services required major additional expenditures, calling instead for significant improvements in efficiency.

Apart from stressing the problem of fiscal pro-cyclicality, the reports' observations, even allowing for the customary discreet tone of IMF-speak, were at most very mildly

---

[2] The staff noted 'concerns... about transparency since the [benchmarking] report did not supply evidence of pay gaps *vis-à-vis* the private sector. (In fact, *all* groups were judged to qualify for a pay raise)... staff *urged* the authorities to strictly enforce... conditionality, including by insisting that [productivity] improvements be substantive and publicly verifiable...'(IMF 2007: 19).

critical.[3] It was unfortunate that their analysis did not explore the possible consequences for the budget of a major collapse in the property market, accompanied (as it surely would be) by a massive slowdown in growth. Nor, apart from querying the benchmarking methodology, did the reports draw attention to or address the implications for fiscal sustainability of the increases in public sector pay. From a similar perspective, the appropriateness of the rapid rise in the range and size of social protection benefits never warranted mention.

The OECD

The OECD published three Economic Surveys of Ireland in 2003, 2006, and 2008, respectively. Teams visited Dublin on each occasion prior to preparing their report. Drafts of IMF staff reports typically are not shown to the authorities prior to their issuance to the IMF's Board (except to correct for factual errors or possible mischaracterization of national official views). However, draft OECD country reports are provided to national authorities for comment before finalization and considerable back and forth discussion can take place during this process.[4] Thus, arguably, compared to the IMF, there may be greater 'censorship' (or, at least, accommodation of national official views) involved in the OECD exercise.[5]

The assessments of the OECD on fiscal policy throughout were broadly similar to those of the IMF. However, their reports focused in some detail on specific tax and expenditure issues by and large not dealt with by the IMF. This partly reflects the OECD's specialized expertise in certain areas as well as the fact that, generally speaking, it devoted considerably more resources than the IMF to ensuring more comprehensive coverage of topics.

The OECD reports consistently noted the generally strong overall fiscal position but injected some words of caution. Thus, the 2003 report (OECD 2003: 3) expressed concern over the sharp deterioration between 2000 and 2002, from a budgetary surplus of 4.4 per cent of GDP to an éstimated small deficit, while noting that this was partly due to adverse exogenous factors. Although there were encouraging signs in prospect for 2003, 'even so' the report foresaw a small rise in the deficit.

The 2006 report conveyed a more nuanced message. It described the fiscal position as 'healthy' (OECD 2006: 1) and noted the small estimated overall surplus in 2005. However, the anticipated loosening of fiscal policy in 2006–08 was described as 'untimely', because of pro-cyclicality considerations. Warning noises were made about the 'locking in' of long-term social expenditure commitments at 'what could

---

[3] The IMF has conducted a fairly searching assessment of why, as a general matter, they failed to foresee the extent of the looming crisis, not only in Ireland but in other countries as well (see IMF 2011).

[4] One example relates to when the Department of Finance insisted on removal of a specific sentence relating to the property market.

[5] However, while the IMF process may be more independent in a formal sense, it has been argued that pressures not to 'offend' the authorities may still operate, albeit more subtly, especially when larger, more important countries are concerned. On the other hand, some national authorities (for example, those of the UK and the USA) on several occasions have not hesitated to disagree forcefully and publicly with the views expressed in the IMF reports for their countries.

be the peak of a revenue cycle'. The report stated fairly directly that there were 'large downside risks to fiscal policy' and, in quite a prescient comment, urged the authorities to 'leave sufficient room for manoeuvre—i.e., to plan for the worst but hope for the best. In practice this means returning to balance or running a small surplus'.

The last OECD report prior to the onset of the crash (OECD 2008: 60–61) noted the sharp budgetary deterioration in 2007. However, despite the fact that 'a small fiscal deficit was likely in the coming years' the authors opined that 'the underlying fiscal position remains sound, although the budgetary situation is more challenging...'. No major collapse was foreshadowed. The report further observed that since 'revenue growth had moderated... spending [would need to rise] more slowly'. The changing composition of revenue in favour of highly cyclical sources related to the housing market could lead to a situation where 'a weak economy combined with a housing correction could create a... large shortfall in revenues'.

OECD reports fairly consistently (but especially in 2008) subjected various aspects of taxation and expenditure policies not only to considerable scrutiny but often criticism. An underlying theme, not necessarily stated explicitly, was that since Ireland's boom was not eternal, greater efforts were required to ensure more efficient usage of government resources in the face of slower revenue growth, while avoiding policies which distorted incentives. In addition to the cyclicality of taxation, topics covered included: the growing role of tax expenditures; the inappropriate bias towards home ownership implied by the tax system (including the absence of a household property tax); the real increases of around 25 per cent in social sector expenditures such as health and education between 2004 and 2007; the two benchmarking exercises (the 2002 exercise was singled out for special criticism); and the consistent, but according to the reports largely unmet, need to reform budgeting procedures and improve efficiency and value for money. The importance of addressing fundamental weaknesses in the pension system was also discussed extensively.

Although differing somewhat in language, coverage, and emphasis, the overall messages of the IMF and OECD assessments throughout the decade prior to the crash were fairly similar. Ireland's budgetary position was fundamentally strong, despite some chiding over inappropriate fiscal expansion, especially around the 2002 and 2007 elections. The worse case scenario considered—including as late as in the 2008 OECD report—was that faced with slower revenue growth, some moderation in the *growth* of expenditures from earlier unsustainably high rates would be needed. Although concerns were expressed about a significant fall in house prices, neither organization's reports raised or hinted at the possible effects of a major property market collapse on overall economic growth and the budget. While the OECD, to its credit, devoted considerable attention to the housing market and the particular issue of property-related taxation, their focus seemed to be more on the distortive effects involved rather than the risk of a massive revenue collapse.

The IMF and the OECD also had a fairly sanguine view of the state of the Irish banking system. It is little wonder that the government appears not to have devoted much attention to whatever relatively mild concerns they expressed regarding fiscal policy. Although the budgetary excesses associated with the elections of 2002 and 2007 were probably not considered desirable, the price involved—a modest slap on the wrist from outside—was a small one to have to pay. The critical shortcoming was that no outsiders were seriously questioning the sustainability of the real spending increases that had occurred throughout the decade.

References

IMF (2003) *Ireland: Staff Report for the Article IV Consultation.*
IMF (2004) *Ireland: Staff Report for the Article IV Consultation.*
IMF (2005) *Ireland: Staff Report for the Article IV Consultation.*
IMF (2006) *Ireland: Staff Report for the Article IV Consultation.*
IMF (2007) *Ireland: Staff Report for the Article IV Consultation.*
IMF (2011) *IMF Performance in the Run Up to the Financial and Economic Crisis: IMF Surveillance in 2004–07.*
OECD (2003) *Economic Survey of Ireland, 2003: Policy Brief.*
OECD (2006) *Economic Survey of Ireland 2006: Keeping Public Finances on Track (Summary).*
OECD (2008) *Economic Surveys: Ireland.*

Interview with the Governor of the Central Bank of Ireland, 18 November 2010

Programme: Morning Ireland **Station:** RTE Radio 1
Date & Time: 18/11/10; 07:00 **Duration:** 12 mins

Subject: Interview with Patrick Honohan (Governor, Central Bank) who discusses the IMF–ECB visit to Dublin today and the possibility of a bailout for Ireland.[1]

Presenter Rachael English: We are going to talk first to Patrick Honohan, the Governor of the Central Bank. He's in Frankfurt where he's attending a meeting of the governing council of the European Central Bank. Good morning to you.

Patrick Honohan (Central Bank Governor): Good Morning.

Rachael English: We've more important matters to discuss. The *Financial Times* this morning is reporting that there is growing concern about bank deposits here. There's a palpable sense amongst people that they're not being given the full picture. One paper talks of the public being treated with contempt. So what are the IMF and the ECB here for today? What will they be doing?

Patrick Honohan: I think the purpose of this whole exercise is to provide reassurance. Reassurance to international markets, reassurance to our partners in Europe and internationally that the policy stance that the government is adopting is designed and will be effective in getting us on a stable trajectory—a situation that can last and is sustainable indefinitely. They also will want to provide assurance to investors and depositors in banks that they, as independent outside examiners, are satisfied of the condition of the banks and that the banks have adequate capital resources to meet any calls that may come to them.

Rachael English: The Taoiseach, over the past couple of days, has been remarkably reluctant to use the phrase bailout. Do you accept that is what we are looking at here, that we are talking about a bailout?

Patrick Honohan: We don't talk about bailouts. When you are talking about the IMF, the IMF talks about loans—not bailouts. Loans get repaid so there hasn't been a bailout from the IMF. Shareholders in the IMF—which are governments—get their return on the money that they have advanced to the IMF.

---

[1] Transcript provided by the Central Bank.

Rachael English: Right, so are we then talking about a loan?

Patrick Honohan: It is a loan, yes.

Rachael English: And you can confirm that they will be giving us a loan?

Patrick Honohan: Well if it's agreed, of course, yes.

Rachael English: And when you say 'if it's agreed', Why else would they be here?

Patrick Honohan: Exactly. The intention is, and the expectation is—on their part (and personally on my part)—that negotiations or discussions will be effective and that a loan will be made available as necessary.

Rachael English: That is your understanding. Is that also the understanding of the government? Because people will be aware over the past few days that there has been a lot of talk from politicians about this loan not being inevitable.

Patrick Honohan: I'm not the government, but I know that these talks are serious talks that the IMF and the European Commission and the ECB would not send a large team if they didn't believe first of all, that they could agree to a package, that there is a programme to them that is fully acceptable that could be designed and would likely to be acceptable to the Irish Government and the Irish people.

Rachael English: So it is your understanding then that there will be a loan and we will have to accept it.

Patrick Honohan: It's my expectation that that will happen, yes absolutely.

Rachael English: How big is this loan likely to be?

Patrick Honohan: It will be a large loan because the purpose of the amount to be advanced or to be made available to be borrowed is to show Ireland has sufficient firepower to deal with any concerns of the market. That's the purpose of it so we're talking about a very substantial loan for sure.

Rachael English: When you say 'very substantial' are we talking tens of billions? Sixty/ Seventy billion maybe?

Patrick Honohan: Tens of billions—yes. I don't know that any precision has been put on it at this stage yet.

Rachael English: And what will be done with that money? Will it all be going into the banks or where will it go?

Patrick Honohan: I don't think there's any question of it all going into the banks as you put it. It's true that the banks need additional confidence. Our efforts—the huge sums of money that have been put in by the government to support the banks—have not generated sufficient confidence yet. The money is enough objectively but the confidence isn't there and it's partially not there because investors are concerned in general about the government finances and the future prospects for growth and employment. So with the market uncertainty generally high, for the last four or five months—effectively since the start of April, I think it is desirable that the banks should have more capital. It's government capital ownership funds available to show to the market—look this is beyond question.

Rachael English: How much are they likely to need in your assessment?

Patrick Honohan: That's actually one of the very specific questions, the technical work is going on at the moment and there are different views. I think maybe the best way to think about this is that this is contingent funding. The capital is probably not required at all, but it can be made available in the form of contingent capital funding that can be shown but not used.

Rachael English: So are we now talking about a larger figure than that given by the government in September, on the so-called 'Black Thursday'?

Patrick Honohan: Not really if you are talking about net losses and what the overall ultimate cost to the taxpayer will be. This is money that is supposed to go in as capital— in other words something that goes in as a buffer, and comes out again when it is not needed. The Americans did this is the autumn of '08. They told all their banks, 'look, we know you think you don't need capital but we think the market thinks you need additional capital, so you have got to accept additional capital.' A lot of investment was made by the US government into their banks and was repaid very promptly in that case.

Rachael English: Talking about the banks, and the banks needing capital, as I was saying at the start, the *Financial Times* is today reporting that there is concern at Bank deposits here dwindling and it mentions in particular the Bank of Ireland, AIB, and Irish Life and Permanent. Do you share these concerns?

Patrick Honohan: Well, first of all I'm not going to talk about any banks. There have been substantial outflows of funds from the Irish banking system since April. That is a matter of general knowledge. And what has happened is: very large investment firms, investment funds, financial institutions, largely abroad who invested and placed deposits in banks in good times, when we were a triple A country, as the ratings of the country fell, they said 'well actually we don't as a matter of practice or course, invest in less than triple A'. And so they just didn't renew their deposits as they fell due, but that was all replaced by borrowing from the European Central Bank facility that is available to all the banks. So that is what's going on.

Rachael English: And is that situation continuing then?

Patrick Honohan: Well there has been a steady drain of deposits, but as I say this is something for which the banks have facilities, and from the Irish Central Bank, I'm in a position to provide exceptional funding to any bank if needed.

Rachael English: And that was needed in some cases, according to the papers today. Is that the case?

Patrick Honohan: All I'll say is there has been such a need, but I don't really want you to press me on that because I'm not allowed to talk about these things on the current basis. Of course I'd have to make sure, just in case it would sound as if I'm exceeding my powers, I would have to make sure that the other members of the ECB, this Governing Council, don't object to making those loans, because that's always on a case by case basis. But of course if I ask them, they will not object.

Rachael English: You're at a meeting today, as we were saying at the start, of the Governing Council of the European Central Bank. Will that be dominated by Ireland's predicament?

Patrick Honohan: No, this is just a regular Governing Council meeting. Of course there'll be some discussion on Ireland, but it's not an exceptional meeting set up to discuss Ireland or anything like that.

Rachael English: And talking of technical matters, but a rather important one in this case, on the question of this loan, how and when will it be decided about the rate of interest that Ireland will be charged?

Patrick Honohan: We know very clearly the IMF's procedures or the rate of interest on their lending—you can talk to somebody else on that in detail because I'll get it wrong because I'm just standing here in Frankfurt. The EFSF and EFSM [European Financial Stability Mechanism], these European facilities, the exact rate of interest hasn't, I think, yet been agreed, how it should be structured. But in broad terms, it's expected to be roughly in the same territory as the IMF standard lending interest rates.

Rachael English: So is that likely then to be around 5 per cent? Isn't that the figure that was mentioned in the Greek context?

Patrick Honohan: The Greek context is slightly different, but in broad terms, it's in that territory, but some of the lending is in the form of SDRs [special drawing rights], some will be in the form of euros, so it gets a little bit complicated.

Rachael English: Ok, and just one final question then, in relation to the loan, because I know already that listeners are getting onto us and they're looking for absolute clarity here: just to confirm that it is your understanding that we will be receiving a multibillion euro loan from the IMF and from the EU?

Patrick Honohan: It's not my call. It's the government's decision at the end. It's my expectation that that is what is definitely likely to happen, that is why the large technical teams are sitting down discussing these matters and I think this is the way forward. Market conditions have not allowed us to go ahead without seeking the support of our international collaborators so that is what's ahead. And I don't see it as something that is really worrisome or should lead to a huge change in direction, because as we know the fiscal discussions about €6 billion in cuts, all of that is part and parcel of what an IMF team would ask for, would suggest if they came in, in the absence of any such discussions. So I'm not saying that they'll rubberstamp, but I think that they will not find all that much to disagree with.

Rachael English: Alright, Patrick Honohan, governor of the Central Bank, thank you very much for joining us on the line from Frankfurt this morning.

IMF Assistance to Ireland—A Hypothetical Scenario[1]

This note outlines, for illustrative purposes, the possible main features of a hypothetical scenario involving the provision of external financial assistance by the International Monetary Fund (IMF) to Ireland at some stage during 2009. Such a scenario—to which no attempt is made to assign a probability—might evolve if (a) the Irish authorities were to conclude that they cannot take further unpopular adjustment measures; (b) the resulting financing gap exceeds what can be raised by willing private lenders at 'reasonable' terms; and (c) the consequent need for official assistance is by recourse to the IMF rather than to the EU/ECB.

In essence, the implication would be that at some point the costs of continued unpopular measures exceed those associated with the so-called 'stigma' of IMF involvement, as discussed in Section 4. However, in Ireland's current circumstances, the substantive intrusionary element associated with the IMF, if handled properly, might be considerably less than that suggested at times by ill-informed and alarmist press commentary.

The aim of this note is to highlight the main features of the IMF's approach which are relatively well known. However, even if assumptions (a) and (b) above were to hold, in practice, it is very probable that some recourse be made to the ECB/EU prior to a conventional overture to the IMF. The note therefore concludes with a brief discussion (of necessity somewhat speculative, since precedents do not exist) of a 'European only' approach, either independently from the IMF or complemented by some form of IMF 'endorsement'.

1 Procedural Aspects

Discussions on possible IMF assistance would take place in Dublin, most likely following prior informal contacts (in Washington, Dublin, or elsewhere). These contacts would seek to establish, before any formal discussions, the main elements of the government's program that the IMF would be asked to support; these would in turn tee off from the assessment and recommendations contained in the IMF's regular consultation report to be prepared following their forthcoming visit. The aim would be to try to ensure in advance that the discussions went smoothly and that any element of

---

[1] Authored by Donal Donovan. Previously unpublished, this note was provided to Alan Ahearne, Special Adviser to the Minister of Finance, on 31 March 2009.

'crisis'/risk of breakdown was minimized. As suggested below, certain features—including the absence of any 'crisis' like situation stemming from a run on the currency (a common feature à la Iceland)—of the Irish situation could bode well for a relatively smooth process.

The IMF team would be led by a senior official of the European Department (probably at Senior Advisor, Deputy Director level). Given the importance of the case, it is possible that that the Director of the Department would participate at some stage. The Irish side would appoint a team led by a senior official of the Department of Finance. The Minister of Finance and the Governor of the Central Bank would be kept closely informed of the progress of the discussions and would likely meet with the team on one or more occasions.

Either before, during, or after the discussions, it would not be unusual for the Minister of Finance to have direct contacts (either by phone or via a visit to Washington) with the leadership of the IMF (the Managing Director, Mr Strauss Kahn) to review progress and discuss any key unresolved aspects.

2 The Substance of the Programme

While every country situation is unique, prior experience suggests clues as to what might be the main elements of an agreed program. Assuming a stand by arrangement (SBA) was requested, a period of three years would be likely (although it could certainly be for a shorter period and in any event could be cancelled by Ireland at any time).

In the case of a three-year SBA the main elements would probably cover:

(a) a fiscal strategy designed to reduce the deficit to an 'acceptable level' over three years or more, encompassing broad annual targets for revenue/GDP and expenditure/GDP consistent with this objectives;
(b) a detailed plan for year one (2009) reflecting more specific fiscal measures;
(c) the specification of government bailout plans for the banking/financial system, and the associated costs;
(d) 'structural policies' aimed, *inter alia*, at restoring competitiveness (private and public), reforming the financial regulatory system, and (possibly) addressing the corporate tax differential issue.

The key question is to what extent the commitments to be established in the IMF—supported program would be more demanding than those already in place/planned by the government. On this some observations are in order:

(1) The government's aim of lowering the deficit to 3 per cent of GDP by 2013 is very unlikely to be questioned;
(2) The fiscal measures already taken so far and those (broadly speaking) planned for April—amounting to 4–5 per cent of GDP on an annual basis—would probably be viewed as the maximum that could reasonably be asked for at this stage. In this context, the US, which plays a major role in IMF policies, has generally been calling for a less deflationary/more inflationary fiscal policy stance in current circumstances than that agreed so far by the EU.

(3) If the situation were to deteriorate further (e.g., if the deficit post the April budget is targeted at around 10 per cent but subsequently were to drift towards 12–14 per cent in the course of 2009), the program would probably call for some additional measures (but not necessarily a full offset). In any case, such a scenario would probably impel the government to act, regardless of outside official involvement.

(4) The estimates/assumptions underlying the government's decisions/plans to inject further funds into the banks (either via additional capital/nationalization or the 'bad bank' approach), while the subject of close scrutiny, would probably not be a major source of contention (given the uncertainty on these issues in all countries currently). However, there would likely be a call for continued review of the magnitude of state liabilities involved and a fairly vague commitment 'to take further measures as necessary'.

(5) As regards structural measures, the recommendations and subsequent decisions arising from the Commission on Taxation and An Bord Snip Nua and the overall strategy on competitiveness (especially flexible labour markets and the 'smart economy' initiatives) could be incorporated more or less as is.

The specification of the government's strategy regarding the path of real sector wages over the next 2–3 years might be somewhat more tricky but, as in other cases, careful wording could be worked out.

(6) The corporate tax issue vis-à-vis the EU is likely to prove more difficult. While this might seem to be a purely EU (and not an IMF) issue, Germany is the third largest shareholder in the IMF, after the US and Japan. Japan could be expected to maintain a fairly low profile, while the Obama administration, which is in principle opposed to preferential tax regimes for US firms abroad, might well also shelter behind a neutral position (to avoid offending the Irish), indicating that this was a matter on which the EU members of the IMF should take the lead. The intrinsic merits of the Irish case for retention may well fall on largely deaf EU ears. However, a political argument can be made, namely, that the 'good feeling/ gratitude' towards EU countries supporting a rescue to a 'friend in need' would help to pass Lisbon. However, this could be dissipated if the price to be paid was peremptory insistence on the removal of the exemption. This is the type of issue that one would expect to be resolved, not by the negotiating team, but following political lobbying in EU capitals to be reflected in the positions of EU members of the IMF Board. A possible compromise could be along the lines of Ireland agreeing 'to review the tax issue [with a view to its possible adaptation] by no later that end 2009' (i.e. after the Lisbon vote).

3 Financial Aspects

The Irish authorities would send a short letter to the IMF requesting a SBA in an amount of SDR x billion (SDR is the accounting currency of the IMF, currently equalling about €1.1) in support of their attached economic programme (the latter is the substantive 'negotiated' document). These documents would normally be published with the country's consent: any deviation from this practice (suggesting the existence of 'secret commitments') is definitely discouraged.

The amount of the SBA is expressed as a per cent of a country's IMF quota (for Ireland SDR838.4 million, equivalent to approximately €900 million). There is considerable discretion as regards the percentage of quota available under an SBA. In the recent case of Iceland, the SBA was for 1190 per cent of quota but for a two year period. For Ireland, assuming the same per cent as Iceland, but pro rata over three years, the amount available would be around €16 billion; higher amounts could well be possible, depending on the case made by Ireland.

The total SBA amount is divided into three annual amounts. Within each year, the annual amount is normally made available in four quarterly instalments. As part of its annual program (to be elaborated each year within the three-year framework) the government sets forth specific quarterly targets or limits (following discussions with the IMF team). In Ireland's case these would most likely be some version(s) of the government deficit/Exchequer borrowing requirement.

During the year, assuming the quarterly targets are met, the quarterly funding instalment is made available automatically without challenge. If a target is not met by a 'small' margin, and the government wishes to draw the instalment, a 'waiver' can be granted, usually without the need for substantive discussions. However, in the case of a significant deviation from target, which could raise concerns that the program might be veering 'off track', and assuming the government still wishes to draw, substantive discussions are likely to be required, perhaps (but not necessarily) involving agreement on additional measures, before a waiver were to be agreed to. If the government, despite a deviation from target, does not wish to draw, the SBA essentially 'lapses' and that is the formal end of the matter.

Finally, apart from discussions to specify an annual program, a six monthly visit within each year is quite normal.

4 The EU/ECB Option

It is difficult to be precise about what such an arrangement might entail, given the lack of precedents. As regards the mechanics, it appears that the process might involve Irish commercial banks buying government paper and subsequently discounting this paper at the ECB. This would ensure that the letter, if not the spirit, of the ECB prohibition on lending to member governments was not violated.

As regards conditionality, this could be expected to be similar in coverage to that of the IMF, but with somewhat more explicit emphasis on the tax issue. Issues concerning the amounts of assistance, frequency of disbursements, and the use of benchmarks to monitor progress à la the IMF are unclear, as is the availability of tried expertise on the EU side to handle the discussions quickly and efficiently.

The EU/ECB option can be viewed as having the advantages of (a) being bailed out by 'friends' and (b) avoiding the 'stigma' associated with the IMF. However, in certain cases, (a) might be less of an advantage as it can be harder/more painful to have difficult financial discussions with your next-door neighbour (whom you see every day) than with relatively anonymous banker who does not live on the same street. Moreover, the stigma under (b) could be significantly reduced if, first, Ireland were not the only EU country involved, and second, if in reality the substantive and procedural aspects turned out to such that the IMF were seen more as giving a stamp of approval to measures already taken independently by the Irish authorities. The latter would, however, require careful thought and advance preparation.

A final possibility—again of an unknown nature—might be a joint EU/IMF arrangement, with the EU providing money and the IMF 'assessing progress' in the programme, but with a 'lighter touch', eg without tying disbursements rigidly to quantitative performance targets. Such an arrangement has been employed occasionally in the past involving commercial lenders and the IMF. However, complications arose regarding, *inter alia*, the nature and clarity of 'signals' provided by the IMF and the approach fell into some disfavour. Nevertheless, in current circumstances, all options might well be considered.

Index

Index